ROUTLEDGE LIBRARY EDITIONS: THE HISTORY OF ECONOMIC THOUGHT

Volume 6

AN ENQUIRY INTO THE NATURE AND EFFECTS OF THE PAPER CREDIT OF GREAT BRITAIN

AN ENQUIRY INTO THE NATURE AND EFFECTS OF THE PAPER CREDIT OF GREAT BRITAIN

HENRY THORNTON

Edited with an introduction
by
F. A. v. HAYEK

LONDON AND NEW YORK

First published in 1939 by George Allen & Unwin Ltd

This edition first published in 2017
by Routledge
2 Park Square, Milton Park, Abingdon, Oxon OX14 4RN

and by Routledge
711 Third Avenue, New York, NY 10017

Routledge is an imprint of the Taylor & Francis Group, an informa business

© 1939 F. A. v. Hayek

All rights reserved. No part of this book may be reprinted or reproduced or utilised in any form or by any electronic, mechanical, or other means, now known or hereafter invented, including photocopying and recording, or in any information storage or retrieval system, without permission in writing from the publishers.

Trademark notice: Product or corporate names may be trademarks or registered trademarks, and are used only for identification and explanation without intent to infringe.

British Library Cataloguing in Publication Data
A catalogue record for this book is available from the British Library

ISBN: 978-1-138-29250-5 (Set)
ISBN: 978-1-315-23288-1 (Set) (ebk)
ISBN: 978-1-138-29144-7 (Volume 6) (hbk)
ISBN: 978-1-138-29152-2 (Volume 6) (pbk)
ISBN: 978-1-315-26526-1 (Volume 6) (ebk)

Publisher's Note
The publisher has gone to great lengths to ensure the quality of this reprint but points out that some imperfections in the original copies may be apparent.

Disclaimer
The publisher has made every effort to trace copyright holders and would welcome correspondence from those they have been unable to trace.

[*From the painting by J. Hoppner*]

AN
ENQUIRY INTO THE NATURE
AND EFFECTS OF THE PAPER
CREDIT OF GREAT BRITAIN
(1802)

by
HENRY THORNTON

TOGETHER WITH HIS EVIDENCE GIVEN BEFORE THE COMMITTEES OF
SECRECY OF THE TWO HOUSES OF PARLIAMENT IN THE BANK
OF ENGLAND, MARCH AND APRIL, 1797, SOME MANUSCRIPT
NOTES, AND HIS SPEECHES ON THE BULLION REPORT,
MAY 1811

EDITED WITH AN INTRODUCTION
by
F. A. v. HAYEK

LONDON
GEORGE ALLEN & UNWIN LTD
MUSEUM STREET

THIS EDITION FIRST PUBLISHED IN 1939

All rights reserved

PRINTED IN GREAT BRITAIN BY
UNWIN BROTHERS LTD., WOKING

THE LIBRARY OF ECONOMICS

THE interest in the study of economic problems has increased steadily throughout this century. But truth and wisdom are prerogatives of no single generation, and we can profit by applying to the *masters of economic science* of preceding generations the same continuous and constructive criticism as is available for contemporary thought. This is the more important in economics, because present writers have matured under that oral tradition which has long characterized the teaching of economics in both Great Britain and the U.S.A. As a result neither they nor their pupils have always been aware of the sources of contemporary inspiration.

Although few copies of any one of these older books may have survived, there are nevertheless a great many such works. It is impossible for the modern student, unless he is a specialist in the history of theory, to feel his way to the classics which are fruitful of inspiration for to-day—those from which to-day's "growing points" are nourished.

The Editorial Board is sufficient guarantee of the skill and knowledge with which the selection of the volumes for this Library has been made. The Editors have chosen, *first*, those books which have directly influenced contemporary thought, but are no longer at all easily obtainable. *Secondly*, writers who, starting from different premisses and in a different tradition, concerned themselves with analytical problems of special significance for to-day. To the discussion of these problems the older writers can make an especially valuable contribution, because the lapse of time has freed the incidental examples they use from associations which confuse the issue or introduce contemporary political controversy.

A number of *outstanding* modern contributions to knowledge will make their first appearance in the second Section of the Library.

The first work in Section One is:

Nassau Senior: *An Outline of the Science of Political Economy*, with an Appendix "On Certain Terms which are liable to be used ambiguously" in political economy, being Appendix I to Whately's "The Elements of Logic." This carefully prepared new edition also contains a Bibliographical Note and an Index. *Price 7s. 6d.*

The present work will be followed by:

John Stuart Mill: *Essays on Some Unsettled Questions of Political Economy* (1844) with Appendices, reprinting for the first time his *Essay on the Commercial Crisis of 1825* and the *Currency Debates* from "Parliamentary History and Review," 1825–1826.

Approximate price 7s. 6d.

E. v. Böhm-Bawerk: *The Positive Theory of Capital.* Translated by Hugh Gaitskell. With notes and an Appendix on the recent developments of the theory by the Translator. *Approximate price 25s.*

Jeremy Bentham: *A Manual of Political Economy*, re-edited from original manuscripts by P. N. Rosenstein-Rodan. This volume also contains a reprint of *The Defence of Usury*.

The standard for Section Two will be set by the following works:

Erik Lindahl: *Studies in the Theory of Money and Capital. Price 10s. 6d.*

P. N. Rosenstein-Rodan: *History of Economic Theory from Aristotle to Adam Smith.* *Approximate price 12s. 6d.*

THE PUBLISHERS

CONTENTS

	PAGE
INTRODUCTION BY F. A. VON HAYEK	11
AN ENQUIRY INTO THE NATURE AND EFFECTS OF THE PAPER CREDIT OF GREAT BRITAIN.	65
APPENDIX I: THE EVIDENCE GIVEN BY HENRY THORNTON BEFORE THE COMMITTEES OF SECRECY OF THE TWO HOUSES OF PARLIAMENT ON THE BANK OF ENGLAND, MARCH AND APRIL 1797	277
APPENDIX II: NOTES ON LORD KING'S THOUGHTS ON THE EFFECTS OF THE BANK RESTRICTION	311
APPENDIX III: TWO SPEECHES OF HENRY THORNTON ON THE BULLION REPORT, MAY 1811	323

NOTE

THE varied nature of the material reproduced in this volume has made it necessary to reset it in new type and it has consequently been impossible to preserve the original pagination. The original spelling has, however, been preserved, and every care has been taken by the publishers to secure faithful reproduction of the original. The alphabetical index at the end of this volume has been compiled by Mr. H. P. H. Gough, B.Sc.(Econ.).

The publishers also wish to express their thanks to Mrs. P. M. Thornton for permission to reproduce J. Hoppner's portrait of Henry Thornton as a frontispiece to this volume, and to the Goldsmiths' Librarian of the University of London for permission to reproduce Henry Thornton's manuscript notes from the copy of Lord King's *Thoughts on the Effects of the Bank Restriction* in the Goldsmiths' Library of the University of London.

INTRODUCTION

I

To most of the contemporaries of Henry Thornton his authorship of the book which is now reprinted after one hundred and thirty-six years would by no means have been regarded as his major title to fame. To them the fact that he was a successful banker and a great expert on finance probably appeared as the indispensable but comparatively uninteresting background which put him in the position to be a great philanthropist and the effective advocate of every good cause; certainly it enabled him to provide at his comfortable Clapham home the meeting place for the active and influential group of Evangelicals, who, quite apart from the great rôle they played in their own time, were probably one of the most profound influences which fashioned the outlook and character that was typical of the English upper middle class of the nineteenth century.* It would be an interesting and instructive task to attempt a full-length Life of Henry Thornton, and, considering how many minor figures of the circle of which he and William Wilberforce were the centre have been honoured with biographies,† it is surprising that it has never been accomplished.‡ But the men who became the historians of the late eighteenth and early nineteenth century were on the whole not too sympathetic towards that austere view of life, which in many instances must have overshadowed their own youth, and which perhaps found its most perfect embodiment in the person of Henry Thornton. It may well

---

* The influence of the Clapham Sect in this respect is well brought out in E. Halévy's *History of the English People in 1815.*

† See Bibliographical Note at the end of this Introduction.

‡ W. Wilberforce at one time intended to write a biography of his friend Thornton, but never completed it. See on this *Life of Wilberforce* by his sons, vol. ii, p. 329; the *Correspondence of William Wilberforce*, edited by the same, London 1840, vol. ii, p. 422; and the Preface to Henry Thornton's *Family Prayers*, by R. H. Inglis.

be, however, that a more detached future historian will recognize that in their immediate influence the "party of saints" of which Thornton may be regarded as the prototype, at least rival their better-known contemporaries, the philosophical radicals. But even if such a complete biography of Henry Thornton would, as seems likely, contribute a great deal to our understanding of the social and economic views, the *Wirtschaftsgesinnung*, that dominated the nineteenth century, it can certainly not be attempted here. In this essay we can do no more than give an outline of those sides of Henry Thornton's life which throw light on the circumstances in which the *Paper Credit of Great Britain* was written, and on the influence which the views of its author exerted on contemporary thought.

"We are all City people and connected with merchants, and nothing but merchants on every side" was Henry Thornton's own comment on the ambitions of his brothers to become members of high Society.* Although descended from a succession of Yorkshire clergymen, John Thornton, the common ancestor of the London Thorntons, was a merchant in Hull in the late seventeenth and early eighteenth century.† His two sons, Godfrey and Robert, the latter the grandfather of Henry, both went to London and appear to have engaged in the trade with Russia and the Baltic. Both were directors of the Bank of England, as was also the son of the former, the younger Godfrey, in whose counting-house his cousin's son Henry, the subject of this memoir, was to serve his apprenticeship, "chiefly employed in carrying out bills to be accepted and taking the weight of Hemp, Flax, etc., at the Custome House."‡ Robert's son, another John and the father of Henry, was also a "Russian merchant" in the firm of Thornton, Cornwall

---

* MS. *Recollections of Marianne Thornton* (1857).

† *The Genealogical and Heraldic History of the Landed Gentry*, by the late Sir J. Bernard Burke; and P. M. Thornton, *Some Things We Remember*.

‡ MS. *Diary of Henry Thornton* (see Bibliography at the end of this Introduction). The author wishes here to express his gratitude to three descendants of Henry Thornton, Mrs. P. M. Thornton, Mrs. D. Demarest, and Mr. E. M. Forster for the loan of this and other documents and for permission to quote from them.

& Co. He is known as the friend and benefactor of the poet William Cowper* and as a member of the first generation of Evangelicals—that Wesleyan wing within the Established Church who, just because they remained within the Church, probably did more to impress the stamp of Puritanism on nineteenth-century English society than Nonconformism. His father, Robert, had already settled in Clapham, then the country residence of numerous City magnates, and here this branch of the Thornton family resided for another four generations. It was probably the then curate of Clapham, Henry Venn, who in the 1750's won John Thornton over to the tenets of Evangelicalism. But it was not until many years later, when their sons John Venn and Henry Thornton lived at Clapham, that their circle became known as the "Clapham Sect."†

John Thornton, "the Great and the Good," as he was called, was celebrated for his magnificent generosity, and he is reputed to have spent on charity in the course of his life the sum of £100,000 or even £150,000.‡ His charity and his deep piety were fully

* The connection with Cowper came about through John Newton, one of the many clergymen whom John Thornton supported. Newton had, after a youth spent in the slave trade, become parson of Olney and when he took Cowper into his house Thornton gave him an extra allowance to support the poet. See the *Correspondence of W. Cowper*, edited by T. Wright, and T. Wright, *The Life of William Cowper*, also *Memorials of the Rev. William Bull of Newport Pagnell*, compiled chiefly from his own letters and those of his friend Newton, Cowper, and Thornton, 1783–1814, by his grandson the Rev. Josiah Bull, M.A., London, 1864.

† The term "Clapham Sect" was apparently first used by Sydney Smith in an article in the *Edinburgh Review*.

‡ According to John Newton and Henry Venn respectively. See Telford, *Sect that Moved the World*, p. 71, also R. de M. Rudolf's article on the Clapham Sect in *Clapham and the Clapham Sect*, and [Henry Venn] *The Love of Christ the Source of Genuine Philanthropy*, A Discourse on II Cor. chap. 5, ver. 14, 15, occasioned by the death of John Thornton, Esq., containing observations on his Character and Principles. London, 1791, and Thos. Scott, *Discourses Occasioned by the Death of John Thornton, Esq.*, London, 1791. John Thornton also adapted in 1775 for English use an earlier translation of C. H. von Bogatzky's *Güldenes Schatzkästlein der Kinder Gottes* as the *Golden Treasury Interleaved*, and it is reported that "He employed the extensive commerce in which he was engaged as a powerful instrument for conveying immense quantities of Bibles, Prayer Books, and the most useful publications, to every place visited by our trade. He printed, at his own sole expense, large editions of the latter for that purpose and it may safely be affirmed that there is scarcely

inherited by his son, and the lines which in an elegy on his death in 1790 Cowper wrote of John Thornton

> "Thou hadst an industry in doing good,
> Restless as his who toils and sweats for food"

were equally true of Henry, who also succeeded his father to the friendship with Cowper. But in other respects the simple, passionate and occasionally even violent older man must have presented a curious contrast to his highly intellectual and disciplined son, who regarded enthusiasm and eagerness as grave sins. And although John, in spite of his princely munificence, succeeded in passing on to his children much increased the considerable fortune he had inherited,* his sterner son regarded him as a Jack of all trades who never thrives and as being somewhat too impulsive and unmethodical in his generosity.

Of John's three sons† Samuel (1754–1839), the eldest, became like his father a "Russian merchant," was M.P. for Hull and later for Surrey; and as a director and, from 1799 to 1801, Governor of the Bank of England, he was a figure of considerable importance in the City.‡ As he outlived his younger brother Henry by eighteen years and after the latter's death gave important evidence on monetary problems to the Commons Committee on the Resumption of Specie Payments in 1819, he seems to have been the more familiar figure to the economists of the 'twenties and 'thirties. It must be due to a confusion with him that J. R. MacCulloch started the legend, since copied by

---

a part of the known world, where such books could be introduced, which did not feel the salutary influence of this single individual" (*Life of John Newton*, written by himself, with a continuation by R. Cecil, Edinburgh, N.D.).

* According to an evidently exaggerated statement in the obituary notice in the *Gentleman's Magazine* (November 1790) "he began the world with £100,000 and left it with £600,000. His gains as a merchant were immense. He was the greatest merchant in Europe, except Mr. Hope, of Amsterdam; and generally one-half of his profits was dedicated to the poor."

† Of the two daughters, Jane, married Lord Balgonie, later Earl of Leven, and the other died as a child.

‡ See the *Book of Yearly Recollections of Samuel Thornton, Esq.*

practically everyone who ever mentioned Henry Thornton, that the latter was a director and Governor of the Bank of England.*

Robert, the second son, M.P. for Colchester and at one time Governor of the East India Company, although by residence a member of the Clapham circle, seems to have been rather different from the rest of the family. He collected a magnificent library, his "villa in Clapham was celebrated for the beauty of its garden and conservatory," and he "lavishly entertained royalty and many others" there with the result that he outran his fortune, tried to recoup it in daring speculations in the funds, failed, and ultimately died in America.†

Henry, the youngest son, was born on March 10, 1760. The parents apparently had rather unusual ideas about education, and while they seem to have spared no expense, and even sent their eldest son for three years to the Royal Pedagogue in Halle, Saxony,‡ they took a somewhat unfortunate line in the case of Henry. After eight years at a fairly efficient school run by a Mr. Devis in Wandsworth, where he began to learn Latin at five, he was sent to a Mr. Roberts at Point Pleasant, who

* J. R. MacCulloch, *The Literature of Political Economy*, London, 1845, p. 169, who already suggests that Henry Thornton was in consequence unduly partial to the Bank of England. The error has entered even Leslie Stephen's article on Henry Thornton in the *D.N.B.* and has since again and again been made the basis of unfounded accusations of bias on the part of Thornton, especially by J. W. Angell, *The Theory of International Prices*, Cambridge, 126, p. 46. That Henry Thornton was never a director of the Bank of England is apparent from the complete list of directors given by W. M. Acres, *The Bank of England from Within*, 1694–1900, London, 1931, vol. ii, pp. 613–30, and has been confirmed on enquiry by the Secretary of the Bank of England. The falsity of the statement should, however, have been obvious from the fact that according to a firmly established tradition a banker (in the strict English sense of the word, as distinguished from a "merchant-banker") could not become a director of the Bank.

† Cf. R. de M. Rudolf in *Clapham and the Clapham Sect*, p. 107; Colquhoun, *Wilberforce*, p. 270; W. G. Black in *Notes and Queries*, 5th Series, vol. vii, January 6, 1877, p. 6; and *MS. Recollections of Marianne Thornton*.

‡ *Book of Yearly Recollections of Samuel Thornton*, p. 1. The University of Halle was then the centre of German Pietism, in a sense a precursor of the Evanglical Revival in England.

"professed to keep a school different from other Schools, and seemed a sort of miracle from the circumstance of his being himself the teacher of every thing. He taught Latin, Greek, French, Rhetoric, drawing, arithmetic, reading, writing, speaking, geography, bowing, walking, fencing. He also gave us a few lessons in Hebrew, and in mathematics."[*]

Henry resided in this academy from his thirteenth to well into his nineteenth year, but because of his superior previous knowledge of Greek and Latin he was tempted to be very idle during the whole of this period. He complains later that he left school with an extremely small stock of knowledge and that he knew little or nothing of English, History, Mathematics, Natural Philosophy, Belles Lettres, and Politics.

His school years had only been interrupted, in the interval between the two schools, by a family visit to France, where in the company of Cowper's friend, the Rev. Mr. Unwin, they spent some weeks in Paris in 1773.

The two years from the spring of 1778 to the spring of 1780 Henry spent in the firm of his relative, Godfrey Thornton, and then he entered his father's counting-house, that is, as he explains,

"a counting house in which he conducts some business in his own name, apart from that of the House of Thornton, Cornwall & Co. There is a proverb that 'Jack of all trades never thrives.' This proverb was verified in my father's case. He was in his private capacity a merchant in general. He made, that is to say, occasional and sometimes large speculations in any article which happened to take his fancy. During the two or three years in which I was his partner he embarked on a great speculation in wheat by which he lost £2,000 or £3,000—in a speculation in Tobacco by which he also lost money; in the sale also of British articles sent to the West Indies. . . ."

"Mortified to find that little pecuniary advantage was to be expected from my connection with my Father, I gave a very willing ear to a proposition made to me by Mr. Poole of Woodford for entering into a Banking concern with Mr. Down, my present partner. My Father was averse to it, and my Mother also. I did not, however, very greatly respect their judgment and they did not forbid my becoming a Banker. My Father as I suspect chiefly feared that I should be placed under peculiar temptation

[*] *MS. Diary of Henry Thornton.*

to keep improper Company by my being a Banker, a point in which he was mistaken. My Mother's prejudices led her to think that to cease being a Merchant in order to become a Banker was to descend in life. She was well read in the *Spectator*, and had learnt to think that Sir Andrew Freeport was one of the first characters in the world."*

It was in 1784 that he joined the banking house of Down and Free,† which soon became Down, Thornton, and Free, and of which he remained an active partner till his death. Two years earlier, however, he had entered the House of Commons and it was, as he records, partly this fact which recommended him to his partners. He had, indeed, made an even earlier attempt to enter Parliament when he was little more than twenty-one. Such an early entry into political life was at that time by no means uncommon. At the elections of 1780 the two friends, William Pitt and William Wilberforce, had both been successful at the age of twenty-one—Wilberforce, a second cousin‡ of Henry Thornton, at Hull, where Wilberforce senior and the father of Mrs. John Thornton were both eminent merchants. When a year later the second seat for Hull became vacant, Henry's ambitious mother urged him to become a candidate. But after a little canvassing he discovered that he was universally expected to give two guineas to every voter, a custom with which he was neither willing nor able to comply, and consequently withdrew. In the autumn of 1782 another vacancy occurred, however, by the death of the member for Southwark, and again his mother urged him on, and prepared the way for him through her connections in Dissenting circles. His father, Henry, records,

* *MS. Diary of Henry Thornton,* January 1802.
† Established in 1773 as Marlor, Lascelles, Pell and Down.
‡ William Wilberforce I, the grandfather of the more famous William Wilberforce III here discussed, had married Sarah Thornton, a sister of Robert, the grandfather of Henry Thornton. In the next generation a daughter of Robert Thornton and half-sister of Henry's father, Hannah Thornton, married her cousin William Wilberforce II, an uncle of William Wilberforce III, who spent part of his boyhood in the house of his aunt and there came for the first time under the influence of the Evangelicals. Most of the years of his boyhood were spent in the house of Mr. Joseph Sykes, at West Ella, near Hull, where he grew up with the numerous children of the family, one of whom was to be the future Mrs. Henry Thornton.

Enquiry into Paper Credit 17 B

"appeared to me not at all opposed to my mother's propositions and he gave me a recommendatory letter to Mr. Ellis, the only person in Southwark with whom he was acquainted. My father, however, observed that according to his opinion the only mode in which it was right to enter into Parliament was that of Sir John Barnard, who was riding about Clapham Common while his election was going on, and who instead of soliciting his Electors was solicited by them. I perceived so plainly the impossibility of success in my own case if a principle of this kind was to be prescribed to me, that I considered my father's objections as extravagant, and the evil of the two guineas not subsisting in Southwark I thought little of any other Evils and committed my cause to the hands of a large and self-created Committee which took upon itself to manage my election for me. A very able Lawyer Mr. Serjeant Adair was my opponent. Mrs. Thrale at whose house I dined on this occasion in company with Dr. Johnson, gave me her support.* The dissenters in general were favourable to me. The Thrale party† who had supported Lord North in the American war, were most of them also on my side, and the popular sentiment was in favour of a Merchant rather than a Lawyer. Some religious people moreover sided with me for my father's sake, and the known largeness of his charities were a further recommendation. I carried my election by a great majority. . . ."‡

"The first vote I ever gave in Parliament," he writes somewhat later in his diary, "was in favour of the treaty of peace with America. I imme-

---

* Cf. the following note by Fanny Burney : December 2, 1782, "Mrs. Thrale had a large party. . . . The rest were : . . . Mr. Thornton, the new member for the borough, a man of Presbyterian extraction upon which he has grafted of late much *ton* and *nonchalance,* and who was pleased to follow me about with a sort of hard and unmeaning curiosity, very disagreeable to me, and to himself very much like nothing . . ." *Diary and Letters of Madame D'Arblay,* edited by C. Barret, Preface and Notes by Austin Dobson, 1904, vol. ii, p. 130.

† Henry Thrale had been M.P. for Southwark from 1768 to 1780.

‡ *MS. Diary of Henry Thornton.* The passage quoted in the text continues : "There is no doubt that the law which forbids treating was violated by me on this occasion, a subject into which my Father and Mother did not enquire. Mr. Adair, in the speech which he made on retiring from the Hustings intimated that he might if he pleased set aside my Election by petitioning against me and I believe he took the question of an appeal to the House of Commons into consideration, but that he relinquished his purpose partly on the ground of his party having also treated though in a less degree, and partly on that of my majority proving so considerable that I could not be said to owe my success to this illegal practice. A short time after my Election, but antecedently to my taking my Seat I was invited by a friend to dine at his House in private with Mr. Pitt, and I was much gratified by the idea of being introduced to so great a person."

diately became in some measure enlisted with the friends of Mr. Pitt and an opponent of the Coalition party. I divided against Mr. Fox's India Bill (November 1783) and again supported Mr. Pitt on his return to power, except in a few instances."

Thornton's active participation in the debates of these years seems in the main to have been confined to questions of taxation, particularly the discussion of the receipts tax and the shop tax. Even then, as he suggests, his allegiance to Pitt was by no means absolute, and in these years that little but influential group of independent members, the "party of the Saints," gradually formed, of which Thornton and Wilberforce were for many years to be the leading figures.

In the winter of 1785–6 Wilberforce, after his final conversion to the views of the Evangelicals, had found a retreat in the house of John Thornton, and there the two young men drew close together and round them the "Clapham Sect" began to form. Looking back many years later,* Thornton writes:

"Few men have been blessed with worthier and better friends than it has been my lot to be. Mr. Wilberforce stands at the head of these, for he was the friend of my youth. I owed much to him in every sense soon after I came out in life, for my education had been narrow, and his enlarged mind, his affectionate and understanding manners and his very superior piety were exactly calculated to supply what was wanting to my improvement and my establishment in a right course. It is chiefly through him that I have been introduced to a variety of other most valuable associates, to my friends Babington† and Gisborne‡ and their worthy families, to Lord

---

* *MS. Diary of Henry Thornton.*

† Thomas Babington (1758–1838), landowner in Rothley Temple, Leicestershire, since 1800 M.P. for Leicester, member of Wilberforce's "Philanthropic Cabinet," prominent abolitionist and writer on education. On Babington and the others mentioned below see the full accounts in Colquhoun, *Wilberforce and his Friends.*

‡ Thomas Gisborne (1758–1846), curate of Barton-under-Needwood, Staffordshire, lives at Yoxall Lodge which, like his friend Babington's house Rothley Temple, provides frequently a country retreat for Wilberforce and other members of the group; author of *Principles of Moral Philosophy*, 1789, and *An Enquiry into the Duties of Men in the Higher Ranks and Middle Classes*, 1794.

Teignmouth* and his family, to Mrs. Hannah More† and her sisters; to Mr. Stephen‡ and to not a few respectable members of Parliament. Second only to Mr. Wilberforce in my esteem is now the family of Mr. Grant."§

For the early years the names of T. Clarkson‖ and Granville Sharp,¶ while somewhat later Zachary Macaulay,** John Venn,†† William Smith,‡‡ and John Bowdler§§ would have to be included, to give a fairly complete list of Thornton's closer associates. It was a truly remarkable group of people, whose connections were made even closer by numerous intermarriages between their families,‖‖ and who to the present day show the strength of their

* Sir John Shore, later created Lord Teignmouth (1751–1834), after early experience in India under Warren Hastings, Viceroy from 1793–1798, retired to Clapham in 1802, first President of the Bible Society.

† Hannah More (1745–1833), authoress and dramatist, who after a youth in the midst of the London literary circles, as a friend of Garrick, Dr. Johnson, and Horace Walpole, became one of the most influential religious writers and most active advocates of popular education.

‡ James Stephen (1758–1832), Master in Chancery and M.P. for Tralee since 1808, and for East Grinstead since 1812, became interested in the abolitionist cause by experiences as a barrister in the West Indies, later for many years one of the closest allies of Wilberforce.

§ Charles Grant (1746–1823) lived in Clapham after a long life in India and as one of the most influential directors and at one time Governor of East India Company; father of Lord Glenelg, Secretary for the Colonies, and Sir Robert Grant, Governor of Bombay.

‖ Thomas Clarkson (1760–1846), with Granville Sharp and Wilberforce the leading figure in the abolitionist movement.

¶ Granville Sharp (1735–1813), originator of the anti-slavery agitation.

** Zachary Macaulay (1768–1838), joins anti-slavery movement because of experience as employee on an estate in Jamaica, appointed Governor of Sierra Leone Company by Henry Thornton, and after his return for many years editor of the *Christian Observer;* Father of T. B. Macaulay.

†† John Venn (1759–1813), son of Henry Venn, the author of the *Complete Duty of Man,* "the trusted exposition of the Characteristic theology of the Clapham Sect," Rector of Clapham since 1792.

‡‡ William Smith (1756–1835), merchant and stockbroker, from 1784 M.P. in succession for Sudbury, Camelford, and Norwich, noted lover of nature and patron of the arts, lived at Clapham.

§§ John Bowdler (1783–1815), lawyer and poet, cousin of Thomas Bowdler of "Family Shakespeare" fame. In John Bowdler's writings Henry Thornton appears under the name of "Sophron."

‖‖ T. Gisborne married Babington's sister, and Babington Macaulay's, who in turn married, if not a real member of the group, at least a favourite pupil of Hannah More's; James Stephen married as his second wife a sister of Wilberforce who, it will be remembered, was a second cousin of Henry Thornton.

20

native gifts by the extraordinarily long list of their famous descendants.*

Early in 1792 Henry Thornton bought a house at Battersea Rise,† on Clapham Common, which had formerly belonged to Lubbock, the banker, and for the next five years, till they both married, Wilberforce shared it with him, "contributing so much toward expenses." Two other houses on the estate which Thornton had acquired, Glenelg and Broomfield, were let to two friends, Charles Grant and Edward Eliot, the latter the brother-in-law of Pitt. After Eliot's death in 1797 Broomfield was taken by Wilberforce. Thornton added to his house and it is said that Pitt on one of his visits to his brother-in-law designed the oval library of Battersea Rise, which became the famous meeting-place of the group. It was here that the campaign for the abolition of slavery was planned and directed and that the numerous other activities of the Evangelical party were discussed.

It is quite impossible to make more than a mere mention in this sketch of the more important movements which the Clapham Sect initiated and in which Henry Thornton took a leading part. Their main achievement is, of course, the abolition of the slave trade,‡

James Stephen's son of the same name, the author of the Essay on the Clapham Sect, married a granddaughter of John Venn, whose son Henry was married to Martha Sykes, a niece of Mrs. Henry Thornton.

* The most famous of these is of course T. B. Macaulay, who in a school originally provided for negro children but then continued for the Clapham boys had James Stephen the younger, Samuel Wilberforce, the bishop ("Soapy Sam"), and the younger Lord Teignmouth for his contemporaries. In the third generation there is Florence Nightingale, the grand-daughter of William Smith, and in addition James Fitzjames and Leslie Stephen, G. O. Trevelyan, A. V. Dicey, and John Venn the logician may be mentioned as figures of great intellectual eminence. Of living authors the names of Mrs. Virginia Woolf as a descendant of the Stephens's and of Mr. E. M. Forster as a direct descendant of Henry Thornton may be added.

† A charming description of *Battersea Rise* (which disappeared only in 1907) is given from her own recollection by Miss Dorothy Pym, another descendant of Henry Thornton, in a book of that title (London, 1934). Photographs of the famous library will be found in *Clapham and the Clapham Sect*, p. 109, and in J. Telford, *A Sect that Moved the World*, p. 116.

‡ Cf. F. J. Klingberg, *The Anti-Slavery Movement in England*, New Haven and London, 1926, and R. Coupland, *The British Anti-Slavery Movement*, London (Home University Library), 1933.

and from the beginning of the association of Thornton and Wilberforce up till the passing of the Act of 1807,* the greater part of their energies were devoted to this leading goal. If Wilberforce was the driving spirit, Thornton was the wise and practical counsellor on whom Wilberforce placed absolute reliance. When in 1791 the experiment of settling a number of liberated slaves in St. George's Bay led to the foundation of the Sierra Leone Company, the first of the African Chartered Companies, Henry Thornton became its Chairman; and through all its vicissitudes, till Sierra Leone was taken over as a Crown Colony in 1808, he remained Chairman of the Company, and devoted much of his time to its business and the many Parliamentary discussions to which its problems gave rise.† And when in 1798 the abolitionists almost despaired of ever succeeding, Henry Thornton revived their hopes by successfully piloting a bill for the exclusion of the slave trade from certain parts of the African coast through the House of Commons, although it eventually failed to pass the Lords.‡

If this is the best known of the achievements of the group, there are others of not much less importance. Faith in popular education, and sabbatarian zeal, led in 1785 to the foundation of the Sunday School Society of which Henry Thornton was the

---

* The following anecdote, connected with the final passage of the long fought for bill, which is rather characteristic of Henry Thornton and his relation to Wilberforce, may have a place here. After the division "a good many came over to Palace Yard after the House got up and congratulated [Wilberforce]. John Thornton and Heber, Sharp, Macaulay, Grant and Robert Grant, Robert Bird and William Smith who were in the gallery. 'Well, Henry,' Mr. Wilberforce asked playfully of Mr. Thornton, 'what shall we abolish next?' 'The lottery, I think,' gravely replied his sterner friend." (*Life of Wilberforce*, vol. iii, p. 298.)

† On the History of the Sierra Leone Company see F. W. Butt Thompson, *Sierra Leone in History and Tradition*, 1926.

‡ That Henry Thornton was the originator of the bill is commonly affirmed in the literature, but not evident from the *Parliamentary Debates*. But according to the *Annual Register* (vol. 40, 1798, p. 237) Henry Thornton moved, on May 4, 1798, "that the House resolve itself into a committee in which he should move to bring in a bill to prohibit the carrying on the slave trade on the Northern Coast of Africa." See also the *Journals of the House of Commons*, vol. liii, 1797–8, p. 540.

first President.* He provided for twenty-five years the means which enabled Hannah More to run her schools for the poor.† And when in 1795 the same old friend‡ embarked upon her *Cheap Repository* tracts, in addition to writing some of the tracts.§

"Mr. T[hornton] and two or three others condescended to spend hours with the hawkers to learn the mysteries of their trade; the result is, we purpose next month to print two different editions of the same tract, one of handsome appearance for the rich, the other on coarser paper, but so excessively cheap by wholesale, as fully to meet the hawkers on their own ground."‖

With such advice the group succeeded in selling no less than two millions of the Cheap Repository Tracts during the first year of their existence. Out of this grew in 1799 the Religious Tract Society;¶ in the same year the Church Missionary Society,** and in 1804 the British and Foreign Bible Society†† were founded by the Clapham group, and in all three organizations Henry Thornton served as Treasurer. And the Charity of the Sect did not remain confined to the English on the one side and the Heathen on the other. When during the Napoleonic wars news came of frightful destitution in Germany, it was again Henry Thornton and Zachary Macaulay who organized public meetings and subscriptions to raise funds for relief.‡‡

---

* M. G. Jones, *The Charity School Movement*, Cambridge, 1938, p. 152.

† Roberts, *Memoirs of H. More*, vol. iii, p. 451.

‡ "He and H. More are like brother and sister, or mother and son" is the description of the friendship by Lady Hesketh (*Letters of Lady Hesketh to the Rev. John Johnson*, edited by C. B. Johnson, 1901, p. 89).

§ According to his Diary, in addition to revising for Hannah More some of her own tracts, particularly the *Shepherd of Salisbury Plain* and the *Lancashire Collier Girl*, he seems to have written himself at least three tracts in 1795, one of them containing dialogues and another on the *Religious Advantages of the Inhabitants of Great Britain*.

‖ Hannah More in a letter to Z. Macaulay, dated January 6, 1706 (*Life and Correspondence*, edited by Roberts, vol. ii, p. 460).

¶ See A. de Morgan in *Notes and Queries*, 3rd Series, vol. vi, pp. 241–6.

** E. Stock, *The History of the Church Missionary Society*, London, 1899, vol. i, p. 69.

†† W. Canton, *History of the British and Foreign Bible Society*, 1904, vol. i.

‡‡ Lady Knutsford, *Z. Macaulay*, p. 310.

But we must leave the activities in which Henry Thornton participated mainly as a leading member of a group, and return to the main events of his life and his more personal views and activities in Parliament. He had entered the banking business at the beginning of a period of ten years of great prosperity and rapid expansion of the credit system of England. At the death of his father in 1790, Henry inherited a substantial sum which may well have helped him in building up what appears to have been a comparatively small banking house into one of the largest in the City. Of the three older partners two, of whom he says that

"they both were very kind to me—both however lent no very willing ear to the religious observations which I sometimes endeavoured to press upon them,"*

died in the first few years of the new century, and, the third being an invalid, left him as the dominant figure in the business. Looking back over his career as a banker he writes in 1809:

"My Banking business has been very profitable to me. I discovered before I entered that the antecedent gains had been extremely small; probably they were not more than £1,500 or £2,000 per year in all of which half had belonged to Mr. Down. The business gradually increased when my name and that of Mr. Free were added to the firm. We owed much to the kindness of our friends and much also to the circumstance of many country banks rising up at the time, with which we were wise enough to become connected. In the year 1793, a season of great commercial distress, we experienced greater difficulties than most other bankers in consequence of the sudden reductions of very large sums which we had held at interest for some very considerable banks. The evil partly consisted in the inadequacy of our capital. Mr. Down was not at that time very rich and my savings had been far from considerable.

"The world naturally expects that a House trusted so largely and conducting such expensive operations, should have funds of its own either in hand or within call, bearing some proportions to its concern and there is something, as I now think, like want of honesty in claiming an almost unbounded credit without laying a proportional foundation for it. The banking business is an extremely desirable one. It is remarkably suited

* *MS. Diary of Henry Thornton*, March 21, 1803.

24

to my infirmity of health, and the Providence of God has dealt most mercifully with me in thus accommodating my profession to my circumstances. My eldest son seems well qualified by nature to take my place in this concern. A little good sense, regular attendance, a spirit of liberality and kindness not degenerating into profusion and servility, together with an exact integrity are the chief points to be regarded.

"There is no necessity for becoming an *intimate acquaintance* of all who are disposed to be the good customer of the house. Many of them may be very unfit to be friends. It may be, on the other hand, expedient to cultivate the friendship of a few respectable connections of the House and it will not be difficult to discover which of these are in point of private character the most desirable as guest at our table, or intimate associates in our family. . . ."

"I have, by the blessings of good Providence, enjoyed a considerable and generally increasing income for the last twenty years. But I have made it my rule not to amass any large fortune. When my father died, I received from him about £40,000, having antecedently derived from him only the very moderate sum of £6,000. My income has grown to £8, 10, or even 11 or 12,000 per an. of which £4 or £5,000 generally suffices for my expenses and about £2 or £3,000 is given in charity. My bounty was much larger before I married and now and then perhaps approached to profusion. The number of my children (now 8) and the infirmity of my health, together with the consideration that some may derive from me a tender constitution, which may be the source of more than ordinary expense, disposes me now to lay by £2 or £3,000 per an. for, in the midst of my compassion for the poor, I desire always to remember that saying of the Apostle 'He that provideth not for his own household is worse than an infidel.' "

It is recorded that till his marriage in 1796 Thornton had made it a rule to give away as charity six-sevenths of his income.* His

---

* This is a statement frequently made in the literature on Henry Thornton. In a letter to *The Guardian* of June 19, 1907, p. 1023, "A Granddaughter of Henry Thornton" gives the following extracts from Henry Thornton's accounts for the four years from 1790:

Charity	£2,260.	All other expenses		£1,543
,,	3,960	,,	,,	,,	1,817
,,	7,508	,,	,,	,,	1,616
,,	6,680	,,	,,	,,	1,988

and about the following year, 1794, he says in his *MS. Diary*: "I have spent work at the Banking House does not appear to have taken up too much of his time. If we may trust his Diary, to attend there regularly from 11 a.m. to 3 p.m. seems to have been a good intention rarely achieved. And even so, we find occasionally entries as the following: "I did little yesterday at my Banking House except correcting a Sermon on Self Denial."*

Of his business habits two anecdotes have come down to us, one of them referring to an embarrassment similar to that reported

£1,300 this year more than I have got and I find I have been indiscreet in my loans of money, especially formerly—

I have spent 2,200 besides 560 repairs, is about	2,800
Clapham House and furniture rent	600
gave in Charity 3,750	
lost by old bad debts now wrote off about 1,550	5,300
	8,700

which is about £1,300 more than I have got, but I have been rather imprudent and I ought to trace this to a fault in my character."

In a MS. letter in the British Museum (Egerton Collection, 1966), by Robert Harry Inglis, apparently written shortly after Henry Thornton's death, it is said of him that "He was liberality embodied—his charities were munificent beyond any example as we now know since his death. One of the items of his bounty as it was told me by a common friend who had personal means of knowing it, was £1,400 per annum for the education of pious men for the Church. His charities before his marriage were 10,000 per annum and the most extraordinary part of this is that he gave nothing without enquiry—it was not a large appropriation of a particular sum to the relief of others which satisfied his conscience—he felt that he was not only a Steward to set apart for the general class of indigence a large portion of his means, but that he was equally a Steward in the detailed distribution of it—it was not enough that he did not spend it on himself, but in spending it on others he made it go as far as possible. He therefore gave his time as well as his money—a sacrifice which Mr. Macaulay said he did not think overstated at 5,000 per annum more —as his undivided attention to the business of his Banking house would have enabled him to realize many more profits and to avoid many more losses—if he had left a very large fortune, it might have been said that these charities magnificent as they are were yet mainly his superfluities; but his income was mainly for life and his fortune is comparatively very inconsiderable; but he left his children a name more valuable and an example more precious than any other employment of his time would have enabled him to leave."

* MS. Diary, January 23, 1795. Shortly later the following entry occurs, February 15, 1795. "Went to Sierra Leone House and attended an hour and a half on Committee of Trade—I think my attendance was useful—It was certainly a self-denial, and yet how pleasant would some people think even my acts of self-denial to be—so favoured am I by Providence."

above, which occurred during the crisis of 1810. In the autumn of that year

"he was on his road with his family to Scotland. It was a time of severe pressure upon banks and trading interests. Straitened by the obstacles of the war, hampered by the embargoes by which Napoleon had deranged the course of trade, many commercial houses, long reckoned safe, sunk; others could only save themselves by flying to the banks for accommodation. The bank in which Mr. Thornton was a partner felt the pressure, and felt it severely, just after their most able partner had left London for the North. Had Mr. Thornton known what was impending, he would not have absented himself. The news reached him on his route to Scotland, and caused him some embarrassment. To return from a journey undertaken and generally known, would have spread rumours which might have brought on the very crisis that was to be feared. This course, therefore, could not be thought of. He decided to continue his journey, but he opened himself in confidence to one valued friend, and stated his wish that some thousands of pounds might be placed at demand at the disposal of his partners in the bank. No sooner was the hint given than it was met by ample support. Funds poured in from all quarters— Wilberforce, with generous ardour, hastening to lead the way; and the money came in such a flood, that his bank saw itself lifted above the sands on which it was settling, and floated into deep waters with abundant resources."*

The other anecdote is told by the younger James Stephen without a date:

"Tidings of the commercial failure of a near kinsman embarked him at once on any enquiry—how far he was obliged to indemnify those who might have given credit to his relative, in reliance, however, unauthorized, on his own resources; and again the coffers of the banker were un- locked by the astuteness of the casuist. A mercantile partnership (many a year has passed since the disclosure could injure or affect any one), which without his knowledge had obtained from his firm large and improvident advances, became so hopelessly embarrassed, that their bankruptcy was pressed upon him as the only chance of averting from his own house the most serious disasters. He overruled the proposal, on the ground that they whose rashness had given to their debtors an unmerited credit, had no right to call on others to divide with them the consequent

* Colquhoun, *Wilberforce*, p. 248.

loss. To the last farthing he therefore dissolved the liabilities of the insolvents, at a cost of which his own share exceeded twenty thousand pounds. Yet he was then declining in health, and the father of nine young children."*

As will be seen more fully in the second part of this essay, it was probably the experience of the crisis of 1793 which directed Thornton's mind to credit problems. And in 1797, when the suspension of cash payments by the Bank of England led to separate enquiries by the House of Commons and the House of Lords, we find him prepared to give in his evidence before both committees a most lucid outline of the main ideas, which shows that by this time his thoughts had already crystallized. It immediately attracted wide attention and established his reputation as the foremost authority on these matters.† This side of his activities will, however, be taken up in the next section and we must now bring this general account of his life to a close.

Henry Thornton had married in the spring of 1796 Marianne Sykes, like his mother the daughter of a "Russian merchant" in Hull. It seems that she was a woman of considerable intelligence and education, but like her husband of very delicate health. In spite of this, however, Battersea Rise was soon peopled with nine children who all survived their parents. In the education of his children Henry took a great interest, and it is said that he "endeavoured to interest them at the earliest possible age in politics, and even in currency. He wrote a paper, advocating this practice, in the *Christian Observer*."‡

To the busy father the country house in Battersea Rise served, however, only as a retreat from his labours in the City and in

* J. Stephen, *Essays*, p. 191. From the last sentence of the passage it appears that the event must have taken place between 1809 and 1815. The first sentence very likely refers to the bankruptcy of his brother Robert.

† In the House of Lords Debate on the Bank on May 15, 1797, already, Lord Auckland refers to "Mr. Henry Thornton of whom and of whose evidence it was difficult to speak in terms of adequate respect."—*Parliamentary History*, vol. xxiii, 1897–8, p. 534.

‡ Leslie Stephen in the article on Henry Thornton in the *D.N.B.* and *Manuscript Recollections of Marianne Thornton.*

Parliament, and during the months when he resided at Clapham he would daily ride on horseback into town. He spent most of his time at a house in King's Arms Yard, Coleman Street, near the seat of his Bank in Bartholomew Lane, and later, when his increasing parliamentary duties made it desirable to live in Westminster, at a house in Old Palace Yard which he had taken over from Wilberforce. His activities and his influence in Parliament, and at the same time his political independence, had been constantly growing since the evidence of 1797 had established his reputation. In that same year he supported Grey's motion for parliamentary reform, and on questions such as abuses in elections and the general abolition of sinecures he frequently found himself in disagreement with the Government. His reformatory zeal led him to support Catholic emancipation at an early stage (1805) and to take a lively interest in questions such as debtors relief and prison reform. In the great struggle with France all his efforts were directed towards the restoration, and later to the maintenance of peace. On questions like the attack on Copenhagen he differed not only with the Government but also with the members of his closest circle, his brothers, Wilberforce, Babington, and Grant. In the discussion of Pitt's income tax he strongly advocated a graduation of the rate according to the character of the income, and when he failed to carry his point, he silently raised his own payment to the figure to which it would have amounted under his scheme.* In the new century, however, his parliamentary activity became more and more connected with the problems of currency and banking. He was a member of the Committee of 1804 on the Irish exchange,† he was elected in February 1807 a member of the committee of 21 "to examine and control the several branches of public expenditure," and there took "a considerable lead in the report made by

---

* There is only a short reference in the report in *Hansard* of his speech on December 22, 1798, to the distinction between fluctuating and fixed incomes, but some additional information can be gathered from J. Stephen's *Essays*, p. 190, L. Stephen's article in the *D.N.B.*, and an article by Miss J. Wedgwood in the *Contemporary Review*, vol. lxviii, October 1895.

† See *Journals of the House of Commons*, vol. lix, 1803–4, pp. 129–30.

them on the Bank affairs, by which £240,000 a year has been saved to the state. I had in this case to oppose the views of my family and city connection."* In 1810 at last he took a leading part not only in the work of the Bullion Committee, of which we shall have to speak more fully later, but also in the work of the Committee on the State of Commercial Credit appointed by Perceval's Government a little later in the same year. His active years in Parliament extended just long enough not only to be a member of the Committee of 1813 "to enquire into the Corn Trade of the United Kingdom," but also to speak in the great debate on the Corn Laws in June 1814. This was almost his last speech in Parliament; it was followed by only one a little later in the same month on a bill on London Prisons.

During these fourteen years which Henry Thornton lived into the nineteenth century, his work in Parliament and his literary activities must have taken up almost all his time. In the repeated elections of these years, in 1802, 1806, 1807, and 1812 he found it harder and harder to retain his seat with declining majorities. He was not a figure who appealed to the popular imagination, and even though the universal respect in which he was held secured him his seat till his death, his diary shows that he was greatly worried by his declining support. Yet we need hardly be surprised that in times of intense party strife and widespread political corruption to retain his seat was difficult for a man who refused to give undivided allegiance to any party and whose supporters attempted to recommend him to a greedy populace by doggerel verses like these:

> "Nor place nor pension e'er got he
> For self or for connection;
> We shall not tax the Treasury
> By Thornton's re-election."†

It has been said by one of the admirers of Henry Thornton that

---

* *MS. Diary,* 1809.

† *MS. Recollections of Marianne Thornton;* also Colquhoun, *Wilberforce,* p. 283.

he wrote a good deal, "but nothing likely to descend to posterity."*
That the *Paper Credit*, the only book† which Thornton appears
himself to have published, might be an exception probably never
occurred to the author of this statement. He clearly had in mind
the devotional and more popular writings of Henry Thornton,
which, indeed, were voluminous. It has happened to a bibliophile
economist that a stout volume of *Collected Works of Henry Thornton,
Esq., M.P.*, which he eagerly pulled from the shelves of a second-
hand bookshop proved to contain Family Prayers and Family
Commentaries on the Sermon on the Mount and on Portions of the
Pentateuch. These strictly religious writings of Henry Thornton
were published from his manuscripts after his death by R. H.
Inglis. But in addition he wrote a considerable amount for the
organ of the Clapham Sect, the *Christian Observer*, which he helped
to found and which for many years was edited by Zachary Macaulay.
It is said that from 1802, when this journal started, till his death,
Thornton contributed no less than eighty-two articles on a wide
range of subjects:

"sketches of public affairs, of the state of the parties in the stormy times
of 1803, 1806, 1810, and 1813; the difficult questions of the Orders in
Council; and the Middlesex election; biographies of Pitt and Fox, written
with the thoughtfulness as well as the impartiality of history, critiques
on the *Edinburgh Review*, on books, on the temper of religious parties, are
interspersed with advice as wise as Addison's, less playful, but more
sound."‡

During these later years of his life Thornton's contacts and
influence must have extended far beyond the narrower circle of
the Sect. As early as 1800 we find Jeremy Bentham writing to him
in connection with his Pannopticon project.§ And if a difference of
religious views had probably prevented closer contacts, he was a

---

* M. Seeley, *Later Evangelical Fathers*, London, 1879, p. 36.
† See Bibliographical Note at the end of this Introduction.
‡ Colquhoun, *Wilberforce*, p. 303.
§ *Catalogue of the Manuscripts of Jeremy Bentham* in the Library of University
College, London, compiled by A. Taylor Milne, University College, London,
1937, pp. 41, 141.

well-known and respected figure in the camp of the Philosophical Radicals. Lord Brougham seems to have known him well*, and in 1812 we find Ricardo inviting Malthus to dine with him and Thornton, a dinner party which the busy Thornton asks to have transferred to his house.†

It is astounding that all this activity should have come from a man who throughout the greater part of his life seems to have been in exceedingly weak health. But apart from occasional visits to Buxton or Bath, Brighton or the Isle of Wight, enforced by the state of his health, he did not give himself any rest. Even these annual journeys, although often extended to include visits to the sisters More and other friends, were not entirely devoted to recreation. In a letter to Charles Grant written from Buxton in September 1806, Henry Thornton writes:

"Dr. Lovell, whom partly to satisfy the kind anxiety of friends, I consulted about my own health, advised Buxton Waters, and after seeing some beautiful scenes in Monmouthshire and one especially which I never shall forget we moved slowly hither. We bought a grey poney on which my little Girl‡ has cantered many a half stage and I have to thank the poney for having made me much better acquainted with my Daughter than I was before. We have also gone together to see a variety of Manufactures and have been learning to feel for those who dig in mines, who toil in Quarries, perspire in Salt works, wear out their Eyes in looking at Furnaces or pass their whole morning noon and Even in the limited Employment of putting on the head of a Pin, or drawing over and over the same pattern on a piece of China. I fear that the Less pleasant part of Education has been neglected. I trust however that seeing the world in this sense will be very usefull. It also has not a little entertained Mrs. T. and I trust that the View which we have taken of our fellow creatures has inspired some thankfulness for the temporal as well as spiritual Advantages of our own condition."§

* See *Brougham and His Early Friends*. Letters to James Loch, 1798–1809. Collected and arranged by R. H. M. Buddle and G. A. Jackson, Privately Printed, 1908, vol. ii, letters of December 14 and 22, 1904.

† *Letters of David Ricardo to Thomas Robert Malthus*, 1810–23, edited by James Bonar, Oxford, 1887, pp. 25, 26, December 17, 1812.

‡ This is Henry Thornton's first child, Marianne, then nine years of age.

§ MS. letter of Henry Thornton to Charles Grant, dated Buxton September 17, 1806, in the possession of Mr. E. M. Forster.

The anxiety of Henry Thornton's friends was however only too well justified and the lingering complaint, apparently consumption, grew gradually worse. In the autumn of 1814 his constitution finally broke down, and after a prolonged illness he died on January 16, 1815, in his fifty-fifth year.*

"A more upright, independent, and truly virtuous man has never adorned the Senate," says the writer of the obituary notice in the *Gentleman's Magazine.*† The various attempts to describe his character depict him as a man of almost unearthly goodness. "He has indeed a mind so disciplined and trained," writes one of Thornton's friends to his wife, "so godly, so divested of self, and so active to glorify God and benefit men that a near view of him is a most humbling lesson."‡ James Stephen§ and J. C. Colquhoun‖ describe the bent of his mind as pre-eminently judicial and "essentially philosophic." But we shall perhaps have a more life-like picture of the man if from the almost unbroken stream of deserved praise we quote the one or two more critical passages. Henry Brougham describes him as "the most eminent in every respect" of Wilberforce's small party,

"a man of strong understanding, great powers of reasoning and of investi-

---

* On the day of Thornton's death we find young T. B. Macaulay writing to Mrs. Hannah More: "Clapham, January 16, 1815. My dear Madam, My mamma was on the point of writing to inform you that a supposed favourable alteration has taken place in Mr. Henry Thornton's case. His physicians are still sanguine in their expectations; but his friends, who examine his disorders by the rules of commonsense, and not by those of medicine, are very weak in their hopes. The warm bath has been prescribed; and it is the wish and prayer of all who know him that so excellent and valuable a character may be preserved to the world."—*Letters of Hannah More to Zachary Macaulay*, edited by A. Roberts, London, 1860, p. 68. Mrs. Henry Thornton followed her husband after a few months and the orphaned children were taken care of by Mr. and Mrs. R. H. Inglis (later Sir Robert Inglis, and M.P. for Oxford), who moved into Battersea Rise and succeeded in preserving it as a centre of humanitarian and intellectual activity. It may be of interest to note that the apothecary Pennington who attended Henry Thornton in his last illness was probably the brother of the economist, James Pennington.

† *Gentleman's Magazine*, February 1815, vol. lxxxv, Part 1, p. 182.

‡ Morris, *The Life of Charles Grant*, London, 1904, p. 177. Letter of Charles Grant to Mrs. Grant of September 1794.

§ *Essays*, p. 189.   ‖ *Wilberforce*, p. 271.

Enquiry into Paper Credit

gation; an accurate and curious observer, but who neither had cultivated oratory at all nor had received a refined education, nor had extended his reading beyond the subjects connected with moral, political and theological learning. The trade of a banker, which he followed, engrossed much of his time; and his exertions both in Parliament and through the press, were chiefly confined to the celebrated controversy upon the currency, in which his well-known work led the way, and to a bill for restricting the Slave Trade to part of the African coast, which he introduced when the abolitionists were wearied out with their repeated failure; and had well-nigh abandoned all hopes of carrying the great measure itself."*

And James Stephen at the end of the description of Thornton in his once celebrated Essay on the Clapham Sect pictures him as

"Affectionate, but passionless—with a fine and indeed a fastidious taste, but destitute of all creative imagination—gifted rather with fortitude to endure calamity, than with courage to exult in the struggle with danger— a lover of mankind but not an enthusiast in the cause of our common humanity—his serene and perspicacious spirit was never haunted by the visions, nor borne away by the resistless impulses, of which heroic natures, and they alone, are conscious. Well qualified to impart to the highest energies of others a wise direction, and inflexible perseverance, he had to borrow from them the glowing temperament which hopes against hope, and is wise in despite of prudence."†

A note may perhaps be added to this on the fate of Henry Thornton's firm. After his death it had become Pole, Thornton, Free, Down & Scott, with Sir Peter Pole as leading partner, and young Henry Sykes Thornton, Henry's eldest son, who was only fifteen at the time of his death, became an active partner early in 1825. The house seems to have greatly prospered—it is said during the years 1818–24 to have yielded £40,000 a year,‡ and it was regarded as "one of the oldest and most extensive Banking Houses in London."§ It is suggested, however, in some of the contemporary literature that the means of the partners were not fully

---

* Henry Brougham, *Historical Sketches of Statesmen who Flourished in the Time of George III*, London, 1855, vol. i, article on Wilberforce, p. 346.
† *Essays*, p. 193.
‡ J. Francis, *History of the Bank of England* (1845), vol. ii, p. 9.
§ T. Joplin, *Analysis and History of the Currency Question*, 1832, p. 206.

adequate to the increased volume of business, and that they had invested "in securities not strictly convertible to a larger extent than was prudent."* However this may be, when in the late autumn of 1825 an acute stringency in the money market occurred and a number of the more important country banks failed, suspicion was aroused against the London house which by its extensive connections was bound to be particularly affected by the heavy drain of funds from London. For some time the firm was able to meet the steadily increasing demands; but on the evening of Saturday, December 3rd, the Deputy-Governor† of the Bank of England was informed that Pole & Co. were in need of assistance. An emergency meeting of the available directors on Sunday morning decided to put on Monday at the disposal of the firm, against ample security, the sum of £300,000.‡ And if we may believe a much later report, "it was not thought that the extent of the financial crisis should be known, and before the subordinates of the Bank were in their places, the Governor and the Deputy-Governor themselves counted out and handed over the gold, which was carried away in silence and secrecy."§ But this only prolonged the struggle for a week and on the following Monday the firm stopped

---

* See J. H. Palmer's statement in *Report from the Committee of Secrecy on the Bank of England Charter*, ordered (by the House of Commons) to be printed June 17, 1833. Q.607. In a pamphlet by an anonymous writer Henry Thornton is blamed as being responsible for the failure of the firm ten years after his death: "The failure of Pole, Thornton, and Co. is in no degree whatever to be ascribed to their country correspondents, but mainly to the circumstances of that kind-hearted, amiable and good man Henry Thornton, having left the concern of Down, Thornton, and Co. in a state of great perplexity, to say no more; and Sir Peter Pole having joined the concern, on the death of Mr. Thornton, in a state that imperatively required the most rigid adherence to pure banking principles, to insure safety and prosperity to the establishment, being weak enough to depart from those principles for the purpose of speculation." *A Letter to the Earl of Liverpool, on the Erroneous Information that His Majesty's Ministers have adopted regarding the Country Banks and the Currency in the Manufacturing Districts*. By a Manufacturer in the North of England. London, 1826, p. 11.

† The Governor, Cornelius Buller, is reported to have been connected with the House of Pole & Co. by marriage and "other circumstances of relationship."

‡ *Report on the Bank Charter*, 1833, Q.5006.

§ J. Wedgwood, *Contemporary Review*, vol. lxviii, October 1895, p. 525.

payment* with the effect of bringing the panic to its height and causing the closure of several other banking houses on the next day, including one of about equal size, Williams, Burgess & Williams. Although Pole & Co. was ultimately not only found to be fully solvent but even to realize a handsome surplus over its liabilities, it did not re-open. It was in effect merged with Williams & Co., which at the beginning of 1826 re-opened as Williams, Deacon & Co.,† and it was in this firm that Henry Thornton the younger spent another fifty-five years of successful banking life till he died in 1881. His relations to another more famous son of a member of the Clapham Sect, his class-mate, Lord Macaulay, to whom he acted as banker, will be familiar to many readers of G. O. Trevelyan's *Life of Macaulay*.

II

It is not too much to say that the appearance of the *Paper Credit* in 1802 marks the beginning of a new epoch in the development of monetary theory. Although Thornton's merits have long been overshadowed by the greater fame of Ricardo, it has now come to be recognized‡ that in the field of money the main achievement of the classical period is due to Thornton, and that even the modi-

* T. Joplin, in discussing this crisis (*Analysis and History*, p. 235), rightly points out that it was similar to that of 1793 in that it was brought about by a contraction of the issues of the Bank of England, and he adds that "Mr. Thornton, being a banker—a partner, it is curious to remark, of the house that failed on this occasion—had his attention particularly called to the subject; and a very considerable portion of his work, on public credit, is devoted to show, that, in a period of panic, the Bank ought rather to lean to the side of enlarging, than contracting its issues."

† This is according to a circular dated December 31, 1825, and signed by Robt. Williams and C. M. Williams, a copy of which was kindly supplied to the present author by the Manager of Williams, Deacon's Bank Ltd. Mr. John Deacon who joined the firm at the same time is described as a later partner of Messrs. Baring Brothers & Co., and the Hon. John Thornton Melville, who also became a partner at the same time, was the son-in-law and former partner of Samuel Thornton, and apparently related to the Thorntons in other ways also.

‡ The more correct appreciation of Thornton's merits in modern times is mainly due to Professor Jacob Viner's *Canada's Balance of International Indebtedness*, 1924.

36

fications of his theories by his better-known successors were not always improvements. The remarkable fact is that almost as soon as, after a long period of quiescence, circumstances once again made monetary problems the subject of general interest, he was ready to put forward a new body of doctrine which not only provided the framework during the next fifteen years for what may still be regarded as the greatest of all monetary debates, but which also represents the most important single contribution to these discussions.

Since the contributions of Cantillon, Galiani, and Hume in the middle of the eighteenth century little progress had been made in monetary science. Joseph Harris's *Essay on Money and Coins*, published in 1757–8, which was one of the first systematic treatises on money in the English language, might still be regarded, at the end of the century, as representative of the existing state of knowledge. The suggestive and interesting, but essentially wrong-headed chapters on money in James Steuart's *Political Economy* had no very wide influence. And the treatment of money in the *Wealth of Nations*, which dominated opinion on these matters in the last quarter of the century, contains comparatively little of theoretical interest.* But even the descriptive parts of the *Wealth*

---

* On the literature of this period see J. H. Hollander, "The Development of the Theory of Money from Adam Smith to David Ricardo," *Quarterly Journal of Economics*, vol. xxv, May 1911. I am here disregarding some of the more interesting French writers of the period, who seem to have had practically no influence on discussion in England (with the exception probably of Turgot). For the same reason I am also neglecting Henry Lloyd's interesting *Essay on the Theory of Money*, 1771, which appears to have remained almost completely unnoticed.

Henry Thornton probably had no very extensive acquaintance with the early literature. A manuscript "list of all the books in the library" of Battersea Rise, drawn up about twenty years after Henry Thornton's death, which presumably contains most of the works on economics which he possessed, and which very appropriately begins with Trimmer's *Economy of Charity*, contains from among the early economic works only: the *Wealth of Nations*, Montesquieu's *Spirit of the Laws*, the *Works* of John Locke, A. Anderson, *Origin of Commerce*, and M. Postlethwayt, *Universal Dictionary of Trade and Commerce*. If we add Hume's *Essays* (which would probably not be admitted to so pious a household) these are practically the same books as those quoted in the *Paper Credit*.

of Nations were no longer adequate by the end of the century. The twenty years following its appearance had brought gradual but fundamental changes in the structure of the English credit system. The rapid increase in the number of country banks, the abandonment of the issue of notes on the part of the London bankers, the rapid growth of the use of the cheque, and the establishment of the London Clearing House all fall into this period. And it was during the same period that the Bank of England became the Bankers' Bank, the *dernier resort* as Sir Francis Baring described it in 1797,* where in an emergency everybody expected to obtain ready money.

Another phenomenon to which Adam Smith had given comparatively little attention were the economic crises which occurred with surprising regularity in 1763, 1772, 1783, and 1793. And in consequence of the changed position of the Bank of England new problems arose on the occasion of these crises. It is said that in the crisis of 1783 the Bank for the first time deliberately and successfully met an outflow of gold by a contraction of credit. Whether or not this was a new discovery, there can be little doubt that ten years later, in somewhat different circumstances, the Bank applied this method rather harshly.

The years preceding the crisis of 1792–3 had been years of great prosperity, which, in the last twelve months before the crisis, assumed the character of an inflationary boom. The tide had, however, already turned in the last few months of 1792, and the outbreak of the war with France led in February 1793 to a financial panic, caused by the failure first of a well-known house in London, then of a big banker in Newcastle and finally of numerous country banks all over England. The general state of alarm, and the discredit into which the notes of the country banks fell, led to an extensive and prolonged demand for guineas and Bank of England notes. The directors of the Bank, who for the past six months had seen their demand liabilities mount and their cash

* Francis Baring, *Observations on the Establishment of the Bank of England*, 1797, second edition, pp. 22 and 47.

reserves dwindle, finally lost their heads and suddenly refused to grant further accommodation, leaving "the unfortunate public to shift for itself."* The result was an unheard of intensification of the financial panic and the danger of universal failure. After pressure by the Government on the Bank to relax its attitude had failed to produce any result, a rapidly appointed committee of the House of Commons† recommended that Exchequer bills to the amount of £5,000,000 should be issued (under the direction of a board of commissioners appointed for the purpose) to provide the mercantile community with the means to raise cash. The mere announcement that this step would be taken went far to stay the panic, and, in fact, only a fraction of the authorized amount of Exchequer bills had to be issued before normal conditions were restored.

This drain on the resources of the Bank of England had occurred at a time when the exchanges were favourable and when in fact gold was being imported in small quantities. It was a classical case of what was later to become known as an "internal" as distinguished from an "external" drain. But it took some years more for the Bank of England to learn that the way to meet such an internal drain was to grant credits liberally, and then, in learning this lesson, it forgot that in the case of an external drain exactly the opposite measures were called for.

The first two years of the war with France, although free from major financial disturbances, gradually created a situation of considerable difficulty for the Bank. On the one hand expenditure for the English army on the Continent, subsidies to the allies, bad harvests in England, and France's return to a gold currency led to a continual and increasing drain of gold from England. On the other hand insistent and repeated demands from the Government for loans not only made it impossible for the Bank to contract the note circulation, but actually led to a considerable expansion.

* *A Letter to the R. H. William Pitt on the Conduct of the Bank Directors*, 1796 p. 11.
† See *Report of the Committee on the State of Commercial Credit*, 1793.

When finally, towards the end of 1795, the foreign exchanges began to fall rapidly and the export of gold assumed alarming proportions, and repeated protests to the Government had failed to lessen the demands from that quarter, the Bank (which was still prevented by the usury law from charging a rate of interest in excess of five per cent) made the sensational announcement, on the last day of that year, that in future

"whenever bills sent in for discount shall in any day amount to a larger sum than it shall be resolved to discount on that day, a pro rata proportion of such bills in each parcel as are not otherwise objectionable, will be returned to the person sending in the same, without regard to the respectability of the party sending in the bills, or the solidity of the bills themselves."*

This recourse to a rationing of credit caused renewed stringency in the money market in the spring of 1796 and evoked loud protests from the City. A committee of merchants and bankers even proposed a plan for a new Board of Credit, a kind of rival institution to the Bank of England, which was to relieve the dearth of cash.

It is not easy to reconcile these complaints about the continued scarcity of money during this period with the no less insistent complaints about the high prices, and with the continued unfavourable course of the exchanges. While, however, a really satisfactory account of the exact course of events could only be given after a good deal of research, there can be no doubt that the immediate cause of the final suspension of cash payments by the Bank in 1797 was a renewed internal drain. The latter part of 1796 had brought a new wave of failures of mercantile and banking houses all over the country. The apprehension of a French invasion heightened the alarm, and when in February 1797 a single French frigate actually landed 1,200 men in Fishguard in Wales, a run on the Bank of England started, which in the course of a few days reduced its already much impaired reserves by one half.

It is idle to speculate to-day as to whether the Bank, if it had continued to pay in cash so long as it could, would have been able

* See T. Tooke, *History of Prices*, vol. i, 1838, p. 200.

to allay the panic before its reserves of coin had been exhausted.*
The fact is that Pitt, being informed of the state of affairs by a
deputation from the Bank on Sunday, February 26, 1797, forbade
the directors, by an Order in Council of that date, to continue

"issuing any cash payments until the sense of Parliament can be taken on
that subject, and the proper measures thereon, for maintaining the means
of circulation, and supporting the public and commercial credit of the
kingdom at this important conjuncture."†

On the following day the contents of this Order in Council were
conveyed to the House of Commons in a special Message from
the King, and the House thereupon immediately resolved to
appoint a committee "to examine and state the total amount of
the outstanding demands of the Bank of England, and likewise of
the funds for discharging the same." A Committee of Secrecy of
fifteen members was accordingly chosen by ballot on March 1st,
and proceeded at once with its task. A special committee was also
appointed by the House of Lords on the following day, and on
March 7th was supplanted by a Committee of Secrecy of fifteen
"to enquire into the causes which produced the Order in Council
of 26th of February last."

In the course of March and April both committees took extensive
evidence, the Commons committee calling nineteen witnesses and
the Lords sixteen. Both committees called largely the same persons,
primarily representatives of the Bank of England, merchants, the
secretary of the Country Banks Association, and Henry Thornton,
who seems to have been the sole representative of the London
Bankers. The reason why he was selected is probably that, in
addition to his being a member of the House of Commons, his
firm was particularly widely connected with country banks. The
list, which he gave in the course of his evidence, of places in which

---

* As Ricardo later thought it might have done. See *Proposals for a Secure and
Economical Currency*, in *Works*, edited McCulloch, p. 406.

† The texts of the various documents connected with the Bank Restriction
have been conveniently collected together by A. Allardyce, *An Address to
the Proprietors of the Bank of England*, 3rd edition with additions, 1798.

41

his bank had country correspondents in 1797 is largely the same as that for 1800, the first year for which we can reconstruct a complete list. In that year, Down, Thornton & Free had altogether twenty-three country correspondents. They were mainly in the Midlands, the North, and Scotland, with a few in the South-west.*

But Thornton had something more to offer than just the knowledge and experience of a banker with wide connections all over the country. It is clear from his evidence that he had already thought deeply about the problems of credit. Indeed, there is some reason for believing, despite a statement in the preface to the *Paper Credit* which gives a contrary impression, that he was perhaps at that time already engaged on a work on the subject. This at least seems to follow from a statement, which we no longer have any means of checking

"that while, during one of his elections, he had been engaged all day in a hot canvass, toiling through the streets of Southwark, he writes to his wife that he secured a couple of hours in the evening to carry on his work on Paper Credit."†

As the elections of 1802 took place some months after the book had appeared, this statement must evidently refer to the elections of 1796, so that Thornton would appear to have worked on the book for six years.‡

* I am indebted to Mr. H. A. Shannon for a complete list of the country correspondents of Down, Thornton and Free, and later of Pole and Co., from 1800 to 1825. In 1800, in addition to the places mentioned in the evidence, they had correspondents in Aberdeen, Brecon (Wales), Sheffield and Stafford. And as regards the towns mentioned in the evidence they now had two correspondents in both Bristol and Edinburgh, but apparently no longer had any in Ashburton and Sleaford (assuming that the bankers in these places mentioned in 1793 were "correspondents" and not merely "acquaintances"). The number grew from twenty-three in 1800 to a maximum of forty-nine in 1813, and was still forty-one in 1825 when the firm went out of business. In that year fourteen of their country correspondents seem to have failed or otherwise come to an end, eight to have transferred to Williams, Deacon and Co., and the rest to other London banks.

† J. C. Colquhoun, *Wilberforce and His Friends*, p. 283.

‡ Certainly the statement cannot refer to an earlier date, for Thornton did not marry until March 1796; nor is there any indication in his diary for 1795 that he was then occupied with questions of this kind.

Whether this is true or not, Thornton's evidence, which is reprinted in full in Appendix I of this volume, gives, in the course of the discussion of the causes of the panic of 1797, a careful analysis of the interrelations between the different parts of the monetary circulation and of the factors determining the demand for the different kinds of media of circulation. Incidentally he also throws a certain amount of light on such problems as the factors which affect "the disposition of persons to detain bank notes," the rôle of the rate of interest, and in particular the difference between the position of a private banker and the position of the Bank of England. He does not yet, however, deal with the question of the depreciation of the currency and the factors influencing the foreign exchanges, which were to be the main topics of discussion in the years to come, and on which he was to make the major contribution in his book of 1802.

There had been, indeed, even before this time, much concern about the unfavourable state of the exchanges and even suggestions that this might have been due to an over-issue of bank notes.* We must not forget that the recent spectacle of the depreciation of the French *assignats* had made the phenomenon of inflation as familiar to the English public as it is at the present time, and that it certainly did not require any very profound knowledge to realize that an increase of paper money would lead to a fall in its value. But at the time of the crisis of 1797, the exchanges had recovered and remained fairly favourable for more than two years; and the Bank was even able to replenish its much depleted gold reserves. The restriction of cash payments, however, which may have been justified as a temporary expedient, was renewed again and again, and remained in force for altogether twenty-four years.

Up till the end of 1799 it can hardly be said that there existed any appreciable degree of inflation. The demands for accommodation of the Government were kept within fairly narrow limits

---

* Cf. [W. Anderson?] *The iniquity of banking; or banknotes proved to be an injury to the public, and the real cause of the present exorbitant prices of provisions*, London, 1797.

and, since the general depression of trade also kept private demands for credit low, there was little temptation for the bank to expand its circulation. Towards the beginning of the year 1800, however, the situation altered. Increased war expenditures and the unsatisfactory receipts from the new taxes led to renewed Government borrowing from the Bank on a large scale, and as early as the middle of 1799 the exchanges began to fall and prices to rise. Most attention was attracted by the rise in the price of gold bullion which in the autumn of 1800 reached a premium of 10 per cent. This led to attacks on the Bank in a host of pamphlets. The one which drew most attention was a pamphlet by Walter Boyd, who had already taken a prominent part in the discussion of the measures of 1797, and had become known as one of the sponsors of the proposed rival note-issuing institution.* Boyd claimed, with somewhat questionable justification, that it had been reserved to him

"to assign, as the cause of the general rise, which almost all things have experienced within the last two or three years (and which grain, as the article that comes most frequently in contact with money, feels the soonest and the most) the existence of a great Bank, invested with the power of issuing paper, professing to be payable on demand, but which, in fact, the Bank which issues it, is not obliged to pay."†

Boyd had the satisfaction that, even before his *Letter to Pitt* appeared in print, his argument was apparently confirmed by a statement which the Bank of England submitted at the request of the House of Commons, and which showed that the note cir-

* Walter Boyd, *A Letter to the Right Honourable William Pitt on the Influence of the Stoppage of Specie at the Bank of England on the Prices of Provisions and Other Commodities*, London, 1801. See also two earlier pamphlets, *The Cause of the Present Threatened Famine Traced to its Real Source, viz. an Actual Depreciation of our Circulation, Occasioned by the Paper Currency, etc., etc.*, by Common Sense, London, 1800, and *Thoughts on the Present Prices of Provisions, their Causes and Remedies*, by an Independent Gentleman [J. Symons?], London 1800; and of a slightly later date: *Profusion of Paper Money, not Deficiency in Harvests; Taxation, not Speculation, the Principal Causes of the Sufferings of the People, containing . . . and an important inference from Mr. H. Thornton's speech in Parliament on March 26th*, by a Banker, London, 1802. (The reference is actually to Thornton's speech on March 23, 1801, quoted below.)

† Loc. cit., p. 60.

culation had increased from the date of the restriction to December 6, 1800, from £8·6 to £15·5 millions. In the debate in the House which followed, Henry Thornton agreed that

"as to the assertion that the increased issue of Bank paper was the cause of the dearness of provisions, he would not deny that it might have some foundation; but he would contend that its effect was far from being as great as was being alleged; and as to the depreciation of Bank paper arising from the exchange being against this country, it was at present only 12 per cent. and was produced, not by the mismanagement of the Bank, but by the difference between imports and exports, the latter of which had risen above the former from the extraordinary importations of provisions."*

There is reason to doubt whether this condensed report of Henry Thornton's speech does justice to his argument. It is clearly unfair to regard Thornton as an apologist of the Bank of England, and the too often repeated accusation of bias is particularly baseless when it is founded on the wrong assumption that he was a director or even Governor of the Bank. It is, nevertheless, evident that he regarded the argument of Boyd and others, who attributed all the difficulties merely to an excessive issue, as unduly simplified and misleading. He was still too much impressed by the acute scarcity of money which had only recently been felt; and events, indeed, proved that before inflation was to set in on a scale such that there could be no doubt about its existence, the pound was to make at least a partial recovery.

It is very likely that, at least in the shape in which it was ultimately published, the *Paper Credit* was intended partly as a reply to Boyd. Others, who had attempted to reply, had not been particularly successful,† and for some twelve months Boyd's argument seemed to hold the field. But when, in February or March 1802,

---

* Cf. *The Parliamentary Register; or, History of the Proceedings and Debates of the Houses of Lords and Commons*, printed for J. Debrett; First Session, First Parliament of the United Kingdom and Ireland, vol. xiv, vol. 76 of series, 1801, p. 556. The report there is fuller than in *Hansard*. An even fuller report, judging by contemporary references, appears to be contained in yet another publication, referred to as *Woodfall's Parliamentary Debates*, which I have not been able to trace.

† See particularly Sir Francis Baring, *Observations on the Publication of Walter Boyd*, London, 1801.

45

Thornton's work appeared, it immediately took first place and provided the basis from which all further discussion proceeded.

This Introduction cannot attempt to summarize the argument of the work or even to point out all its merits. It would take a great deal of space merely to mention all the points in respect to which Thornton's treatment constituted an important advance on earlier discussions, and it must suffice to indicate a few passages which deserve special attention. It may be true, as has often been asserted, that his exposition lacks system and in places is even obscure, but too much can be made of this defect. And there will be few readers who will not be impressed by the acumen and the balance of mind displayed throughout the exposition. Thornton's achievement lies much more in his contribution to general theory than in his diagnosis of the situation of the particular moment. And if, as may well be the case, it can be argued that his judgment of the situation of the moment and his forecasts were less correct than those of some of his contemporaries who used cruder reasoning, this does not detract from the lasting value of his work. We have to judge it not as a controversial pamphlet on the questions of the day, but as one of the works in which problems of the moment have led the author to go down to fundamentals and to treat them for their general significance.

It seems that on the whole the arrangement of the book follows the order in which the author's thoughts developed. The first part, after two short introductory chapters, is mainly devoted to pointing out the dangers of an excessive contraction of the issue of paper, and the causes of what became known as an "internal drain."* It is in this context that Thornton develops his important views about the "motives for holding" money, the factors which determine the relative demand for the different kinds of media of circulation, and a fairly elaborate theory of the effects of changes in the "rapidity of circulation."† He discusses the effects of the "state of confidence" on the willingness to "provide for contingencies" by holding money or assets which can be more or less

* Chapter IV.   † Pages 96, 232.

easily converted into money, and in certain later passages he takes account of the "loss sustained by keeping money" and the effects of an increase of money on the rate of interest.* And it is in these discussions that he makes his main contributions to the theory of credit properly so-called: that is, to that branch of monetary theory which has only just recently again begun to attract attention under the title of "liquidity preference." It is largely in this connection also that he incidentally provides a great deal of descriptive information on the organization of the English monetary and banking system. One does not realize how full this description is until one finds it summarized in systematic form in the review article by Francis Horner which has yet to be mentioned. Of special interest in this connection is the explanation of how "by the transfer of debts in the books of the banker a large part of what are termed cash payments are effected," and the implied recognition of the essential similarity of bank notes and bank-deposits.†

There are several other little points in these early chapters, such as the remark about the relative rigidity of wages,‡ and the reference to the movement of commodity stocks,§ which show surprising insight into the problems of industrial fluctuations. But Thornton's best-known achievement does not come until later when he deals with the problems relating to the foreign exchanges. He first takes up this topic in Chapter V, where he treats the effects of an external drain, i.e. an outflow of gold which is primarily caused by an unfavourable change in the balance of trade.‖ This is the situation which he rightly thought to exist in the years immediately before and after the abandonment of the gold standard in 1797. He is fully aware that a relative excess of bank notes "may arise from other causes besides that of a too great emission of paper,"¶ and that in such a situation "the bank should not only not increase, but that it should, perhaps, very greatly diminish it,

---

* Pages 83, 91, 96, 232, 234, 235. † Pages 101 and 134 footnote.
‡ Pages 119 and 189–90. § Footnote on p. 120.
‖ Page 150 note. ¶ Page 225.

47

if it would endeavour to prevent gold from going out."* His very modern doubts about such a policy of deflation (doubts by reference to which he attempts partly to justify the Bank of England's policy), are "whether the bank, in the attempt to produce this very low price, may not, in a country circumstanced as Great Britain is, so exceedingly distress trade and discourage manufactures as to impair . . . those sources of our returning wealth to which we must chiefly trust for the restoration of our balance"† as to frustrate the main purpose.

The problem of the effects of an absolute increase of the circulation, as it was the last to arise in his experience, is also the last to be taken up in his book. What is most impressive here is the methodical development of the argument. He commences by giving a brilliant exposition of the mechanism of the change in relative prices in the two countries concerned, which already contains practically all of the doctrine which, one hundred and twenty years later, was "rediscovered" as the purchasing power parity theory.‡ Then after showing how a local change of prices in a particular part of any country will soon be corrected by a reduction of sales to, and an increase of purchases from, other parts of the country,§ he proceeds to apply the same argument to the relations between two different countries.

All of this is, of course, the theory of the mechanism of international gold movements, and of the foreign exchanges, which later became associated with the names of Ricardo and John Stuart Mill. It has now become clear that in so far as Mill (and later Professor Taussig) differed from and improved upon Ricardo they just resumed Thornton's argument. Ricardo's unwillingness to recognize that the excess of the circulation might be an effect as well as a cause of the unfavourable balance of trade, which led him to criticize Thornton at some length, || caused this whole

* Pages 151.   † Page 152.   ‡ Pages 198–9.   § Pages 208–11.
|| *The High Price of Bullion* (1810), *Works,* edited by McCulloch, pp. 268–9. For further criticisms of Thornton's views by Ricardo, see the latter's notes on Thornton's book as reproduced in *Minor Papers on the Currency Question, 1809–1823,* by David Ricardo, edited by Jacob H. Hollander, Baltimore, 1932.

theory to remain for a long time in a much more rigid and unsatisfactory form than that which it had originally received at the hands of Thornton.

Great as this achievement is, to many readers Thornton will appear to reach the height of his intellectual power in the penultimate chapter in which he proceeds to meet various objections, and in particular to refute the erroneous argument "that a proper limitation of bank notes may be sufficiently secured by attending merely to the nature of the security for which they are given."* It is here that, in summarizing earlier points, he sometimes finds the happiest formulations; he also breaks entirely new ground in an attempt to elucidate the effects of a credit expansion in greater detail. He sees that the expansion of credit will in the first instance lead to the employment of "antecedently idle persons," but adds that as these are limited in number, the increased issue "will set to work labourers, of whom a part will be drawn from other, and perhaps, not less useful occupations."† This leads him (after some animadversions on Hume's suggestion that it is only in "the intermediate situation between the acquisition of money and the rise of prices that the increasing quantity of gold and silver is favourable to industry") to one of the earliest expositions of what has become known as the doctrine of "forced saving." The "augmentation of stock," which may be brought about by an excessive issue of paper, is due to the fact that the labourer "may be forced by his necessity to consume fewer articles, though he may exercise the same industry" and "this saving" may be supplemented by "a similar defalcation of the revenues of the unproductive members of society."‡ And Thornton is careful to add that the increase in output will never be proportional to the increase in the quantity of money and that therefore a general rise in prices is inevitable.§

The discussion of the proper limitation of issues leads on to the second point of primary importance in this chapter, the discussion

* Page 244.   † Pages 236.
‡ Page 239.   § Pages 239 et seq.

Enquiry into Paper Credit

of the rôle of the rate of interest. The statutory limitation of the rate of interest which the Bank may charge has the effect, he says, that at times this rate will be much lower than the mercantile rate of profits, and will in consequence lead to an undesirable expansion of credit unless the Bank takes other measures to keep down the volume of credit.* This is a remarkable anticipation of the distinction between the market rate and the "natural" or "equilibrium" rate of interest which since the work of Knut Wicksell has played such an important rôle in the discussions of these problems. With this idea, along with the idea of forced saving, Thornton was for the first time in possession of the two main elements which it was left for Wicksell, nearly a hundred years later, successfully to combine into one of the most promising contributions to the theory of credit and industrial fluctuations.†

The points we have mentioned, though they are the most important, do not by any means exhaust Thornton's contributions to knowledge. They may, however, serve as an indication of the character of the work which put the discussion of monetary problems on a new plane. Its outstanding merit was soon recognized. On June 28, 1802, we find Jeremy Bentham writing to Dumont:

"This is a book of real merit—a controversy with him would be really instructive. I have tumbled it over but very imperfectly, that not being the order of the day, and for fear of calling off my attention, and absorbing my capacity of exertion. But one of these days I may not improbably grapple with him. Admitting all his facts, with thanks,—agreeing with him in almost all his conclusions,—but disputing with him what seems (as far as I have yet seen) to be his most material conclusions, viz., that paper money does more harm than good. Here is a book of real instruction, if the French were wise enough to translate it; the style is clear, plain, without ornament or pretension, the reasoning is close."‡

* Pages 253–6.

† On the significance of Thornton's views on this point, and the further development of these theories, see the first chapter of my *Prices and Production*, 2nd edition, 1935, and "A Note on the Development of the Doctrine of 'Forced Saving,'" *Quarterly Journal of Economics*, November 1932.

‡ J. Bentham, *Works*, edited by J. Bowring, vol. x, p. 389.

A fact which was of great importance in leading to the rapid diffusion of Thornton's ideas was that Francis Horner devoted to it, in the first number of the new *Edinburgh Review*, a brilliant article of thirty pages in which, even if he perhaps passed over some of the finer points in Thornton's analysis, he gave an exposition of the main argument of the book in a form which was considerably more systematic and coherent than the original version.* Although to some extent critical, he gave the work the deserved praise as "the most valuable unquestionably of all the publications which the momentous event of the Bank Restriction had produced." In particular his reproduction *verbatim* of one of the most important passages on the effect of price movements on the balance of trade and the foreign exchanges probably exerted as much influence as the book itself.

The developments of the years immediately following the publication of the *Paper Credit* had the result of causing further discussion to centre almost entirely upon the effects of an over-issue on the foreign exchanges and the price of bullion. The immediate cause of the renewed discussion was not so much the situation in England as developments in Ireland. The restriction of cash payments had been extended (merely for the sake of uniformity and despite the fact that the exchanges had been favourable to Dublin) to the Bank of Ireland. This institution seems very rapidly to have taken advantage of the new situation, and in the first six years it quadrupled its note circulation. The result was that by 1803 the rate of exchange on London had fallen by about 20 per cent. The fact that this was due to the mismanagement of the note issue was particularly clear in this case because the exchanges on Belfast, which had its own circulation consisting largely of coin and notes of local banks, had remained at par, and

* *The Edinburgh Review*, vol. i, No. 1, October 1802, pp. 172–201. It was at one time intended to reprint Horner's article in this volume, but this plan had to be abandoned in favour of the inclusion of Thornton's speeches on the Bullion Report. It is, however, to be hoped that not only this, but also some of the other very interesting articles on economic questions which Francis Horner contributed to the *Edinburgh Review*, will some day be reprinted.

the Dublin exchange showed the same depreciation in Belfast as in London.

Sometime before this, however, and shortly after the appearance of the *Paper Credit*, Henry Thornton had already expressed, in one of the parliamentary debates, his concern about developments in Ireland. In the second reading of the Bank of Ireland Restriction Bill on April 26, 1802,

"Mr. Henry Thornton observed that this bill had been introduced to accompany the restriction on the Bank of England. With respect to the restriction on the Bank of England no danger could result from it; that Bank was a body extremely respectable, who were sufficiently disposed to restrain the circulation of their own paper, and to limit within due bounds the circulation of the country, which they were better enabled to do, as they possessed a monopoly of the issue of paper in the metropolis. With respect to the Bank of Ireland, the case was different; other banks issued paper in the same place where that existed, and a restriction on that bank would therefore be ineffectual. It was important, however, for the House to bear in mind, that too great an emission of paper produced the ground on which the continuance of the restriction on the Bank was founded, as, by raising the price of commodities, it impeded their exportation, and consequently turned exchanges against us. Ireland appeared extremely liable to dangers of this kind; when, however, the discontinuance of the restriction on the Bank of England should be under discussion, the circumstances of the course of exchanges against Ireland ought not to operate as a reason against that discontinuance, and they must provide in that country, as in this, cash for their paper. . . ."*

As time went on, however, it became increasingly clear that the Bank of England, too, was not keeping its circulation within safe limits. And in April 1804 Thornton (in the marginal annotations of a copy of Lord King's *Thoughts on the Effects of the Bank Restriction* which he evidently made for a friend)† already expresses

---

* *Parliamentary Register* (Second Session of First Parliament of United Kingdom and Ireland, vol. xviii), vol. 80 of series, p. 95.

† See Appendix II below, p. 312, where these manuscript notes are reproduced and a full description of the volume from which they are taken is given. It appears from this that Henry Thornton gave the annotated copy of Lord King's book to a friend, Mr. Scott Moncrieff, whose name also appears in

52

his apprehension of the Directors of "the Bank perhaps not sufficiently perceiving that a limitation of Paper will improve the exchanges," although he still thinks that, compared with the Bank of Ireland, "the Directors of the Bank of England, if they have erred at all, have erred but a little." But at the same time he admits that

"if the Committee of the House of Commons on Irish Currency now sitting were to state in their Report to the House in distinct language that they are persuaded that a Reduction of Bank Paper must have a tendency to improve the Exchange even this hint coming from such a quarter and applying itself as is necessary to the Bank of England as well as that of Ireland would have all the desired effect."

Of this Committee on the Irish Currency to which Thornton here refers and which had been appointed early in the year Thornton himself was a members. It seems even that he was one of the most influential and active member,[*] and in view of this confessed intention to give a hint to the Bank of England, the Report of this Committee, which has justly been celebrated as anticipating the more famous Bullion Report in almost every important respect gains still further significance. It is, however, not known what part, if any, Henry Thornton took in the drafting of the Report, and in view of the fact that the Committee counted among its

Thornton's diary, who in turn sent it to J. A. Maconochie, evidently the same James Allan Maconochie, advocate and Sheriff of Orkney, who owned the manuscript notes of Adam Smith's Glasgow Lectures (see Edwin Cannan's Introduction to his edition of Adam Smith's *Lectures on Justice, Police, Revenue and Arms*, Oxford 1896, p. xvi). The passages quoted above occur on pp. 29 and 126 of the pamphlet, see pp. 316 and 321 below. Acknowledgment is due to the Goldsmiths' Librarian of the University of London for permission to reproduce the notes from the copy in his library.

[*] Among the letters of Francis Horner in the possession of Lady Eleanor Langman there is an unpublished letter to his brother Leonard, undated but probably written in April 1804, in which he writes about the Irish Committee: "The inquiries of this Committee will give us a good many curious facts. Thornton attends these constantly; and he understands these matters better than anybody else in London." For this quotation I am indebted to Professor F. W. Fetter, who has had an opportunity to inspect the unpublished letters of Francis Horner.

members other competent writers on Currency, in particular, Henry Parnell, who in the same year also published a pamphlet on the Irish Currency,* we cannot even venture a surmise.

Of the development of Thornton's ideas in the next six years we know nothing. Nor is this the place for writing a history of the monetary developments of these years or of the further discussions to which they gave rise. This has been done well by others. Suffice it to say that in 1810 the continued rise of prices and fall of the exchanges caused increasing and widespread apprehension, and that eventually, on a motion of Francis Horner, on February 19th of that year, a Select Committee was "appointed to enquire into the Cause of the High Price of Gold Bullion, and to take into consideration the State of the Circulating Medium and of the Exchanges between Great Britain and Foreign Parts."

Of the deliberations of this famous Bullion Committee, and the exact responsibility of its individual members for the writing of the Report, we also know very little. Francis Horner was elected chairman, and on the twenty-two days (from February 22nd to March 26th) on which the Committee took evidence, he usually took the chair, although his place was occasionally taken by Huskisson and three times by Thornton.

On the drafting of the report there is an oft-quoted passage from one of the published letters of Francis Horner which deserves to be included here:

"The Report is in truth very clumsily and prolixly drawn; stating nothing but very old doctrines on the subject it treats of, and stating them in a more imperfect form than they have frequently appeared before. It is a motley composition by Huskisson, Thornton, and myself; each having written parts which are tacked together without any care to give them an uniform style or a very exact connection. One great merit the Report, however, possesses; that it declares in very plain and pointed terms, both the true doctrine and the existence of a great evil growing out of the neglect of that doctrine. By keeping up the discussion, which I mean to

* H. Parnell, *Observations upon the State of Currency in Ireland and upon the Course of Exchange between Dublin and London*, Dublin, 1804.

do, and by forcing it on the attention of Parliament, we shall in time (I trust) effect the restoration of the old and only safe system."*

There is also a somewhat obscure and probably incorrect statement of Colquhoun, who speaks of the "long deliberations in the bullion committee in which Horner and Henry Thornton carried their motions against the Government 11 to 4."† As the total membership of the Committee numbered twenty-two, this statement, allowing for a number of absentees, is not absurd on the face of it, although nothing else is known of any motions on which the Committee voted.

The report was not submitted to the House until the evening of the day (June 8th) preceding the prorogation of Parliament. But, it is alleged,

"the substance of the report was immediately circulated in the newspapers and the alarm which it occasioned among the bankers and the merchants, who were accustomed to look to the Bank for discounting their bills, was followed by many failures of mercantile houses in London, as well as of some country banks."‡

The publication of the report led to an intense discussion of the problems it raised in a host of pamphlets, but as it had been too late to discuss it in the session in which it had been presented, it was some time before it was taken up in the House. In fact, it was not until May 6, 1811, that Francis Horner moved the House into Committee to consider the report. There occurred a four-day debate in which Thornton, Horner, Huskisson, Canning, and a number of the other members of the Bullion Committee took part. A carefully prepared speech which Thornton delivered on the second day, together with another made a week later, was

* Francis Horner to J. A. Murray in a letter dated June 26, 1810, reprinted in *Memoirs and Correspondence of Francis Horner*, edited by L. Horner, London, 1843, vol. ii, p. 47. † Colquhoun, *Wilberforce*, p. 301.

‡ T. H. B. Oldfield, *Representative History of Great Britain and Ireland*, London, 1816, vol. ii, p. 345. The crisis mentioned occurred only in September and is the same as that in which, as we have seen, Henry Thornton's firm experienced difficulties, and in which, as may be added here, the firm of his eldest brother Samuel came to grief. See also, W. Smart, *Economic Annals of the Nineteenth Century*, 1801–1820, London, 1910, p. 255.

55

published by him in pamphlet form. This first part of the debate revolved around sixteen resolutions moved by Horner, of which the last and most important proposed

"That in order to revert gradually to this Security, and to enforce meanwhile a due Limitation of the Paper of the Bank of England, as well as of all the other Bank Paper of the Country, it is expedient to amend the Act which suspends the Cash Payments of the Bank, by altering the time, till which the suspension shall continue, from Six Months after the Ratification of a Definitive Treaty of Peace, to that of Two Years from the present Time."

By this time, although he had not altered his theoretical position in any essential respect, Thornton had become thoroughly convinced of the mismanagement of the note issue and the overwhelming danger of an excessive circulation in general, and was no longer afraid to apply the remedy of a severe contraction. His speech, which is really a lecture on the dangers of a paper currency, is particularly interesting for the increased importance which he had now come to attach to the rate of interest. He not only emphasized the power of a high rate of interest to attract gold,[*] but described the whole "subject of the rate of interest" as "a very great and turning point."[†] He supplemented his theory, as given in the *Paper Credit*, of how a rate of interest lower than the mercantile rate of profits, led to an indefinite expansion of credit, by a discussion of the effect of an expectation of rising prices on the rate of interest, which in all important points anticipated Professor Irving Fisher's well-known distinction between the real and nominal rate of interest.[‡]

In the vote which followed Horner's resolutions were all defeated, the first fifteen (which embodied the theoretical basis of his recommendations) by 151 to 75, the last and decisive one by 180 to 45. And to make quite certain of the victory, Vansittart,

---

[*] Page 331. [†] Page 335.

[‡] Page 335–6. See also page 339, where Thornton speaks of "a rate of interest lower than that which was the natural one at the moment," and page 342–3.

for the Government, moved on May 13th seventeen counter-resolutions, which in effect asserted that there was no divergence of value between notes and coin and that the high price of bullion was not due to any over-issue of notes. These resolutions led to a further debate, in the course of which Thornton took the opportunity to reply to a number of objections. The most interesting feature of this second speech is that in it Thornton explicitly retracts "an error to which he himself had once inclined," namely, the idea that an increase of the circulation, by stimulating production, might help to correct the exchanges.*

With these two speeches Thornton's known contributions to monetary theory come to an end. If, in the remaining three years of his life, he took any active part in the discussion which continued, nothing has been preserved in print. But although in Parliament his views had been defeated, largely for reasons of high policy, he lived long enough to see them widely accepted. And among those of his contemporaries who took an interest in these matters there existed little doubt that the new body of thought was mainly his creation. Even a comparative outsider, like Dr. Miller in his *Philosophy of History*, did justice to his contribution by describing his book, in 1816, as "forming an epoch in the history of the Science to which it belongs."† If some of his fellow-economists, and particularly Ricardo, do not appear to have given him full credit and to have mentioned him only to criticize him, we can be sure that this was only due to the fact that among the public for which they wrote they could take a thorough acquaintance with Thornton's work for granted. But the effect was that in the course of time his fame faded before that of men whose contributions covered a much greater part of political economy, and then even the distinct contribution, which was undoubtedly his, began to be credited to his successors. For a long time John Stuart Mill, who in 1848, in his *Principles of Political Economy*, described the *Paper Credit* as even at his time "the clearest

* Below, page 353.
† George Miller, *Lectures on the Philosophy of Modern History*, Dublin, 1816.

exposition that I am acquainted with, in the English language, of the modes in which credit is given and taken in a mercantile community,"* was the last author to do anything like justice to Henry Thornton. And even Mill does not appear to have been quite aware that in his exposition of the mechanism of international gold movements he followed Thornton more than Ricardo. It was not until just before, and particularly since, the Great War, that, with the great interest which a number of American economists (particularly Professors Hollander and Viner) have shown in the history of English monetary policy and monetary doctrines, his importance came again to be fully recognized.†

III

BIBLIOGRAPHICAL NOTES

A. The Works of Henry Thornton.—*The Enquiry into the Nature and Effect of the Paper Credit of Great Britain* was published in February or March 1802‡ by J. Hatchard, of Piccadilly, as an octavo volume of 320 pages (I–XII and 13–320), price in boards 7s. An American edition appeared in Philadelphia, 1807, 272 pp., and it was reprinted by J. R. McCulloch in *A Select Collection of Scarce and Valuable Tracts on Paper Currency and Banking*, London, 1857, pp. 137–340. A French translation was undertaken, at Bentham's suggestion (see p. 50 above), by P. E. L. Dumont, and six extracts of this translation appeared in the *Bibliothèque Britannique ou Receuil*, vol. xxi, pp. 408–499, vol. xxii, pp. 25–75, 145–216, 301–332, and 413–464, and vol. xxiii, 3–31. This translation was then published in book form under the title *Recherches sur la nature et les effets du credit du papier*, etc., Geneva, 1803, and seems now to be exceedingly rare. A German translation by L. H. Jakob, with notes and appendices,

---

* Ashley's edition, p. 515 note.
† See Bibliographical Note D at the end of this Introduction.
‡ Cf. *The Christian Observer*, No. 1, published February 1, 1802, p. 3: "An Essay on Paper Credit by Henry Thornton, Esq., M.P., is expected to appear in a few days."

58

appeared under the title *Der Papier Credit von Grossbrittannien,* Halle 1803.

The Substance of two Speeches of Henry Thornton, Esq., in the Debate in the House of Commons on the Report of the Bullion Committee on May 7 and 14, 1811, were also published by Hatchard, as an octavo pamphlet of vii + 79 pages.

The Catalogue of the Library of the British Museum and the *Dictionary of National Biography* ascribe to Henry Thornton also the authorship of an anonymous pamphlet *On the Probable Effects of the Peace, with Respect to the Commercial Interest of Great Britain,* London (Hatchard), 1802. There seems, however, to be no ground for this ascription and internal evidence makes it rather unlikely that this pamphlet should be by Henry Thornton, since it deals largely with the effects of the peace on particular commodities in which Henry Thornton was not likely to be interested. The author may, however, well have been one of the merchant members of the Thornton family.

Apart from unsigned and mostly unidentified* contributions to the *Cheap Repository* tracts and the *Christian Observer,* Henry Thornton appears to have published nothing else. But after his death the following religious writings were edited by the guardian of his children, R. H. Inglis:

Family Prayers, by the late Henry Thornton, Esq., M.P., edited by R. H. I., London, 1934, xii + 164 pp. This reached its 31st edition in 1854, and it has been said that "indeed the use of that book was the distinctive sign of true Evangelism" (G. W. E. Russell, *The Household of Faith,* London, 1902).

Family Commentary upon the Sermon of the Mount, London, 1835.

Family Commentary on Portions of the Pentateuch, in Lectures, with Prayers adapted to the subject, by Henry Thornton, edited by R. H. I., London, 1837.

The volume entitled *Works of the late Henry Thornton, Esq., M.P.,* is a consecutively paginated reprint of the three works last named (856 pp.) of which only twelve copies were issued.

The *Lectures on the Ten Commandments* contained in the

---

* See, however, above.

59

Commentary on the Pentateuch were originally written for Hannah More's *Cheap Repository*, and later also reprinted separately with prayers by R. H. Inglis, London, 1843.

Finally, a series of seven articles which Thornton had contributed to the *Christian Observer* were republished under the title *Three Female Characters*, London, 1846.

All the works of Henry Thornton as well as the *Christian Observer* were published by John Hatchard, the first bookseller of that name, and "a sound evangelical and resident of Clapham."

B. The Manuscript Diary of Henry Thornton and other Family Papers.—The main source for the present sketch of the life of Henry Thornton are various manuscripts preserved by members of the family which the author has been privileged to use. Among these is a diary kept by Henry Thornton from January 1795 till February 1796 (i.e. the date of his marriage), containing almost daily entries for the first six months, and somewhat more irregular notes made during the later periods, with a few additions made in 1802, 1803, 1810, 1812, and 1814.

In this diary, the original of which is in the possession of Mr. E. M. Foster, Henry Thornton refers to a connected history of his life, which in 1803 he was writing for the benefit of his children. The original of this does not seem to have been preserved, but a copy of it is prefixed to a copy of the diary proper which is in the possession of Mrs. D. Demarest. It was written at intervals between 1802 and 1809 and most of the longer quotations in the text are from this connected history. As, however, all the quotations used were taken from this copy before it was discovered that it contains copies of two different documents, the reference is throughout to the "MS. Diary of Henry Thornton." Earlier authors, particularly the sons of Wilberforce in the *Life* of their father and James Stephen who have used the same documents refer to them as "Private and Conversational Memoranda of Henry Thornton."

The author has also been able to use MS. Recollections of Marianne Thornton, the daughter of Henry Thornton, written in 1857, and a few family letters, which are all in the possession of Mr. E. M. Forster.

C. Printed Sources on Henry Thornton and the Clapham Sect.—The main printed sources on the life of Henry Thornton are James Stephen's essay on the Clapham Sect, first published in the *Edinburgh Review*, vol. 80, 1842, and many times reprinted in his *Essays in Ecclesiastical Biography* (page references in the text are to the Silver Library Edition, 1907, vol. ii) and J. C. Colquhoun, *Wilberforce and his Friends*. John Telford, *A Sect that Moved the World*, London, 1907, the volume on *Clapham and the Clapham Sect*, published for the Clapham Antiquarian Society by Edmund Balwin, Clapham, 1927, and M. Seeley, *Later Evangelical Fathers*, 1879, are useful collections of information on the Clapham Sect, mostly from earlier printed sources. The chapter on Henry Thornton in H. R. Fox Bourne, *London Merchants*, 1869 (second edition 1876) is unreliable. Some information on Henry Thornton is to be found in two memoirs of other members of his family, namely *The Book of Yearly Recollections of Samuel Thornton, Esq.*, edited for private circulation with a Preface and Introduction by his grandson John Thornton and printed by W. Clowes & Sons, Ltd., 1891, and in P. M. Thornton, *Some Things we have Remembered: Samuel Thornton, Admiral 1797–1859, and Percy Melville Thornton 1841–1911*, London, 1912.

Of the biographies of Henry Thornton's friends those containing most information are: *The Life of William Wilberforce*, by his sons R. I. and S. Wilberforce, 5 vols., London, 1838, *The Correspondence of William Wilberforce*, edited by the same, London, 1840, and *The Private Papers of William Wilberforce*, edited by A. M. Wilberforce, London, 1897; *The Life and Letters of Zachary Macaulay*, by his granddaughter Viscountess Knutsford, London, 1901; the *Memoirs of the Life and Correspondence of Hannah More*, third edition, 1835, and the *Life of Hannah More*, by H. Thompson, by W. Roberts, London, 1838.

There are several modern biographies of Wilberforce of which only the one by R. Coupland (1923) need be mentioned. A Life of the elder James Stephen has been written by Sir George Stephen (Victoria, 1875) and sketches of his life will be found in the introductory chapters of the biographies of his son of the same name by C. E. Stephen (1906) and of his grandsons James Fitzjames

Stephen, by Leslie Stephen (1895), and Leslie Stephen, by F. W. Maitland (1906). Biographies are also available of T. Clarkson, by J. Elmes (1854) and E. L. Griggs (1936), of Granville Sharp, by Prince Hoare (1820), and E. C. P. Lascelles (1929); of Charles Grant, by H. Morris (1904); of John Shore (Lord Teignmouth) by his son (1843); a Life of John Venn is prefixed to the collection of his Sermons; and a Memoir of John Bowdler to the edition of his Works (1857).

D. WORKS ON THE MONETARY HISTORY AND LITERATURE OF THE BANK RESTRICTION PERIOD.—1. *History*: In addition to the well-known works on the history of currency, banking, and industrial fluctuations by T. Tooke, H. D. Macleod, R. Bischop, A. Andreades, M. Bouniatian, and A. E. Feaveryear the following should be especially mentioned: E. Cannan, Introduction to *The Paper Pound 1797–1821*. A Reprint of the Bullion Report. Second edition, London, 1925; R. G. Hawtrey, *Currency and Credit*, third edition, London, 1928, chapter xviii; W. Smart, *Economic Annals of the Nineteenth Century 1801–1820*, London, 1910; N. J. Silberling, British Financial Experience, 1790–1830, *The Review of Economic Statistics*, prel. vol. i, 1919; British Prices and Business Cycles, in the same journal, prel. vol. v, 1923; and Financial and Monetary Experience of Great Britain during the Napoleonic Wars, *Quarterly Journal of Economics*, vol. 38, 1924; A. Cunningham, *British Credit in the last Napoleonic War*, Cambridge, 1910; A. W. Acworth, *Financial Reconstruction in England 1815–22*, London, 1925; G. O'Brien, The Last Years of the Irish Currency, *Economic History* (A Supplement to the *Economic Journal*), vol. i, No. 2, 1927; L. Wolowski, *Un chapitre de l'histoire financiere de l'Angleterre, La suspension des payments de la Banque et le Bullion Report*, Paris, 1865; M. Phillips, *The Token Money of the Bank of England 1797–1816*, London, 1900; P. Aretz, *Die Entwicklung der Diskontpolitik der Bank von England*, 1780–1850, Berlin, 1916; E. Kellenberger, Die Aufhebung der Barzahlung in England 1797 und ihre Folgen, *Jahrbücher für Nationalökonomie und Statistik*, III. F. vol. 51, 1916; J. Wolter, *Das staatliche Geldwesen Englands zu Zeit der Bankrestriktion*,

Strassburg, 1917; A. M. de Jong, De Engelsche Bank Restriction van 1797, *De Economist*, 72nd year, Feb.–Apr. 1923.

2. *Development of Monetary Theory*, J. H. Hollander; The Development of the Theory of Money from Adam Smith to David Ricardo, *Quarterly Journal of Economics*, vol. 25, May 1911; J. Viner, *Canada's Balance of International Indebtedness*, 1900–1911, Cambridge, 1924; and *Studies in the Theory of International Trade*, London, 1937; J. W. Angell, *The Theory of International Prices*, Cambridge, 1926; C. Rist, *Histoire des Doctrines relatives au Crédit er la Monnaie*, Paris, 1938; A. Loria, *Studi sulla valore della moneta*, Turin, 1891; G. Krügel, *Der Bullion Bericht*, Rostock, 1930; H. Leroi-Fürst, Die Entwicklung der Lehr von der Zahlungsbilanz im 19. Jahrhundert bis 1873, *Archiv für Sozialwissenschaften und Sozialpolitik*, vol. 56, 1926; E. Fossati, Ricardo und die Entstehung des Bullion Reports, *Zeitschrift für Nationalökonomie*, vols. iv and v, 1933–4.

AN

ENQUIRY

INTO

THE NATURE AND EFFECTS

of

THE PAPER CREDIT

OF

GREAT BRITAIN.

BY

HENRY THORNTON, ESQ.
M. P.

LONDON:

PRINTED FOR J. HATCHARD, BOOKSELLER TO THE QUEEN,
(Opposite York House)
PICCADILLY;

AND MESSRS. F. AND C. RIVINGTON,
ST. PAUL's CHURCH YARD.

1802

INTRODUCTION

THE first intention of the Writer of the following pages was merely to expose some popular errors which related chiefly to the suspension of the cash payments of the Bank of England, and to the influence of our paper currency on the price of provisions. But in pursuing his purpose, many questions occurred which it seemed important to discuss, partly on account of their having some bearing on the topics under consideration, and partly because they appeared to be of general importance, and had either been left unexplained, or had been inaccurately stated by those English writers who have treated of paper credit. This work has, therefore, assumed, in some degree, the character of a general treatise.

The first Chapter contains a few preliminary observations on commercial credit. The object of the two following Chapters is distinctly to describe the several kinds of paper credit; to lay down some general principles respecting it; and, in particular, to point out the important consequences which result from the different degrees of rapidity in the circulation of different kinds of circulating medium, and also in the circulation of the same medium at different periods of time.

The nature of the institution of the Bank of England is then explained; the necessity of maintaining the accustomed, or nearly the accustomed, quantity of its notes, however great may be the fluctuations of its cash, is insisted on; and the suspension of its cash payments is shewn to have resulted neither from a deficiency in its resources, nor from a too great extension of its loans to government, nor from rashness or improvidence in its directors, but from circumstances which they had little power of controuling: this event being one to which a national establishment, like the

Bank of England, is, in some situations of the country, unavoidably subject.

The manner in which an unfavourable balance of trade affects the course of exchange, and in which an unfavourable exchange creates an excess of the market price above the mint price of gold, and a profit on the exportation of our coin, are the subjects of a succeeding Chapter.

The circumstances, also, which have led to the multiplication of our country banks, and the several advantages and disadvantages of those institutions, are fully stated.

The earlier parts of the work having tended to shew the evil of a too great and sudden diminution of our circulating medium, some of the latter Chapters are employed in pointing out the consequences of a too great augmentation of it. The limitation of the amount of the notes of the Bank of England is shewn to be the means of restricting the quantity of the circulating paper of the kingdom, of preventing a rise in the price of commodities in Great Britain, and of thus extending our exports and restraining our imports, and rendering the exchange more favourable. Some objections to the limitation of the Bank of England paper are likewise stated and answered.

The last Chapter treats of the influence of paper credit on the price of all the articles of life: a subject, the difficulties of which are in some degree removed by the antecedent discussions.

In the course of this enquiry, several passages in the work of Dr. A. Smith on the Wealth of Nations are animadverted on, as are also some observations made by Mr. Hume in his Essays on Money and on the Balance of Trade, and by Sir James Stewart in his book on Political Œconomy, as well as some remarks in the writings of Locke and Montesquieu.

The mode in which the subjects of coin, of paper credit, of the balance of trade, and of exchanges (subjects intimately connected with each other), have been treated by those writers, was suggested by the circumstances of more early times: and we ought not to be surprised, if, in treatises necessarily in some degree theoretical, or written for the purpose of establishing a particular truth, certain incidental observations should not be just, nor even if some main principles should have been laid down in terms not sufficiently guarded.

A person who presumes to differ from the authorities which have been mentioned, and who proposes to correct the public opinion on the important subject of our paper credit, ought, undoubtedly, to be very cautious lest he should propagate new errors while he is endeavouring to remove the old. A sense of the duty of mature consideration has caused some delay in the publication of the following work. That its leading doctrines are just, the writer feels a confident persuasion. That it may have imperfections, and some, perhaps, which greater care on his part might have corrected, he cannot doubt. But he trusts, that a man who is much occupied on the practical business of life, will be excused by the public, if he should present to them a treatise less elaborate, and, in many respects, more incomplete, than those on which he has found it necessary to remark. Future enquirers may possibly pursue, with advantage, some particular topics on which he has felt a certain degree of distrust.

It may not be irrelevant or improper to observe, that the present work has been written by a person whose situation in life has supplied information on several of the topics under discussion, and that much use has been made of those means of correcting the errors of former writers which recent events have afforded.

CONTENTS

CHAP. I.

PAGE

OF *Commercial Credit;—of Paper Credit, as arising out of it.— Of Commercial Capital* — — — — — 75

CHAP. II.

Of Trade by Barter.—Of Money.—Of Bills of Exchange and Notes.—Of Bills and Notes, considered as discountable Articles. —Of Fictitious Bills, or Bills of Accommodation — — 81

CHAP. III.

Of circulating Paper.—Of Bank Notes.—Of Bills considered as circulating Paper.—Of the different Degrees of Rapidity in the Circulation of different Times.—Error of Dr. A. Smith.— Difference in the Quantity wanted for effecting the Payments of a Country in Consequence of this Difference of Rapidity.—Proof of this taken from Events of 1793.—Fallacy involved, in the Supposition that Paper Credit might be abolished — — 90

CHAP. IV.

Observation of Dr. Smith, respecting the Bank of England.—Of the Nature of that Institution.—Reasons for never greatly diminishing its Notes.—its Liability to be exhausted of Guineas.—the Suspension of its Cash Payments not owning to too great Issue of Paper,—nor to too great Loans.—Propriety of parliamentary Interference — — — — — — — 103

CHAP. V.

Of the Balance of Trade.—Of the Course of Exchange.—Tendency of an unfavourable Exchange to take away Gold;—of the Prob-

PAGE

ability of the Return of Gold;—of the Manner in which it may be supposed that the exported Gold is employed on the Continent.— Reasons for having renewed the Law for suspending the Cash Payments of the Bank of England — — — — — 141

CHAP. VI.

Error of imagining that Gold can be provided at the Time of actual Distress.—Reasons for not admitting the Presumption that the Directors of the Bank must have been to blame, for not making, beforehand, a more adequate Provision — — — — 161

CHAP. VII.

Of Country Banks.—their Advantages and Disadvantages — — 168

CHAP. VIII.

Of the Tendency of a too great Issue of Bank Paper to produce an Excess of the Market Price above the Mint Price of Gold,—of the Means by which it creates this Excess, viz. by its Operation on the Price of Goods, and on the Course of Exchange.—Errors of Dr. A. Smith on the Subject of Excessive Paper.—Of the Manner in which the Limitation of the Quantity of the Bank of England Paper serves to limit the Quantity, and sustain the Value of all the Paper in the Kingdom — — — — — 193

CHAP. IX.

Of the Circumstances which cause the Paper of the Bank of England, as well as all the other Paper of the Country, to fail of having their Value regulated according to any exact Proportion to the Quantity of Bank of England Notes — — — — 212

CHAP. X.

Objections to the Doctrine of the two preceding Chapters answered.— Of the Circumstances which render it necessary that the Bank

PAGE

*should impose its own Limit on the Quantity of its Paper.—Effect
of the Law against Usury.—Proof of the Necessity of restricting the
Bank Loans, drawn from the Case of the Transfer of Capital to
Foreign Countries*   —   —   —   —   —   —   230

CHAP. XI.

*Of the Influence of Paper Credit on the Price of Commodities.—
Observations on some Passages of Montesquieu and Hume.—
Conclusion*   —   —   —   —   —   —   —   260

AN ENQUIRY INTO THE NATURE AND EFFECTS OF THE PAPER CREDIT OF GREAT BRITAIN (1802)

CHAP. I

Of Commercial Credit.—Of Paper Credit, as arising out of it.—Of Commercial Capital.

COMMERCIAL credit may be defined to be that confidence which subsists among commercial men in respect to their mercantile affairs. This confidence operates in several ways. It disposes them to lend money to each other, to bring themselves under various pecuniary engagements by the acceptance and indorsement of bills, and also to sell and deliver goods in consideration of an equivalent promised to be given at a subsequent period. Even in that early and rude state of society, in which neither bills nor money are as yet known, it may be assumed, that if there be commerce, a certain degree of commercial credit will also subsist. In the interchange, for example, of commodities between the farmer and the manufacturer, the manufacturer, probably, will sometimes deliver goods to the farmer on the credit of the growing crop, in confidence that the farmer will come into possession of the fruits of his labour, and will be either compelled by the law of the land, or induced by a sense of justice, to fulfil his part of the contract when the harvest shall be over. In a variety of other cases it must happen, even in the infancy of society, that one man will deliver property to his neighbour without receiving, on the spot, the equivalent which is agreed to be given in return. It will occasionally be the interest of the one party thus to wait the other's convenience: for he that reposes the confidence will receive

75

in the price an adequate compensation for the disadvantages incurred by the risk and the delay. In a society in which law and the sense of moral duty are weak, and property is consequently insecure, there will, of course, be little confidence or credit, and there will also be little commerce.

This commercial credit is the foundation of *paper credit* ; paper serving to express that confidence which is in the mind, and to reduce to writing those engagements to pay, which might otherwise be merely verbal. It will hereafter be explained in what manner, and to how very great a degree, paper credit also spares the use of the expensive article of gold; and how the multiplication of paper securities serves to enlarge, confirm, and diffuse that confidence among traders, which, in some measure, existed independently of paper, and would, to a certain degree, remain, though paper should be abolished.

If there may be a convenience in giving credit in the infancy of society, when the interchange of commodities is small, there may be, at least, the same convenience when goods begin to be multiplied, when wealth is more variously distributed, and society is advanced.

The day on which it suits the British merchant to purchase and send away a large quantity of goods, may not be that on which he finds it convenient to pay for them. If it is made necessary for him to give ready money in return, he must always have in his hands a very large stock of money; and for the expence of keeping this fund (an expence consisting chiefly in the loss of interest) he must be repaid in the price of the commodities in which he deals. He avoids this charge, and also obtains time for preparing and adjusting his pecuniary concerns, by buying on credit; that is to say, by paying for his goods not by money, but by the delivery of a note in which he promises the money on a future day. He is thus set more at liberty in his speculations: his judgement as to the propriety of buying or not buying, or of selling or not selling, and also as to the time of doing either, may be more freely exercised.

The general principle, according to which the length of the

76

customary credit in different trades has adjusted itself, seems clearly to have been that of mutual advantage and convenience. For example, if we suppose the merchant importers of any particular article for home consumption to be generally rich, and the retailers of it to be poor—that is, to have a capital insufficient to enable them to keep the assortment and stock of goods necessary in their retail commerce—the credit customarily given by the importers, and taken by the retail traders, will naturally be long. In other words, it will be the custom of the importers to lend part of their capital to the retail dealers, in consideration of an advantage in the price proportionate to the benefit conferred by the loan. Sometimes two or more customs prevail, as to the period of credit, in the same trade; and to each custom there are individual exceptions. The deviations from the rule obviously arise out of that principle of mutual advantage and convenience on which the rule itself has been founded.

The option of buying and of selling on longer or shorter credit, as it multiplies the number of persons able to buy and to sell, promotes free competition, and thus contributes to lower the price of articles. A variety of degrees in the length of credit which is afforded, tends more especially to give to some of the poorer traders a greater power of purchasing, and cherishes that particular sort of competition most adapted to lower prices, namely, the competition of dealers likely to be contented with a very moderate rate of gain. Opulent merchants sometimes complain of the intrusion of dealers who possess a small capital and take long credit, for this very reason, that such dealers reduce the profits of trade.

But the custom of taking and giving long credit has its inconveniences as well as its advantages. It encreases the amount of the bad debts incurred in the course of commercial transactions. The apprehension of loss, is, therefore, continually operating on the mind of the lender as a restraint on the custom of giving credit, while the compensation he receives for the use of the capital which he supplies, acts as an encouragement to the practice. The subsisting state of credit may, in general, be considered as resulting out of a comparison made both by lenders and borrowers of the advantages and disadvantages which each discover that they derive from giving and taking credit.

Mercantile confidence, however, is not always dealt out in that proportion in which there is reasonable ground for it. At some periods it has risen to a most unwarrantable height, and has given occasion to the most extravagant and hurtful speculations. Of these the cases of the Ayr bank, and of the South Sea scheme, are instances. Evils of this kind, however, have a tendency to correct themselves. In a country possessed of commercial knowledge and experience, confidence, in most instances, will not be misplaced.

Some persons are of opinion, that, when the custom of buying on credit is pushed very far, and a great quantity of individual dealings is in consequence carried on by persons having comparatively little property, the national commerce is to be considered as unsupported by a proper capital; and that a nation, under such circumstances, whatever may be its ostensible riches, exhibits the delusive appearance of wealth.

It must, however, be remembered, that the practice of buying on credit, in the internal commerce of the country, supposes the habit of selling on credit also to subsist; and to prevail, on the whole, in an exactly equal degree. In respect to the foreign trade of a country, the practice of dealing on credit indicates poverty or riches, in proportion as the credit generally taken is longer or shorter than the credit given. The custom which tradesmen have of selling to the consumers on credit, is also an indication of wealth in the commercial world: the traders must possess a surplus of wealth, either their own or borrowed, which bears an exact proportion to the amount of debts due to them by the consumers. Thus that practice of trading on credit which prevails among us, so far as it subsists between trader and trader, is an indication neither of wealth nor of poverty in the mercantile body; so far as it respects our transactions with foreign countries, is an indication of extraordinary wealth belonging to the merchants of Great Britain; and so far as it respects the trade between the retailer and the consumer, implies a deficiency of wealth in the consumers, and a proportionate surplus of it among commercial men. The existing customs imply, that, on the whole, there is among our traders a great abundance of wealth.

It may conduce to the prevention of error, in the subsequent discussions, to define, in this place, what is meant by commercial capital. This consists, first, in the goods (part of them in the course of manufacture) which are in the hands of our manufacturers and dealers, and are in their way to consumption. The amount of these is necessarily larger or smaller in proportion as the general expenditure is more or less considerable, and in proportion, also, as commodities pass more or less quickly into the hands of the consumer. It further consists in the ships, buildings, machinery, and other dead stock maintained for the purpose of carrying on our manufactures and commerce, under which head may be included the gold found necessary for the purposes of commerce, but at all times forming a very small item in this great account. It comprehends also the debts due to our traders for goods sold and delivered by them on credit; debts finally to be discharged by articles of value given in return.

Commercial capital, let it then be understood, consists not in paper, and is not augmented by the multiplication of this medium of payment. In one sense, indeed, it may be encreased by paper. I mean, that the nominal value of the existing goods may be enlarged through a reduction which is caused by paper in the value of that standard by which all property is estimated. The paper itself forms no part of the estimate.

This mode of computing the amount of the national capital engaged in commerce, is substantially the same with that in which each commercial man estimates the value of his own property. Paper constitutes, it is true, an article on the credit side of the books of some men; but it forms an exactly equal item on the debit side of the books of others. It constitutes, therefore, on the whole, neither a debit nor a credit. The banker who issues twenty thousand pounds in notes, and lends in consequence twenty thousand pounds to the merchants on the security of bills accepted by them, states himself in his books to be debtor to the various holders of his notes to the extent of the sum in question; and states himself to be the creditor of the accepters of the bills in his possession to the same amount. His valuation, therefore, of his own property, is the same as if neither the bills nor the bank notes had any existence. Again; the merchants, in making their estimate of property, deduct the bills payable by themselves which are in the drawer of the banker, and add to their estimate the notes of the banker which are in their own drawer; so that the valuation, likewise, of the capital of the merchants is the same as if the paper had no existence. The use of paper does not, therefore, introduce any principle of delusion into that estimate of property which is made by individuals. The case of gold, on the other hand, differs from that of paper inasmuch as the possessor of gold takes credit for that for which no man debits himself. The several commercial capitals of traders, as estimated in their books, would, unquestionably, be found, if deducted from their other property and added together, to correspond, in amount, with a general estimate of the commercial stock of the country, calculated under the several heads already stated.

It is true, that men, in estimating their share in the public funds of the country, add to their estimate a debt due to them which no *individual* deducts from his valuation. On this head, it may be observed, that the nation is the debtor. But the commercial capital, which has been described, exists independently of capital in the public funds. The man in trade has property in trade. If he has property in the stocks, he has the property in trade in addition to it. In speaking, therefore, of the commercial capital, whether of the nation or of an individual, the idea that any part of it is composed either of the paper credit or of the stocks of the country, is to be totally excluded.

CHAP. II

Of Trade by Barter.—Of Money.—Of Bills of Exchange and Notes.— Of Bills and Notes, considered as discountable Articles.—Of fictitious Bills, or Bills of Accommodation.

SOCIETY, in its rudest state, carries on its trade by the means only of barter. When most advanced, it still conducts its commerce on the same principle; for gold and silver coin, bankers' notes, and bills of exchange, may be considered merely as instruments employed for the purpose of facilitating the barter. The object is to exchange such a quantity of one sort of goods for such a quantity of another, as may be deemed, under all circumstances, a suitable equivalent*.

Barter being soon felt to be inconvenient, the precious metals are resorted to as a measure of value, they being, at once, portable, steady in their price, and capable of subdivisions. The state fixes a stamp upon them, in order thus to certify the quantity and fineness of each piece.

The precious metals, when uncoined (or in the state of bullion) are themselves commodities; but when converted into money they are to be considered merely as a measure of the value of other articles. They may, indeed, be converted back into commodities;

---

* By the term suitable equivalent, is not intended that equivalent which an impartial umpire, determining according to the strict rule of equity, might dictate. The equivalent obtained by men dealing in the way of barter is not exactly of this sort; for that power which the proprietors of a scarce and necessary commodity have over the consumers of it, will always lead them to demand a much higher price than the production of it may have cost.

In Africa, for example, where the mode of barter prevails, the price of rice is at some times equal to about two pounds, and at others to about sixteen pounds per ton. It cannot be supposed that the variations in the crops of different seasons can bear any proportion to this variation of prices. Monopoly also is an evil which is incident to trade as trade. It is, indeed, more particularly apt to exist in the infancy of commerce.

and it is one recommendation of their use as coin, that they are capable of this conversion.

We shall now advert to some of the simplest forms in which it may be supposed that paper credit will first exist.

To speak first of bills of exchange.

It is obvious, that, however portable gold may be in comparison of any other article which might be made a measure of value, to carry it in quantities to a great distance must prove incommodious. Let it be supposed, that there are in London ten manufacturers who sell their article to ten shopkeepers in York, by whom it is retailed; and that there are in York ten manufacturers of another commodity, who sell it to ten shopkeepers in London. There would be no occasion for the ten shopkeepers in London to send yearly as many guineas to London. It would only be necessary for the York manufacturers to receive from each of the shopkeepers, at their own door, the money in question (for we may assume a sufficient quantity to be usually circulating in the place): giving in return letters which should acknowledge the receipt of it; and which should also direct the money, lying ready in the hands of their debtors in London, to be paid to the London shopkeepers, so as to cancel the debt in London in the same manner as that at York. The expence and the risk of all transmission of money would thus be saved; and the traders in question would of course be, on the whole, enabled to sell their article at a price proportionably lower than that which they would otherwise require. Letters ordering the transfer of the debt, are termed, in the language of the present day, bills of exchange. They are bills by which the debt of one person is exchanged for the debt of another; and the debt, perhaps, which is due in one place for the debt due in another.

To speak next of *Promissory Notes*.

When goods are delivered in consideration of an equivalent in money to be received at a subsequent period, it becomes desirable that, for the sake of precisely recording the day on which payment is to be made, and the exact amount of the sum, a note, expressing each of these particulars, should be given. The term "value received" is introduced into the note, as also into every bill of exchange; that expression being deemed necessary in law to make the bill or the note binding.

Bills of exchange and notes have been hitherto considered as created only for those simple purposes for which they seem originally to have been drawn, and which are professed by the form always used in drawing them. Both these sorts of paper must now be spoken of as possessing an additional character, namely, that of being *Discountable Articles*, or articles which there is an opportunity of converting, at any time, into money; such a discount or deduction from the amount of the bill or note as is equal to the interest upon it, during the period for which it has to run, being paid as the price of the conversion. The bills of exchange, which were described as drawn from York on London, and as serving to transfer debts, would equally answer that purpose at whatever date they might be payable. It is customary, however, to make almost all bills payable at a period somewhat distant. Country bankers, for instance, and shopkeepers, who often act in this respect as bankers, indemnify themselves for the trouble and expence attending the drawing of bills, not by a commission, but by a protraction of the time at which the bills are to become payable. Thus is created a paper credit, which shall remain in existence for perhaps one or more months, and may serve, during any part of that time, as a discountable article.

Promissory notes were before represented as drawn on the occasion of the sale of goods, and made payable at a distant period. In returning to the more careful consideration of them, we shall discover the existence of the same disposition to multiply paper credit.

When a merchant in this country sells his goods on credit, it is, perhaps, not very important to him that he should receive from the buyer a promissory note (or an accepted bill, which is the same thing), if the only object of taking the note or bill is the ascertainment of the exact amount of the debt, and of the period of payment.

83

It is true that the law gives superior facility to the recovery of debts for which promissory notes have been given. Nevertheless, if the sum be small, and the party in credit, all these advantages, in the present high state of confidence, would, in many cases, be thought scarcely to compensate even the trifling expence of the note stamp. The debt will be a book debt, if no note be taken; and, as such, may be sufficiently secure.

Notes, even for goods sold and delivered, are therefore to be considered as given chiefly for the sake of a convenience of another kind, which the seller finds in having them. The note, like the bill of exchange just spoken of, is a discountable article. It may be turned, if circumstances require, into money; or into bank notes, which answer the same purpose. It is not, perhaps, fully intended to turn the note or bill into money; they are taken rather as a provision against a contingency. The holder is rendered secure against the effect of disappointments in the receipt of cash. It is in this manner that his credit is fortified, and that he is enabled to fulfil with punctuality his pecuniary engagements; for there is a certain sort and quantity of bills and notes, on the turning of which into money, at the common rate of discount, the holder, if he be a man of credit, may almost as confidently rely on the changing of a bank note into guineas, or of a guinea into silver.

The interest which traders have in being always possessed of a number of notes and bills, has naturally led to a great multiplication of them; and not only to the multiplication of notes given for goods sold, or of regular bills of exchange, but to the creation of numerous other notes and bills. Of these, some are termed notes and bills of accommodation: and the term fictitious is often applied to them. It may be useful to describe them particularly.

It was before shewn, that the principal motive for fabricating what must here be called the real note, that is, the note drawn in consequence of a real sale of goods, is the wish to have the means of turning it into money. The seller, therefore, who desires to have a note for goods sold, may be considered as taking occasion to ingraft on the transaction of the sale, the convenient condition of receiving from the buyer a discountable note of the same amount with the value of the goods. A fictitious note, or note of accommodation, is a note drawn for the same purpose of being discounted; though it is not also sanctioned by the circumstance of having been drawn in consequence of an actual sale of goods. Notes of accommodation are, indeed, of various kinds. The following description of one may suffice.

A, being in want of 100*l.*, requests B to accept a note or bill drawn at two months, which B, therefore, on the face of it, is bound to pay; it is understood, however, that A will take care either to discharge the bill himself, or to furnish B with the means of paying it. A obtains ready money for the bill on the joint credit of the two parties. A fulfills his promise of paying it when due, and thus concludes the transaction. This service rendered by B to A is, however, not unlikely to be requited at a more or less distant period by a similar acceptance of a bill on A, drawn and discounted for B's convenience.

Let us now compare such a bill with a real bill. Let us consider in what points they differ, or seem to differ; and in what they agree.

They agree, inasmuch as each is a discountable article; each has also been created for the purpose of being discounted; and each is, perhaps, discounted in fact. Each, therefore, serves equally to supply means of speculation to the merchant. So far, moreover, as bills and notes constitute what is called the circulating medium, or paper currency, of the country (a topic which shall not be here anticipated), and prevent the use of guineas, the fictitious and the real bill are upon an equality; and if the price of commodities be raised in proportion to the quantity of paper currency, the one contributes to that rise exactly in the same manner as the other.

Before we come to the points in which they differ, let us advert to one point in which they are commonly supposed to be unlike; but in which they cannot be said always or necessarily to differ.

"Real notes," it is sometimes said, "represent actual property. "There are actual goods in existence, which are the counterpart "to every real note. Notes which are not drawn, in consequence "of a sale of goods, are a species of false wealth, by which a nation "is deceived. These supply only an imaginary capital; the others "indicate one that is real."

In answer to this statement it may be observed, first, that the notes given in consequence of a real sale of goods cannot be considered as, on that account, *certainly* representing any actual property, Suppose that A sells one hundred pounds worth of goods to B at six months credit, and takes a bill at six months for it; and that B, within a month after, sells the same goods, at a like credit, to C, taking a like bill; and again, that C, after another month, sells them to D, taking a like bill, and so on. There may then, at the end of six months, be six bills of 100*l.* each existing at the same time; and every one of these may possibly have been discounted. Of all these bills, then, one only represents any actual property.

In the next place it is obvious, that the number of those bills which are given in consequence of sales of goods, and which, nevertheless, do not represent property, is liable to be encreased through the extension of the length of credit given on the sale of goods. If, for instance, we had supposed the credit given to be a credit of twelve months instead of six, 1,200*l.* instead of 600*l.* would have been the amount of the bills drawn on the occasion of the sale of goods; and 1,100*l.* would have been the amount of that part of these which would represent no property.

In order to justify the supposition that a real bill (as it is called) represents actual property, there ought to be some power in the bill-holder to prevent the property which the bill represents, from being turned to other purposes than that of paying the bill in question. No such power exists; neither the man who holds the real bill, nor the man who discounts it, has any property in the specific goods for which it was given: he as much trusts to the general ability to pay of the giver of the bill, as the holder of any fictitious bill does. The fictitious bill may, in many cases, be a bill given by a person having a large and known capital, a part of which the fictitious bill may be said, in that case, to represent. The supposition that real bills represent property, and that fictitious bills do not, seems, therefore, to be one by which more than justice is done to one of these species of bills, and something less than justice to the other.

We come next to some points in which they differ.

First, the fictitious note, or note of accommodation, is liable to the objection that it professes to be what it is not. This objection, however, lies only against those fictitious bills which are passed as real. In many cases, it is sufficiently obvious what they are. Secondly, the fictitious bill is, in general, less likely to be punctually paid than the real one. There is a general presumption, that the dealer in fictitious bills is a man who is a more adventurous speculator than he who carefully abstains from them. It follows, thirdly, that fictitious bills, besides being less safe, are less subject to limitation as to their quantity. The extent of a man's actual sales form some limit to the amount of his real notes; and, as it is highly desirable in commerce that credit should be dealt out to all persons in some sort of regular and due proportion, the measure of a man's actual sales, certified by the appearance of his bills drawn in virtue of those sales, is some rule in the case, though a very imperfect one in many respects.

A fictitious bill, or bill of accommodation, is evidently, in substance, the same as any common promissory note; and even better, in this respect,—that there is but one security to the promissory note, whereas, in the case of the bill of accommodation, there are two. So much jealousy subsists lest traders should push their means of raising money too far, that paper, the same in its general nature with that which is given, being the only paper which can be given, by men out of business, is deemed somewhat discreditable when coming from a merchant. And because such paper, when in the merchant's hand, necessarily imitates the paper which passes on the occasion of a sale of goods, the epithet fictitious has been cast upon it; an epithet which has seemed to countenance the confused and mistaken notion, that there is something altogether false and delusive in the nature of a certain part both of the paper and of the apparent wealth of the country.

Bills of exchange are drawn upon London to a great amount, from all parts, not only of Great Britain, but of the world; and the grounds on which they have been drawn in a great degree elude observation. A large proportion of them, no doubt partakes of the nature of bills of accommodation. They have, however, in general, that shape communicated to them, whatever it may be, which is thought likely to render them discountable; and it is not difficult, as the preceding observations will have shewn, to make of some real, and, at the same time, of many seeming, transactions of commerce as a ground for drawing, and as a means of multiplying such bills.

The practice of creating a paper credit, by drawing and re-drawing, has been particularly described by Dr. Adam Smith; and is stated by him to have a tendency which is very ruinous to the party resorting to it. This practice, however, is often carried on at much less expence to those engaged in it than Dr. Smith imagines. A, for instance, of London, draws a bill at two months on B, of Amsterdam, and receives immediate money for the bill. B enables himself to pay the bill by drawing, when it is nearly due, a bill at two months on A for the same sum, which bill he sells or dis-counts; and A again finds the means of payment by again drawing a bill, at two months, on B. The transaction is, in substance, obviously the same as if A and B had borrowed, on their joint security, the sum in question for six months. The ground on which transactions of this sort have been stated by Dr. Adam Smith to be ruinous is, that of the heavy expence of a commission on every bill drawn, which is paid by him who raises money in this manner. If, for instance, one-half per cent. is the commission, and the bills are drawn at two months, and a discount of five per cent. per annum is paid, the money is raised at an interest of eight per cent. Such transactions, however, are often carried on alternately for the benefit of each of the two parties; that is to say, at one time the transaction is on the account of A, who pays a commission to B; at another it is on the account of B, who pays a commission to A. Thus each party, on the whole, gains about as much as he pays in the shape of such commissions; and the discount in turning the bill into money, which is the same as that on any other bill, may, therefore, be considered as the whole expence incurred. Money may be raised in this manner at an interest of only five per cent. In the case recently proposed, the drawing and re-drawing were imagined to be only between A, of London, and B, of Amsterdam. This practice, however, is often carried on between three or more parties drawing from three or more places. In such case, the draft is drawn on the place on which the existing course of exchange shews that it will best answer to draw it. An operation of this sort may obviously be carried on partly for the purpose of raising money, and partly for that of profiting by a small turn in the exchange. Transactions which are the converse to this, are, on the other hand, entered into by those who happen to possess ready money. They remit, if the exchange seems to favour their remittance, and draw in consequence of having remitted. To determine what bills are fictitious, or bills of accommodation, and what are real, is often a point of difficulty. Even the drawers and remitters themselves frequently either do not know, or do not take the trouble to reflect, whether the bills ought more properly to be considered as of the one class or of the other; and the private discounter, or banker, to whom they are offered, still more frequently finds the credit of the bills to be the only rule which it is possible to follow in judging whether he ought to discount them.

CHAP. III

Of circulating Paper—of Bank Notes—of Bills considered as circulating Paper—different Degrees of Rapidity in the Circulation of different Sorts of circulating Medium, and of the same Sort of circulating Medium at different Times.—Error of Dr. A. Smith.—Difference in the Quantities wanted for effecting the Payments of a Country in Consequence of this Difference of Rapidity.—Proof of this taken from Events of 1793.—Fallacy involved in the Supposition that Paper Credit might be abolished.

W E proceed next to speak of circulating paper, and first of *Notes payable to Bearer on Demand,* whether issued by a public bank or by a private banker.

When confidence rises to a certain height in a country, it occurs to some persons, that profit may be obtained by issuing notes, which purport to be exchangeable for money; and which, through the known facility of thus exchanging them, may circulate in its stead; a part only of the money, of which the notes supply the place, being kept in store as a provision for the current payments. On the remainder interest is gained, and this interest constitutes the profit of the issuer. Some powerful and well accredited company will probably be the first issuers of paper of this sort, the numerous proprietors of the company exerting their influence for the sake of the dividends which they expect, in giving currency to the new paper credit. The establishment of a great public bank has a tendency to promote the institution of private banks. The public bank, obliged to provide itself largely with money for its own payments, becomes a reservoir of gold to which private banks may resort with little difficulty, expence, or delay, for the supply of their several necessities.

Dr. A. Smith, in his chapter on Paper Credit, considers the national stock of money in the same light with those machines and instruments of trade which require a certain expence, first, to erect, and afterwards to support them. And he proceeds to observe, that the substitution of paper, in the room of gold and silver coin, serves to replace a very expensive instrument of commerce with one much less costly, and sometimes equally convenient. "Thus," he says, "a banker, by issuing 100,000*l.* in notes, keeping "20,000*l.* in hand for his current payments, causes 20,000*l.* in gold "and silver to perform all the functions which 100,000*l.* would "otherwise have performed; in consequence of which, 80,000*l.* "of gold and silver can be spared, which will not fail to be exchanged "for foreign goods, and become a new fund for a new trade, pro- "ducing profit to the country."*

Dr. Smith, although he discusses at some length the subject of Paper Circulation, does not at all advert to the tendency of bills of exchange to spare the use of bank paper, or to their faculty of supplying its place in many cases.

In the former Chapter it was shewn that bills, though professedly drawn for the purpose of exchanging a debt due to one person for a debt due to another, are, in fact, created rather for the sake of serving as a discountable article, and of forming a provision against contingencies; and that, by being at any time convertible into cash (that is, into either money or bank notes) they render that supply of cash which is necessary to be kept in store much less considerable.

But they not only spare the use of ready money; they also

* Dr. Smith, in confirmation of this, remarks how greatly Scotland had been enriched in the twenty-five or thirty years preceding the time at which he wrote, by the erection of new banks in almost every considerable town, and even in some country villages, the effects having been, as he affirms, precisely those which he had described. The trade of Glasgow he states to have been doubled in about fifteen years after the erection of its first bank, and the trade of Scotland to be thought to have been more than quadrupled since the first erection of its two first public banking companies. This effect, indeed, he conceives to be too good to be accounted for by that cause alone; though he deems it indisputable, that the banks have essentially contributed to the augmentation of the trade and industry of Scotland. The gold and silver of Scotland, circulating before the union, is estimated by him at full a million; the quantity since the union at less than half a million; and the paper circulating in Scotland since the union at about one million and a half.

occupy its place in many cases. Let us imagine a farmer in the country to discharge a debt of 10*l*. to his neighbouring grocer, by giving to him a bill for that sum, drawn on his cornfactor in London for grain sold in the metropolis; and the grocer to transmit the bill, he having previously indorsed it, to a neighbouring sugar-baker, in discharge of a like debt; and the sugar-baker to send it, when again indorsed, to a West India merchant in an outport, and the West India merchant to deliver it to his country banker, who also indorses it, and sends it into further circulation. The bill in this case will have effected five payments exactly as if it were a 10*l*. note payable to bearer on demand. It will, however, have circulated in consequence chiefly of the confidence placed by each receiver of it in the last indorser, his own correspondent in trade; whereas, the circulation of a bank note is owing rather to the circumstance of the name of the issuer being so well known as to give to it an universal credit. A multitude of bills pass between trader and trader in the country in the manner which has been described; and they evidently form, in the strictest sense, a part of the circulating medium of the kingdom*.

Bills, however, and especially those which are drawn for large sums, may be considered as in general circulating more slowly than either gold or bank notes, and for a reason which it is material to explain. Bank notes, though they yield an interest to the issuer,

---

* Mr. Boyd, in his publication addressed to Mr. Pitt on the Subject of the Bank of England Issues, propagates the same error into which many others have fallen, of considering bills as no part of the circulating medium of the country. He says, "by the words "means of circulation," "circulating medium," and "currency," (which are used as synonymous terms in this Letter) I under-"stand always ready money, whether consisting of bank notes or specie, in "contradiction to *bills of exchange*, navy bills, exchequer bills, or any nego-"tiable paper which form no part of the circulating medium, as I have always "understood that term. The latter is the circulator; the former are merely "objects of circulation." . . . See note to the first page of Mr. Boyd's Letter to Mr. Pitt.

It will be seen, in the progress of this work, that it was necessary to clear away much confusion which has arisen from the want of a sufficiently full acquaintance with the several kinds of paper credit; and, in particular, to remove, by a considerable detail, the prevailing errors respecting the nature of bills, before it could be possible to reason properly upon the effects of paper credit.

afford none to the man who detains them in his possession; they are to him as unproductive as guineas. The possessor of a bank note, therefore, makes haste to part with it. The possessor of a bill of exchange possesses, on the contrary, that which is always growing more valuable. The bill, when it is first drawn, is worth something less than a bank note, on account of its not being due until a distant day; and the first receiver of it may be supposed to obtain a compensation for the inferiority of its value in the price of the article with which the bill is purchased. When he parts with it, he may be considered as granting to the next receiver a like compensation, which is proportionate to the time which the bill has still to run. Each holder of a bill has, therefore, an interest in detaining it.

Bills, it is true, generally pass among traders in the country without there being any calculation or regular allowance of discount; the reason of which circumstance is, that there is a generally understood period of time for which those bills may have to run, which, according to the custom of traders, are accepted as current payment. If any bill given in payment has a longer time than usual to run, he who receives it is considered as so far favouring the person from whom he takes it; and the favoured person has to compensate for this advantage, not, perhaps, by a recompence of the same kind accurately calculated, but in the general adjustment of the pecuniary affairs of the two parties.

This quality in bills of exchange (and it might be added of interest notes, &c.) of occupying the place of bank paper, and of also throwing the interest accruing during their detention into the pocket of the *holder*, contributes greatly to the use of them. The whole trading world may be considered as having an interest in encouraging them. To possess some article which, so long as it is detained, shall produce a regular interest, which shall be subject to no fluctuations in price, which, by the custom of commerce, shall pass in certain cases as a payment, and shall likewise be convertible into ready money by the sacrifice of a small discount, is the true policy of the merchant. Goods will not serve this purpose, because they do not grow more valuable by detention; nor stocks, because, though they yield an interest, they fluctuate much in value; and, also, because the expence of brokerage is incurred in selling them, not to mention the inconveniences arising from the circumstance of their being transferable only in the books of the Bank of England. Stocks, however, by being at all times a saleable and ready money article, are, to a certain degree, held by persons in London on the same principle as bills, and serve, therefore, in some measure, like bills, if we consider these as a discountable article, to spare the use of bank notes. Exchequer bills will not fully answer the purpose, because there is a commission on the sale of these, as on the sale of stocks; and because, not to speak of some other inferior objections to them, they fluctuate, in some small degree, in price.

Bills, since they circulate chiefly among the trading world, come little under the observation of the public. The amount of bills in existence may yet, perhaps, be at all times greater than the amount of all the bank notes of every kind, and of all the circulating guineas*.

The amount of what is called the circulating medium of a country has been supposed by some to bear a regular proportion to the quantity of trade and of payments. It has, however, been shewn, that such part of the circulating medium as yields an interest to the holder will effect much fewer payments, in proportion to its amount, than the part which yields to the holder no interest. A number of country bank notes, amounting to 100*l.*, may, for instance, effect on an average one payment in three days; while a bill of 100*l.* may, through the disposition of each holder to detain it, effect only one payment in nine days.

There is a passage in the work of Dr. Adam Smith which serves to inculcate the error of which I have been speaking; a passage on which it may be useful to comment with some particularity.

---

* Liverpool and Manchester effect the whole of their larger mercantile payments not by country bank notes, of which none are issued by the banks of those places, but by bills at one or two months date, drawn on London. The bills annually drawn by the banks of each of those towns amount to many millions. The banks obtain a small commission on these bills.

He says, "The whole paper money of *every kind* which can "*easily* circulate in any country, never can exceed the value of the "gold and silver of which it supplies the place, or which (the "commerce being supposed the same) would circulate there, if "there was no paper money."

Does Dr. Smith mean to include, in his idea of "the *whole* "paper money of *every kind* which can easily circulate," all the bills of exchange of a country, or does he not? And does he also include interest notes, exchequer bills, and India bonds, and those other articles which very much resemble bills of exchange? In an earlier part of his chapter he has this observation—"There are "different sorts of paper money; but the circulating notes of "banks and bankers are the species which is best known, and "which seems best adapted for this purpose." We are led to judge by this passage, and also by the term "paper money of *every kind*" in the passage before quoted, that it was his purpose to include bills of exchange; on the other hand, if *all* the bills of exchange of a country are to be added to the bank notes which circulate, it becomes then so manifest, that the whole of the paper must be more than equal to the amount of the money which would cir- culate if there were no paper, that we feel surprised that the erroneousness of the position did not strike Dr. Smith himself. He introduces, indeed, the qualifying word "easily;" he speaks of "the whole paper money of every kind which can *easily* circulate." But this term, as I apprehend, is meant only to refer to an easy, in contradistinction to a forced, paper circulation; for it is on the subject of a forced circulation that a great part of his observations turn. He seems, on the other hand, to have paid no regard to the distinction on which I have dwelt, of a more slow and a more rapid circulation; a thing which is quite different from an easy and a difficult circulation. He appears, in short, not at all to have reflected how false his maxim is rendered (if laid down in the terms which he has used) both by the different degrees of rapidity of circulation which generally belong to the two different classes of paper of which I have spoken, and also by the different degrees of rapidity which may likewise belong to the circulation of the same kinds of paper, and even of the same guineas, at different times.

The error of Dr. Smith, then, is this:—he represents the whole paper, which can easily circulate when there are no guineas, to be the same in quantity with the guineas which would circulate if there were no paper; whereas, it is the quantity not of "the "thing which circulates," that is, of the thing which is *capable* of circulation, but of the actual circulation which should rather be spoken of as the same in both cases. The quantity of circulating paper, that is, of paper capable of circulation, may be great, and yet the quantity of actual circulation may be small, or *vice versa*. The same note may either effect ten payments in one day, or one payment in ten days; and one note, therefore, will effect the same payments in the one case, which it would require a hundred notes to effect in the other.

I have spoken of the different degrees of rapidity in the circulation of *different kinds* of paper, and of the consequent difference of the quantity of each which is wanted in order to effect the same payments. I shall speak next of the different degrees of rapidity in the circulation of the *same* mediums at *different times:* and, first, of bank notes.

The causes which lead to a variation in the rapidity of the circulation of bank notes may be several. In general, it may be observed, that a high state of confidence serves to quicken their circulation; and this happens upon a principle which shall be fully explained. It must be premised, that by the phrase a more or less quick circulation of notes will be meant a more or less quick circulation of the whole of them on an average. Whatever encreases that reserve, for instance, of Bank of England notes which remains in the drawer of the London banker as his provision against contingencies, contributes to what will here be termed the less quick circulation of the whole. Now a high state of confidence contributes to make men provide less amply against contingencies. At such a time, they trust, that if the demand upon them for a payment, which is now doubtful and contingent, should actually be made, they shall be able to provide for it at the moment; and they are loth to be at the expence of selling an article, or of getting a bill discounted, in order to make the provision much before the period at which it shall be wanted. When, on the contrary, a season of distrust arises, prudence suggests, that the loss of interest arising from a detention of notes for a few additional days should not be regarded.

It is well known that guineas are hoarded, in times of alarm, on this principle. Notes, it is true, are not hoarded to the same extent; partly because notes are not supposed equally likely, in the event of any general confusion, to find their value, and partly because the class of persons who are the holders of notes is less subject to weak and extravagant alarms. In difficult times, however, the disposition to hoard, or rather to be largely provided with Bank of England notes, will, perhaps, prevail in no inconsiderable degree.

This remark has been applied to Bank of England notes, because these are always in high credit; and it ought, perhaps, to be chiefly confined to these. They constitute the coin in which the great mercantile payments in London, which are payments on account of the whole country, are effected. If, therefore, a difficulty in converting bills of exchange into notes is apprehended, the effect both on bankers, merchants, and tradesmen, is somewhat the same as the effect of an apprehension entertained by the lower class of a difficulty in converting Bank of England notes or bankers' notes into guineas. The apprehension of the approaching difficulty makes men eager to do that to-day, which otherwise they would do to-morrow.

The truth of this observation, as applied to Bank of England notes, as well as the importance of attending to it, may be made manifest by adverting to the events of the year 1793, when, through the failure of many country banks, much general distrust took place. The alarm, the first material one of the kind which had for a long time happened, was extremely great. It does not appear that the Bank of England notes, at that time in circulation,

Enquiry into Paper Credit   97   G

were fewer than usual. It is certain, however, that the existing number became, at the period of apprehension, insufficient for giving punctuality to the payments of the metropolis; and it is not to be doubted, that the insufficiency must have arisen, in some measure, from that slowness in the circulation of notes, naturally attending an alarm, which has been just described. Every one fearing lest he should not have his notes ready when the day of payment should come, would endeavour to provide himself with them somewhat beforehand. A few merchants, from a natural though hurtful timidity, would keep in their own hands some of those notes, which, in other times, they would have lodged with their bankers; and the effect would be, to cause the same quantity of bank paper to transact fewer payments, or, in other words, to lessen the rapidity of the circulation of notes on the whole, and thus to encrease the number of notes wanted. Probably, also, some Bank of England paper would be used as a substitute for country bank notes suppressed.

The success of the remedy which the parliament administered, denotes what was the nature of the evil. A loan of exchequer bills was directed to be made to as many mercantile persons, giving proper security, as should apply. It is a fact, worthy of serious attention, that the failures abated greatly, and mercantile credit began to be restored, not at the period when the exchequer bills were actually delivered, but at a time antecedent to that æra. It also deserves notice, that though the failures had originated in an extraordinary demand for guineas, it was not any supply of gold which effected the cure. That fear of not being able to obtain guineas, which arose in the country, led, in its consequences, to an extraordinary demand for bank notes in London; and the want of bank notes in London became, after a time, the chief evil. The very expectation of a supply of exchequer bills, that is, of a supply of an article which almost any trader might obtain, and which it was known that he might then sell, and thus turn into bank notes, and after turning into bank notes might also convert into guineas, created an idea of general solvency. This expectation cured, in the first instance, the distress of London, and it then lessened the demand for guineas in the country, through that punctuality in effecting the London payments which it produced, and the universal confidence which it thus inspired. The sum permitted by parliament to be advanced in exchequer bills was five millions, of which not one half was taken. Of the sum taken, no part was lost. On the contrary, the small compensation, or extra interest, which was paid to government for lending its credit (for it was mere credit, and not either money or bank notes that the government advanced), amounted to something more than was necessary to defray the charges, and a small balance of profit accrued to the public. For this seasonable interference, a measure at first not well understood and opposed at the time, chiefly on the ground of constitutional jealousy, the mercantile as well as the manufacturing interests of the country were certainly much indebted to the parliament, and to the government*.

That a state of distrust causes a slowness in the circulation of *guineas*, and that at such a time a greater quantity of money will be wanted in order to effect only the same money payments, is a position which scarcely needs to be proved. Some observations, however, on this subject may not be useless. When a season of extraordinary alarm arises, and the money of the country in some measure disappears, the guineas, it is commonly said, are hoarded.

---

* The commissioners named in the act state in their report, " that the know-"ledge that loans might have been obtained, sufficed, in several instances, to "render them unnecessary; that the whole number of applications was three "hundred and thirty-two, for sums amounting to £.3,855,624; of which two "hundred and thirty-eight were granted, amounting to £.2,202,000; forty-"five for sums to the amount of £.1,215,100 were withdrawn; and forty-nine "were rejected for various reasons. That the whole sum advanced on loans was "paid, a considerable part before it was due, and the remainder regularly at "the stated periods, without apparent difficulty or distress."

They observe that, "the advantages of this measure were evinced by a speedy "restoration of confidence in mercantile transactions, which produced a facility "in raising money that was presently felt, not only in the metropolis, but "through the whole extent of Great Britain. Nor was the operation of the act "less beneficial with respect to a variety of eminent manufacturers, who, *having* "*in a great degree suspended their works*, were enabled to resume them, and to "afford employment to a number of workmen who must otherwise have been "thrown on the public."

In a certain degree this assertion may be literally true. But the scarcity of gold probably results chiefly from the circumstance of a considerable variety of persons, country bankers, shopkeepers, and others, augmenting, some in a smaller and some in a more ample measure, that supply which it had been customary to keep by them. The stock thus enlarged is not a fund which its possessor purposes, in no case, to diminish, but a fund which, if he has occasion to lessen it, he endeavours, as he has opportunity, to replace. It is thus that a more slow circulation of guineas is occasioned; and the slower the circulation, the greater the quantity wanted, in order to effect the same number of money payments.

Thus, then, it appears, that the sentiment which Dr. Smith leads his readers to entertain, namely, that there is in every country a certain fixed quantity of paper, supplying the place of gold, which is all that "can easily circulate" (or circulate without being *forced* into circulation), and which is all (for such, likewise, seems to be the intended inference) that should ever be allowed to be sent into circulation, is, in a variety of respects, incorrect. The existence of various hoards of gold in the coffers of bankers, and of the Bank of England, while there are no corresponding hoards of paper, would of itself forbid any thing like accurate comparison between them. Many additional, though smaller, circumstances might be mentioned as contributing to prevent the quantity of notes which will circulate from being the same as the quantity of gold which would circulate if there were no notes; such as their superior convenience in a variety of respects, the facility of sending them by post, the faculty which they have of being either used as guineas, or of supplying the place of bills of exchange, and furnishing a remittance to distant places.

There is a further objection to the same remark of Dr. Smith. It would lead an uninformed person to conceive, that the trade of a country, and of this country in particular, circumstanced as it now is, might be carried on altogether by guineas, if bank notes of all kinds were by any means annihilated. It may already have occurred, that if bank paper were abolished, a substitute for it would be likely to be found, to a certain degree, in bills of exchange; and that these, on account of their slower circulation, must, in that case, be much larger in amount than the notes of which they would take the place. But further; if bills and bank notes were extinguished, other substitutes than gold would unquestionably be found. Recourse would be had to devices of various kinds by which men would save themselves the trouble of counting, weighing, and transporting guineas, in all the larger operations of commerce, so that the amount of guineas brought into use would not at all correspond with the amount of the bills and notes suppressed. Banks would be instituted, not of the description which now exist, but of that kind and number which should serve best to spare both the trouble of gold, and the expence incurred by the loss of interest upon the quantity of it in possession. Merely by the transfer of the debts of one merchant to another, in the books of the banker, a large portion of what are termed cash payments is effected at this time without the use of any bank paper[*], and a much larger sum would be thus transferred, if guineas were the only circulating medium of the country. Credit would still exist; credit in books, credit depending on the testimony of witnesses, or on the mere verbal promise of parties. It might not be paper credit; but still it might be such credit as would spare, more or less, the use of

[*] The following custom, now prevailing among the bankers within the city of London, may serve to illustrate this observation, and also to shew the strength of the disposition which exists in those who are not the issuers of bank notes to spare the use both of paper and guineas. It is the practice of each of these bankers to send a clerk, at an agreed hour in the afternoon, to a room provided for their use. Each clerk there exchanges the drafts on other bankers received at his own house, for the drafts on his own house received at the houses of other bankers. The balances of the several bankers are transferred in the same room from one to another, in a manner which it is unnecessary to explain in detail, and the several balances are finally wound up by each clerk into one balance. The difference between the whole sum which each banker has to pay to all other city bankers, and the whole sum which he has to receive of all other city bankers, is, therefore, all that is discharged in bank notes or money; a difference much less in its amount than the *several* differences would be equal to. This device, which serves to spare the use of bank notes, may suggest the practicability of a great variety of contrivances for sparing the use of gold, to which men having confidence in each other would naturally resort, if we could suppose bank paper to be abolished.

guineas. It might be credit of a worse kind, less accurately dealt out in proportion to the desert of different persons, and therefore, in some instances, at least, still more extended; it might be credit less contributing to punctuality of payments, and to the due fulfilment of engagements; less conducive to the interests of trade, and to the cheapening of articles; and it would, perhaps, also be credit quite as liable to interruption on the occasion of any sudden alarm or material change in the commercial prospects and circumstances of the country.

CHAP. IV

Observation of Dr. Smith respecting the Bank of England—of the Nature of that Institution.—Reasons for never greatly diminishing its Notes —its Liability to be exhausted of Guineas—the Suspension of its Cash Payments not owing to too great Issue of Paper—nor to too great Loans.—Propriety of parliamentary Interference.

DR Adam Smith, after laying down the principle which has been lately animadverted on, "that the quantity of paper "which can easily circulate in a country never can exceed the "gold and silver which would circulate if there were no paper," proceeds to observe, that the Bank of England, "by issuing too "great a quantity of paper, of which the excess was continually "returning, in order to be exchanged for gold and silver, was "for many years together, obliged to coin gold to the extent of "between eight hundred thousand pounds and a million a year. "For this great coinage the bank was frequently obliged to purchase "gold bullion at 4*l.* an ounce, which it soon after issued in coin "at 3*l.* 17*s.* 10½*d.* an ounce, losing two and a half and three per "cent. on the coinage." Dr. Smith probably could not be acquainted with the secret of the actual quantity of those bank notes, of the number of which he complains; he must, therefore, have taken it for granted, that they were what he terms excessive, on the ground of the price of gold being high, and the coinage great. He does not proceed, in any respect, to guard or to limit the observation in question; an observation which, when thus unqualified, may lead the reader to suppose, that whenever the bank finds itself subjected to any great demand for gold in consequence of a high price of bullion, the cause of this evil is an excess of circulating paper, and the remedy a reduction of bank notes. There is also danger, lest it should be conceived, that if the remedy should appear to fail, it can fail only because the reduction is not sufficiently great.

103

The point of which we are speaking is of great importance, and will be the subject of much future discussion. One object of the present and succeeding Chapter will be to shew, that, however just may be the principle of Dr. Smith when properly limited and explained, the reduction of the quantity of Bank of England paper is by no means a measure which ought to be resorted to on the occasion of every demand upon the bank for guineas arising from the high price of bullion, and that such reduction may even aggravate that sort of rise which is caused by an alarm in the country.

It will be proper, first, to describe the nature of the institution of the Bank of England, and the relation in which it stands to the public; in this detail, the event of the late stoppage of its cash payments will be particularly noticed.

Bills are drawn on London from every quarter of the kingdom, and remittances are sent to the metropolis to provide for them, while London draws no bills, or next to none, upon the country. London is, in this respect, to the whole island, in some degree, what the centre of a city is to the suburbs. The traders may dwell in the suburbs, and lodge many goods there, and they may carry on at home a variety of smaller payments, while their chief cash account is with the banker, who fixes his residence among the other bankers, in the heart of the city. London also is become, especially of late, the trading metropolis of Europe, and, indeed, of the whole world; the foreign drafts, on account of merchants living in our out-ports and other trading towns, and carrying on business there, being made, with scarcely any exceptions, payable in London. The metropolis, moreover, through the extent of its own commerce, and the greatness of its wealth and population, has immense receipts and payments on its own account; and the circumstance of its being the seat of government, and the place where the public dividends are paid, serves to encrease its pecuniary transactions. The practice, indeed, of transferring the payments of the country to London being once begun, was likely to extend itself. For, in proportion as the amount and number of payments and receipts is augmented in any one particular place, the business of paying and receiving is more easily and cheaply transacted, the necessary guineas becoming fewer in proportion to the sums to be received and paid, and the bank notes wanted, though encreasing on the whole, becoming fewer in proportion also. On the punctuality with which the accustomed payments of London are effected, depends, therefore, most essentially the whole commercial credit of Great Britain. The larger London payments are effected exclusively through the paper of the Bank of England; for the superiority of its credit is such, that, by common agreement among the bankers, whose practice, in this respect, almost invariably guides that of other persons, no note of a private house will pass in payment as a paper circulation in London.

The bank has a capital of near twelve millions, to which it has added near four millions of undivided profits or savings: all this capital and savings must be lost before the creditors can sustain any loss.

The Bank of England is quite independent of the executive government. It has an interest, undoubtedly (of the same kind with that of many private individuals), in the maintenance of our financial as well as commercial credit. It is also in the habit of lending out a large portion of its ample funds on government securities of various kinds, a comparatively small part only, though a sum not small in itself, being lent to the merchants in the way of discount. The ground on which the bank lends so much to government is clearly that of mutual convenience, as well as long habit. It is the only lender in the country on a large scale; the government is the only borrower on a scale equally extended; and the two parties, like two wholesale traders in a town, the one the only great buyer, and the other the only great seller of the same article, naturally deal much with each other, and have comparatively small transactions with those who carry on only a more contracted business. The bank, moreover, in time of peace, is much benefited by lending to government. It naturally, therefore, continues those loans, during war, which it had been used to grant at all antecedent periods. It occasionally furnishes a considerable sum to the East India company. If, indeed, it lent more to the merchants during war, and less to the government, the difference would not be so great as might, perhaps, at first view be supposed. If, for instance, it furnished a smaller sum on the security of exchequer bills, that article might then be supposed to fall in price, or, in other words, to yield a higher and more tempting interest; and the bankers, in that case, would buy more exchequer bills, and would grant less aid to the merchants; they would, at least, in some degree, take up whichever trade the Bank of England should relinquish. The preference given by the bank to the government securities, is, therefore, no symptom of a want of independence in its directors: they are subject, in a much greater degree, to their own proprietors than to any administration. The strong manner in which the directors of the bank* at the time antecedent to the suspension of their cash payments, insisted on having four millions and a half paid up to them by the government—a payment which, though demanded at a very inconvenient time, was accordingly made—may be mentioned as one sufficiently striking mark of the independence of that company. There is, however, another much more important circumstance to be noticed, which is conclusive on this subject. The government of Great Britain is under little or no *temptation* either to dictate to the Bank of England, or to lean upon it in any way which is inconvenient or dangerous to the bank itself. The minister has been able to raise annually, without the smallest difficulty, by means of our funding system, the sum of no less than between twenty and thirty millions. The government, therefore, is always able to lessen, by a loan from the public, if it should be deemed necessary, the amount of its debt running with the bank. To suppose that bank notes are issued to excess, with a view to furnish means of lending money to the minister, is, in a high degree, unreasonable. The utmost sum which he

* See the correspondence of the bank on this subject, in the Appendix to the Report of the House of Commons respecting the order of council for authorising the suspension of the cash payments of the bank.

could hope to gain in the way of loan from the bank, by means of an extraordinary issue of bank notes, could hardly be more than four or five millions; and it is not easy to believe, that a government which can raise at once twenty or thirty millions, will be likely, for the sake of only four or five millions (for the loan of which it must pay nearly the same interest as for a loan from the public), to derange the system, distress the credit, or endanger the safety of the Bank of England*. This banking company differs in this most important point from every one of those national banks, which issue paper, on the continent. I understand that the banks of Petersburgh, Copenhagen, Stockholm, Vienna, Madrid, and Lisbon, each of which issues circulating notes, which pass as current payment, are all in the most direct and strict sense government banks†. It is also well known, that the governments residing in these several places have not those easy means of raising money, by a loan from the people, which the minister of Great Britain so remarkably possesses. Those governments, therefore, have, in times even of moderate difficulty, no other resource than that of extending the issue of the paper of their own banks; which extension of issue naturally produces a nearly correspondent depreciation of the value of the notes, and a fall in the exchange with other countries, if computed at the paper price. The notes, moreover, being once thus depreciated, the government, even supposing its embarrassments

* The same remark has been made in a short pamphlet lately published by Sir Francis Baring.

† The bank of Amsterdam did not issue circulating notes, but was a mere bank for deposits, the whole of which it was supposed by some to keep always in specie. It was discovered, however, when the French possessed themselves of Holland, that it had been used privately to lend a certain part of them to the city of Amsterdam, and a part to the old Dutch government. These loans ought certainly rather to have been furnished in that open manner in which those of our bank are made. Neither of the two debts, as I understand, have yet been discharged. The bank of Amsterdam had no capital of its own.

In whatever way we may suppose the property of the bank of Amsterdam, or that of any other public bank or private individual, to be employed, it is not easy to imagine that it can altogether escape the hands of a needy and successful invader. If the property of a public bank is kept in money, a rapacious enemy may seize that money. If lent to the merchants, the enemy, by their requisitions, may draw it from the merchants; and by thus incapacitating the merchants to pay their debts to the bank, may cause the failure of the bank.

to cease, is seldom disposed to bring them back to their former limits, to do which implies some sacrifice on their part at the time of effecting the reduction; but it contents itself, perhaps, with either a little lessening, or with not further adding to, the evil. The expectation of the people on the continent, therefore, generally is, that the paper, which is falling in value, will, in better times only cease to fall, or, if it rises, will experience only an immaterial rise, and this expectation serves of course to accelerate its fall. Hence it has happened, that in all the places of Europe, of which mention has been made, there exists a great and established, and generally, an increasing discount or agio between the current coin and the paper money of the kingdom. Nor, indeed, is this all: several of the governments of Europe have not only extended their paper in the manner which has been described, but have, besides this, depreciated, from time to time, their very coin; and thus there has been a two-fold cause for a rise in the nominal price of their commodities when exchanged with the current paper. There is, therefore, a fundamental difference between the nature of the paper of the Bank of England, and that of all the national or government banks on the continent. No one supposes that the English guinea contains less and less gold than heretofore, through frauds practised by government in the coinage; and as little is it to be suspected that the Bank of England paper is about to be depreciated by an excessive issue either ordered or needed by the government. There is, moreover, at present, this further ground for assuming that the issue of Bank of England notes is not likely to be excessive,—that it has lately become a practice to make the number of them public. Their quantity, as it now appears, has never, in any short time, varied very greatly; has seldom, in late years, been below ten or eleven millions, even when no one pound and two pound notes were issued; and has at no moment exceeded the sum of about fifteen millions and a half, including two millions and a half of one pound and two pound notes. It is not impossible that the discredit into which the paper of the government banks of the continent of Europe has fallen, into which also the paper of the American banks sunk at the time of the American war, through the same extension of its issues by the successive French revolutionary governments, may have, in some degree, contributed, though most unjustly, to that fall in the exchange which Great Britain has experienced. Foreigners not adverting to that independence of the Bank of England, the grounds of which have been stated, and misled possibly by the abundant misrepresentations which have taken place in this country, may have thought that it was the government which, by its loans, involved the bank in difficulties (a point which shall be discussed presently), and that the bank is merely an instrument in the hands of the government; an instrument which may be turned, as the government banks on the continent have been, to the purpose of issuing notes to an extravagant extent. If such should, in any degree, be their sentiment, it would be just in them to infer from thence, that the Bank of England notes are not unlikely to fall in their value in the same manner as the notes of the continental banks, An unwillingness to leave in this country whatever sums they may have a right to draw from us (sums probably small in the whole) may have been the consequence of this fear, and a great unwillingness to trust with us even a small quantity of property, may happen to cause, under certain circumstances, a considerable fall in the exchange.

It may be mentioned as an additional ground of confidence in the Bank of England, and as a circumstance of importance in many respects, that the numerous proprietors who chuse the directors, and have the power of controlling them (a power of which they have prudently forborne to make any frequent use), are men whose general stake in the country far exceeds that particular one which they have in the stock of the company. They are men, therefore, who feel themselves to be most deeply interested not merely in the increase of the dividends or in the maintenance of the credit of the Bank of England, but in the support of commercial as well as of public credit in general. There is, indeed, both among them and among the whole commercial world, who make so large a portion of this country, a remarkable determination to sustain credit, and especially the credit of the bank; and this general agreement to support the bank is one of the pillars of its strength, and one pledge of its safety. The proprietors of it themselves are not likely to approve of any dangerous extension even of their own paper; both they and the directors know the importance of confining the bank paper, generally speaking, within its accustomed limits, and must necessarily be supposed to prefer its credit, and the paper credit of the nation, to the comparatively trifling consideration of a small increase in their own dividends; an increase which would prove delusory, if it should arise from that extravagant issue of bank notes which would have the effect of depreciating all the circulating medium of the country, since it would thus raise upon the proprietors of bank stock, as well as on others, the price of all the articles of life*. While the proprietors and directors of the bank have thus an interest, on the one hand, in limiting the quantity of paper issued, they are also naturally anxious, on the other, in common with the whole commercial world, to give the utmost possible credit to it; and although an opinion should prevail, even to some extent, among persons out of business, that the appearance of gold is the only test of wealth, and that the absence of it, however temporary, implies great danger to the country, the mercantile interest, and in particular the bank proprietors, the bankers, and the traders of London, by whose transactions the value of the London paper is upheld, may be considered as combined in the support of a juster sentiment. The bank itself is known to have experienced, at former times (as appears from the evidence of the directors given to parliament), very great fluctuations in its cash;

* If the bank notes were increased even five millions, the additional profit which would accrue to the proprietors would not be more than two per cent. A proprietor qualified to vote in the bank court (that is, having 500*l.* stock) would, therefore, gain by this extravagant issue, supposing it to be maintained for a year, the sum of 10*l.* A large proportion of the bank proprietors do not hold more than 1,000*l.* stock. The gain of each of these would not be more than 20*l.*; a sum perfectly insignificant, compared with the interest which they have in the maintenance of the general commercial credit of the country.

and, in one period of returning peace and prosperity, a reduction of it below that which took place at the time of the late suspension of its cash payments: the amount of gold in the bank, at any one particular æra, is, perhaps, therefore, on the ground of this experience, not now considered by the commercial world as having all that importance which was given to it when the bank affairs were involved in greater mystery. It is perfectly well understood among all commercial men, that gold coin is not an article in which all payments (though it is so promised) are at any time intended really to be made; that no fund ever was or can be provided by the bank which shall be sufficient for such a purpose; and that gold coin is to be viewed chiefly as a standard by which all bills and paper money should have their value regulated as exactly as possible; and that the main, and, indeed, the only, point is to take all reasonable care that money shall in fact serve as that standard.

This is the great maxim to be laid down on the subject of paper credit. Let it, then, be next considered what is necessary, in order sufficiently to secure that, whatever the circulating paper may be, gold shall be the standard to which the value of that paper shall conform itself. It is no doubt important, that there should be usually in the country a certain degree of interchange of gold for paper, for this is one of the means which will serve to fix the value of the latter. Whether the interchange wanted to produce this effect must be more or less large and frequent, depends much on the habits and dispositions of the country, and, in particular, on the degree of knowledge of the nature of paper credit generally prevailing, and on the degree of confidence in it.

In order to secure that this interchange shall at all times take place, it is important that, generally speaking, a considerable fund of gold should be kept in the country, and there is in this kingdom no other depository for it but the Bank of England. This fund should be a provision not only against the common and more trifling fluctuations in the demand for coin, but also against the two following contingencies. First, it should serve to counteract the effects of an unfavourable balance of trade, for this infallibly will sometimes occur, and it is what one or more bad harvests cannot fail to cause. It is also desirable, secondly, that the reserve of gold should be sufficient to meet any extraordinary demand at home, though a demand in this quarter, if it should arise from great and sudden fright, may undoubtedly be so unreasonable and indefinite as to defy all calculation. If, moreover, alarm should ever happen at a period in which the stock of gold should have been reduced by the other great cause of its reduction, namely, that of a call having been recently made for gold to discharge an unfavourable balance of trade, the powers of any bank, however ample its general provision should have been, may easily be supposed to prove insufficient for this double purpose.

To revert, then, to the Bank of England. A short time before the suspension of its cash payments, the gold in its coffers had been reduced materially through an unfavourable balance of trade. The exchange with Europe had, however, so far improved for some time preceding the suspension, as to have caused gold to begin again to flow into the country. When it was thus only beginning to return, the fear of an invasion took place, and it led to the sudden failure of some country banks in the north of England. Other parts felt the influence of the alarm, those in Scotland, in a great measure, excepted, where, through long use, the confidence of the people, even in paper money of a guinea value, is so great (a circumstance to which the peculiar respectability of the Scotch banks has contributed), that the distress for gold was little felt in that part of the island. A great demand on the Bank of England for guineas was thus created; a demand which every one who can possess himself of a bank note is entitled to make by the very terms in which the note is expressed. In London, it is observable that much distress was beginning to arise, which was in its nature somewhat different from that in the country. In London, con-fidence in the Bank of England being high, and its notes main-taining their accustomed credit, its guineas were little called for with a view to the mere object of London payments. The guineas applied for by persons in London, was, generally speaking, on the account of people in the country. The distress arising in London, like that which took place in 1793, was a distress for notes of the Bank of England. So great was the demand for notes, that the interest of money, for a few days before the suspension of the payments of the bank, may be estimated (by calculating the price of exchequer bills, the best test that can be referred to, as well as by comparing the money price of stocks with their time price) to have been about sixteen or seventeen per cent. per ann. The bank, on this occasion, pursued, though only in a small degree, the path which a reader of Dr. Smith would consider him to prescribe, as in all cases the proper and effectual means of detaining or bringing back guineas. They lessened the number of their notes, which, having been for some years before near eleven millions, and having been reduced, for some time, to between nine and ten millions, were at this particular moment brought down to between eight and nine millions.

It has been shewn already, that, in order to effect the vast and accustomed payments daily made in London, payments which are most of them promised beforehand, a circulating sum in bank notes, nearly equal to whatever may have been its customary amount is necessary. But a much more clear idea of this subject will be gained by entering into some detail.

There are in London between sixty and seventy bankers, and it is almost entirely through them that the larger payments of London are effected. It may be estimated (though the conjecture is necessarily a loose one) that the sums paid daily by the bankers of London may not be less than four or five millions. The notes in their hands form, probably, a very large proportion of the whole circulating notes in the metropolis. It is certain, at least, that only a very small proportion of Bank of England notes circulate far from London, and that it is to the metropolis itself that all the larger ones are confined. The amount of the bank notes in the hands of each banker, of course, fluctuates considerably; but the amount in the hands of all probably varies very little; and this amount cannot be much diminished consistently with their ideas of what

Enquiry into Paper Credit 113 H

is necessary to the punctuality of their payments, and to the complete security of their houses. Thus there is little room for reduction as to the whole of that larger part of the notes of the Bank of England which is in the hands of the London bankers: the notes which may chance to circulate among other persons, especially among persons carrying on any commerce, if we suppose the usual punctuality of payments to be maintained, and the ordinary system of effecting them to proceed, can admit also of little diminution. A deficiency of notes in London is a very different thing from a deficiency either of country bank notes or of coin in the country. A large proportion of the London payments are payments of bills accepted by considerable houses, and a failure in the punctuality of any one such payment is deemed an act of insolvency in the party. The London payments are, moreover, carried on by a comparatively small quantity of notes; and they, perhaps, cannot easily be effected, with due regularity, by a much smaller number, so complete has been the system of economy in the use of them which time and experience have introduced among the bankers. There is, moreover, no substitute for them. They have an exclusive, though limited, circulation. They serve, at the same time, both to sustain and regulate the whole paper credit of the country. It is plain, from the circumstances which have just been stated, that any very great and sudden diminution of Bank of England notes would be attended with the most serious effects both on the metropolis and on the whole kingdom. A reduction of them which may seem moderate to men who have not reflected on this subject—a diminution, for instance, of one-third or two-fifths, might, perhaps, be sufficient to produce a very general insolvency in London, of which the effect would be the suspension of confidence, the derangement of commerce, and the stagnation of manufactures throughout the country. Gold, in such case, would unquestionably be hoarded through the great consternation which would be excited; and it would, probably, not again appear until confidence should be restored by the *previous* introduction of some additional or some new paper circulation.

114

The case which has been put is, however, merely hypothetical; for there is too strong and evident an interest in every quarter to maintain, in some way or other, the regular course of London payments, to make it probable that this scene of confusion should occur; or, even if it should arise, that it should continue. Whether there might chance to be much or little gold in the country, steps would be taken to induce the bank to issue its usual quantity of paper, or measures would be resorted to for providing, by some other means, a substitute for it. The credit, however, of even the best substitute, would be far inferior to that of the old and known Bank of England notes; for the new paper would be guaranteed by a capital probably far less ample than that of the Bank of England: it would also be just as impossible for the issuers of it to procure, at the time in question, a supply of guineas to be given in payment of it, as it would for the Bank of England to provide a supply of guineas for payment of their notes. The new paper, then, though it should be the same in its general nature, would be inferior to that of the bank. It would yield, indeed, a profit to the issuers, a profit which the bank would lose the opportunity of gaining; and the desire of this profit might co-operate in producing a disposition in new bodies of men to proceed to the creation of it. If we suppose it to be created, and to form one part of the current circulating medium of the metropolis; and if we suppose, also, as we necessarily must, a reduced quantity of Bank of England notes to continue current at the same time, the new paper would then be easily exchangeable for the Bank of England paper; and every holder of the new paper would, therefore, be able, by first exchanging it for the bank paper, to draw gold out of the bank. The directors of the bank, therefore, by proceeding to such a reduction of their notes, as should create a necessity for the bankers and merchants to create a new paper among themselves, would only increase the general paper circulation in London. They have now, by their exclusive power of furnishing a circulating medium to the metropolis, the means of, in some degree, limiting and regulating its quantity; a power of which they would be totally divested, if, by exercising it too severely, they should once cause other paper to become current in the same manner as their own. Projects for the introduction of a new circulating medium into the metropolis have, at different times, been formed; all such schemes, however, must necessarily fail, as long as there continues to be an unwillingness among the bankers to unite in giving currency to the new paper. This unwillingness would, of course, diminish in proportion as the pressure should become general and severe.

The idea which some persons have entertained of its being at all times a paramount duty of the Bank of England to diminish its notes, in some sort of regular proportion to that diminution which it experiences in its gold, is, then, an idea which is merely theoretic. It must be admitted, however, to be very natural.

It has been supposed by some, that the pressure on the mercantile world which a great diminution of notes must cause, would, especially if it were a severe one, induce the merchants to send for gold from abroad, in order to supply their own want of money. The supposition, when thus put, is stated in much too vague a manner to be susceptible of that close examination which I wish to give to it. There can be no doubt that we shall find it altogether false, when pushed to the extent of assuming that the extreme *severity* of the pressure is to be the remedy. Let us consider this point in as practical a way as possible.

It was supposed that the difficulty of obtaining bank notes would cause *the* merchants to send abroad for gold, in order to effect their payments. But *what* merchants? Certainly not those merchants whose goods are unfit for a foreign market, and are in no demand there. They must first exchange these unsuitable goods for goods which are suitable, that is, they must sell them, in the first instance, for money, or what passes as money, and answers, in their view, all the same purposes. Thus they get possession of the very thing, to supply their want of which they are supposed to send abroad. The trader acts, in this respect, like any one who is not a trader. If distressed for the means of effecting what is called

116

a cash payment, he no more turns his thoughts to a foreign country for a supply of gold, than the farmer or landed gentleman who is equally pressed. He considers only what part of his property he can turn into bank notes. These he sees to be at hand; of the gold which is in foreign countries he knows nothing.

It will be allowed, then, that it is not on our traders in general that the pressure will so operate as to induce them to send for gold from the continent. It will, perhaps, however, be said to operate on our foreign merchants: but we must now distinguish, also, between one foreign merchant and another. The export trade to foreign countries is, generally speaking, one trade; the trade of importing from foreign countries is a second; the trade of sending out and bringing home bullion, in order to pay or receive the difference between the exports and imports, may be considered as a third. This third trade is carried on upon the same principles with any other branch of commerce, that is, it is entered into just so far as it is lucrative to the speculator in bullion, and no farther. The point, therefore, to be enquired into is clearly this,—whether the pressure arising from a scarcity of bank notes tends to render the importation of bullion a more profitable speculation.

In solving this question, there is not, perhaps, all the difficulty which might be supposed; for it is obvious that, generally speaking, it will answer to import gold into a country just in proportion as the goods sent out of it, in the way of trade (that is, the goods which must be paid for), are greater in value than the goods which are, in the way of trade, brought into it. We may, therefore, now dismiss also the case of the mere dealer in bullion from our consideration. We have only to examine in what way the pressure arising from the suppression of bank notes will affect the quantity of goods which are in the way of trade either exported or imported.

That a certain degree of pressure will urge the British merchants in general who buy of the manufacturers, as well as the manufacturers themselves, to sell their goods in order to raise money; that it will thus have some influence in lowering prices at home; and that the low prices at home may tempt merchants to export their articles in the hope of a better price abroad, is by no means an unreasonable supposition. But, then, it is to be observed on the other hand, first, that this more than ordinary eagerness of all our traders to sell, which seems so desirable, is necessarily coupled with a general reluctance to buy, which is exactly proportionate to it: it must be obvious, that, when the general body of merchants, being urged by the pecuniary difficulties of the time, are selling their goods in order to raise money, they will naturally also delay making the accustomed purchases of the manufacturer. They require of him, at least, that he shall give them a more than usually extended credit; but the manufacturer, experiencing the same difficulty with the merchants, is quite unable to give this credit. The *sales* of the manufacturer are, therefore, suspended; but though these are stopped, his daily and weekly payments continue, provided his manufacture proceeds. In other words, his money is going out while no money is coming in; and this happens at an æra when the general state of credit is such, that he is not only not able to borrow, in order to supply his extraordinary need, but when he is also pressed for a prompter payment than before of all the raw materials of his manufacture. Thus the manufacturer, on account of the unusual scarcity of money, may even, though the selling price of his article should be profitable, be absolutely compelled by necessity to slacken, if not suspend, his operations. To inflict such a pressure on the mercantile world as necessarily causes an intermission of manufacturing labour, is obviously not the way to increase that exportable produce, by the excess of which, above the imported articles, gold is to be brought into the country.

But, secondly, that very diminution in the *price* of manufactures which is supposed to cause them to be exported, may also, if carried very far, produce a suspension of the labour of those who fabricate them. The masters naturally turn off their hands when they find their article selling exceedingly ill. It is true, that if we could suppose the diminution of bank paper to produce permanently a diminution in the value of all articles whatsoever, and a diminution, as it would then be fair that it should do, in the rate of wages also, the encouragement to future manufactures would be the same, though there would be a loss on the stock in hand. The tendency, however, of a very great and sudden reduction of the accustomed number of bank notes, is to create an *unusual* and *temporary* distress, and a fall of price arising from that distress. But a fall arising from temporary distress, will be attended probably with no correspondent fall in the rate of wages; for the fall of price, and the distress, will be understood to be temporary, and the rate of wages, we know, is not so variable as the price of goods. There is reason, therefore, to fear that the unnatural and extraordinary low price* arising from the sort of distress of which we now speak, would occasion much discouragement of the fabrication of manufactures.

Thirdly, a great diminution of notes prevents much of that industry of the country which had been exerted from being so productive as it would otherwise be. When a time either of multi-

---

* It may, perhaps, be supposed, that a diminution of the quantity of Bank of England notes, if permanent, would produce that permanent diminution of the price of articles which is so much desired, and the observation made above may be thought to give some countenance to this supposition. Such permanent reduction in the price of commodities could not, however, as I apprehend, be by any such means effected. The general and permanent value of bank notes must be the same as the general and permanent value of that gold for which they are exchangeable, and the value of gold in England is regulated by the general and permanent value of it all over the world; and, therefore, although it is admitted that a great and sudden reduction of bank notes may produce a great local and temporary fall in the price of articles (a fall, that is to say, even in their gold price, for we are here supposing gold and paper to be interchanged), the gold price must, in a short time, find its level with the gold price over the rest of the world. The continuance of the great limitation of the number of bank notes would, therefore, lead either, as has already been observed, to the creation of some new London paper, or possibly to some new modes of economy in the use of the existing notes: the effect of which economy on prices would be the same, in all respects, as that of the restoration of the usual quantity of bank notes. What seems most probable is, that the continuance of any great limitation of the number of bank notes would lead to the transfer of the present cash payments of London to some other place or places in which the means of effecting payments should not be obstructed through the too limited exercise of that exclusive power of furnishing a paper circulation with which the Bank of England has, by its charter, been invested. This subject of the influence of paper credit on prices will be more fully entered into in a future chapter.

119

plied failures, or even of much disappointment in the expected means of effecting payments arises, plans of commerce and manufacture, as well as of general improvement of every kind, which had been entered upon, are changed or suspended, and part of the labour which had been bestowed proves, therefore, to have been thrown away. If, for instance, expensive machinery had been erected, under an expectation of regular employment for it, a pressing want of the means of effecting payments may cause that machinery to stand idle. The goods which ought to form part of the assortment of the factor or the shopkeeper, and to be occupying their premises, are loading the warehouse of the manufacturer*, and, perhaps, are suffering damage by too long detention. On the other hand, some sales are forced; and thus the goods prepared for one market, and best suited to it, are sold at another. There

* When an interruption of the usual credit arises, it naturally happens that the individuals having the least property, and the fewest resources, are the most pressed; and it is sometimes assumed by the public, rather too readily, that those who suffer are justly punished for the too great extent of their speculations. It is true, undoubtedly, that those who prove to be the first to fail, have probably been men of too eager and adventurous a spirit. Let the spirit of adventure among traders, however, have been either more or less, the interruption of the usual credit cannot fail to cause distress; and that distress will fall upon those who have merely been, *comparatively*, the more adventurous part of the trading world. It is often also assumed by the public (and without the least foundation) that the want not of gold merely but of *bonâ fide* mercantile capital in the country is betrayed by a failure of paper credit. The error of this supposition is not only plain, from the general principles laid down in the first chapter of this work, but it is also distinctly proved by the circumstance stated above, that while the premises of the factor and of the shopkeeper are becoming empty of goods, the warehouse of the manufacturer is growing proportionably full. The time soon comes, indeed, when that suspension of labour (which, it should be remembered, is the *consequence* of the suspension of credit) causes the general stock of goods (or the mercantile capital of the country) to be diminished. The evil, therefore, consists not in the want of *bonâ fide* capital, but in the want of such a quantity of the circulating medium as shall be sufficient, at the time, to furnish the means of transferring the goods of the manufacturer from his own warehouse to that of the factor and the shopkeeper. The quantity wanted to be employed in the circulation, and especially the quantity of gold, becomes more, as was observed in the third chapter, when confidence is less, because the rapidity of the circulation is less. The substitution of gold for paper, and of better paper for that which is worse, and some temporary increase of the gold and good paper actually circulating, are obviously the remedy.

cease, at such a time, to be that regularity and exactness in proportioning and adapting the supply to the consumption, and that dispatch in bringing every article from the hands of the fabricator into actual use, which are some of the great means of rendering industry productive, and of adding to the general substance of a country. Every great and sudden check given to paper credit not only operates as a check to industry, but leads also to much of this misapplication of it. Some diminution of the general property of the country must follow from this cause; and, of course, a deduction also from that part of it which forms the stock for exportation. It can hardly be necessary to repeat, that on the quantity of exported stock depends the quantity of gold imported from foreign countries.

It will be supposed, perhaps, that the limitation of bank notes, by lessening the means of payment of the importing merchant, may induce him to suspend his imports; and that, since it is the excess of exports above the imports which causes gold to enter the country, the limitation of paper may, with a view to the diminution of imports, be very desirable. There is, probably, some justice in this supposition. It should, however, be observed on this subject, that Great Britain, at that period of an unfavourable balance which we are now supposing, may be considered as importing chiefly either, first, corn, of which no one would wish to check the import by a limitation of paper; or, secondly, that class of articles which are brought from one country in order to be transported to another; articles which come chiefly from very distant parts, and of which the payment cannot be declined, it having been promised long before hand; articles, also, which soon serve to swell the exports in a somewhat greater degree than they had increased the imports; or, thirdly, that rude produce of other countries which forms the raw materials of our own manufacture, and serves, after a short time, to supply exportable articles to a very increased amount.

The limitation of credit at home will chiefly be of use by urging the exporting merchant to press the sale of the goods which he has abroad, and to direct them to be sold, if he can, at a short credit; and also by its urging, in like manner, the importing merchant to delay buying abroad, as long as he can, and to buy at a long credit. In other words, it may be of use in leading English merchants, in their dealings with foreigners, to anticipate their receipts, and to delay their payments; on the other hand, it is carefully to be remembered, that an anticipation of receipts, and a delay of payments, are only a temporary benefit; while a suspension of manufactures operates, as far as it goes, as so much permanent and entire loss to the country. It is, moreover, to be borne in mind, that a very severe pressure is *sure* to produce a suspension of manufactures, while it is not sure to cause British merchants to obtain an extension of credit from foreigners. And *very extraordinary* suppression of bank notes must produce distrust abroad through the failures at home, to which it is known abroad to give rise. It, therefore, indisposes foreign merchants to lend money to England, and it induces those foreigners, who have debts due to them from Englishmen, to urge the payment of those debts. England, during the prevalence of any great distrust, is obliged to send abroad manufacturers not for the payment of goods imported or for the puchase of gold, but for the extinction of debt.

Although, therefore, it may possibly admit of a doubt whether some moderate restriction of the paper of the bank may not be expedient with a view to mend for the time an unfavourable balance, it seems sufficiently clear that any very sudden and violent reduction of bank notes must tend, by the convulsion to which it will lead, to prevent gold from coming into the country rather than to invite it, and thus to increase the danger of the bank itself. The observation which was before made may, therefore, be repeated, *that it is not the severity of the pressure which is to be the remedy.* It is, indeed, in every respect plain that it must be important to maintain, and to maintain carefully, the credit of the country, at that time in particular, when its guineas are few, and are also leaving it; that is the time when our own funds are necessarily low, when the most regular industry should by every means be promoted, and when there is the most need of the aid both of our domestic and foreign credit; and it belongs to the Bank of England, in particular, to guard and to superintend the interests of the country in this respect. The very policy of the bank differs, in this particular, from that of the individual country banker, whose own share of the evil resulting to the country, from the sudden suppression of his own notes, is small; who may trust, moreover, that there will be a substitution either of guineas or of other paper in the place of his own paper which is suppressed; and who, it may be remarked, supplies himself with the means of discharging his own notes by obtaining guineas from the Bank of England.

But the Bank of England has no bank to which it can resort for a supply of guineas proportioned to its wants in the same manner in which it is resorted to by the country banks; nor have the bankers and traders in London, to whom at present is transferred the business of effecting the great cash payments of the whole country, the same resource in case Bank of England notes are suppressed which traders in the country have, supposing country bank notes to be withdrawn. The country payments being not strictly promised before hand, may, many of them, bear to be postponed. Bills of exchange on London may also form some substitute for country bank notes, and may pass as such in the manner which was some time ago described; but if Bank of England notes are suppressed, and are suppressed, as we have been supposing them to be, in consequence of guineas being scarce, there then remain no means whatever of effecting the London payments. There can be no doubt that the extinction or very great diminution of bank notes would be a far greater evil, in the present circumstances of the metropolis, than the disappearing of guineas. If guineas disappear, notes may be substituted in their place; and through that general confidence which may be inspired by the agreement of bankers and other leading persons to take them, they will not fail, provided the issues are moderate, and the balance of trade is not very unfavourable to the country, to maintain exactly the gold price. The punctuality thus introduced into all the larger operations of commerce, will facilitate contrivances for effecting the smaller payments.

Differences of opinion, undoubtedly, may exist as to the exact degree in which the notes of the Bank of England ought, under any given circumstances, to be diminished. It may be hoped, however, that at least one point has now been fully and completely established, namely, that there may be an error on the side of too much diminishing bank notes, as well as on the side of too much increasing them. There is an excessive limitation of them, as every one must admit, which will produce failures; failures must cause consternation, and consternation must lead to a run upon the bank for guineas. There must, in short, then, be some point at which the bank must stop in respect to the reduction of its notes, however progressive may be the drain upon it for guineas.

But if its notes are not lessened, or if even they are lessened, but are not entirely extinguished, it is then in the power of any one who can possess himself of a bank note to possess himself also of guineas, as long as the bank pays in guineas; and it will be found to follow, moreover, that the bank is thus rendered liable to be totally exhausted of guineas. I mean, that it is liable to be totally exhausted of them, however great their number may have been, if it determines to *maintain* even the *smallest* number of notes. By maintaining, that is to say, five millions, or two millions, or even one million, of notes, the bank cannot avoid being exhausted (supposing the alarm to rise high enough to do it) of even five millions, or ten millions, or, if it had them, of twenty or fifty millions of guineas. It will depend, in such case, on the degree of alarm, and not on the maintenance of the greater or of the less quantity of notes, whether the guineas shall be more or less rapidly called for from the bank; or, in other words, the bank may be as much exhausted of guineas if it maintains five millions of notes as if it maintains ten millions, provided the alarm is only the same in the one case as in the other. If, therefore, the maintenance of the five millions of notes is sure to produce more alarm than the maintenance of ten, then the maintenance of the larger quantity of notes will serve to diminish the demand for guineas, and the maintenance of the smaller number to increase it.

The following is the manner in which that operation, which is finally to exhaust all the guineas of the bank, may be supposed to proceed. A, for instance, the holder of a note of 1000*l.* (and it is what any man may obtain by selling goods) carries it to the bank and demands 1000*l.* in gold. The bank gives the gold; which gold, let it be remarked, either goes abroad to pay for an unfavourable balance of trade, or, as we are now rather supposing, fills a void in the circulation of the country, occasioned by the withdrawing of country bank notes in consequence of alarm, or serves as an addition to the fund of country banks, or forms a hoard in the hands of individuals. The 1000*l.* in gold, thus furnished by the bank, does not supply, in any degree, the place of the 1000*l.* note for which it was given; for the 1000*l.* note had been employed in London in making the larger payments. It is hardly ever, in almost any degree, as a substitute for Bank of England notes, that the gold taken from the bank is wanted. The bank, therefore, having paid away this 1000*l.* in gold, and having received for it their own note for 1000*l.* must now re-issue this note, if they are resolved to *maintain the amount of their paper circulation.* How, then, is the bank to issue it? The only means which the bank, on its part, is able to take for the extension of its paper circulation, is to enlarge its loans. It must, therefore, re-issue the 1000*l.* note, in the shape of a loan, to some person who offers a bill to discount. It receives, therefore, a bill of 1000*l.* and gives a note of 1000*l.* in return for it. For the same note, thus re-issued, we may suppose 1000*l.* in money to be again demanded, and to be again paid. The paper circulation of the bank is now again diminished 1000*l.* and, therefore, there arises a necessity for issuing the same 1000*l.* note, or some other note or notes to like amount, a third time, in order to maintain the amount of notes in circulation. The like transaction, or rather a number of such transactions, may be supposed to be repeated either five, or fifty, or a hundred, or a thousand times. Even if we should suppose the bank to bring down its paper circulation to one hundred thousand pounds, and to *maintain it at that sum*, it is obvious that this same operation might be so reiterated, from day to day, as to extract at length from the bank even the greatest imaginable number of guineas. Thus, then, the bank is rendered liable to be exhausted of its guineas, by its determination to maintain the number of its notes, whether that number be greater or smaller; and here, also, let it be remarked by the way (a point on which more shall be said presently), that the bank, in consequence of its determination to maintain a given number of notes, is placed under an absolute necessity of increasing its loans to the very same extent to which it is deprived of its guineas. The bank, let it be remembered, was stated to lend an additional 1000*l.* on the occasion of each reiterated demand upon it for 1000*l.* in guineas. It thus clearly appears that the Bank of England is placed, by the very nature of its institution, in a situation in which it may not be possible to avoid a temporary failure in the regularity of its cash payments.

An idea has, indeed, prevailed, than which nothing can be more natural, that because an individual merchant is presumed to be blameable if he is not able to make good his payments, therefore also, a national bank, in case of failure, may be presumed to be censurable in like manner; and, on account of the greater importance of its transactions, to be censurable even in a still higher degree. But the total disparity in the circumstances of the two cases should be taken into consideration. Private houses may, in general, be fairly presumed to be in fault if they fail in the punctuality of their cash payments, supposing the Bank of England to pay in money, because, if they have made on their part a tolerably prudent provision, they may be in general considered as having in the bank a sure resource. Take away from them that resource and they will then be not only as liable as the Bank of England to the like accident, but they will be much more so; their means of supplying themselves with guineas becoming then exceedingly precarious. It may be apprehended, also, that, if instead one national bank two or more should be instituted, each having a small capital; each would then exercise a separate judgment; each would trust in some measure to the chance of getting a supply of guineas from the other, and each would allow itself to pursue its own particular interest, instead of taking upon itself the superintendance of general credit, and seeking its own safety through the medium of the safety of the public; unless, indeed, we should suppose such a good understanding to subsist between them as to make them act as if they were one body, and resemble, in many respects, one single institution.

The accident of a failure in the means of making the cash payments of a country, though it is one against which there can be no security which is complete, seems, therefore, to be best provided against by the establishment of one principal bank. It, however, becomes the public not to judge the bank, which is thus rendered its servant, and is completely subjected to its interests, by the same rules by which it judges of smaller banking and commercial establishments, but to advert to the peculiarity of its case.

If there has been any fault in the conduct of the Bank of England, the fault, as I conceive, has rather been, as has just been stated, on the side of too much restricting its notes in the late seasons of alarm, than on that of too much enlarging them. In doing this, it has happened to act (though but in part) according to what seems likely to have been the advice of Dr. A. Smith in the case. It has also taken that course which is the natural one for smaller banks, and which might, perhaps, have been the proper one for the Bank of England itself, in the infancy of its establishment, when the country was less dependent upon it for the means of effecting its payments. It has, probably, pursued a principle which had been acted upon, by its own directors, in all former times. It has also followed what was, at the very period in question, the common opinion of the public on the subject. It has, moreover, only diminished those notes, perhaps, in too great a degree, which there might possibly be found to be some argument for restraining with a more gentle hand. I venture, however, with deference, to express a suspicion that the bank may have, in some measure, aggravated, perhaps, rather than lessened, the demand upon itself for guineas through the suppression of too many notes at the time preceding the suspension of its cash payments; and I will hazard an opinion, that it might also, with propriety, have somewhat extended the temporary issue of its paper in the year 1793, when that alarm, arising from the failure of country banks, which has been already spoken of, took place. It is clear, at least, that it did not, in the more recent instance, succeed by the diminution of its notes in curing the evil which it thus aimed to remedy.

A suspicion prevailed, at the time of which we have been chiefly speaking, that the loans afforded by the bank to the government had caused the distress of the bank. But the government, it should be remembered, has no supply of guineas with which it can discharge any debt. It is circumstanced, in this respect, like any other debtor of the bank. It must, if forced to pay its debt, pay it in bank notes, an article which the bank cannot refuse to take. And the government must collect these notes wherever they are to be obtained; that is, from the bankers and traders, and other persons in possession of them, to whom it must, in return, give new stock or exchequer bills, which it may, at all times, easily create; though, at a period of mercantile distress, this would be done at a somewhat unfavourable price. We learn, from the evidence given to parliament, that the government was urged by the bank to pay up four and a half millions of existing debt a short time before the period in question, and that it complied with the demand; that is, the government collected some of the bank notes which were in circulation, and paid them into the bank; and then a part, but only a part, of the notes so paid in were re-issued to the merchants. If the whole of the notes paid into the bank by the government had been immediately re-issued in loans to private traders, *then the sum of notes in circulation* would have been the same. The government is only one large borrower from the bank; the merchants are a number of similar, though smaller, borrowers. Whether, therefore, the bank lent more to individuals and less to government, or less to government and more to individuals, the effect as to the number of notes allowed to be in circulation, must have been equal. The Exchequer, after receiving notes from the bank, almost as quickly pays them away, and thus sends them into the common circulation as the merchant does; and it is the total quantity of circulating notes, and not the manner in which they come into circulation, that is the material point.

It may be thought, indeed, that commerce would be encouraged, and commercial credit, as well as general paper credit, would be supported in a much greater degree by the bank sending their notes into circulation, through the medium of a loan to the merchants, than through that of a loan to government. But the difference would not, as I apprehend, be so great as many commercial men themselves at that time imagined. Those merchants who obtained an increase of the accustomed advances from the bank, would, some of them, probably invest, in the new exchequer bills which were created, a part of that very sum with which the bank favoured them. The merchants in higher credit, of course, would have the preference at the bank; and they were certainly under a very strong temptation to borrow of the bank at five per cent. interest for the sake of investing the sum so borrowed in exchequer bills, yielding five and a half or six, or, for a time, even seven or eight per cent. or more. As far as this was the case, it is obvious that the bank, instead of lending to the government, would only lend to those who lent to the government, the government paying an additional interest, and the merchants receiving it. Where this did not take place, that might happen which would be exactly equivalent. The bankers finding that the merchants were, many of them, allowed to become larger borrowers at the bank than before, would think it less necessary to lend to them, and would, therefore, add to the sum which they themselves kept in exchequer bills, the great profit on that article tempting them, at the same time, to do this. The bank, on this supposition, would lend to the merchants, who would forbear to borrow of the banker (which is the same thing for the present purpose as lending to the

Enquiry into Paper Credit

banker), who would lend to the government. But let us put a third case. Let us imagine it to be a gentleman in the country who invested the property in the new exchequer bills. That property would probably, since we must suppose it easily applicable to such investment, have been lying in some private hand at interest. Let us imagine it to consist of 100*l.* which had been in the hands of a country banker; the country banker, in this case, would draw upon his London banker; the country banker's account with the London banker would then be worse by 100*l.*; and the London banker having 100*l.* less deposits, would be able to lend 100*l.* less to the London merchants. In other words, the Bank of England, in this case, instead of lending to the government, would lend to the London merchant, who would forbear to borrow of the London banker, who would lend to, or, perhaps, forbear to borrow of the country banker, who would forbear to borrow of the country gentleman, who would lend to the government; which also seems to be much the same as if the Bank of England themselves lent to the government. This detailed case has been put partly for the sake of observing upon it, that the necessity which would be created for the transfer of this 100*l.*, through so many hands, would produce a want of some degree of *additional* circulating medium in order to effect these several payments. It would, however, be chiefly by the means of a bill on London that the transaction just now supposed would be conducted; but the bill must finally be paid by a Bank of England note.——Let us imagine a fourth case. Let us suppose a sum to be invested in the new exchequer bills by a person obtaining money for the purpose of the investment, not by calling in a sum lying at interest, as was last assumed, but by selling goods, land, or any other article. We must, then, necessarily suppose a buyer of those goods, of that land, or of that other article to be created by such sale. We shall find, also, that it is necessary to suppose either that buyer to become a borrower, or to become the seller to one who would become a borrower; or, at least, we must come to a borrower at last. We are supposing one man to *sell* goods for 100*l.*, and not to *restore* this 100*l. to* trade, but to *lend* it out.

We must, then, necessarily suppose some other man to borrow 100*l.* and by thus borrowing to add that 100*l.* capital to trade which the other had taken from it; for since the trade goods in the country remain the same, the capital invested in trade must be the same also. The body of lenders, therefore, whoever they might be, who lent the four and a half millions to government, necessarily created a body of borrowers to exactly the same amount in what may be called the general money market of the country. Thus a pressure was, on the whole, created, which was just equal to that which was relieved: a pressure, in the first instance, falling in some degree (though by no means entirely, or even principally) in a different quarter than before; a pressure, however, very soon extending itself to the same persons; for there is a competition among the several classes both of borrowers and of lenders in the money market, which, notwithstanding some inequality occasioned by the usury laws, causes the increased distress brought upon any one class of the accustomed borrowers very soon to distribute itself among all. The bank, it is true, would, by lending the four and a half millions in bills at two months, possess more means of at any time diminishing its loans, and of thus lessening also its notes, than if the same sum had been invested in exchequer bills, since the latter are at a longer date; and it was natural for the bank to call in its loan to government for this reason. If, however, the calling in of the loan to government was only to furnish the means of limiting the notes, then that question returns which has already been discussed, namely, whether the diminution of the notes was not carried possibly somewhat farther than was desirable, even for the sake of the bank itself. During the existence of this loan to government, that reduction of notes, which has been supposed to have been too great, may have been, perhaps, to a certain degree obstructed, though by no means necessarily precluded since an opportunity of diminishing the discounts to the merchants, and of thus lessening the notes, at all times existed. On the whole, there appears to be no reason to infer, from the circumstance of the demand for the four and a half millions having been made upon

131

government, that the government was either the more remote or the more immediate cause of the suspension of the cash payments of the bank, except, undoubtedly, so far as the war in general, or the particular circumstance of a remittance of a subsidy to the Emperor a short time before the event in question, might be considered as affecting the balance of trade, and thus contributing to draw gold out of the country.

It is, on public grounds, so important to shew that the more than usual largeness of the bank loans to government (for it can hardly fail to be true that they were more than commonly extended) was not the cause of the suspension of the cash payments of the bank, that I shall dwell for some time longer on this subject. This was continually charged as the cause, and it was not unnatural to suppose it to be so. The paper circulation of the bank, however, it has been observed, was at this time not increased. It was, on the contrary, much reduced. It was by no means higher than was necessary for securing the regularity of the payments of the metropolis. Now, if it be allowed that there was this necessity for maintaining the existing quantity of notes, it then was not the notes which must be considered as issued for the purpose of making the loans, but the loans must be considered as made in consequence of the issue of notes. When the notes of the bank are increased, the loans must be increased also; when the notes are maintained, the loans must be maintained in as great proportion; when the notes are decreased, the loans can be decreased *only in that proportion*. There can, then, be no matter of blame on account of the magnitude of the loans, unless there be matter of blame on account of the magnitude of the notes. But the notes I have stated to have been probably rather too few than too many. If the reader has agreed with me in this, he must then agree with me that the loans were too scanty rather than too large. In other words, then, the bank, at the time of the failure of its cash payments, had lent too little rather than too much. If the bank would have somewhat diminished its danger by issuing more notes, the granting of more loans would have also diminished its danger. Thus the very converse to the common opinion on this subject seems to be the truth.

There is, however, another point of importance here to be remarked. The loans which the bank had made on the whole, that is, the loans to government and to individuals taken together, at the time of the suspension of its cash payments, were not only maintained in that proportion in which the notes were maintained, but they were increased beyond that proportion. This increase beyond that proportion was also a matter of necessity.

The loans of the bank do not simply keep pace with the notes. The loans necessarily increase or diminish through another cause; they diminish as gold flows into the bank, and increase as gold goes out, supposing, as we generally may, the article of deposits to remain the same; that is, they necessarily increase and diminish in a ratio directly contrary to that which a theorist would prescribe and which the public naturally would suppose.

To those who are but slightly acquainted with these subjects, this truth will probably be made much clearer by a statement of the whole disposeable effects of the Bank of England, and of the manner in which those effects are employed. The statement is important, because it will serve to prove, beyond the possibility of contradiction, that the extraordinary largeness of the loans of the bank, at the critical period in question, ought to be considered not as a consequence of any disposition in the bank to be great and adventurous lenders at a time when their guineas grew low, but as arising out of the necessity under which they were placed. I mean that they could not avoid lending to the whole extent to which they did, provided even that small number of notes which they kept in circulation was maintained.

The effects of the bank on the 25th February 1797, I mean those effects which were their own, as well as those placed in their hands belonging to other persons, may, in conformity to the account rendered by themselves to parliament, be stated, in round numbers, to have been as follows.

(It may be premised, that they had a capital of their own of about

11,626,000*l.* which shall be excluded from our present consideration, it being lent to government at three per cent. per annum interest.)

1. They had a sum of undivided profits which formed an additional and disposeable capital of nearly   L.3,800,000

2. They had of deposits lodged with them by customers of various classes about - - - - -   5,100,000

These deposits include, as may be presumed, the dividends belonging to many proprietors of stock, which may be viewed in the same light with the cash kept by an individual in the hands of his banker.

3. They had what may be considered as disposeable effects, or deposits placed in their hands in return for bank notes issued* - - - - - -   8,600,000

Thus the bank had, at that time, disposeable effects amounting in all to - - - - - - - L.17,500,000

* The reader, perhaps, may not understand upon what principle it is that the amount of the notes of the Bank of England is classed among the deposits. The amount of them was placed on this side of the account in the statement given to parliament by the bank, and very properly, or rather very necessarily. It is not, however, the notes which themselves form deposits. They are given *in return for* deposits; and they are, therefore, the measure of those deposits. It is in substance the same thing whether a person deposits 100*l.* in money with the bank, taking no note, but obtaining a right to draw a draft on a banking account which is opened in his name, or whether he deposits the same 100*l.* and receives for it a bank note. The possession of the right to draw obtained in the one case, is exactly equivalent to the possession of the note obtained in the other. The notes, it is true, are commonly issued not in consideration of money received, but of bills discounted; but the deposits, it may also be observed, are generally formed by the same means of bills discounted. The manner of transacting the discounting business at the bank is this:—the discounter opens a banking account with the bank, and usually keeps a small balance upon it; when he sends bills to be discounted, those bills, if the bank consents to discount them, are placed to the credit of his banking account; and when he draws for them, or for any part of them, the bearer of his draft receives the amount of it in bank notes. The numerous balances, therefore (in general small ones), which the discounters keep with the bank, are included, no doubt, in the bank account, under the head of deposits, and form a part of the second item in the statement above. The sum which I have considered as deposited in the bank, by those who take away the notes, they opening no account, is not termed deposits in the bank statement. I have, however, thought it necessary so to term it, in order to make the subject more clear to the reader.

134

It will much illustrate what is about to be added, if the following observations respecting these three several heads of disposeable effects are here made.

First. Let it be remarked, that the first sum of 3,800,000*l.* does not fluctuate; it only increases gradually, and in a small degree.

Secondly. The second sum of 5,100,000*l.* fluctuates probably but little; and as far as it does so, it fluctuates not at the pleasure of the bank, but at the will of its customers.

Thirdly. The third, then, is the only one of the three component parts of the disposeable effects of the bank which it is in the power of the bank to increase or diminish at its own option. The bank exercised their power of diminishing this article, at the time in question, so far as to bring it down to about 8,600,000*l.* To reduce it thus far was, as has been repeatedly stated, to reduce it, perhaps, somewhat too much; but let us assume only, that the reduction was sufficient, or nearly sufficient. The bank, then, it must be admitted, had 17,500,000*l.* of disposeable effects, and it was not to be ascribed to them as a matter of blame that these effects then stood at about the sum at which they did.

Having, then, these effects, and being under a necessity of disposing of them in some way or other, let us state next how they did in fact employ them.

In proceeding to make this statement, it will be necessary, with a view to the object for which it is made, to name some specific sum (it matters not whether more or less than the real one) for the amount of that part of the effects of the bank which was, on the 25th February, 1797, invested in bullion. In the account rendered to parliament, the value of the bullion and of the bills discounted, &c. are put together, and are stated at nearly seven millions. Let it be supposed that the bullion was either one, two, or three millions; and that the bills discounted, &c. were, therefore, either four, five, or six millions. The mode of disposing of the 17,500,000*l.* will then be as follows.

The bank invested in government securities, that is, in exchequer bills, in loans to government made on the security of the

135

land and malt tax which was coming in, and in treasury bills of
exchange growing due, about - - - - - - L.10,500,000
    They invested, as shall for the present be
assumed in conformity to the estimate which it was
before proposed to make, "in bills discounted to the
merchants," in what is termed in their account,
"money lent," and in some other (probably small)
"articles," - - - - - - - - - - - - - 4,000,000
    And they had property invested in bullion, as shall
for the present be assumed, amounting to - - - 3,000,000

    Making together, as the investment necessarily
must, the same sum exactly which the disposeable
effects were before stated to amount to, namely - L.17,500,000
    This same account of the investment may be given more briefly
and conveniently for our present purpose, in the following manner,
viz. the total sum lent both to government and to individuals, or,
in other words, the total loans were

                                            L.14,500,000
The total of the bullion was - - - - - - 3,000,000

Making together - - - - - - - - - L.17,500,000
    It will now be obvious to the reader, that if the bullion, instead
of three millions, is supposed to have been only two millions, then
the total of the loans must be supposed to be increased one million;
and that if the bullion, instead of three millions, is supposed to be
only one million, then the loans must be supposed to be increased
two millions.
    In other words, the account of the investment may either
be stated as has been just done, or it may be stated as follows:
Total loans - - - - - - - - - - - L.15,500,000
Bullion - - - - - - - - - - - - - 2,000,000

Making together, as before, - - - - - - - 17,500,000

136

Or total loans - - - - - - - - - - - - 16,500,000
Bullion - - - - - - - - - - - - - 1,000,000

Making together, as before, - - - - - - - L.17,500,000

It thus appears, that the loans necessarily must increase in proportion as the gold decreases, provided the disposeable effects remain the same.

It follows, on the principle which has just been explained, that if we suppose, as we necessarily must, the bullion to have been, twelve months before the time of the suspension of the cash payments of the bank, much higher than at the period of the suspension, the loans would, during the course of those twelve months, necessarily increase. Let us (for the sake of illustration) suppose the gold to have been a year before the suspension eight millions, and to have fallen on the 26th February, 1797, to the sum of two millions. In that case, if we were to suppose the disposeable effects of the bank to have been at both periods the same, there must necessarily have been, in the course of the year, an increase of the bank loans of no less than six millions. But the effects of the bank were not quite the same at the two periods. They probably were higher by about two millions at the former period; for the notes were higher by nearly that sum. The notes, then, fell in the year two millions, but the bullion fell six. The loans, therefore, would be decreased two millions, through the decrease of notes, but would be increased six millions through the decrease of bullion; that is, they would *necessarily* be increased, in the course of the year four millions. I have dwelt thus particularly on this circumstance, because the whole of the suspicion, that the magnitude of the bank loans were the cause of the failure of its cash, seems to me to rest upon it. The largeness of those loans was not the *cause* of the guineas going from them, as has been ordinarily supposed; it was the *effect*. Nothing could be more natural than for the public to call that the cause, in this instance, which was the effect, and that the effect which was the cause. In the case of private persons it is often very justly said, that a man fails in his payments because he has lent so largely; and it would seem very strange to reply that this was not the case, for that the man in question had found it necessary to lend largely, because his cash failed him; and that the failure of the cash was the cause, and the lending merely an effect. That, however, which could not be affirmed of an individual, is true in the case of the bank, and the circumstances which give occasion for this peculiarity in our reasonings respecting that institution, are these two; first, the difficulty in obtaining a supply of guineas which the bank experiences, a difficulty totally unknown to individuals who draw their guineas from the bank itself; and, secondly, the singular necessity under which the bank is placed of maintaining at all times its notes.

It was thought by some, that the interference on the part of the government and parliament was improper, inasmuch as the bank ought not to have been prevented from continuing to pay in cash as long as it had any remaining ability to do so. Every bank note, it was urged, is a contract to pay money entered into between the bank and the possessor of it, in consequence of what has been deemed a valuable consideration; and no authority of parliament ought, except in a case of the last necessity, to interpose itself to prevent the fulfilment of such a contract. To this it seems to be a fair answer to say, that the question is not whether any one holder of a note shall have his claim to receive money for it interfered with, but that it is a question respecting *all* the holders of notes, *as well as all other persons having a right to demand any cash payments in any quarter whatever.* Now, there are few or no creditors who are not also debtors; and a very large proportion of debtors owe as much to others, as others owe to them. Bankers and traders are greater debtors than other men; but they are also greater creditors. The bank itself is a great creditor, its credits, indeed, being far greater than its debts, and it is intitled to receive a part of its debts almost immediately. The case, then, is this: a comparatively very small portion of the persons having a right to demand cash, are led, by sudden alarm, to urge their claim for guineas to such an extent as to invest even a large portion of their capital in that article of which a quantity has been provided which is sufficient only for the purpose of the ordinary kind of payments. All the cash in the world would not satisfy claims of this sort, if all men, having a right to urge them, were disposed equally to do so. The very persons who press for these payments do not reflect, that they themselves, perhaps, have creditors who might, with equal justice, exact the immediate money payment of a still larger debt against them. The law authorizing the suspension of the cash payments of the bank, seems, therefore, to have only given effect to what must have been the general wish of the nation in the new and extraordinary circumstances in which it found itself. If every bill and engagement is a contract to pay money, the two parties to the contract may be understood as agreeing, for the sake of a common and almost universal interest, to relax as to the literal interpretation of it, and as consenting that "money should mean money's worth," and not the very pieces of metal: and the parliament may be considered as interposing in order to execute this common wish of the public.

By authorising the suspension of the cash payments of the bank, while a certain quantity of guineas still remained in its coffers, the parliament, moreover, much diminished the shock which this extraordinary event might naturally be expected to occasion; and also provided the means of furnishing the guineas actually necessary after that æra for some smaller current payments, as well as the means of securing the credit of bank notes, thus rendering them a more valuable medium of exchange for goods, and a fairer substitute for guineas than they might otherwise have been. The parliament, then, were led by the practical view which they took of the subject, to disregard theory, as well as some popular prejudice, for the sake of more effectually guarding the public safety, and promoting real justice.

The danger chiefly to be apprehended in London, was, that the common class of people, not receiving their pay in the usual article of coin, and not knowing at the first that one and two pound notes would purchase every thing in the same manner as gold, might be excited to some tumultuous proceedings. It was also feared that, through the discredit cast on small notes by the common people, this new paper might fall, at the first issue of it, to a discount. It was important, therefore, to continue for a time to pay the labouring people in money; and to circulate the new one and two pound notes, in the first instance, by the medium of the higher classes. Of the sum remaining in the bank, a small part was issued to each of the bankers, after the suspension took place, for the convenience of common workmen. It was obviously desirable, that a farther sum should be reserved in the bank as a provision for any subsequent and important uses.

Immediately after this event, the bank extended the quantity of its notes nearly to the amount of the sum usually in circulation: and not only was credit revived, but in no long time guineas became remarkably abundant. The bank, as is commonly supposed, was replenished with them. And there is this infallible proof, that gold flowed into the country; that the course of exchange became much in favour of it.

CHAP. V

Of the Balance of Trade.—Of the Course of Exchange.—Tendency of an unfavourable Exchange to take away Gold.—Of the Probability of the Return of Gold.—Of the Manner in which it may be supposed that exported Gold is employed on the Continent.—Reasons for having renewed the Law for suspending the Cash Payments of the Bank of England.

THE law which authorised the suspension of the cash payments of the bank having been re-enacted; the high price of provisions having given occasion to much speculation on the subject of paper credit; the course of exchange having again turned greatly against the country; and gold having to a material degree disappeared, its place being occupied by small paper notes; it is not surprising that suspicions of the necessity of an alteration in the system of our paper credit should have become prevalent. Some consideration shall here be given to that unfavourable state of the exchange between this country and Europe, which operated during the last two years of the war, in again drawing away our guineas.

It may be laid down as a general truth, that the commercial exports and imports of a state (that is to say, the exported and imported commodities, for which one country receives an equivalent from another) naturally proportion themselves in some degree to each other; and that the balance of trade, therefore (by which is meant the difference between these commercial exports and imports), cannot continue for a very long time to be either highly favourable or highly unfavourable to a country. For that balance must be paid in bullion, or else must constitute a debt. To suppose a very great balance to be paid, year after year, in bullion, is to assume such a diminution of bullion in one country, and such an accumulation of it in another, as are not easy to be imagined: it may even be questioned whether the commercial prosperity of a state does not tend, on the whole, to reduce, rather than augment, the quantity of gold in use, through that extension of paper credit to which it leads. To suppose large and successive balances to be formed into a debt, is to assume an accumulation of debt, which is almost equally incredible. A prosperous nation commonly employs its growing wealth, not so much in augmenting the debts due to it from abroad, as in the enlargement of its capital at home; I mean, in the cultivation of its lands, in the encrease of its buildings, the extension of its machinery, the multiplication of its docks and its canals, and in a variety of other improvements, which become the sure sources of an encreasing income. The state may be progressive in these respects, even in years in which the balance of trade is unfavourable. There is a customary length of credit in foreign parts which the British exporter, however overflowing his capital may be, is not very willing to enlarge. And events fail not occasionally to arise, which remind him of the danger of committing too great a portion of his property into the hands of those who are not subject to the same laws with himself; and whose country may suddenly be involved, at any moment, in a war with Great Britain.

The equalization of the commercial exports and imports is promoted not only by the unwillingness of the richer state to lend to an unlimited extent, but also by a disinclination to borrow in the poorer. There is in the mass of the people, of all countries, a disposition to adapt their individual expenditure to their income. Importations conducted with a view to the consumption of the country into which the articles are imported (and such, perhaps, are the chief importations of a poor country), are limited by the ability of the individuals of that country to pay for them out of their income. Importations, with a view to subsequent exportation, are in like manner limited by the ability to pay which subsists among the individuals of the several countries to which the imported goods are afterwards exported. The income of individuals is the general limit in all cases. If, therefore, through any unfortunate circumstance, if through war, scarcity, or any other extensive calamity, the value of the annual income of the inhabitants of a country is diminished, either new economy on the one hand, or new exertions of individual industry on the other, fail not, after a certain time, in some measure, to restore the balance. And this equality between private expenditures and private incomes tends ultimately to produce equality between the commercial exports and imports.

But though the value of the commercial exports and imports of a country will have this general tendency to proportion themselves to each other, there will not fail occasionally to arise a very great inequality between them. A good or a bad harvest, in particular, will have a considerable influence in producing this temporary difference. The extra quantity of corn and other articles imported into Great Britain in this and the last year, with a view to supply the deficiency of our own crops, must have amounted in value to so many millions, that it may justly excite surprise that we should have been able, during an expensive war, to provide the means of cancelling our foreign debt so far even as we have done; especially when the peculiar interruptions to our commerce are also considered. In this country, however, as in all others, the two principles of economy and exertion are always operating in proportion to the occasion for them. But the economy and exertion follow rather than accompany the evil which they have to cure. If the harvest fails, and imports are necessary, in order to supply the deficiency, payment for those imports is almost immediately required: but the means of payment are to be supplied more gradually through the limitation of private expenditure, or the encrease of individual industry. Hence a temporary pressure arises at the time of any very unfavourable balance. To understand how to provide against this pressure, and how to encounter it, is a great part of the wisdom of a commercial state.

By the commercial exports and imports which have been spoken of, those articles have been intended for which an equivalent is given; not those which form a remittance, for which nothing is obtained in exchange. Many of our exported and some of our imported commodities are of that class which furnish no return.

For example, numerous stores were shipped, during the war, for the support of our navy and army in foreign parts. Remittances were made, in the way of loan and subsidy, to our allies. Some dividends may be supposed to have been transmitted to the foreign proprietors of British stock. Much property is also sent out of the kingdom, which constitutes a capital employed in the cultivation of lands in the West Indies. On the other hand, capital is transmitted *to* Great Britain from the East Indies, both by the India Company and by individuals.

Although exports and imports of this class form no part of the commercial exports and imports which have been spoken of, they affect the quantity of those commercial exports and imports, and they contribute, exactly like the circumstance of a bad harvest, to render the balance of trade unfavourable*; they tend, that is to

* This point may be illustrated in the following manner:—

Let us suppose a subsidy, for example, of two millions to be remitted to the Emperor of Germany, through the medium of bills to that amount, directed to be drawn by Vienna on London. By these bills, Great Britain is laid under a necessity of exporting two millions, either of goods or of bullion, or of both, for which no foreign commodities will be given in return. These two millions of exports diminish our fund of exportable goods; and they also satisfy a part of the foreign demand for British articles. They tend, in both these respects, to reduce the quantity of goods which can be exported by us in the way of ordinary commerce, and to turn the balance of trade against us. Capital transferred to our colonies, dividends transmitted to foreigners, and articles shipped for the use of our fleets and armies, contribute in the same manner as foreign subsidies to render the balance of trade unfavourable. It may be added, that articles consumed at home, in the support of similar fleets and armies, as well as all other expenditure in Great Britain, must have the same general tendency.

It may be worthy of remark, that since an additional internal expenditure, in the same manner as the remittance of a subsidy to foreign parts, contributes to an unfavourable balance of trade, and therefore, also, to the exportation of our gold, it follows, that, if the remittance of a small subsidy tends to produce at home a large saving; if, for instance, it spares the expence of maintaining a great naval and military force for the defence of our own island, through the continental diversion to which it leads, the subsidy may conduce to render our balance of trade more favourable; and may, on the whole, prevent rather than promote the exportation of our coin—A circumstance which, in considering the policy of furnishing an aid to foreign allies, is not always taken into contemplation.

144

say, in the same manner, to bring Great Britain into debt to foreign countries, and to promote the exportation of our bullion. Our mercantile exports and imports, nevertheless, by whatever means they may be rendered disproportionate, necessarily become, in the long run, tolerably equal; for it is evident that there is a limit, both to the debt which foreigners will permit British merchants to incur, and also to the quantity of British bullion which is exportable.

Gold has been spoken of in this Chapter as that article by which a balance of trade is discharged, and not as itself constituting a commodity. Gold, however, when exported and imported, may be considered in the same light with all other commodities; for it is an article of intrinsic value: its price, like that of other commodities, rises and falls according to the proportion between the supply and the demand; it naturally seeks, like them, that country in which it is the dearest; and it is, in point of fact, like them, exported by our merchants accordingly as the export or import is likely to yield a profit. Some description of the circumstances which cause the export of gold to become a profitable speculation to the merchant may serve to illustrate this subject.

When a bill is drawn by one country on another—by Hamburgh, for instance, on London—it is sold (or discounted) in the place in which it is drawn, to some person in the same place; and the buyer or discounter gives for the bill that article, whatever it may be, which forms the current payment of the spot. This article may consist either of gold or silver coin, or of bank paper, or, which is much the same thing as bank paper, of a credit in the books of some public bank.

Let us now suppose that the exporter of corn from Hamburgh to London draws a bill for 100*l.* on London, and offers it for sale on the Hamburgh Exchange at the season when great exportations of corn to London are taking place. The persons in Hamburgh having occasion to buy bills are fewer, in such a case, than those who want to sell them; and the price of the bill, like that of any other article, fluctuates according to the proportion subsisting between the supply and the demand. The disproportion, then,

Enquiry into Paper Credit   145   K

between the number of those persons at Hamburgh who want to sell London bills for Hamburgh coin, and the number of those who want to sell Hamburgh coin for London bills, causes the price of London bills to fall, and of Hamburgh coin to rise. Thus gold is said to rise at Hamburgh; and the exchange between London and Hamburgh becomes unfavourable to London. This fluctuation in the exchange will, in the first instance, be small. It will be limited to that trifling sum which it costs to transport bullion from one place to the other, so long as there is bullion to be transported. But let us now suppose the number of Hamburgh bills on London, drawn for the payment of the goods imported into the latter place, to be so numerous, that the exportation of all the bullion which is purchasable in Great Britain, has not sufficed for their payment. Gold coin, in this case, will be exported, being first melted down for the purpose. Coin, indeed, is not allowed to be exported from Great Britain, nor gold which has been melted down from coin; an oath being required of every exporter of gold, that the gold which he exports does not consist of guineas which have been melted. There are, however, many ways of escaping the law which imposes this oath. The law is dishonestly evaded either by the clandestine exportation of guineas, no oath at all being taken; or by taking a false oath; or by contriving that the person taking the oath shall be, in some degree, ignorant of the melting which has been practised. The operation of the law is avoided without this dishonesty, through the exportation of gold which had been turned, or had been about to be turned, to the purposes of gilded and golden ornaments, the place of this gold being supplied by gold melted down from coin. The state of the British law unquestionably serves to discourage and limit, though not effectually to hinder, that exportation of guineas which is encouraged by an unfavourable balance of trade; and, perhaps, scarcely lessens it when the profit on exportation becomes very great. The law tends, indeed, to produce a greater interchange of gold for paper at home. But it encreases whatever evil arises from an unfavourable state of the exchange with foreign countries.

Let it now be considered how this high price of gold in London must operate in respect to the Bank of England. Great demands for guineas will be made on the bank; and, in general, probably by persons not intending to melt or export guineas themselves, but wishing only to supply that want which all have begun to experience in consequence of the large illicit exportations carried on by a few unknown persons. It is assumed, for the present, that the bank is paying in guineas. What, then, is the course which the bank will naturally pursue? Finding the guineas in their coffers to lessen every day, they must naturally be supposed to be desirous of replacing them by all effectual and not extravagantly expensive means. They will be disposed, to a certain degree, to buy gold, though at a losing price, and to coin it into new guineas; but they will have to do this at the very moment when many are privately melting what is coined. The one party will be melting and selling, while the other is buying and coining. And each of these two contending businesses will now be carried on not on account of an actual exportation of each melted guinea to Hamburgh, but the operation (or, at least, a great part of it) will be confined to London; the coiners and the melters living on the same spot, and giving constant employment to each other.

The bank, if we suppose it, as we now do, to carry on this sort of contest with the melters, is obviously waging a very unequal war; and even though it should not be tired early, it will be likely to be tired sooner than its adversaries.

The dilemma in which the bank is thus placed, is evidently one which implies no deficiency in its wealth, in its credit, or in the strength of its resources. The public, during all this time, may have the highest confidence in it. The notes of the bank may be of the same number as usual, possibly somewhat lower in number; its capital and savings may be immensely great, and perfectly well known; its stock may be selling at much above par; its clear annual profits may be considerable. Its gold, nevertheless, through the operation of that one cause which has just been named, may be growing less and less. And it is not at all impossible, if an alarm

147

at home should draw away the gold at the same time, that, however ample its general fund may have been, it may be reduced to its last guinea; and may actually be brought under the necessity of making a temporary suspension of its payments.

An important subject of enquiry here suggests itself. Dr. Smith, as was remarked in the beginning of the former chapter, in some degree leads his reader to assume the Bank of England to be in fault (that is, to have issued too many notes) whenever an excess of the market price above the mint price of gold takes place, an excess which produces, as shall immediately be shewn, that difficulty in replenishing the coffers of the bank which has been recently described. If the observation of Dr. Smith be, without exception or qualification, true, then the quantity of paper issued by the Bank of England has undoubtedly been excessive throughout the last two years; for the excess of the market price above the mint price of gold has been, during that time, considerable. Then, also, it is the bank which has placed in its own way that obstacle to the purchase of gold which has been spoken of. Any enquiry tending to indicate the causes which place the bank under this singular difficulty, seems to be important.

I shall here endeavour clearly to explain what is meant by the high and the low price of gold; and also by that difference between the mint price and the market price, which has such material consequences.

Gold must be considered as dear, in proportion as goods for which it is exchangeable are cheap; and as cheap, in proportion as goods are dear. Any circumstance, therefore, which serves to make goods generally dear, must serve to make gold generally cheap, and *vice versa*; and any circumstance which serves to make goods dear at any particular time or place, must serve to make gold cheap at that time or place, and *vice versa*.

The reason of the difference between the mint price and the market price of gold, does not easily occur. If the bank, from time to time, buys gold at a high price, that is, if it gives for gold a large quantity of goods (or something convertible into a large quantity, which is the same thing); it is natural, on the first view, to suppose that the high price given by the bank, which is the principal and almost the only English purchaser, must form the current English price; and that this high current price of gold in England will prove the means both of bringing it hither, and of detaining it here; causing goods, which are cheap, to go abroad; and gold, which is dear, to come hither, and also to remain in the country. Undoubtedly gold would remain in England, when tempted hither by the high price given for it by the bank, if it were not for the following circumstance. Gold is bought by the bank, in order to be converted into coin; and, when turned into coin, it forms a part of the circulating medium of the country, paper constituting another part. If, then, this paper is by any means rendered cheap, and if the paper so rendered cheap is currently interchanged for one sort of gold, namely, for gold which has been coined, then the coined gold will partake in the cheapness of the paper; that is, it will buy, when in the shape of coin, a smaller quantity of goods than it will purchase when in the form of bullion. In other words, an ounce of gold coming from the mint in the shape of guineas, and making $3l.$ $17s.$ $10\frac{1}{2}d.$ (for that is the sum into which an ounce always is coined at the mint), will be worth less than the same ounce of gold was worth before it went to the mint, and less than it would again be worth if converted back into bullion. There arises, therefore, a temptation to convert back into bullion, and then to export; or, which is the same thing, to export, and then convert back into bullion; or, which is also the same thing, to convert back into bullion, and then sell to the bank, at the price which would be obtained by exportation, that gold which the bank had turned from bullion into coin. In proportion as the difficulty of collecting, melting, and sending abroad the gold coin is augmented (and it increases as the quantity of coin diminishes), the difference between the mint and market price of bullion will become more considerable, supposing the demand for gold in foreign countries to continue. Thus it is through the interchangeableness of gold coin with paper, that gold coin is made cheap in England; or, in other words, that goods, in comparison with gold coin, are made dear. The goods which are dear remain, therefore, in England; and the gold coin, which is cheap (for the bank is indisposed to buy it, on account of the loss sustained on each coinage), goes abroad.

There is, undoubtedly, much ground for the supposition of Dr. Smith, that a diminution of the quantity of paper has a tendency to cure this evil*. It tends to render the paper more valuable, and, therefore, to make that gold coin more valuable for which the paper is interchangeable, and thus to destroy that excess of the market price above the mint prince of gold, which forms the obstacle to the introduction of a supply of gold into the coffers of the bank. There seems, nevertheless, to be much of inaccuracy and error in the doctrine of Dr. Smith on this subject. He begins by representing the quantity of paper which may properly circulate, as to be measured by that of the gold which would circulate if there were no paper. The reader is, therefore, led to believe, that a difference between the mint price and the market price of gold arises from an issue of a greater quantity. Dr. Smith also too much countenances an idea, that the excess consists of paper *forced* into circulation; for he terms the proper quantity that paper which will "easily circulate." He, moreover, induces his reader to suppose, that the excessive issue is an issue to a more than usual amount. At the time of a very unfavourable balance of trade (an event which Dr. Smith leaves totally out of his consideration), it is very possible,

* That the diminution of the circulating paper has a tendency to bring down the price of goods at home, and to cause those goods to go abroad for the sake of a better market, was observed in the preceding Chapter, and will again be insisted on when we proceed to treat of the importance of properly limiting the quantity of Bank of England notes. Many remarks, however, were added, in the former Chapter, respecting those detrimental effects of a reduction of paper, which are to be set against the good consequences of it. In the present Chapter the same arguments, on each side, are about to recur, and they will, therefore, be but slightly touched upon.

In the former Chapter, the difficulties which the bank experiences in consequence of a run occasioned by an alarm, were chiefly considered; in the present, the difficulties arising from that sort of drain which proceeds from an unfavourable balance of trade are investigated. In some future Chapters, the difficulties to which the bank is exposed by a similar drain, resulting from a too greate mission of paper, will be the subject of examination.

as I apprehend, that the excess of paper, if such it is to be called, is merely an excess above that very low and reduced quantity to which it is necessary that it should be brought down, in order to prevent the existence of an excess of the market price above the mint price of gold. I conceive, therefore, that this excess, if it arises on the occasion of an unfavourable balance of trade, and at a time when there has been no extraordinary emission of notes, may fairly be considered as an excess created by that unfavourable balance, though it is one which a reduction of notes tends to cure.

The fair statement of the case seems to be this. At the time of a very unfavourable balance (produced, for example, through a failure of the harvest), a country has occasion for large supplies of corn from abroad: but either it has not the means of supplying at the instant a sufficient quantity of goods in return, or, which is much the more probable case, and the case which I suppose more applicable to England, the goods which the country having the unfavourable balance is able to furnish as means of cancelling its debt, are not in such demand abroad as to afford the prospect of a tempting or even of a tolerable price; and this want of a demand may happen possibly through some political circumstance which has produced, in a particular quarter, the temporary interruption of an established branch of commerce. The country, therefore, which has the favourable balance, being, to a certain degree, eager for payment, but not in immediate want of all that supply of goods which would be necessary to pay the balance, prefers gold as part, at least, of the payment; for gold can always be turned to a more beneficial use than a very great overplus of any other commodity. In order, then, to induce the country having the favourable balance to take all its payment in goods, and no part of it in gold, it would be requisite not only to prevent goods from being very dear, but even to render them excessively cheap. It would be necessary, therefore, that the bank should not only not encrease its paper, but that it should, perhaps, very greatly diminish it, if it would endeavour to prevent gold from going out in part of payment of the unfavourable balance. And if the bank do this, then there will arise those other questions, which Dr. Smith leaves totally out of his consideration; namely, whether the bank, in the attempt to produce this very low price, may not, in a country circumstanced as Great Britain is, so exceedingly distress trade and discourage manufactures as to impair, in the manner already specified, those sources of our returning wealth to which we must chiefly trust for the restoration of our balance of trade, and for bringing back the tide of gold into Great Britain. It is also necessary to notice in this place, that the favourable effect which a limitation of bank paper produces on the exchange is certainly not instantaneous, and may, probably, only be experienced after some considerable interval of time; it may, therefore, in many cases, be expected that the exchange will rectify itself before the reduction of bank paper can have any operation. It is also to be recollected (a point, indeed, which Dr. Smith himself states), that gold is retained or drawn away, not by the limitation or the encrease of the Bank of England paper alone, but by that of their paper, conjointly with that of the other paper of the country. The bank paper serves, it is true, to regulate, in a great degree, that other paper; but not with exactness. The bank, by proceeding to that reduction of its own paper which is necessary to bring gold into the country, may possibly annihilate, before it is aware, a part or even almost the whole of the circulating country bank notes, and much other paper also; and it may, in that case, have to supply gold sufficient to fill the whole void, perhaps more than the whole void, which it has created; for it may be called upon to furnish large additional sums which may forthwith be hoarded in consequence of the alarm thus occasioned. Hence, even though it should encrease the supply of gold from abroad; it may augment, in a far greater degree, the demand for it at home. For this reason, it may be the true policy and duty of the bank to permit, for a time, and to a certain extent, the continuance of that unfavourable exchange, which causes gold to leave the country, and to be drawn out of its own coffers: and it must, in that case, necessarily encrease its loans to the same extent to which its gold is diminished. The bank, however, ought generally to be provided with a fund of gold so ample, as to enable it to pursue this line of conduct, with safety to itself, through the period of an unfavourable balance; a period, the duration of which may, to a certain degree, be estimated, though disappointment in a second harvest may cause much error in the calculation.

The more particular examination of this subject of an unfavourable exchange, brings us, therefore, to the same conclusion to which we were led in the former Chapter; namely, that the bank ought to avoid too contracted an issue of bank notes. The absence of gold, though itself an evil, may prevent other evils of greater moment; and may thus conduce, under certain circumstances, to the good of the country. Our gold has lately furnished the prompt payment for a part of that corn, which has been necessary for our consumption. The common manufacturer, if he understood his own interest, would approve rather than complain of the temporary substitution of paper for gold, which has been thus occasioned; for the export of gold has served to ease him in the first instance: his labour, indeed, must hereafter purchase back again the gold which has been exported, but he will have to buy it back by exertions less severe than would otherwise have been needful. The price of the goods which he manufactures, and, consequently, the price also of his own labour, is rendered somewhat higher by not glutting the foreign market with a quantity of articles altogether disproportionate to the demand. It should farther be remembered, that gold is an unproductive part of our capital: that the interest upon the sum exported is so much saved to the country: and that the export of gold serves, as far as it goes, to improve the exchange, by discharging the debt due on account of an unfavourable balance of trade; and to prevent the depreciation of our own paper currency, as compared with the current money payments of other countries.

It may probably be thought that the exported gold will not return. This subject may deserve a careful enquiry. It should be observed, in the first place, that, in order to produce an improvement in the exchange, we have only to suppose the present degree of the *pressure for payment* of goods imported to abate. It may happen, for instance, that in consequence of Hamburgh having become richer through the favourable harvest enjoyed in the surrounding countries, and through the high price obtained for its exported corn, while Britain has become poorer; the antecedent custom of Hamburgh merchants being in debt to London merchants may change, and a contrary custom may become prevalent. If this new debt of London to Hamburgh should be permitted to exist in the same manner as the Hamburgh debt may be supposed to have existed before, the exchange will not be affected by it. The debt which affects the exchange is only that sort of debt, the payment of which is more or less eagerly demanded. A country, therefore, seems likely soon to arrive at a limit in this respect. It has only to diminish not the debt itself, but the pressure of the demand for payment, and the exchange begins to mend. Let the two countries become equally satisfied to allow the debt to continue as it is, and the exchange finds its level. Again; let the country in debt prove itself to be somewhat more desirous to pay its debt, a debt of course running at interest, than the creditor country is to receive payment; and the exchange will be even in favour of the debtor country.

It may naturally be enquired what becomes of the gold which has been supposed to go from this country to Hamburgh; and how it comes to pass that it is there demanded in such large quantities. When Britain has already spared out of its circulation, and out of the coffers of its principal bank, many millions, perhaps, of gold; whence happens it that Europe, having only the same trade as before, uses all that is sent, and continues to call, by means of the exchange, for a still encreasing supply?

I understand that, at the period of every very favourable exchange to Hamburgh, most of the gold poured in thither is melted down into the several sorts of coin which are current on the continent; and that it then becomes an article of remittance to various places. It is, of course, remitted to those parts in which the balance of trade with Hamburgh is unfavourable to that city. Still, however, the difficulty of accounting for the new and *general* demand for gold seems to remain. The following considerations may afford some solution of it. When the trade of the world, or of many separate and considerable places, is more than usually fluctuating, as in times of political uncertainty or convulsion it can hardly fail to be, a larger quantity of gold is wanted than when confidence is high, and when the several exports and imports of different countries more nearly balance each other. Gold, during any extraordinary irregularity in trade between independent states, is the most commodious of all articles of remittance. It is a species of return which Hamburgh, for instance, can send to every place from which its spirit of speculation may have called for articles of commerce. It is, indeed, only the balance of the accounts which is paid in money; but, at different times, there may be balances of different sizes to be thus discharged. Whatever event, therefore, so disturbs the course of trade over the continent as to cause an encrease in the balances of the trade of independent countries, seems likely to cause an augmentation of the general demand for gold. But the general demand for gold is also affected by the degree of confidence at the same time subsisting. It has been already shewn, that the quantity of gold requisite for the circulation of any single country may be very different at different periods, and that the difference is proportioned to the degree of confidence between man and man existing at the several seasons. The quantity of gold wanted for the general trade of the world may also fluctuate, in some degree, from the same cause. It is, however, likely also to vary from a variation in the confidence subsisting between independent countries. For the sake of illustration, let us suppose that Hamburgh owes to some town in Prussia, one hundred miles distant, 100,000*l.* sterling, in consequence of an unfavourable balance of trade occasioned by corn purchased there, and exported by Hamburgh merchants to London; a balance which, if the creditors in the Prussian town were willing to wait six months, would probably by that time be repaid, and even more than repaid, through the importation into the same town of West India articles which Hamburgh would have received within that period from Great Britain. If confidence is high, the merchants of this town will be content, for the sake, perhaps, of an addition of one per cent. to the stipulated interest, to permit the debt to remain unextinguished for the six months; and in this case the course of exchange between the Prussian town and Hamburgh will alter to the extent of one per cent. But if, through the want of confidence subsisting between the Prussian town and Hamburgh, an addition not of one, but of two per cent. to the current interest should be considered to be the adequate compensation for the risk incurred, the exchange will fluctuate two per cent.; and a variation of two per cent. in the exchange will produce, let it be supposed, to the Hamburgh debtors a greater loss than would be incurred by the expence of transporting 100,000*l.* in gold to the Prussian town in question. Gold is, therefore, in that case, transported. On the two circumstances, taken together, of the largeness of the balance between the independent places, and the degree of confidence subsisting between them, appears to depend the quantity of bullion required. It seems, therefore, by no means difficult to account for the manner in which large quantities of gold exported from this country may be employed on the continent in seasons of general distrust, even though we should not suppose any great portion to be hoarded.

Bullion to a very large amount was retained in the Spanish settlements, during the latter period of the war, through the fear of capture; and perhaps, therefore, we might trace in part the want of gold, of which we have complained, to those successful exertions in watching the ports of the enemy which have been made by the British navy.

The immediate cause, however, of the exportation of our coin has been an unfavourable exchange, produced partly by our heavy expenditure, though chiefly by the superadded circumstance of two successively bad harvests. When the recurrence of a favourable balance of trade is long delayed, the fluctuation of the exchange may be expected to be not an immaterial one. The exchange is, in some degree, sustained for a time, which is thought likely to be short, through the readiness of foreigners to speculate in it; but protracted speculations of this sort do not equally answer, unless the fluctuation in the exchange is very considerable. If, for example, a foreigner remits money to London, at a period when the exchange has become unfavourable to England to the extent of three per cent., places it at interest in the hands of a British merchant, and draws for it in six months afterwards, the exchange having by that time returned to its usual level, he gains two and a half per cent. for half a year's interest on his money, and also three per cent. by the course of exchange, which is five and a half per cent. in half a year, or eleven per cent. per annum. But if the same foreigner remits money to England when the exchange has, in like manner, varied three per cent., and draws for it not in six months but in two years, the exchange having returned to its usual level only at the end of that long period, the foreigner than gains ten per cent. interest on his money, and three per cent. by the exchange, or thirteen per cent. in two years: that is to say, he gains in this case six and a half per cent. per annum, but in the other eleven per cent. per annum. If a variation of three per cent. is supposed necessary to induce foreigners to speculate for a period which is expected to end in six months, a variation of no less than twelve per cent. would be necessary to induce them to speculate for a period which is expected to end in two years. The improvement of our exchange with Europe having been delayed through a second bad harvest, it is not surprising that the expectation of its recovery within a short time should have been weakened in the mind of foreigners. Indeed, many circumstances, some of which have been already touched upon*, concurred,

* A mistaken idea of the bank payments having been suspended through the improper largeness of its loans to government, and of its resembling the continental banks which have issued excessive quantities of paper for the service of their several governments, was before stated to be not unlikely to have prevailed abroad, too much countenance having been given in this country to such a sentiment. Foreigners, if such was their opinion, would conceive that our exchange was a permanently declining one, and that it would, there-

157

towards the conclusion of the war, in rendering our exchange unfavourable.

Some gold, it may be presumed, was retained in the bank coffers, which, if the cash payments of that company had not been suspended, would have found its way to foreign countries, and have contributed to remedy the existing evil.

We depended chiefly, as will be shewn hereafter, on the proper limitation of the quantity of our circulating paper, though partly, also, on the degree of expectation which was kept up abroad of the future improvement of our exchange; an expectation which might be rendered greater or less by a variety of circumstances. Great Britain has had this great advantage over those countries which are in the habit either of depreciating their coin or of allowing a discount on their paper, that they, in anticipating the return of a more favourable state of their trade, look forward only to a time when their uncertain and unstable rate of exchange may be meliorated in a degree not easy to be calculated; whereas we have anticipated a period when an intrinsically valuable and specific standard would be restored, when our banks would be obliged to pay fully in guineas containing the same weight of gold as before, and when our exchange, therefore, might be expected completely to return to its former level.

Undoubtedly, circumstances of so great and extraordinary a nature may arise as to prevent the return of gold at an early or assignable period. It may, however, be safely affirmed, that when the main sources of a country's wealth are unimpaired; when its population, its industry, its manufacturing and trading capital, its general commerce, its credit, its colonial possessions, its political strength and independence, its laws and constitution remain; and when, moreover, its paper is confined within its accustomed

fore, answer better to them to draw than to remit, and to draw immediately than to delay drawing. The idea that foreign property might be seized in England, as an act of retaliation for the British property seized in the north of Europe, may also have had some influence. The expectation of seizures on each side would prejudice the exchange of whichever country was in debt, and the country in debt happened to be Great Britain.

bounds; the absence of its gold, more especially if it be the obvious consequence of one or more unfavourable seasons, is an evil which is likely neither to be durable, nor in any respect very important.

Under such circumstances, to alter materially the old and accustomed system of paper credit, and, in particular, to restrain in any very extraordinary degree the issues of paper of more responsible banks, is to deprive a country of those means of recovering itself which it naturally possesses. This seems to be the fair inference from the observations which have been stated in the present and preceding Chapters. The return of gold is to be promoted not so much by any legislative measure directed to that immediate object, as by cherishing the general industry, and attending to the higher and more leading interests of the community.

It may be proper here to add, that the experience of past times, both of war and peace, leads us to suppose, that the exchange between Great Britain and foreign countries is not likely to remain for any long period unfavourable to Great Britain. Experience has likewise proved, that the return of gold has not been precluded by the law which authorized the continuance of the suspension of the cash payments of the bank; for, while that law was in force, there occurred one season during which gold flowed with a remarkably strong tide into the country.

It seems scarcely necessary now to dwell on the reasons which evince that the repeal of the law in question, in the last period of the war, would have been inexpedient. It would have been to repeal it at a time not a little resembling that in which the parliament first thought proper to enact it: for it would have been to repeal it when gold had been recently drawn out of the country by an unfavourable exchange; and when we were subjected, as before, to alarms of invasion. To have opened the bank would have been, moreover, to have subjected it not only to a demand for gold on these two accounts, but also to such extra calls as might have arisen from the anxiety of the country banks to provide for the event of the first opening more amply than might have been permanently necessary. The renewal, therefore, of the law for suspending the cash payments of the bank stood on the ground of the particular circumstances of the times, and not on any principle which necessarily implied the permanence or even the long continuance of the suspension.

CHAP. VI

Error of imagining that Gold can be provided at the Time of actual Distress—Reasons for not admitting the Presumption that the Directors of the Bank must have been to blame for not making beforehand a more adequate Provision.

THE impracticability of encreasing the fund of gold in the Bank of England, when an alarm at home has already taken place, or even during the period of a very unfavourable balance of trade, has been manifested in the preceding pages.

There is a peculiar inconsistency in the supposition that a country ought, at such a season, to take its measures for encreasing the quantity of its gold. The argument for such an attempt would run thus—"The stock of gold has been in past time too low, as "appears by the experience of the present period; for it is not now "sufficient to supply what is necessary for our own circulation, and "to enable us also to pay our unfavourable balance. We ought, "therefore, to take due care that, in time to come, there shall be "a larger provision of gold in the country." So far, undoubtedly, there may be some general justice in the reasoning. But if the further inference is added, that we must, therefore, *now* begin to make the provision, this is to propose to take measures to provide against a want, which is future and contingent, at a time when that very want which we would prevent is actually pressing upon us. With as fair an appearance of justice it might have been argued in respect to the stock of corn in hand in the country—"The "stock of corn has been, as now appears, for some time too low; "for it is, at the present season, insufficient for the due supply of "the country. We ought, therefore, to take care that, in time to "come, there shall be a better provision for such contingencies "as the present." So far, undoubtedly, there might be justice in the observation. But to proceed in our reasoning as to corn, in the

Enquiry into Paper Credit   161   L

same manner as is sometimes done in respect to guineas, would be to add—"Therefore, now, while the scarcity is pressing upon "us, let us begin to make this provision; let us instantly stock our "granaries with a surplus quantity of corn; let us divert the little "grain which we possess from those most necessary uses to which "it is now destined. Let us encrease our present difficulty, in "order that the country may be put, for the future, out of the "reach of the danger which it is experiencing at the present hour." The two cases are not, indeed, precisely parallel; but there seems to be sufficient resemblance to justify the elucidation.

There is, however, another ground on which the directors of the bank may possibly be thought censurable—that of having failed to supply themselves with a sufficient quantity of gold at an antecedent period. Let us, therefore, enquire whether the public has sufficient reasons for entertaining this suspicion.

Let it be premised, that, since the directors of the Bank of England can have no particular temptation to improvidence; and since our national bank is, from its very nature, liable to that accident which has lately, for the first time, befallen it, a liability which, for obvious reasons, it may have been the custom too studiously to conceal, there is not all that previous presumption of blame which might be supposed. There can be no doubt that the credit of the Bank of England has been, at all periods, most anxiously consulted by its directors; and that present profit has uniformly been only the second consideration.

There are, however, certain limits which, even when gold is most easily purchased, the bank naturally prescribed to itself in respect to its stock of that article. The amount of the disposable effects of the bank, on the 26th of February, 1797, was stated under three heads in a former place; and it was then observed, that the only part of them which the bank itself could enlarge was the deposits lodged in return for bank notes issued. But even the bank notes cannot safely be encreased in a degree which is very considerable. Indeed, experience has proved, that there may be some sort of limit to the demand for them; for the applications for loans have often amounted, during peace, to less than the bank has been disposed to afford on the credit of good bills at the existing rate of discount.

Let us, then, proceed to illustrate our subject by supposing the disposable effects of the bank to have usually stood, for some years antecedent to the suspension of its cash payments, at the sum of about nineteen millions; that is to say, let us allow them to have been about a million and a half more than they amounted to at that period.

It must not be imagined that these nineteen millions could, at any time, be with propriety invested in gold. For the Bank of England, like every other mercantile establishment, carries on its business on such principles as will produce a profit. And the very lowest profit which can serve as a sufficient inducement to pursue the trade of banking, must be somewhat higher than the mere current interest of money. Let us reckon this *necessary profit* of the bank to be six per cent. The bank makes no more than three per cent. interest on the capital subscribed by its members, which is permanently lent to the government. It must, then, so manage its disposable effects as to gain an annual sum equal to an additional three per cent. upon its own capital, that is, about 350,000*l*. This it must do by lending out at interest a part of the nineteen millions; and it must lend out, at interest, a still farther part of it, both in order to defray the annual charges of its establishment, and in order also to furnish the means of paying those occasional sums to government which are required as the price of the renewal of its charter. It will be found, perhaps, that not less than ten or twelve of the nineteen millions must be always at interest in order to provide for these objects; and, consequently, that eight or nine millions will have formed the highest average sum which the bank can have kept in gold, consistently with the acquisition of merely the necessary profit on its capital. But neither is it fair to suppose, that these eight or nine millions ought to have been the general or average sum kept in gold. The cash of the bank fluctuates very greatly; and in order to secure the keeping of cash and bullion

163

to the average amount of eight or nine millions, it will occasionally have been necessary to keep twelve or fourteen millions, or possibly even more. This sum would be most unreasonably large; for, during the time when twelve or fourteen millions are invested in gold, the bank, instead of gaining six per cent. on its capital, will not gain above three or four; and, moreover, it cannot exactly know how long this extraordinary quantity of gold may continue in its coffers. It certainly can never count beforehand on those great reductions of cash which may serve, by increasing the sum at interest, to compensate for what is lost by a large detention of bullion: for the reduction of cash happens not through any measures taken by the bank, but in consequence of events difficult to be foreseen, and, as has been already shewn, by no means easy to be controlled. The bank, therefore, without impeachment of the character of its directors, may be reasonably presumed to have been at least somewhat indisposed to make investments in bullion, which, while they lasted, should reduce its income very far below the necessary annual profit.

Thus the bank, in endeavouring to secure what has been termed the necessary annual profit, would naturally be led to make, on the whole, something more than that profit; and, indeed, a variety of circumstances have lately occurred which have had a tendency to encrease its gains to a degree which must have been unexpected by the bank itself. Let us, then, suppose that the profits which the bank, considering all circumstances, may fairly and properly have derived from its business for some years past, may have been not six per cent. (which was spoken of as the lowest sum necessary for carrying on the trade of banking), but seven or eight per cent. Now seven or eight per cent. or a little more, seems likely to be that profit which the bank has, in point of fact, been gaining. The dividends which it has paid to the proprietors have been, for some time, seven per cent., and it has also added 3,800,000*l* to its capital. This addition has been accruing, no doubt, during a long course of years. If we assume that it has accumulated at the rate of about 116,000*l*. per annum, the bank will have gained annually one per cent. on its capital, besides the seven per cent. which has been divided; if at 232,000*l.** per annum, the bank will have gained annually two per cent. on its capital, besides the seven per cent. which has been divided.

The bank, then, let it be supposed, has been gaining eight or nine per cent. when seven or eight per cent. is as much as it is reasonable that it should have acquired. I have entered into this detail, which, in various parts, may be somewhat erroneous, merely for the sake of shewing that any proposed enquiry whether the quantity of gold kept by the bank may or may not have been too small, must necessarily be much narrower than many persons may imagine. According to the supposition just made, it can relate only to the propriety of a past annual gain of about one per cent. or at most of two per cent. on the bank capital. A gain of one per cent. would have been about 116,000*l.* per annum; and consequently the bank, by taking this gain, have, on an average, kept a stock of gold which has been smaller than it would otherwise have possessed by about 2,300,000*l.* Whether this sum of 2,300,000*l.* or whether any sum somewhat greater than this, or somewhat short of it, ought or ought not, in time past, to have been invested in gold in addition to the sum which was invested, is a point on which all that it seems safe to affirm with confidence, is, that no person unacquainted with the affairs of the bank can be capable of pronouncing any clear judgement. There must have existed many arguments, and some standing even on the ground of safety and credit, against maintaining the additional fund which has been mentioned.

If the whole profits of the bank had been lately restricted to seven per cent., they would have been limited to that sum which the bank proprietors had been for some time in the habit of receiving. They would have been confined to a sum which would not easily have admitted of accumulations. By obtaining a higher profit the

---

* This is to suppose that the savings of the bank have been between sixteen and seventeen years in accumulating, a period certainly much too short; but the accumulation must have been more rapid during the last years.

directors have secured to the proprietors the continuation of the same regular dividend, and have thus prevented that uncertainty which would have encouraged gambling in bank stock. They have also made, in the course of years, an important addition to their capital; an addition which has caused it to maintain nearly an uniform proportion to the growing extent of the transactions of the bank, and to the advancing commerce of the country; an addition also, by the help of which they have lately lent to government three millions without interest, for a short term of years, as the price of the renewal of their charter. They have thus strengthened that security which the creditors of the bank possess, so far as additional capital can strengthen it; and they will be able hereafter, if it shall seem necessary, to invest in gold, in addition to what they could otherwise have invested, a much larger sum than they could with any propriety have so invested in time past.

It must farther be borne in mind, that the necessity under which the bank has been placed of providing gold which is to fill the void occasioned by the disappearing of country bank notes, has been, in part, a new necessity, country bank notes not having circulated, at remoter periods, in so great a degree as they have lately; and that the additional sum of two or even of three or four millions would have been no security against the effects of a general alarm in the country. The fluctuation in the balance of trade with foreign countries, which we experience, is also become, in consequence of the greater extent of our population and commerce, larger than heretofore. The scale of all things having encreased, the scale of this balance may have encreased also to a degree unexpected by the bank. A war, moreover, unprecedented as that in which we have lately been engaged was not to be anticipated; and the case of a succession of two bad harvests, and of an importation of corn, amounting in two years to the value of fifteen or twenty millions, is felt by all to have been an extraordinary event. We need not wonder, then, if events unforeseen by others, were not foreseen by the Bank of England; nor if for unforeseen events an adequate provision was not at hand.

On the whole, it may be suggested to those who cast blame on the bank for its improvidence in time past, that they should consider well the several points which have here been briefly pointed out; and that if, afterwards, they continue to think the bank censurable, they should ask themselves, before they become the censurers, whether they are sure that, in taking upon themselves the office they exercise that candour with which they would expect to be judged if they had been themselves, during the late difficult and trying period, directors of that institution.

It has already been observed, that, in that crisis during which the conduct of the directors has been more particularly known, they proceeded, perhaps, with too great fear and caution rather than with too little. There seems, therefore, to be a presumption, that a character, if not for caution, at least for tolerable prudence, must have generally been their due. To say the least, there appears to be no ground for charging them with having acted in antecedent times on a directly opposite principle.

CHAP. VII

Of Country Banks—their Advantages and Disadvantages.

THE country banks in Great Britain appear to have amounted, in the year 1797, to three hundred and fifty-three. By a numeration taken in 1799, they appear to have been three hundred and sixty-six. By a third numeration taken in 1800, they were three hundred and eighty-six*. It seems, therefore, that no material addition to their number has arisen in these three years.

A great increase of country banks took place during the time which intervened between the American and the present war, and chiefly in the latter part of it; a period during which the trade, the agriculture, and the population of the country must have advanced very considerably. The circumstance of so many of our country banks having originated at such a time, affords a presumption that they are consequences and tokens of the prosperity, rather than indications of the declining state of the country. No banks have arisen in France during the period of its troubles, though several attempts to erect them have been made. It was with difficulty that any banks supported themselves in America during the war; but after the establishment of peace, banks were instituted in most of the American states. They seem naturally to belong to all commercial countries; but are more particularly likely to be multiplied in a state like ours, in which the mercantile transactions are extended, the population is great, and the expenditure of individuals considerable; and where also a principal bank exists, which, through the necessity imposed on it by its situation, undertakes the task of providing a constant reservoir of gold accessible to every smaller

---

* This statement of the number of country banks is taken from three printed accounts of them, the first of which may not have been very accurate, but may be presumed to state them at too low rather than too high a number. The two later enumerations were made in a more careful manner.

168

banking establishment. The creation of the large bank operates as a premium on the institution of the smaller.

A description of the origin of one of our smaller country banks may elucidate the subject before us. In every town, and in many villages, there existed, antecedently to the creation of what were afterwards termed banks, some trader, manufacturer, or shopkeeper, who acted, in many respects, as a banker to the neighbourhood. The shopkeeper, for example, being in the habit of drawing bills on London, and of remitting bills thither, for the purposes of his own trade, and receiving also much money at his shop, would occasionally give gold to his customers, taking in return their bills on the metropolis, which were mixed with his other bills, and sent to his London correspondent.

Persons who were not customers being also found to want either money for bills, or bills for money, the shopkeeper was led to charge something for his trouble on accommodating them: and the trade of taking and drawing bills being thus rendered profitable, it became an object to encrease it. For the sake of drawing custom to his house, the shopkeeper, having as yet possibly little or no view to the issuing of bank notes, printed "The Bank" over his door, and engraved these words on the checks on which he drew his bills.

It may be assumed, also, to have been not uncommon, before country banks were established, for the principal shopkeeper in a town to take at interest some of the money of his neighbours, on the condition, however, that he should not be required to pay it back without some notice. The money thus deposited with him, or borrowed by him (it is difficult to say which term is the more proper), might either be thrown into his trade, or employed in discounting bills soon to become due; but the latter would evidently be the more safe and prudent way of investing it.

All these parts of the banking business arose out of the situation and circumstances of the country; and existed in many places before the name of banker was assumed.

The practice of issuing country bank notes, that is to say,

notes payable to the bearer on demand, may, undoubtedly, be considered as a separate branch of business. These notes, however, have been shown to be not so very different in their nature from other paper as is commonly imagined.

For the sake of more particularly proving this point, let us advert to the nature of interest notes, a species of paper which some country banks have issued to a great extent. Even the shopkeeper, it was lately observed, would take sums at interest. For each of these sums, especially if he became a banker, he would give out his note, in which would be expressed the sum lent or deposited, the rate of interest upon it, and the time which was to intervene before payment could be demanded. This note would be transferable to any third person. There would, however, be some impediments to its circulation. The interest must be calculated as often as it should change hands. Some of the persons to whom it was offered might not be disposed to accept it as a payment, especially if it had a long time to run. Although these notes might circulate, they would circulate heavily. In order to promote their circulation, and thus encrease the whole number of issuable notes, the banker would be inclined to lessen the time within which they should be payable; and he would find that, in proportion as he adopted this practice, a lower rate of interest on the notes would suffice to induce persons to take them. Notes carrying no interest would circulate, if due within a short time, better than notes bearing interest which should be due at a very distant period. But the only notes which would circulate freely would be those which should be payable, or at least paid, without any notice. Some banks wishing, on the one hand, to encourage the circulation of their paper, and, on the other, to avoid the inconvenience of a strict obligation to pay without notice have issued notes payable after a certain time, and yet have been in the regular practice of giving money for them whenever payment was demanded, and have taken no discount for the accommodation.

Thus, then, the shorter the notice is, the greater is the currency of the note; and, in proportion, therefore, as the circumstances of a country render it more safe for the banks to shorten their notice,

170

in the same proportion it may be expected that notes to the bearer on demand will be issued, and gold displaced.

Some speculative persons have imagined, that the practice pursued by bankers of emitting notes payable on demand is founded on an altogether vicious and unwarrantable principle, inasmuch as such paper is issued with a view to a profit which is to be obtained only by lending out part of the sum necessary for the payment. A number of promises, it is said, are thus made, which the banker has evidently placed it out of his power to perform, supposing the fulfilment of them all to be required at the same time, an event by no means impossible. This objection implies that the banker ought not, after receiving the deposits left with him by his customers, to lend out part of the sum necessary for the payment of these deposits; for he is much bound to discharge demands for deposits without notice, as to pay without notice all his notes. The Bank of England, the London banker, the country banker, the merchant, and also the individual of every class, proceed, in respect to all their promises to pay money, not on any principle of moral certainty, but on that of reasonable and sufficient probability. The objection to bank notes, *as such*, if pushed to that extent to which, if it is at all just, it might be carried, would apply to all verbal promises to pay money, and, indeed, to almost all promises whatever; for there is scarcely any class of these for the performance of which a *perfectly sure* provision is always made at the time of giving the promise. The objection implies, therefore, that men ought to be prohibited from acting in their commercial concerns according to that rule of sufficient probability by which all the other affairs of human life are conducted*.

---

* In some of the democratic pamphlets of the present day, bank notes of every kind are spoken of not merely as liable to be carried to excess, or to be issued by irresponsible persons, or as producing particular evils, but as radically and incurably vicious; they are considered in the light of a complete fraud upon the public, which is practised by the rich, and connived at by the government; and the very issue of them has been stigmatized as equivalent to the crime of forgery. The resemblance of bank notes to other paper, and the resemblance of a promise on paper to any other promise, have been here touched upon with a view of exposing the absurdity of those doctrines.

It is completely understood by the holders of notes, as well as by the customers of banks, that instant payment is provided for only a part of that sum which may, by possibility, be demanded; and the banker, therefore, seems fully justified if he makes such provision as the general and known usage of others in the same profession (for he is supposed, by those who. trust him, to follow this usage), and a prudent regard to all the circumstances of his own case teach him to consider as sufficient.

The practice of issuing notes payable to bearer on demand became very common a few years antecedent to the present war, when various circumstances united to encourage this part of the country banker's employment. Confidence was then high, the number of traders in the country had been greatly multiplied, the income and expenditure of individuals were much increased, and every branch, therefore, of the banking business had naturally enlarged itself. Some addition had been made to the number of London bankers; and a few of these took forward and active measures to encourage the formation even of very small banks in the country, with a view to the benefit expected from a connection with them. In many of our great towns a fair opening was afforded for the erection of additional banks. These new establishments having taken place, various country traders, who had before made use of their own correspondents in London, fell into the practice of transacting their business with the metropolis through the medium of the country banker with whom they kept their cash. The country banker drew largely on a London banker on the account of the country traders, and the London banker was willing to execute the extensive country business which he thus acquired, in consideration of a much lower commission than had before been paid by the several country traders to their separate correspondents in London, who had been, for the most part, London merchants. The reduction of the rate of commission arose from two causes: first, from the new security which was afforded to the transactions between the town and the country, by the interposition of the credit of rich and responsible country banks; and, secondly, from the transfer to one house of that labour of keeping accounts, writing letters, and receiving and paying bills, which had, before, been divided among many. The risk and trouble being diminished, a proportionate abatement in the rate of commission could be afforded.

The multiplication even of country banks, purposing to deal chiefly in bills, would tend, in many ways, to produce an encreased issue of notes on demand. Some deposit of gold would be kept by banks of every class, with the view of satisfying the demands of their customers; and the stock, maintained for this purpose, would would form a part of the necessary provision for the payment of notes payable on demand, and it would, therefore, become an encouragement to the issue of them. The multiplication of deposits of gold through the country would, moreover, furnish, in many cases, more prompt means of obtaining gold on any sudden emergency; since one country bank might often procure a supply from a neighbouring one, especially if a good understanding on this subject should subsist between them. The establishment of mail coaches afforded, at the same time, a more cheap and ready method than before, of bringing gold from London, as well as of transmitting thither any superfluity of it which might arise in the country. In proportion to the facility of obtaining gold, the unproductive stock of it kept in hand might be reduced; or, if the same stock should be maintained, the issue of notes payable on demand would be less hazardous. Indeed, a few old and respectable country banks had long been in the habit of emitting much paper of this sort, and had seldom experienced any inconvenience from doing it. The new ones, therefore, many of which were not at all inferior in property to the old, were led into the practice partly by example.

The circumstance which chiefly operated in procuring currency to the new circulating paper, was that participation of the benefit resulting from it which was enjoyed by the customers of the country banker; for he lent among them the capital which was acquired by the issue of his paper, and they became his instruments in sending it into circulation, by accepting it as a ready-money payment in return for bills discounted. In consideration of their obligations to

173

the banker, and of the interest which they had in his stability, they were also forward, on most occasions, in the support of his credit. Such appear to have been the chief circumstances which led to that great encrease of our country banks, and to that substitution of paper in the place of gold, which have been, for some years past, so much the subject of complaint.

In order to assist the reader in judging whether a preponderance of good or of evil results from our numerous country banks, an endeavour shall now be made to enumerate the principal benefits as well as inconveniences of them.

That country banks have, in a variety of respects, been highly advantageous, can scarcely admit of a doubt. They have afforded an accommodation to many descriptions of persons; but more especially to those who are engaged in commerce. They may be regarded as an effect of that division of labour which naturally takes place in every opulent country. The receipts and the payments of money are now no longer conducted at home, even by the middling trader, but are become a separate branch of business in the hands of bankers. It was to be expected that they to whom this employment has been transferred would find means of abridging labour, and of sparing the use of coin, the most expensive circulating medium. By their skill in attaining these objects, they transact an important portion of the business of the trader at an expense far inferior to that which he must incur were he to conduct it by his own clerks; and they derive a profit to themselves, which, no less than the saving to the customer, may be regarded as clear gain to the kingdom.

Country banks are also useful by furnishing to many persons the means of laying out at interest, and in a safe manner, such money as they may have to spare. Those banks, in particular, which give interest notes for very small sums, afford to the middling and to the lower class of people an encouragement to begin to lay up property, and thus to make provision for the time of sickness or old age. Country banks also furnish a very convenient method of distributing to one class of men the superfluity of another. All who have money to spare know where they can place it, without expence or loss of time, not only in security, but often with pecuniary advantage: and all commercial persons of credit understand in what quarter they can obtain such sums, in the way of loan, as their circumstances will fairly warrant them in borrowing. While country banks thus render a benefit of the first magnitude to fair and prudent commerce, they are important barriers against rash speculation, though not unfrequently they are loudly accused of favouring it. However some few banks may have subjected themselves to this charge, banks in general, and particularly those which have been long established, take care to lend the sums which have been deposited in their hands, not to the imprudent speculator, or to the spendthrift, by whom they are in danger of suffering loss, but to those who, being known to possess some wealth and to manage their concerns with prudence, give proof that they are likely to repay the loan. Borrowers of this class are not apt to enter into very large and perilous undertakings; for they are unwilling to risk the loss of their own capital. Bankers, especially men of eminence, feel a special motive to circumspection, in addition to that which operates with other lenders. The banker always lends under an impression that, if he places in anyone a boundless or immoderate confidence, the imprudence will necessarily be known, in case the borrower should fail, as the affairs of every bankrupt are laid open to the body of creditors; and that his rashness is, therefore, liable to become the subject of conversation among his customers. Indiscretion of this kind, even if the particular instance be of no prominent magnitude, may thus prove an occasion of injuring the character and credit of the banking house, and of lessening the general profits of the business.

The banker also enjoys, from the nature of his situation, very superior means of distinguishing the careful trader from him who is improvident. The bill transactions of the neighbourhood pass under his view: the knowledge, thus obtained, aids his judgment; and confidence may, therefore, be measured out by him more nearly than by another person, in the proportion in which ground for it exists. Through the creation of banks, the appreciation of the credit of numberless persons engaged in commerce has become a science; and to the height to which this science is now carried in Great Britain we are in no small degree indebted for the flourishing state of our internal commerce, for the general reputation of our merchants abroad, and for the preference which in that respect they enjoy over the traders of all other nations. It is certainly the interest, and, I believe, it is also the general practice, of banks to limit not only the loan which any one trader shall obtain from themselves, but the total amount also, as far as they are able, of the sum which the same person shall borrow in different places; at the same time, reciprocally to communicate intelligence for their mutual assistance; and, above all, to discourage bills of accommodation. While the transactions of the surrounding traders are thus subject to the view of the country banks, those of the country banks themselves come under the eye of their respective correspondents, the London bankers; and, in some measure, likewise, of the Bank of England. The Bank of England restricts, according to its discretion, the credit given to the London banker. Thus a system of checks is established, which, though certainly very imperfect, answers many important purposes, and, in particular, opposes many impediments to wild speculation.

Country banks, also, as well as the Bank of England, have been highly beneficial, by adding, through the issue of their paper, to the productive capital of the country*. By this accession our manu-

* Dr. Smith remarks, that it is not by augmenting the capital of the country, but by rendering a greater part of that capital active and productive than would otherwise be so, that the most judicious operations of banking can increase the industry of the country. "Dead stock," he observes, "is converted into active and productive stock." Whether the introduction of the use of paper is spoken of as turning dead and unproductive stock into stock which is active and productive, or as *adding* to the stock of the country, is much the same thing. The less the stock of gold is, the greater will be the stock of other kinds; and if a less stock of gold will, through the aid of paper, equally well perform the work of a larger stock, it may be fairly said that the use of paper furnishes even *additional* stock to the country. Thus, for example, the use of a new sort of machinery which costs less in the erection than that which was employed before, and which just as effectually does the work required, since it enables the owner to have always more goods in the course of manufacture, while he has exactly the same means of manufacturing them, might not improperly be described as adding to the stock of the country.

factures, unquestionably, have been very much extended, our foreign trade has enlarged itself, and the landed interest of the country has had a share of the benefit. The common charge which is brought against country banks, of having raised up a fictitious capital in the country, admits of the following answer. They have substituted, it is true, much paper in the place of gold : but the gold which has gone abroad has brought back, as Dr. Smith observes, valuable commodities in return. The guinea spared from circulation has contributed to bring home the timber which has been used in building, the iron or the steel which has been instrumental to the purposes of machinery, and the cotton and the wool which the hand of the manufacturer has worked up. The paper has thus given to the country a *bonâ fide* capital which has been exactly equal to the gold which it has caused to go abroad; and this additional capital has contributed, just like any other part of the national stock, to give life to industry.

It has lately been objected to paper credit, that, by supplying the farmers with large loans, it has enabled them to keep back their corn from the market, and enhance the price. It is true, that farmers, both in the last and many preceding years, may have obtained larger loans than they would have procured if no country bank notes had existed. The capital so furnished to the farmers may possibly have induced some of them, at certain times, to keep in hand a larger quantity of grain than they would otherwise have found it convenient to hold. We know, however, that the general stock of grain in the autumn of 1800 was particularly low. Since, therefore, but a small part of the capital of the farmers, whether borrowed or their own, was then vested in grain, the principal share would probably be laid out on their land, and would encrease its produce; for, unquestionably, the value of a crop obtained from a farm depends chiefly on the sum employed in cultivation and improvement. Country bank notes have thus added to the general supply of grain; and, by doing so, have contributed to prevent a rise in its price: they have, probably, in this manner, afforded much more than a compensation for any temporary advance in price to which they may have given occasion by enabling farmers to keep a larger quantity in hand. The very possession of a large quantity in hand is to be considered as, in general, a benefit rather than a disadvantage; for it is our chief security against scarcity, and, consequently, also against dearness. To the want of a large surplus stock at the end of the years 1799 and 1800 is to be ascribed, in a great degree, the subsequent high price of provisions. The tendency, therefore, of country bank paper to encrease generally the stock of grain in the hands of the farmer is to be ranked among the advantages of country banks. The tendency to encrease it at the particular time of actual scarcity, is to be classed among the evils which they produce; and it is an inconsiderable evil, which is inseparable from a great and extensive good. To those who are disposed to magnify this occasional evil, it may be further observed, that the farmer is enabled to enlarge his stock by the encrease of his own as well as of the general wealth, much more, no doubt, than by the share which he obtains of that particular part of the new capital of the kingdom which is created through the substitution of country bank notes for gold; only a portion, therefore, of the mischief complained of is to be referred to country bank notes. It is principally to be ascribed to the growing riches and prosperity both of the farmers and other inhabitants of the country.

It is no small additional recommendation of the use of our paper, that the public draws a large yearly revenue from the tax imposed on bills and notes. If paper credit did not exist, a sum equal to that which is thus raised must be supplied by taxes either burthening the industry, or paid out of the property of the people. The public has, since the late additional tax, become a very considerable sharer in the profits of the country bankers' business.

Since, therefore, a paper medium has served the purposes which have been described, and has been, generally speaking, quite as convenient an instrument in settling accounts as the gold which it has displaced, the presumption in favour of its utility seems to be very great; and, if it could be added, that no other effects than those which have as yet been stated have arisen or are likely to arise from it, the advantage of it would be beyond dispute. To reproach it with being a merely fictitious thing, because it possesses not the intrinsic value of gold, is to quarrel with it on account of that quality which is the very ground of its merit. Its merit consists in the circumstance of its costing almost nothing. By means of a very cheap article the country has been, for some years, transacting its money concerns, in which a very expensive material had previously been employed. If this were the whole question, the substitution of paper for gold would be as much to be approved as the introduction of any other efficacious and very cheap instrument in the place of a dear one. It would stand on the same footing with the substitution, for example, of cast iron for wrought iron or steel; of water carriage for land carriage; of a steam engine for the labour of men and horses; and might claim a high rank among that multitude of ingenious and economical contrivances to be found among us, by the aid of which we have attained to the present unrivalled state of our manufactures and commerce.

Some very solid objections, however, may be urged against the system of banking in the country.

The first which I shall mention, is, the tendency of country banks to produce, occasionally, that general failure of paper credit, and with it that derangement and suspension of commerce, as well as intermission of manufacturing labour, which have been already spoken of.

Country bank notes, and especially the smaller ones, circulate, in a great measure, among people out of trade, and pass occasionally into the hands of persons of the lower class; a great proportion, therefore, of the holders of them, have few means of judging of the comparative credit of the several issuers, and are commonly almost as ready to take the paper of any one house calling itself a bank as that of another. A certain degree of currency being thus given to inferior paper, even the man who doubts the ultimate solvency of the issuer is disposed to take it; for the time during which he intends to detain it is very short, and his responsibility will cease almost as soon as he shall have parted with it*. Moreover, the amount of each note is so small, that the risk seems, also, on that account, insignificant. The notes of the greater and of the smaller country banks, thus obtaining, in ordinary times, a nearly similar currency, they naturally fall at a season of alarm into almost equal discredit. If any one bank fails, a general run upon the neighbouring ones is apt to take place, which if not checked in the beginning by a pouring into the circulation a large quantity of gold, leads to very extensive mischief. Many country bankers, during a period of danger, prescribe to themselves a principle of more than ordinary reserve in the issue of their notes, because they consider these as the more vulnerable part of their credit. They know, that if the character of their house should be brought into question, through the fears or even the caprice of any of those strangers into whose hands their circulating paper passes, some distrust may be excited among their customers, the effect of which may be a sudden demand for the payment of large deposits. The amount, therefore, of the country bank notes circulating in the kingdom is liable to great fluctuation. The country banker, in case of an alarm, turns a part of the government securities, bills of exchange, or other property which he has in London, into Bank of England notes, and those notes into money; and thus discharges many of his own circulating notes, as well as enlarges the fund of gold in his coffers. The Bank of England has, therefore, to supply these occasional wants of the country banker; and, in order to be fully prepared to do this, it has, ordinarily, to keep a quantity of gold equal to that of the notes liable to be extinguished, as well as a quantity which shall satisfy the other extraordinary demands which may be made at the same season of consternation either by banking houses, or by individuals.

* I apprehend that, supposing a country bank to fail, the holder of one of its notes, who should have parted with it in sufficient time to afford to the next holder an opportunity of applying for the discharge of it before the day of failure, could not be called upon for the payment of the value of it. The responsibility therefore, of him who has been the holder of a country bank note commonly ceases in about one or two days after it has been parted with. That of the holder of a bill continues till after the bill is due, namely, for a period, perhaps, of one or two months.

Thus the country banker by no means bears his own burthen, while the Bank of England sustains a burthen which is not its own, and which we may naturally suppose that it does not very cheerfully endure*.

The national bank, indeed, may fairly be called upon, in consideration of the benefits enjoyed through its monopoly, to submit to a considerable expence in supplying gold for the country; but there must be some bounds to the claims which can equitably be made upon it: and, in estimating the benefit arising to the kingdom from the use of country bank notes, we have either to deduct the loss which the Bank of England incurs by maintaining an additional supply of gold sufficient to answer the demands which they occasion, or else we have to take into consideration the risk which the bank incurs by only keeping a fund of gold which is somewhat inadequate. The country banks may, perhaps, cause the bank in some measure to encrease its general fund of gold, though not to hold so much of this unproductive article as to afford a security equal to that which the bank would enjoy if no country bank notes existed.

It is obvious, that the additional capital given to the kingdom through the use of country bank notes must not be measured by the amount of those notes, but that a deduction must be made of the sum kept in gold in the coffers of the issuers, as their provision for the occasional payments to which their bank paper subjects them. The other deduction, which has been spoken of, is of the same nature. It is a second deduction, which must be made on account of a similar, and, perhaps, no less considerable provision for the payment of country bank notes, which is rendered necessary

---

* At the time of the distress of 1793, some great and opulent country banks applied to the Bank of England for aid, in the shape of discount, which was refused on account of their not offering approved London securities: some immediate and important failures were the consequence. The Bank of England was indisposed to extend its aid to houses in the country. The event, however, shewed that the relief of the country was necessary to the solvency of the metropolis. A sense of the unfairness of the burthen cast on the bank by the large and sudden demands of the banking establishments in the country, probably contributed to produce an unwillingness to grant them relief.

to be kept in the coffers of the Bank of England. In other words, the capital given to the country, through the use of country bank notes, is only equal (and it was so stated in speaking of that subject) to the amount of the gold which they cause to be exported.

I shall endeavour here to explain more particularly than has yet been done, some of those circumstances which cause a great diminution of country bank notes to bring distress on London, and to end in a general failure of commercial credit.

In a former chapter it was observed, that when that alarm among the common people, which produces an unwillingness to take country bank paper, and an eagerness for gold has risen to a considerable height, some distrust is apt to be excited among the higher class of traders; and that any great want of confidence in this quarter produces an encreased demand for that article, which is, among London bankers and merchants, in much the same credit as gold; I mean Bank of England notes, and which forms, at all times, the only circulating medium of the metropolis in all the larger transactions of its commerce. This more than usual demand for Bank of England notes the bank is at such a time particularly unwilling to satisfy, for reasons which I shall endeavour fully to detail. The reader will have been prepared to enter into them by the observations on the subject of the bank, introduced towards the close of the chapter which treated of that institution.

First, the bank may be supposed to be unwilling to satisfy that somewhat *encreased* demand for its notes which a season of consternation is apt to produce, because it is not unlikely to partake, in some degree, in the general alarm, especially since it must necessarily be supposed to have already suffered, and to be still experiencing a formidable reduction of the quantity of its gold. The natural operation of even this general sort of fear must be to incline it to contract its affairs, and to diminish rather than enlarge its notes.

But it must also be recollected, that the bank has necessarily been led already to encrease its loans in the same degree in which its gold has been reduced, provided it has maintained in circulation the accustomed quantity of notes. This point was explained in the

182

chapter on the subject of the bank. The directors, therefore, must seem to themselves to act with extraordinary liberality towards those who apply to them for discounts, if they only go as far as to maintain the usual, or nearly the usual, quantity of notes. The liberality in lending which they must exercise, if, when the gold is low, they even augment their paper, must be very extended indeed.

In order to render this subject more clear, let us suppose that an extra demand on the Bank of England for three millions of gold has been made through the extinction of the paper of country banks, and through the slower circulation and hoarding of gold which have attended the general alarm. Let us assume, also, that the bank, during the time of its supplying this gold, has thought proper to reduce its notes one million. It will, in that case, have necessarily encreased its loans two millions. Let us further assume, as we not very unreasonably may, that the two millions of additional loans have been afforded, not to the government, who owe a large and standing sum to the bank (suppose eight or ten millions besides the bank capital), but exclusively to the merchants; and let the total amount of loans antecedently afforded to the merchants be reckoned at four millions. The bank, in this case, will have raised its discounts to the merchants from four millions to six; that is, it will have encreased them one half, even though it has diminished its notes one million. This extension of the accustomed accommodation to the mercantile world must appear to call for the thanks of that body, rather than to leave any room for complaint; and yet it is plain from reasoning, and, I believe, it might be also proved from experience, that it will not ease the pressure. The difficulties in London, notwithstanding this additional loan of *two* millions to the merchants will be somewhat encreased; for a sum in gold, amounting to *three* millions, has been drawn from the bank by the London agents of the country bankers and traders, and has been sent by those agents into the country. London, therefore, has furnished for the country circulation three millions of gold; and it has done this by getting discounted at the bank two additional millions of bills, for which it has received two of the millions of gold, and by sparing one million

183

of its circulating notes as a means of obtaining the other million. This reduction of the usual quantity of notes is borne by the metropolis with peculiar difficulty at a time of general alarm. However liberally, therefore, the bankers and merchants may acknowledge themselves to have been already relieved by the bank, they will repeat, and will even urge more than ever, their application for discounts.

It may be observed, with a view to the further elucidation of this part of our subject, that both the bank, and they who borrow of it, are naturally led to fix their attention rather on the amount of the loans furnished than on that of the notes in circulation. The bank is used to allow to each borrower a sum bearing some proportion to his supposed credit; but seldom or never exceeding a certain amount. It is true, the various borrowers do not always in an equal degree avail themselves of their power of raising money at the bank; and, therefore, a material enlargement of the sum total of the bank loans may take place at a moment of difficulty, through the encreased use which some of the richer merchants then make of their credit, as well as through the creation of a few new borrowers at the bank. The directors also, in particular cases, may suffer their rule to be relaxed. The circumstance, however, of the general principle on which the bank ordinarily, and, indeed, naturally proceeds, being that of a limitation of the amount of each of its loans to individuals, must tend, as I conceive to place something like a general limit to the total sum lent. It must conduce to prevent the fluctuation in the bank loans from keeping pace with the variation in the necessities of the public, and must contribute to produce a reduction of notes at that season of extraordinary distrust, when the state of the metropolis, as was more fully remarked in a former part of this Work, calls rather for their encrease.

That the borrowers at the bank are likely to pay no attention to the subject of the total quantity of notes in circulation, is easily shewn. They have, indeed, no means of knowing their amount. They can only judge of the liberality of the bank by the extent of its loans; and of this they form an imperfect estimate by the sum which they or their connexions have been able to obtain. Scarcely any one reflects, that there may be a large encrease of the general loans of the bank, as well as possibly an extension of each loan to individuals, while there is a diminution of the number of bank notes; and that the amount of the notes, not that of the loans, is the object on which the eye should be fixed, in order to judge of the facility of effecting the payments of the metropolis.

It was remarked, in a former chapter, that the bank, at the time antecedent to the suspension of its cash payments, having diminished the sum lent by it to government, and enlarged, though not in an equal degree, that furnished to the merchants, the pressure on the merchants was not relieved, as was expected, by the encreased loan afforded them, but even grew more severe. It was also shewn, that this could not fail to be the case, since the bank notes necessary for effecting the current payments of the metropolis were then diminished, and since the additional loans afforded to the merchants only in part compensated for the new pressure which was created in the general money market of the kingdom, by the circumstance of the government being obliged to become a great borrower in that market. Whenever the bank materially lessens its paper, similar pressure is likely to be felt. Neither the transfer of the bank loans from the government to the merchants, nor even a large encrease of its loans, when that encrease is not carried so far as is necessary to the maintenance of the accustomed, or nearly the accustomed, quantity of bank paper, can prevent, as I apprehend, distress in the metropolis; and this distress soon communicates itself to all parts of the kingdom. The short explanation of the subject is this. Many country bank notes having disappeared, a quantity of gold is called for, which is so much new capital suddenly needed in the country. The only place in which any supply of gold exists is the Bank of England. Moreover, the only quarter from whence the loan of the new capital, under all the circumstances of the case, can come, is also the Bank of England; for the gold in the bank is the only dead or sleeping stock in the kingdom which is convertible into the new active capital which is wanted. The bank,

185

therefore, must *lend* the gold which it furnishes; it must lend, that is to say, to some individuals a sum equal to the gold which other individuals have taken from it: otherwise it does not relieve the country.

If it should be asked, Why does not the bank in such case demand something intrinsically valuable, instead of contenting itself with mere paper in return?—the answer is, first, that if the bank were to receive goods in exchange for its gold, or, in other words, were to purchase goods, it would have afterwards to sell them; and it would then become a trading company, which it is forbid to be by its charter: it is allowed to traffic only in bullion. The answer is, secondly, that if it were to take goods as a mere security, and to detain them as such, it would then prevent their passing into consumption with the desirable expedition. By proceeding on either of these plans, it would also involve itself in a degree of trouble which would not be very consistent with the management of the business of a banking company*. It may be answered, thirdly, that the bills which the bank discounts, are, generally speaking, so safe, that the security either of goods, or stocks, or land, none of which are received in pledge by the directors, may be considered as nearly superfluous. A very small proportion of the five per cent. discount, gained upon the bills turned into ready money at the bank, has compensated, as I believe, for the whole of the loss upon them, even in the years of the greatest commercial failures which have yet been known.

The observations which have now been made sufficiently shew what is the nature of that evil of which we are speaking. It is an evil which ought to be charged not to any fault in the mercantile body, but to the defects of the banking system. It is a privation which the merchants occasionally experience of a considerable part of that

---

* Of the parliamentary loan of exchequer bills in 1793, which was directed to be granted on the security either of sufficient bondsmen, or of a deposit of goods, only a small proportion was taken on the latter principle, on account of the great obstruction to the sale of goods, which was thought to arise from warehousing them on the account of the commissioners appointed by parliament. It has been already remarked, that no part of the sum lent was lost.

186

circulating medium which custom has rendered essential to the punctual fulfilment of their engagements. In good times, the country banks furnish this necessary article, which they are enabled to do through the confidence of the people in general; but when an alarm arises, the country banks cease to give it out, the people refusing what they had before received; and the Bank of England, the only body by whose interposition the distress can be relieved, is somewhat unwilling to exercise all the necessary liberality, for the reasons which have been so fully mentioned. The merchants are some of the chief sufferers, and they are generally, also, loaded with no inconsiderable share of censure; but the public, the country banks, and the Bank of England, may more properly divide the blame.

The mischief produced by a general failure of paper credit is very considerable. How much such a failure interrupts trade and manufacturing industry, and, therefore, ultimately also tends to carry gold out of the country, has been already stated at large. It also causes a great, though merely temporary, fall in the market price of many sorts of property; and thus inflicts a partial and very heavy loss on some traders, and throws extraordinary gain into the hands of others; into the hands, I mean, of those who happen to have superior powers of purchasing at the moment of difficulty. By giving to all banking, as well as mercantile, transactions the appearance of perilous undertakings, it deters men of large property, and of a cautious temper, from following the profession of bankers and merchants. It creates no small uneasiness of mind, even among traders who surmount the difficulties of the moment. Above all, it reduces many respectable, prudent, and, ultimately, very solvent persons to the mortifying necessity of stopping payment; thus obliging them to share in that discredit, in which, it is much to be desired, that traders of an opposite character only should be involved. If, indeed, we suppose, as we necessarily must, that, on account of the multitude of failures which happen at the same time, the discredit of them is much diminished, then another evil is produced, which, in a commercial country, is very great. Acts of insolvency, leaving less stigma on the character, become not so much dreaded as might be wished. The case of some, who bring difficulties on themselves, being almost unavoidably confounded with that of persons whose affairs have been involved through the entanglement of paper credit, to stop payment is considered too much as a misfortune or accident, and too little as a fault; and thus a principal incentive to punctuality in mercantile payments is weakened, and an important check to adventurous speculation is in some measure lost.

The observations which have been made will, however, shew that the tendency of country bank paper to produce a general failure of paper credit, is an evil which may be expected to diminish; for, first, if the Bank of England, in future seasons of alarm, should be disposed to extend its discounts in a greater degree than heretofore, then the threatened calamity may be averted through the generosity of that institution*. If, secondly, the country bankers should be taught (as, in some degree, unquestionably they must), by the difficulties which they have experienced, to provide themselves with a larger quantity of that sort of property which is quickly convertible into Bank of England notes, and, therefore, also, into gold, then the country bankers will have in their own hands a greater power of checking the progress of an alarm. Still, indeed, their resource will be the gold which is in the bank. The encreased promptitude, however, with which the greater convertibility of their funds will enable them to possess themselves of a part of the bank treasure, will render a smaller supply of it sufficient; and this smaller supply may be expected to be furnished, without difficulty, either by means of such a trifling addition to the bank loans as the bank will not refuse,

* It is by no means intended to imply, that it would become the Bank of England to relieve every distress which the rashness of country banks may bring upon them : the bank, by doing this, might encourage their improvidence. There seems to be a medium at which a public bank should aim in granting aid to inferior establishments, and which it must often find very difficult to be observed. The relief should neither be so prompt and liberal as to exempt those who misconduct their business from all the natural consequences of their fault, nor so scanty and slow as deeply to involve the general interests. These interests, nevertheless, are sure to be pleaded by every distressed person whose affairs are large, however indifferent or even ruinous may be their state.

188

or by sparing the necessary sum from the paper circulation of the metropolis, which, if commercial confidence is not impaired, will always admit of some slight and temporary reduction. The Bank of England will itself profit by the circumstance of its gold becoming more accessible to the country banks; for the untoward event of a general failure of paper credit will thus be rendered less probable, and, therefore, a smaller stock of gold will be an equally sufficient provision for the extraordinary demands at home to which the bank will be subject. Or if, thirdly, those among whom country bank notes circulate should learn to be less variable as to the confidence placed by them in country paper, or even to appreciate more justly the several degrees of credit due to the notes of different houses, then the evil which was before supposed to be obviated by the liberality of the Bank of England, or by the prudence of the country banker, will abate through the growth of confidence and the diffusion of commercial knowledge among the public. It seems likely that by each of these means, though especially in the second mode which was mentioned, the tendency of country bank notes to produce an occasional failure of commercial credit will be diminished. In time past, the mischief has been suffered to grow till it appeared too formidable to be encountered; and this has happened partly in consequence of our wanting that knowledge and experience which we now possess.

Another evil attending the present banking system in the country is the following.

The multiplication of country banks issuing small notes to bearer on demand, by occasioning a great and permanent diminution in our circulating coin, serves to encrease the danger, lest the standard by which the value of our paper is intended to be at all times regulated should occasionally not be maintained.

The evils of a great depreciation of paper currency are considerable. In proportion as the article which forms the current payment for goods drops in value, the current price of goods rises. If the labourer receives only the same nominal wages as before the depreciation took place, he is underpaid. Antecedent pecuniary contracts, though nominally, and, perhaps, legally fulfilled, are not performed with due equity. It is true, that the general stock of wealth in the country may remain nearly the same; and it is possible that the circulating paper may be restored to its full value when the period of the particular difficulty shall have passed by. Some degree, however, of unfairness and inequality will, in the mean time, have been produced, and much pressure may have been felt by the lower classes of people, whose wages are seldom raised until some time after the occasion for a rise has begun to exist.

In those countries in which the government is the chief banker or issuer of notes, a temptation arises, on the occasion of every public pressure, either to lessen the quantity of precious metal contained in the chief current coin, as one of the means of detaining it in the country, or to allow paper to pass at a considerable and professed discount, which is another mode of preventing the coin from being exported. These are evils from which we consider ourselves as happily secured by the established principles of good faith which prevail in Great Britain. Those principles, however, should, perhaps, lead us even to place ourselves at a distance from that temptation to depreciate coin, or to permit a discount on paper, to which so many other countries have yielded. The possession, in ordinary times, of a very considerable quantity of gold, either in the bank or in general circulation, or both, seems necessary for our complete security in this respect. The substitution of country bank notes for gold tends to lessen that security. The evil of them is not that they create any false and merely ideal riches, or that they do any constant prejudice to the country. They enable the trader to vest a capital in merchandize, which, without them, he would not possess, and thereby add to the annual income of the nation. In their immediate effect, therefore, they are beneficial; but they leave us more exposed to an occasional evil, against which it is prudent to guard, provided we can accomplish that purpose without too great a sacrifice of present advantages,

It seems, on this account, as well as on some others, very undesirable to render permanent the temporary law passed some years since, and subsequently renewed, for the purpose of permitting the issue of English notes under five pounds. When it shall have expired, the power of re-enacting it, which we shall possess, will be a valuable resource. If, moreover, any measure can be devised, which, by encreasing the public confidence in good paper, will lessen the danger of a general failure of paper credit, and of a run upon the bank for gold, and which, also, by obstructing the issue of five and ten pound notes by smaller and less respectable banks, will somewhat extend the use of coin, on the whole, it will have a twofold argument to recommend it*.

The reader will observe, that even our circulating gold coin has here been considered in the light of a provision against an unfavourable balance of trade with foreign countries, and, therefore, as exportable. Part of our coin will, in fact, always be exported when the balance is very unfavourable, and the exportation, under such circumstances, is beneficial to the country. We are apt to think that it is the interchange of the usual gold coin for paper at home which alone maintains the value of our paper; and we are partly, on this account, much more anxious to detain our gold at home, than we are to discharge by means of it an unfavourable balance of trade, and thereby to improve our exchange with foreign countries. I apprehend, however, that an unfavourable course of exchange, which the export of our gold would cure, will, in many cases, tend much more to depreciate our paper, and to produce a rise in the nominal price of articles, than the want of the usual interchange of gold for paper at home. Our coin itself, as has been already remarked, when paper is depreciated, passes not for what

---

* Various objections, however, occur against almost every parliamentary measure for the regulation of country banks. Dr. Smith is of opinion, that a law prohibiting the issue of small notes is alone a sufficient remedy for the evils attending these institutions, and that the danger arising from banks is lessened by the multiplication of them. It is the object of this Work not so much to canvass any question respecting the particular means of regulating paper credit, as to lay down some general principles concerning it.

the gold in it is worth, but at the paper price; though this is not generally observed to be the case. It is the maintenance of our general exchanges, or, in other words, it is the agreement of the mint price with the bullion price of gold which seems to be the true proof that the circulating paper is not depreciated.

CHAP. VIII

Of the Tendency of a too great Issue of Bank Paper to produce an Excess of the Market Price above the Mint Price of Gold.—Of the Means by which it creates this Excess, namely, by its Operation on the Price of Goods and on the Course of Exchange.—Errors of Dr. A. Smith on the Subject of excessive Paper.—Of the Manner in which the Limitation of the Quantity of the Bank of England Paper serves to limit the Quantity and sustain the Value of all the Paper of the Kingdom.

A THIRD objection commonly made to country banks, is, the influence which their notes are supposed to have in raising the price of articles.

By the principles which shall be laid down in this Chapter, I propose to prove, that, though a general encrease of paper has this tendency, the objection, when applied to the paper of country banks, is particularly ill founded.

It will be necessary, in the discussion which is now about to take place, to join the consideration of two subjects, that of the influence which an enlarged emission of paper has in lifting up the price of commodities, and that of its influence, also, in producing an excess of the market price above the mint price of gold, and in thus exposing the bank to failure, and the country to considerable inconvenience. It is through the medium of the enhanced price of commodities that I conceive the ill effect on the mint price of gold to be brought about.

The discussion of these topics will best be introduced by a statement of the principle which regulates the value of all the articles of life.

The price of commodities in the market is formed by means of a certain struggle which takes place between the buyers and the sellers. It is commonly said, that the price of a thing is regulated by the proportion between the supply and the demand. This is, undoubtedly, true; and for the following reason. If the supply of an article or the demand for it is great, it is also known to be great; and if small, it is understood to be small. When, therefore, the supply, for example, is known to be less than the demand, the sellers judge that the buyers are in some degree at their mercy, and they insist on as favourable a price as their power over the buyers is likely to enable them to obtain. The price paid is not at all governed by the equity of the case, but entirely by the degree of command which the one party has over the other. When the demand is less than the supply, the buyers, in their turn, in some degree, command the market, giving not that sum which is calculated to indemnify the seller against loss, but so much only as they think that the seller will accept rather than not sell his article. The question of price is, therefore, in all cases, a question of power, and of power only. It is obvious, that a rise in the price of a scarce commodity will be more or less considerable in proportion as the article is felt to be one of more or less strict necessity.

The principle which has been laid down as governing the price of goods, must be considered as also regulating that of the paper for which they are sold; for it may as properly be said, on the occasion of a sale of goods, that paper is sold for goods, as that goods are sold for paper: thus the sale of a single commodity, as it is called, is a twofold transaction, though not commonly understood to be so: I mean, that the price at which the exchange (or sale) takes place depends on two facts; on the proportion between the supply of the particular commodity and the demand for it, which is one question; and on the proportion, also, between the state of the general supply of the circulating medium and that of the demand for it, which is another.

Paper, moreover (of which I shall here speak as if it were the only circulating medium, it being the only one used in the larger payments), is, to some persons, somewhat in the same manner as bread is to all, an article of necessity. It is necessary to traders, partly because they have come under engagements to make payments which are only to be effected by means of their own previous receipts: and partly because they hold goods which must, within no long time, be sold for money, that is to say, for paper, since a continually growing loss accrues from the detention of them. Paper, therefore, must be bought by the trader: and if there is a difficulty in obtaining it, the buyer of it is brought under the power of the seller, and, in that case, more goods must be given for it.

Let us, now, trace carefully the steps by which an encrease of paper serves to lift up the price of articles. Let us suppose, for example, an encreased number of Bank of England notes to be issued. In such case the traders in the metropolis discover that there is a more than usual facility of obtaining notes at the bank by giving bills for them, and that they may, therefore, rely on finding easy means of performing any pecuniary engagements into which they may enter. Every trader is encouraged by the knowledge of this facility of borrowing, a little to enlarge his speculations; he is rendered, by the plenty of money, somewhat more ready to buy, and rather less eager to sell; he either trusts that there will be a particular profit on the article which is the object of his speculation, or else he judges, that, by extending his general purchases, he shall at least have his share of the ordinary profit of commercial business, a profit which he considers to be proportioned to the quantity of it. The opinion of an encreased facility of effecting payments causes other traders to become greater buyers for the same reason, and at the same time. Thus an inclination to buy is created in all quarters, and an indisposition to sell. Now, since the cost of articles depends on the issue of that general conflict between the buyers and sellers, which was spoken of, it follows, that any circumstance which serves to communicate a greater degree of eagerness to the mind of the one party than to that of the other, will have an influence on price. It is not necessary to suppose either a monopoly, or a combination, or the least unfairness, to exist, or even large and improper speculations. The encrease in the eagerness of each buyer may be trifling. The zeal to buy, being generally diffused, may, nevertheless, have a sensible operation on price.

That, on the other hand, a reduction of the quantity of paper causes a fall in the price of goods, is scarcely necessary to be proved. It may be useful, however, in some degree, to illustrate this point by facts. I understand, that at the time of the great failure of paper credit in 1795, the price of corn fell, in a few places, no less than twenty or thirty per cent. The fall arose from the necessity of selling corn under which some farmers were placed, in order to carry on their payments. Much of the circulating medium being withdrawn, the demand for it was in those places far greater than the supply; and the few persons, therefore, who were in possession of cash, or of what would pass as cash, having command of the market, obliged the farmers to sell at a price thus greatly reduced. It was a new and sudden scarcity of cash, not any new plenty of corn, which caused the price of corn to drop.

It has been already observed, that some few days antecedently to the suspension of the cash payments of the bank, exchequer bills, as well as stocks, when sold for ready money, that is to say, for bank notes, fell in price. Not many days afterwards, although no material event had occurred except that of the stoppage of the bank, they rose. This fall and rise in the price of government securities evidently did not result from any corresponding fluctuation in the national confidence in them; for the fall took place when the national credit would naturally be the highest, namely, when the bank was as yet paying in cash, and the approaching stoppage was not known; and the rise happened when the national credit would be the lowest, namely, within a few days after that discouraging event. The reason of each of the fluctuations unquestionably was the fluctuation in the quantity of the Bank of England notes, which, as it has since appeared, were, during the day or two which preceded the suspension, about a million less than they were either a short time before or a short time afterwards. The notes being fewer during those few days, the price of them was, at the same time, higher. It was, in fact, therefore, the price of notes which rose, rather than that of stocks which fell, on the days immediately preceding the suspension; and it was the price of notes which a few days afterwards fell, rather than that of stocks which rose*.

I shall, for the present, consider the doctrine which has been laid down, as being sufficiently established, namely, that paper fluctuates in price on the same principles as any other article, its value rising as its quantity sinks, and *vice versâ*; or, in other words, that an augmentation of it has a general tendency to raise, and a diminished issue to lower, the nominal cost of commodities, although, partly for reasons which have been already touched upon, and partly for some which shall be hereafter given, an exact correspondence between the quantity of paper and the price of commodities can by no means be expected always to subsist.

The reader possibly may think that, in treating of this subject, I have been mistaking the effect for the cause, an encreased issue of paper being, in his estimation, merely a consequence which

---

* In the event of any great public alarm, such, for instance, as that which might be occasioned by the landing in this country of any considerable body of enemies, it is likely that the price of Bank of England notes, compared with that of stocks, or other articles for which there is a ready money market, would in like manner rise, even though the quantity of paper should continue the same: this would happen in consequence of that encreased demand for bank notes, to which it has been repeatedly observed that a state of consternation always gives occasion. Many bankers, at such a time, would feel a doubt whether they might not be drawn upon more largely than usual by some of their more timid customers; and whether, also, they might not be subjected to more than common difficulty in selling government securities, an article which, in ordinary times, they are used to turn into cash on the shortest notice, and which, while a prompt sale of them is to be depended on, they prefer to bank notes, because an interest is gained by holding the one, and not by detaining the other. During the short crisis of an invasion, the advantage of accruing interest would be little regarded, and each banker, therefore, would make an effort to exchange his exchequer bills, or, perhaps, his stocks, for Bank of England notes, an effort which must prove generally ineffectual, supposing the quantity issued to be the same; but which, however, would have the effect of bringing down the comparative price of the article so eagerly offered in exchange for notes. Thus the price of government securities would appear to fall, when, in part at least, it would rather be the price of bank notes which should be said to rise. Some encrease of the bank issues seems very justifiable at such a time; such an encrease, I mean, as should be sufficient only to prevent what may be termed an unnatural rise in the value of bank notes. This issue would be the means of preventing a misconception among the public respecting the degree of distrust in government securities entertained by the dealers in them, a circumstance which might be of some political importance in a moment of general consternation.

197

follows a rise in the price of goods, and not the circumstance which produces it. That an enlarged emission of paper may often fairly be considered as only, or chiefly, an effect of high prices, is not meant to be denied. It is, however, intended to insist, that, unquestionably, in some cases at least, the greater quantity of paper is, more properly speaking, the cause. A fuller explanation of this apparently difficult and disputable position will be given in the further progress of this Work.

I proceed, in the next place, to shew in what manner a general rise in the cost of commodities, whether proceeding from an extravagant issue of paper, or from any other circumstance, contributes to produce an excess of the market price above the mint price of gold.

It is obvious, that, in proportion as goods are rendered dear in Great Britain, the foreigner becomes unwilling to buy them, the commodities of other countries which come into competition with our's obtaining a preference in the foreign market; and, therefore, that in consequence of a diminution of orders from abroad, our exports will be diminished; unless we assume, as we shall find it necessary to do, that some compensation in the exchange is given to the foreigner for the disadvantage attending the purchase of our articles. But not only will our exports lessen in the case supposed; our imports also will encrease: for the high British price of goods will tempt foreign commodities to come in nearly in the same degree in which it will discourage British articles from going out. I mean only, that these two effects (that of a diminished export, and that of an encreased import) will follow, provided that we suppose, what is not supposable, namely, that, at the time when the price of goods is greatly raised in Great Britain, the course of exchange suffers no alteration. For the following reason, I have said that this is not supposable. Under the circumstances which have been described of a diminished export, and an encreased import, the balance of trade must unavoidably turn against us; the consequence of which must be, that the drawers of bills on Great Britain in foreign countries will become more in number than the persons having occasion to remit bills. This disparity between the number of individuals wanting to draw, and of those wanting to remit, as was remarked in a former Chapter, must produce a fall in the price at which the over-abundant bills on England sell in the foreign market. The fall in the selling price abroad of bills payable here, will operate as an advantage to the foreign buyer of our commodities in the computation of the exchangeable value of that circulating medium of his own country with which he discharges the debt in Britain contracted by his purchase. It will thus obviate the dearness of our articles: it will serve as a compensation to the foreigner for the loss which he would otherwise sustain by buying in our market. The fall of our exchange will, therefore, promote exportation and encourage importation. It will, in a great degree, prevent the high price of goods in Great Britain from producing that unfavourable balance of trade, which, for the sake of illustrating the subject was supposed to exist.

The compensation thus made to the foreigner for the high British price of all articles is necessary as an inducement to him to take them, somewhat in the same manner as a drawback or bounty on exportation is the necessary inducement to take those particular goods which have been rendered too dear for the foreign market by taxes laid on them in this country. In each case the British consumer pays the high price, and the foreigner is spared, because otherwise he will not accept out commodities.

The fall in our exchange was just now defined to be an advantage gained in the computation of the exchangeable value of that foreign circulating medium with which the foreigner discharges his debt in Great Britain, a debt paid in the circulating medium of this country. It implies, therefore, a high valuation of his circulating medium, and a low valuation of our's; a low valuation, that is to say, both of our paper and of the coin which is interchanged with it.

Now, when coin is thus rendered cheap, it by no means follows that bullion is rendered cheap also. Coin is rendered cheap through its constituting a part of our circulating medium; but bullion does not constitute a part of it. Bullion is a commodity, and nothing but a commodity; and it rises and falls in value on the same principle as all other commodities. It becomes, like them, dear in proportion as the circulating medium for which it is exchanged is rendered cheap, and cheap in proportion as the circulating medium is rendered dear.

In the case, therefore, which has now been supposed, we are to consider coin as sinking below its proper and intrinsic worth, while bullion maintains its natural and accustomed price. Hence there arises that temptation, which was formerly noticed, either to convert back into bullion and then to export; or, which is the same thing, to export and then convert back into bullion; or, which is also the same thing, to convert back into bullion, and then sell to the bank, at the price which would be gained by exportation, that gold which the bank has purchased, and has converted from bullion into coin.

In this manner an encrease of paper, supposing it to be such as to raise the price of commodities in Britain above the price at which, unless there is some allowance afforded in the course of exchange, they will be received in foreign countries, contributes to produce an excess of the market price above the mint price of gold, and to prevent, therefore, the introduction of a proper supply of it into the Bank of England, as well as to draw out of its coffers that coin which the directors of the bank would wish to keep in them.

Dr. Smith appears to me to have treated the important subject of the tendency of an excessive paper circulation to send gold out of a country, and thus to embarrass its banking establishments, in a manner which is particularly defective and unsatisfactory. It is true, that he blames the Bank of England for having contributed to bring on itself, during several successive years, a great expence in buying gold through a too great circulation of its paper; and that he also charges the Scotch banks with having had, through their excessive issues, a share in producing this evil. Thus, therefore, he seems to give to his reader some intimation of the tendency of an excessive issue of paper to create an excess of the market price above the mint price of gold*.

It appears, however, in some degree, from the passage in question, though much more clearly from other parts of his work, that he considers every permanent excess, whether of the market price above the mint price, or of the mint price above the market price of gold, as entirely referable to "something in the state of the coin†."

In one place he remarks, that a high price of bullion arises from the difference between the weight of our more light and that of our more heavy guineas; the value of the gold in the heavier guineas, as he represents the case, determining the general current value of both the lighter and the heavier pieces of coin; and the superior quantity of gold in the heavier guineas constituting, therefore, so much profit on the melting of those heavier pieces‡:

* "By issuing too great a quantity of paper, of which the excess was con-"tinually returning in order to be exchanged for gold and silver, the Bank of "England was, for many years together, obliged to coin gold to the extent of "between eight hundred thousand pounds and a million a year. For this great "coinage the bank (in consequence of the worn and degraded state into which "the gold coin had fallen a few years ago) was frequently obliged to purchase "gold bullion at the high price of 4*l*. an ounce, which it soon after issued in "coin at 3*l*. 17*s*. 10½*d*. an ounce, losing, in this manner, between two and a "half and three per cent. Though the bank, therefore, paid no seignorage, "though the government was properly at the expence of the coinage, this "liberality of government did not prevent altogether the expence of the bank."— Enquiry into the Nature and Causes of the Wealth of Nations, by Dr. A. Smith, Vol. I. page 451, 4th edit. Oct.

† "When the market price either of gold or silver bullion continues for "several years together steadily and constantly either more or less above, or "more or less below, the mint price, we may be assured that this steady and "constant either superiority or inferiority of price is the effect of something "in the state of the coin, which, at that time, renders a certain quantity of "coin either of more value or of less value than the precise quantity of bullion "which it ought to contain."—Smith on the Wealth of Nations, Vol. I. page 69, 4th edit. Oct.

‡ "In every country the greater part of the current coin is almost always "more or less worn or otherwise degenerated from its standard. In Great "Britain, it was, before the late reformation, a good deal so, the gold being "more than two per cent. and the silver more than eight per cent. below its "standard weight. But if forty-four guineas and a half containing their full

201

a supposition manifestly erroneous, and contradicted by experience; for it implies that the excess of the market price above the mint price of gold both never is and never can be greater than the excess of the weight of the heavier above the lighter guineas; and, also, that the price of bullion cannot fluctuate while the state of our coinage remains in all respects the same. We have lately experienced fluctuations in our exchange, and correspondent variations in the market price, compared with the mint price of gold, amounting to no less than eight or ten per cent., the state of our coinage continuing, in all respects, the same.

Dr. Smith recommends a seignorage, as tending to raise the value both of the lighter and heavier coin; and thus, also, to diminish, if not destroy, the excess of the market price above the mint price of gold*.

"standard weight, a pound weight of gold, could purchase very little more "than a pound weight of uncoined gold, forty-four guineas and a half wanting "a part of their weight, could not purchase a pound weight, and something "was to be added, in order to make up the deficiency. The current price of "gold bullion at market, therefore, instead of being the same with the mint "price, or 46*l*. 14*s*. 6*d*. was then about 47*l*. 14*s*. and sometimes about 48*l*. "When the greater part of the coin, however, was in this degenerate condition, "forty-four guineas and a half, fresh from the mint, would purchase no more "goods in the market than any other ordinary guineas; because, when they "come into the coffers of the merchant, being confounded with other money, "they could not afterwards be distinguished, without more trouble than the "difference was worth. Like other guineas, they were worth no more than "46*l*. 14*s*. 6*d*. If thrown into the melting pot, however, they produced, without "any sensible loss, a pound weight of standard gold, which could be sold at "any time for between 47*l*. 14*s*. and 48*l*. either in gold or silver. There was an "evident profit, therefore, in melting down new coined money; and it was "done so instantaneously, that no precaution of government could prevent it. "The operations of the mint were, upon this account, somewhat like the web of "Penelope; the work that was done in the day was undone in the night. The "mint was employed not so much in making daily additions to the coin, as in "replacing the very best part of it which was daily melted down."

  * "Were the private people who carry their gold and silver to the mint to "pay themselves for the coinage, it would add to the value of those metals in "the same manner as the fashion does to that of plate. Coined gold and silver "would be more valuable than uncoined. The seignorage, if it was not exorbitant, "would add to the bullion the whole value of the duty, because the government "having every where the exclusive privilege of coining, no coin can come to "market cheaper than they think proper to afford it.

  "A seignorage will, in many cases, take away altogether, and will in all "cases diminish, the profit of melting down the new coin. This profit always

It is remarkable, that this Writer does not, in any degree, advert either to that more immediate cause (a fall of our exchanges), from which I have, in this as well as in a former Chapter, described the excess in question, as, in all cases, arising; or to that more remote one on which I have lately dwelt, namely, a too high price of goods, which produces a fall of our exchanges.

Dr. Smith does not, in any of his observations on this subject, proceed sufficiently, as I conceive, on the practical principle of shewing how it is through the medium of prices (of the prices of goods in general, and of bullion in particular, compared with the

"arises from the difference between the quantity of bullion which the common "currency ought to contain, and that which it actually does contain. If this "difference is less than the seignorage, there will be loss instead of profit. If "it is equal to the seignorage, there will neither be profit nor loss. If it is "greater than the seignorage, there will, indeed, be some profit; but less than "if there were no seignorage."—Smith's Wealth of Nations, Vol. II. Book IV. Chap. VI. pages 333, 334, and 335.

These observations of Dr. Smith, on the subject of a seignorage, seem erroneous in the following respects. Plate, when bought, is purchased in order not to be sold again, but to be retained by the possessor; and the price paid by the original buyer may, therefore, be not unfairly considered, as it is by Dr. Smith, to be the current price of the article. Gold, on the contrary, is no sooner bought and coined, than it is sent into circulation; it is sold, that is to say (or exchanged for commodities), again and again. What we mean, therefore, by the current price of gold coin, is that price at which it passes, not in the original bargain for bullion between the seller of it and the bank, but in the general course of this subsequent circulation. Guineas, moreover, not only circulate at home, but are liable to be sent abroad in the event of any unfavourable balance of trade. They are worth, in that case, just as much as the foreign country will give for them; and the foreign country, in estimating their value, since it means to melt them, does not at all take into its calculation the expence of the coinage of the piece of metal. It acts like a buyer not of new but of old plate, who destines it to the melting pot, and, therefore, refuses to allow any thing for "the fashion."

This foreign price of our coin principally determines the current value of the price of coin in England. It appears to me to do this in the following manner.

When the price which our coin will fetch in foreign countries is such as to tempt it out of the kingdom, the directors of the bank naturally diminish, in some degree, the quantity of their paper, through an anxiety for the safety of their establishment. By diminishing their paper, they raise its value; and in raising its value, they raise also the value in England of the current coin which is exchanged for it. Thus t e value of our gold coin conforms itself to the value of the current paper, and the current paper is rendered by the bank directors of that value which it is necessary that it should bear in order to prevent large price of the current circulating medium), that the operations of importing and exporting gold are brought about. He considers our coin as going abroad simply in consequence of our circulation at home being over full. Payment in coin, according to his doctrine, is demanded of every bank for as much of its paper as is excessive, because the excessive paper can neither be sent abroad nor turned to any use at home; whereas, when it is changed into coin, the coin may be transmitted to a foreign part, and may there be advantageously employed*.

exportations; a value sometimes rising a little above, and sometimes falling a little below, the price which our coin bears abroad; a price, in the formation of which no regard is had to the fashion.

A seignorage, nevertheless, might add to the current value of the coin of the kingdom for the following reason. It might incline the directors of the bank to improve the value of their paper by a stricter limitation of it, for the sake of more effectually exempting themselves from an occasional burthen, which is now borne for them by the government. The point *below* which they would wish to prevent their paper from falling would still be the same as it is now, namely, the selling price of our coin when melted and carried to foreign countries: the care, however, which they would take to prevent its falling below that price would, perhaps, be greater, and would be such as to raise its average price, if, in the event of each depression, they should be subject not only, as they are now, to loss in the purchase of gold, but to a further loss in coining it. There seems no reason, however, to suppose, that the degree of fluctuation which is now apt to subsist between the market price and mint price of gold could, by any efforts of the bank, be materially lessened. It results from the fluctuations in the exchange; and those fluctuations, in general, proceed from variations in the markets of Europe, which affect the balance of trade, and cannot, by any management of bank paper, be exactly counteracted.

* "The coffers of a banking company which issues more paper than can be "employed in the circulation of the country, and of which the excess is con- "tinually returning upon them for payment, though they ought to be filled "much fuller, yet must empty themselves much faster than if their business was "confined within more reasonable bounds, and must require not only a more "violent but a more constant and uninterrupted exertion of expence in order "to replenish them. The coin, too, which is thus continually drawn in such "large quantities from their coffers cannot be employed in the circulation of the "country. It comes in place of a paper which is over and above what can be "employed in that circulation, and is, therefore, over and above what can be "employed in it too. But as that coin will not be allowed to lie idle, it must, "in one shape or another, be sent abroad, in order to find that profitable em- "ployment which it cannot find at home; and this continual exportation of gold "and silver, by enhancing the difficulty, must necessarily enhance still further "the expence of the bank in finding more gold and silver in order to replenish "those coffers which empty themselves so very rapidly."—Vol. I. page 450.

The reader will perceive, that, according to the principle which I have endeavoured to establish, coin does not merely leave the country because, the circulation being full, no use can be found at home for additional circulating medium; but that every encrease of paper has been represented as enhancing the price of goods, which advanced price of goods affords employment to a larger quantity of circulating medium, so that the circulation can never be said to be over full. This advanced price of goods is the same thing as a reduced price of coin; the coin, therefore, in consequence of its reduced price, is carried out of the country for the sake of obtaining for it a better market. The heavier pieces, undoubtedly, will be preferred, if there is a facility of obtaining and transporting them; but the lighter guineas will also be exported, when the state of the exchange shall be sufficiently low to afford a profit on such a transaction. One of the consequences of Dr. Smith's mode of treating the subject, is, that the reader is led into the error of thinking, that when, through an excessive issue of paper, gold has been made to flow away from us, the expence of restoring it consists merely in the charge of collecting it and transporting it from the place to which it is gone. It follows, on the contrary, from the principles which I have laid down, that, in order to bring back gold, the expence not only of importing it may be to be incurred, but that also of purchasing it at a loss, and at a loss which may be either more or less considerable: a circumstance of great importance in the question. If this loss should ever become extremely great, the difficulties of restoring the value of our paper might not easily be surmounted, and a current discount or difference between the coin and paper of the country would scarcely be avoidable

Dr. Smith, indeed, represents the expence of bringing back gold as considerable; but he seems to impute the greatness of it to the circumstance of its recurring again and again: and he describes it as continuing to recur in the case of each individual bank, whether in town or country, which persists in the false policy of issuing more paper than is sufficient to fill the circulation of the neighbouring district. I shall here take occasion to notice some great inaccuracies in one part of his reasoning upon this point.

He says—"A banking company which issues more paper than "can be employed in the circulation of the country, and of which "the excess is continually returning upon them for payment, "ought to encrease the quantity of gold and silver which they "keep at all times in their coffers, not only in proportion to this "excess, but to a much greater proportion. Suppose, for instance, "all the paper of a particular bank, which the circulation of the "country can easily absorb, amounts to forty thousand pounds, "and the bank keeps usually ten thousand pounds in gold and "silver for its occasional demands. If this bank should attempt to "circulate forty-four thousand pounds, the excess of four thousand "pounds will return as fast as it is issued. Fourteen thousand "pounds must then be kept instead of ten thousand pounds, and the "bank will gain nothing by the excessive circulation. On the "contrary, it will lose the whole expence of continually collecting "four thousand pounds in gold and silver, which will be con- "tinually going out of its coffers as fast as they are brought in."

He then adds—"Had every particular bank always understood "and attended to its own interest, the circulation would never "have been overstocked with paper money."

There is, no doubt, some sort of ground for saying that an excess of paper will come back upon the banks which issue it, and that, in coming back, it will involve the issuing banks in expence. Much exception, however might be taken against Dr. Smith's mode of estimating the expence which the quantity which would come back would bring upon the issuing banks. But the objection which I shall in the first place, urge against the remark of Dr. Smith, is, that, even granting it to be just, it can be just only in a case which can scarcely ever occur among the country banks of this kingdom. I mean, that it can apply solely to the case of a single bank of which the paper circulates exclusively through a surrounding district: it obviously cannot hold in the case of many banks, the paper of all of which circulates in the same district.

In order to explain this clearly, let us make the following supposition. Let us imagine the circulation of country bank paper which a certain district will bear to be one hundred thousand pounds, and ten banks to be in that district, each usually circulating and able to keep in circulation ten thousand pounds. Let us also suppose an excessive issue of four thousand pounds, and let us allow the effect of this on the ten banks to be that which Dr Smith describes, a point which might certainly be disputed, namely, that a necessity will arise for *always* keeping (for this is what Dr Smith's language implies) an additional stock of gold amounting to exactly four thousand pounds, and also that a reiterated expence will be incurred (Dr. Smith does not say how frequently reiterated) in collecting and transporting these four thousand pounds of gold. Still it must be observed, that we may suppose the issue of the four thousand pounds excessive paper to be made by some one only of the ten banks, while the charge incurred by such issue may be divided among them all. It may, therefore, on Dr. Smith's own principles, answer to one of several banks emitting paper which circulates in the same place, to issue the paper which is considered by him as excessive; and the practice of doing so may be owing to the country banker's too well knowing his own interest, and not, as Dr. Smith supposes, to his too ill understanding it.

But the case which I have supposed has been put merely by way of illustration. When many banks issue notes circulating over the same district, it is impossible to say whose paper constitutes the excess. Whatever temptation to excess exists, must be a general one. It is, however, counteracted not only by the charge of transporting gold, on which alone Dr. Smith dwells, but likewise by all the other charges, as well as by all the risks to which country bank notes subject the issuers; not to mention the difficulty of finding a channel through which a quantity of paper much larger than common can be sent by the country bank into circulation.

Dr. Smith supposes, in the passage which has just been quoted, that, when there is an excessive circulation of country bank paper, the excess returns upon the banks to be exchanged for gold and silver. The fact is, that it returns to be exchanged not for gold and silver only, but either for gold and silver, or for bills on London. A bill on London is an order to receive in London, after a certain interval, either gold or Bank of England notes. This order imposes on the country banker the task of providing a fund in London sufficient to answer his draft: it serves, however, to spare that expence of transporting gold, as well as to lessen that necessity of maintaining a stock of guineas, which Dr. Smith assumes to be the consequence of every excessive emission of notes, and to be the certain means, if bankers do but understand their interest, of limiting their issue.

The remark which has just been made derives particular importance from the circumstances of the period through which we have passed. For, if the usual means of preventing an excess of country bank notes were nothing else than the liability of the issuers to be called upon for a money payment of them, it might fairly be assumed, that, at a time when the money payment of them has been suspended, we must necessarily have been exposed to the greatest inundation of country paper, and to a proportionate depreciation of it. The unbounded issue of country bank notes has been restrained by the obligation under which country bankers have considered themselves to be of granting bills on London; that is to say, orders to receive in London Bank of England paper in exchange for their notes, if required to do so: and it is certain that they would be required to do so whenever the quantity of their notes should be much greater in proportion to the occasion for them, than the quantity of the notes of the Bank of England in proportion to the occasion for those notes.

For the sake of explaining this, let it be admitted, for a moment, that a country bank has issued a very extraordinary quantity of notes. We must assume these to be employed by the holders of them in making purchases in the place in which alone the country bank paper passes, namely, in the surrounding district. The effect of such purchases, according to the principles established in this Chapter, must be a great local rise in the price of articles. But to suppose a great and merely local rise, is to suppose that which can never happen or which, at least, cannot long continue to exist; for every purchaser will discover that he can buy commodities elsewhere at a cheaper rate; and he will not fail to procure them in the quarter in which they are cheap, and to transport them to the spot in which they are dear, for the sake of the profit on the transaction. In order that he may be enabled to do this, he will demand to have the notes which pass current in the place in which we have supposed goods to have been rendered dear by the extraordinary emission of paper, converted into the circulating medium of the place in which goods are cheap: he will, therefore, require to have his country bank note turned into a Bank of England note, or into a bill on London, which is nearly the same thing, provided Bank of England notes are fewer in proportion to the occasion for them than the country bank notes; that is to say, provided Bank of England notes have less lifted up the price of goods in London than country bank notes have lifted up the price of goods in the country.

This point may be still more fully illustrated in the following manner. Let us imagine a mercantile house to consist of two branches, the one placed in the metropolis, the other in the country, and each branch to be accustomed to make certain payments in the spot in which it is situated, each, however, to be in the habit of borrowing as largely as it is able, the one of a neighbouring country bank, the other of the Bank of England, and of applying these loans to the joint use of the trading concern. Let us next suppose an extraordinary facility of borrowing at the country bank to arise, while the opportunities of obtaining loans at the Bank of England remain the same*. In such case the mercantile house, provided its London payments continue to bear the same proportion as before

* The case here put is assumed to exist only by way of argument. The point intended to be shown, is, that the case cannot happen; or, at least, that such cannot be the case, at the same time, of all the country banks in the kingdom. A single individual, it is true, may find his means of borrowing at a particular country bank to encrease in the manner which is here supposed; for he may obtain a preference over other borrowers. A single bank, also, may find its means of lending to encrease; for its notes may usurp the place of those of other banks. There can, however, be no material enlargement on the whole of the paper of the country, while the facility of borrowing in London remains the same.

to its country payments, which will hardly fail to be the case, will exchange some part of its encreased loans in the country, consisting in country bank notes, for bills on London, or, in other words, for Bank of England notes. It will thus adjust, with the greatest nicety, the quantity of London and of country paper to the amount of the pecuniary demands upon it in each quarter; and, in doing so, it will contribute to prevent the supply of notes in either place from becoming greater in proportion to the demand than in the other. What has been supposed of one house, may be supposed of many similar ones; and not only of houses of the particular description which has been spoken of, but also of the several independent establishments in the two distant places which have pecuniary transactions together, and have an interest in accommodating each other. Their general operations, of a pecuniary kind, must be such as always to check a local rise in the price of commodities in either place, while it is as yet so small as to be scarcely perceptible. In this manner, therefore, the exchangeableness of country paper for London paper will never fail very nearly to equalize the value of them both. It is, moreover, important clearly to point out that their value will be equalized, or nearly equalized, not by a tendency in the London paper to partake in a low value which the country paper has acquired in consequence of its not being limited by any voluntary act of the issuers; nor by a tendency in each to approximate in value to the other; but by a tendency in the country paper to take exactly the high value which the London paper bears in consequence of its being restricted by the issuers. That this must be the case is plain, from the remark which has just been made; for it has been shewn, that the country paper, however it may fail to be limited in quantity by any moderation or prudence of the issuers, becomes no less effectually limited through the circumstance of their being compelled by the holders to exchange as much of it as is excessive for the London paper which is limited; which is limited, I mean, in consequence of a principle of limitation which the directors of the Bank of England have prescribed to themselves.

The country paper, let it then be observed, does not add any thing to the quantity of the London paper; for the effectual limitation of the London paper is the great point, which it must be borne in mind, that we have assumed. The country paper, therefore, does not in any degree diminish the price of the London paper; for its price must remain fixed so long as its quantity continues fixed, supposing, as we do in our present argument, that the demand for it is the same. It has been proved, however, that the country paper is rendered, by its exchangeableness with the London paper, almost exactly equal to it in value. It is, then, rendered almost exactly equal in value to a paper of which the value is completely sustained. Thus, therefore, the limitation of the supply of the single article of London paper, of which, however, we are taking for granted that the demand continues the same, is the means both of sustaining the value of London paper, and also of sustaining the value as well as limiting the quantity of the whole paper of the country.

It is, however, necessary here to point out to the reader, that, in the immediately preceding observations, we have assumed certain facts to exist, for the sake of stating clearly a general principle. It will be the object of a succeeding Chapter to shew in what respects the case which has been supposed differs from the actual one.

CHAP. IX

Of the Circumstances which cause the Paper of the Bank of England, as well as all the other Paper of the Country, to fail of having their Value regulated according to any exact Proportion to the Quantity of Bank of England Notes.

SEVERAL points may be considered as having been assumed, for the sake of describing clearly the principle which was laid down in the close of the former Chapter. They may be stated to have been the following.

First, the notes of the Bank of England were spoken of as forming exclusively the whole circulating medium of the district which surrounds the metropolis, and as having no circulation beyond the boundaries of that district. The object was, then, to evince, that supposing, secondly, the quantity of Bank of England paper to continue the same; and supposing, thirdly, the payments within the district to be the same; and supposing also, fourthly, the general circumstances to be such as to render the same quantity of circulating medium just as sufficient as before to effect the same payments; the Bank of England paper could not fail both to maintain its own value, and also to maintain the value as well to restrict the quantity of the general paper of the country.

In attempting to shew in what respects the case thus put may have differed from the actual one, I shall advert to each of the four points which have just been mentioned.

First, the notes of the Bank of England have a circulation, which is not perfectly exclusive, over any definable district. In the metropolis itself, and in its neighbourhood, they are the only current paper, some coin circulating also. In many distant parts of the country a very small quantity of Bank of England notes circulate, and also much other paper, as well as a certain quantity of coin. This London and country coin, as well as country paper, may happen through various causes to supplant the Bank of England paper, or to be supplanted by it, either in a greater or in a less degree; and every such variation will have an effect which it is necessary to consider. If, for example, a larger quantity than usual of Bank of England notes should circulate in the country; then the quantity of them which remains applicable to the uses of the London district will be smaller, supposing the total amount issued to be the same. In the case, therefore, of more Bank of England notes circulating in the country, and in the case also of some Bank of England notes occupying the place of guineas antecedently current in London, an issue of a larger total quantity of Bank of Engand paper will be necessary, in order to give the same means as before of effecting London payments, and in order to produce the same limitation as before of the total quantity of circulating paper in the country.

All the one and two pound notes of the Bank of England (a species of paper which has been issued only since the suspension of its cash payments) have clearly formed that sort of addition to the bank paper of which I have been speaking. These have circulated, some in London, and many of them in the country, in the place of guineas, which have disappeared; and the amount of them has lately been two millions. In order, therefore, to produce the same effect on the country paper as before the suspension, the total amount of Bank of England notes lately circulating ought to have exceeded the quantity issued before the suspension by about two millions, supposing all other things the same. There are other causes which occasionally produce variations in that part of the Bank of England paper, which assists in supplying the distant country circulation: and these variations may sometimes be considerable, and may not easily be estimated. They probably, however, have not lately been material. For though, while the practice of paying in gold has been suspended, country banks, on the one hand may have been encouraged somewhat more than before to push their notes into circulation, and may thus have supplanted some of the paper of the Bank of England usually passing in their neighbourhood; they certainly, on the other hand, have many of them kept lately in their drawer a fund of Bank of England notes, which was not heretofore deemed necessary, for the sake of being able to offer these in payment of their own paper*.

I have to consider, secondly, how far, allowing for that difference of two millions of which mention has been made, the circulating quantity of Bank of England paper has lately corresponded with that of antecedent periods.

The average amount of Bank of England notes in circulation during three years ending in December 1795, appears to have been 11,975,573*l*. The amount in circulation on the 26th of February 1797, the day antecedent to the suspension of the cash payments of the bank, has been already stated to have been about 8,600,000*l*., this being that very low sum to which they were then reduced. By a statement of their amount on the 6th December 1800, laid before the House of Commons, they appear to have been then 15,450,970*l*. This last mentioned sum includes the two millions of one and two pound notes. If these two millions are deducted, the amount on the 6th December 1800 will exceed the average amount in three years antecedent to the suspension of the cash payments of the bank by 1,475,397*l*. It remains, however, to be observed, that the notes of the Bank of England were stated to the House of Commons by the governor of that company, in the spring of 1801, to have been then reduced to a sum less by about a million and a half than their amount on the 6th December 1800. The total quantity, therefore, of the Bank of England notes in circulation in one part of the spring of 1801, if the two millions be deducted, almost exactly agrees with their average amount during the three years ending December 1795†.

* Some Bank of England notes have also been recently employed in the place of small bills on London, the use of which has been discouraged by the late additional duty on bills and notes.

† This account of the comparative quantities of the Bank of England notes circulating before, and of those circulating after the suspension of the cash payments of the bank, differs greatly from that of Mr. Boyd, who has, in his

We have to consider, thirdly, whether the payments of the metropolis may be likely to have been the same in the last year as in some preceding years.

A subject, in the examination of which there may seem to be some difficulty, shall here, in the first place, be discussed. It has been already observed, that the quantity of Bank of England notes is limited by the bank directors who issue them; and that the quantity of country bank paper, though restricted in an equal degree, is limited not by the act of the issuers, but through the circumstance of its exchangeableness for London paper. By saying that the country paper is limited in an equal degree, I always mean not that one uniform proportion is maintained between the quantity of the London paper and that of the country paper, but only that the quantity of the one, in comparison with the demand for that one, is the same, or nearly the same, as the quantity of the other in proportion to the call for the other.

pamphlet, minutely investigated the same subject. The causes of this disagreement are the following.

He mentions, as I have done, the amount of Bank of England notes to have been, on the 6th December 1800, 15,450,970*l*. He then compares this their highest amount (for such, or nearly such, I consider it to be), first with their lowest amount, namely, with their amount on the 26th February 1797, which was 8,640,250*l*., and then with their average amount for three years antecedent to the suspension of the cash payments of the bank, viz. 11,975,573*l*., the same average amount at which I have reckoned them, for I have adopted Mr. Boyd's own statement. He then infers, that, on the first of his principles of comparison, an addition of nearly four-fifths, and, on the second, of three-tenths, had been made to the sum in circulation.

To this representation the answer is, as will appear from the text, first, that of the 15,450,970*l*. stated to the House of Commons to be the amount of Bank of England notes in circulation on the 6th December 1800, the sum of about two millions, consisting in one and two pound notes, ought to have been deducted by Mr. Boyd in forming his comparison. These notes evidently filled the place which was before occupied by guineas. They were, for that reason, not added to the 13,450,970*l*. in the return made by the bank to parliament, as they have been in the pamphlet of Mr. Boyd, but were set down as a separate article. Bankers have commonly given out these one and two pound notes as a substitute for guineas; and every individual, whether in London or in the country, who has had a note of this description in his pocket, has obviously kept it in the place of gold.

It is to be replied, secondly, that the sum of 8,640,250*l*., with which one of the comparisons of Mr. Boyd is made, is that remarkably low sum to which the

The reader, in reasoning on this state of the case, may, perhaps, be inclined to infer, and it is a question which seems to deserve consideration, that when the Bank of England paper is more than usually restricted, the pressure in London which in such case takes place (for it is there that the general pressure originates), may be likely to relieve itself either by drawing to London a large part of the Bank of England paper usually circulating in the country, the place which it occupied being supplied by country paper, or by causing many of the payments of London to transfer themselves to the country. If either of these two consequences should result from every pressure in London, then, even though the total amount of Bank of England paper should be diminished, that part of it which circulates in London may possibly continue to be just as sufficient as before to perform the task assigned to it of effecting the London payments; and in that case the country paper also, since it always takes the price of the London paper, will so far

bank improperly, as I have ventured to suspect, and certainly to the no small distress of the metropolis, had suffered their notes to fall on the day antecedent to the suspension of their cash payments, a sum of the smallness of which Mr. Boyd himself has complained. Their notes on the 18th February, that is, exactly one week before, were ....£.9,137,950
They were two weeks before 9,431,550
Three weeks before 9,667,460
A month before ....,,................................. 10,024,740
And five weeks before 10,550,830
Their notes, also, immediately after they were at that lowest sum of 8,640,250*l.*, with which Mr. Boyd forms the first of his comparisons, were encreased considerably: they were, on the 4th March, that is, one week after, 10,416,520*l.*, and they were gradually raised still higher.

There can, therefore, be no doubt that the comparison ought to have been made with the number which were in circulation, not at the remarkable æra of the 26th February 1797, but only during an average of years preceding the suspension.

The fact of the Bank of England notes having been reduced near a million and a half in the spring of 1801, a circumstance which renders the amount of them almost exactly equal at the two periods at which both I and Mr. Boyd have made our comparison, could not be known to Mr. Boyd at the time of writing his pamphlet.

Mr. Boyd founds, on the supposed fact of the vast encrease of Bank of England notes, the opinion which he states in the beginning of his Work, that "to the augmentation of bank paper not convertible into specie, more than to any other cause, is to be ascribed the high price of provisions."

encrease itself as to become in the same manner as before commensurate with the country payments. If any considerable effect of this kind should follow from every limitation of the London paper; then the principle which was laid down in the close of the former Chapter in a great measure fails: and the bank has not that power which was ascribed to it of restricting the quantity and regulating the value of the paper of the country.

That a pressure in London is not likely to produce the first of the two effects which have been mentioned, that of drawing to London the Bank of England notes circulating in the country is a point on which I shall not separately dwell, except so far as to observe, that a pressure in London, if it be very sudden and severe, may be suspected of having a tendency directly contrary to that of bringing Bank of England notes from the country to London; for it is apt, through the alarm which it excites, to produce, as was formerly explained, an extraordinary diminution of country bank notes; a diminution, I mean, which is even greater in proportion to the country payments to be effected than that of the notes of the Bank of England in proportion to the London payments. In such case, a necessity is created for the substitution of other circulating medium in the place of the country paper which has been suppressed. The substitute principally demanded will be gold; but some Bank of England paper is not unlikely to be also employed in filling the void.

In proceeding to enquire whether a pressure in London, arising from the restriction of Bank of England paper, is likely to cause the transfer to the country of many of the payments usually made in London, I shall advert to past experience.

It was mentioned in an early Chapter of this Work, that there seems to have existed, for some time, an encreasing disposition to transfer to London the pecuniary part of even those commercial transactions which belong properly to the country. It here naturally occurs to us to enquire for what reason the restriction of the notes of the Bank of England by the issuers in time past, has not served to remove this disposition, and even to cause the

217

quantity of London payments, compared with those of the country, continually to lessen, rather than to encrease. The Bank of England paper, let it here be observed, operated before the suspension of the cash payments of the bank in restricting the country paper, exactly in the same manner as it has done since that event. It is commonly and very naturally supposed, that it was the exchangeableness of the country paper for guineas which used to sustain its value. This, however, was not the case: its value was sustained by its exchangeableness for Bank of England notes. The country paper bore always and necessarily the same value as the notes of the Bank of England; and not always or necessarily the same value as the gold contained in the coin, for which the country paper was exchangeable. It is true, indeed, that the quantity of gold in our coin had an influence on the value of country paper. It had, however, only an influence which was imperfect and indirect. It served to dictate to the directors of the Bank of England what was that quantity of paper which they might properly emit. For, if at any time the exchanges of the country became so unfavourable as to produce a material excess of the market price above the mint price of gold; the directors of the bank, as appears by the evidence of some of their body given to parliament, were disposed to resort to a reduction of their paper as a means of diminishing or removing the excess, and of thus providing for the security of their establishment. They, moreover, have at all times been accustomed to observe some limit as to the quantity of their notes, for the same prudential reasons.

This interest in the prevention of any great excess of the market price above the mint price of gold was in no degree felt by the country banker; for the loss sustained by every new conversion of bullion into coin was borne not by him, but by the Bank of England, out of whose coffers all the guineas called for in every part of the kingdom were supplied. The Bank of England, if coin was demanded of it, had to purchase bullion at a losing price. The country banker, if coin was in like manner required of him, had only to possess himself of a Bank of England note, which was exchangeable at the bank for guineas without any discount. If, therefore, the directors of the Bank of England suffered their paper to be worth less than the gold contained in the coin for which their paper was exchangeable, the country paper was worth less also; or, in other words, the degree of expence and difficulty which the country banker incurred in obtaining guineas, was to be measured by the degree of expence and difficulty incurred in obtaining Bank of England notes, and not by the degree of expence and difficulty incurred in buying and then coining gold. The necessity which the Bank of England felt of curing any great excess of the market price above the mint price of gold, caused the limitation of Bank of England paper; and then this limitation, in proportion as it took place, produced the limitation of the paper of the country. It was in this manner that an excessive issue of the paper of the kingdom was restrained before the suspension of the cash payments of the Bank of England. If, then, the directors of the bank were used before the suspension of their cash payments to limit their issues through a necessity which sometimes urged them, and if thus they limited the paper of the country in the manner which has been described, it follows that, supposing them after that event to have restrained their issues in like manner, though through a somewhat less urgent motive, the general effect must have been the same. There can, therefore, be no more reason to suppose a transfer to have lately taken place of London payments to the country, or of Bank of England notes circulating in the country to London, than there is to suppose the same transfer to have taken place in the time when the bank paid in gold. Both the nature of the pressure, and the principle on which our paper credit stood, were the same at both periods.

It remains for us to enquire, how far the payments of London are likely to have varied through any other cause. It is probable that, under ordinary circumstances, they do not fluctuate in any very considerable degree within a short distance of time. War seems likely, on the whole, to encrease them, both by the additional business in the stocks, and also by the other pecuniary transactions on the account of government (transactions generally carried on entirely in London), to which it gives occasion. It also encreases the payments of London, in common with those of the country, by contributing to a general rise in the price of articles. It is, however, necessary to guard this observation. In respect to the total *quantity* of consumable articles produced and sold in the kingdom, war, perhaps, may be considered as usually making little difference; for, while it gives a spur to some, it operates as a check to other branches of industry; and, while it encreases national consumption, it may possibly diminish, in an almost equal degree, that of individual. It raises, however, the *price* of commodities, and thus enlarges the general amount of payments, though it more particularly augments those payments which are made in the metropolis. This general augmentation, however, of the price of our articles, unattended by a similar rise in the price of the commodities of other countries, obstructs, as has been already shewn, the exportation of our goods; since it renders them less able to stand the competition to which they are subject in foreign markets, unless a compensation for the rise is afforded to the foreigner in the computation of the exchange between the two countries. The reader may, perhaps, be led here to imagine, that the bank ought to prevent this rise, according to the principles which it is the object of this Chapter to establish, a sufficiently considerable reduction of its paper being all that is necessary for the purpose. No doubt the fact is, that the tendency of goods to rise is continually restrained by the limitation of the paper of the Bank of England. And I apprehend that it is restrained just as much as it is proper, or, perhaps, practicable, to restrain it, if the paper of the bank is so far confined as to prevent an excess of the market price above the mint price of gold: for, in that case, it is restrained so far as still to afford to our goods the opportunity of sale in a foreign market, without giving to the foreigner that compensation in the exchange which leads to the exportation of the current coin of the country. To suppose the bank paper to be restrained much farther, is to suppose a profit on the importation of bullion; a profit, to which the continuance of the importations of that article must soon put a period. In saying, therefore, that war enhances the price of goods, and thus causes an encrease of payments, we ought here to bear in mind that it ought only to be allowed to lift them up to that point to which they can be raised consistently with the general maintenance of our exchanges; and that, so far as they *permanently* stand above that point, it is the enlarged and too great quantity of notes of the Bank of England which is to be considered as the cause of the high price of goods, rather than the high price of goods which is to be taken to be the cause of the enlarged quantity of notes of the Bank of England*. There is considerable danger, lest, in this respect, we should, in some degree, at least, mistake the effect for the cause; and should too much incline to consider an advanced price of commodities to be both the cause of an encreased issue of paper and the justification of it.

War, on the contrary, may be supposed to lessen the amount of general payments, or, at least, to check their growth, so far as it obstructs the accumulation of wealth and the natural progress of commerce. We know, however, that, during the late war, the amount of our exported and imported articles continued greatly to encrease. This happened partly, no doubt, through the general tendency of our trade to enlarge itself, partly through the advantages resulting from some new colonial acquisitions, and partly

* It was observed in a former place, that this difficult and disputable point would be again adverted to in the progress of the present Work. The fairest mode, as it appears to me, of determining which ought to be deemed the cause and which the effect, is that which has been adopted in the text; namely, to charge too much paper with being the cause when the price of bullion is rendered permanently higher than that of coin, and, when otherwise, to consider it rather as an effect. By the term "permanently," I, however, mean such a degree of permanence as may serve to shew that the fall of our exchanges, and the rise in the price of bullion, are not referable to any extraordinary and passing event, such as that of one or even of two particularly bad harvests; for these may not unfairly be termed temporary circumstances, though their influence may extend over a period of one or two years. In general it may, perhaps, also be assumed, that an excessive issue of paper has not been the leading cause of a fall in the exchange, if it afterwards turns out that the exchange is able to recover itself without any material reduction of the quantity of paper.

from the circumstance of the commerce of our competitors having been still more interrupted than our own. Our exports and imports, it is true, form no just measure of the total quantity either of our commercial transactions or of our general payments: they afford, however, some presumption of the enlargement of both. If we take into consideration all the points which have been touched upon, there will appear sufficient reason to believe, that, during the late war, a very considerable and progressive augmentation of the payments of the metropolis must have taken place.

It now remains only to consider, fourthly, how far circumstances may have been such as to have rendered the same quantity of Bank of England notes either more or less sufficient for effecting the same quantity of London payments.

Several causes may have contributed to spare the use of notes. First, it is to be remembered, that a small extension of their quantity may be sufficient to effect a comparatively large number of additional payments; for the private bankers in London, who are the chief holders of Bank of England paper, by no means find it necessary to enlarge their stock of it in full proportion to the encreased number of their pecuniary transactions. The talent of œconomizing bank notes is also a continually improving one; and the very circumstance of the suspension of the cash payments of the bank, by serving to strengthen mercantile credit, has favoured the exercise of œconomy in the use of the paper of the Bank of England. When payments were currently made in gold, the country banks were subject to sudden demands for cash through temporary alarms among the holders of their notes. From these they have lately been more exempt, in consequence of no other option having been given to those who demanded payment of country bank paper than that of receiving Bank of England notes in return. Since the suspension of the cash payments of the bank, credit has been less subject to interruption, and the quantity both of country paper and of Bank of England notes has probably been less variable; or, if the fluctuations of the latter have been as considerable as before, they may have more nearly corresponded with the variations in the wants of the public*.

To sum up the observations which have now been made: it thus appears, that, since the suspension of the cash payments of the bank, the number of its notes has been the same, or nearly the same, as before that event, if those two millions of one and two pound notes, which have been a mere substitute for gold, are deducted; that the payments, however, of the metropolis have been much encreased; but that, on the other hand, the same number of notes has probably sufficed of late for more than the same number of payments.

It has not been the object of these remarks to found upon them any exact estimate of the effect which the quantity of Bank of England paper lately issued is likely to have had on the cost of commodities, or on the market price of bullion; but rather, on the contrary, to shew that no such estimate can with confidence be formed, on account of the number of circumstances, some of them very difficult to be appreciated, which affect the question. I believe the fact to be, that very little correspondence has subsisted

---

* Immediately after the payment of the quarterly dividends on the public funds, the amount of Bank of England paper in circulation is considerably encreased; but the expectation that the plenty of it will soon cease, disposes bankers and others to hold for a time a superfluous quantity. In consequence of the additions to the public debt made during the war, the occasional enlargements of the quantity of bank paper, arising from this cause, have become much more considerable. A diminution of notes, if known to be temporary, and if also moderate, produces, on the other hand, little pressure; for the expectation of returning abundance serves to maintain confidence, and to dispose the bankers to deem a somewhat reduced stock of bank paper for the time sufficient. The chief occasion of a diminution of the number of bank notes has been, that of the payment of the instalments on the public loans. The government, during the latter years of the war, issued from week to week a species of exchequer bills, which they received back in part of the payments on the loans. By thus lessening the quantity of paper taken out of circulation at the time of each instalment, they gave new facility to the operation of raising the public money; an operation which, however great, has in itself no other difficulty than that which arises from the too sudden diminution of London paper to which it is apt to lead. It can scarcely be necessary to add, that a great loan may, nevertheless, portend difficulty in other quarters, and that the degree of ease with which the payment of our loans may be accomplished, is, therefore, no true criterion of the state of the public resources.

between the fluctuation in the amount of Bank of England notes in circulation at different times, and the variations in the general price of articles at the same periods; and this want of a very discernible connexion between the cause and the effect, seems not unlikely to have led some persons too hastily to conclude, that the enlargement and diminution of Bank of England paper have not that influence on the exchanges or on the price of commodities which has been spoken of*.

Let it, therefore, be carefully remembered, that I by no means suppose a limitation of London paper to operate simply by causing an equal reduction of country paper, and then such a fall in the price of goods over the kingdom as is exactly commensurate with the general diminution of paper; and, finally, also such a variation in the exchange as is precisely proportionate to the reduction of paper, and to the fall in the price of goods. Counteracting circumstances of various kinds may prevent these proportions from being maintained: and the full effects may not follow their cause until after the lapse of some period of time.

It must, in particular, be borne in mind, that a limitation of Bank of England paper affects prices in a great measure by its operation on the state of commercial confidence; and this influence on the minds of men will be far from uniform. A small limitation of Bank of England paper may give a great shock to confidence, when the state of credit is delicate; and may, therefore, at such a time, much discourage speculation. The very same limitation, under other circumstances of the country, may be almost without effect.

* It is not long since the Bank of England first adopted the custom of issuing notes for five pounds. These have circulated for some years in the place partly of gold, partly of country bank notes, and partly also, though it is impossible to say in what degree, in the place of ten pound Bank of England notes. There is, therefore, an unknown number of notes for five pounds which has formed that sort of addition to the Bank of England paper, which has no influence in raising the price of articles. This is only one of many circumstances, some operating in one direction, and some in the contrary, which render it difficult to draw a correct inference from those accounts of the quantity of Bank of England notes circulating at a variety of periods, which have been lately laid before parliament.

But although there is so great difficulty in estimating the precise influence on the cost of articles, or on the market price of bullion, which each alternation in the quantity of Bank of England notes may produce, there is no reason, on that account, to doubt the general truth of the proposition which was laid down in the close of the former chapter, namely, that the restriction of the paper of the Bank of England is the means both of maintaining its own value, and of maintaining the value, as well as of limiting the quantity, of all the paper in the country. Although it should be difficult, or even impossible, to determine to what point the limitation must be carried in order to produce a given effect, it may be sufficiently clear that the tendency of the limitation is to secure the benefit in question.

The perplexities of this subject being such as I have now described, it naturally occurs to us to reason from the effect to the cause, and to infer a too great issue of paper when we perceive that there is an excess of the market price above the mint price of gold. But this inference is one which, for reasons formerly given, should always be very cautiously made; for it is to be borne in mind, that the excess may arise from other causes besides that of a too great emission of paper. Let the manner in which an extravagant issue of notes operates in producing the excess be recollected. It raises, and probably by slow degrees, the cost of British goods. It thus obstructs the export of them, unless a compensation for the high price is afforded to the foreign buyer in the rate of exchange; and the variation in our exchange produces a low valuation of our coin, compared with that of bullion. The state of the exchange, then, is the immediate cause of the evil in question. Now, a suspension of the foreign demand for British manufactures, or an encrease of the British demand for foreign articles, circumstances which may arise when there is no encrease of bank paper, are the much more frequent as well as the more obvious causes of a fall in our exchange, and, therefore, also of a high price of bullion.

We are thus led back to the point which was dwelt upon some time since. Our two defective harvests, and the interruptions

Enquiry into Paper Credit 225 P

experienced in our export trade, very sufficiently account for the late fluctuation of our exchanges. In these respects there has evidently been much in our situation which has been remarkable; while, as has been proved in the present Chapter, there has been nothing which ought to be deemed extraordinary in the quantity of paper issued by the Bank of England.

It must, however, be admitted, that if an excessive issue of Bank of England notes produces, as it has been shewn to do, an unfavourable exchange; a reduction of them below the accustomed number must have a tendency to improve our exchange, by whatever means it may have been made to turn against us. But, after this admission, it may be remarked, that it may be necessary to encounter much evil in effecting the reduction. We have been lately placed between two dangers; between that of a depreciated paper currency on the one hand, and that of an interruption to our paper credit, and a consequent stagnation of our commerce and manufactures, on the other. And, on the whole, we have, perhaps, owed much to that liberal policy of the directors of the Bank of England, which has led them to maintain a quantity of notes in appearance encreased, and in reality not diminished, in spite of some political as well as popular prejudices on this subject; at a time, also, when their conduct was observed with particular jealousy, on account of the suspension of their cash payments, and even when the course of exchange was much against us. Whether the bank may have erred a little on the one side or on the other, is a point which it would be invidious very critically to examine, and difficult to determine with certainty. It seems sufficiently clear, that if, at the period of the late northern confederacy, when our exchanges were the least favourable, the bank had materially diminished its paper, the embarrassment of our manufacturers and merchants, which the state of the continent had begun to render great, would have immediately become far greater; and that manufacturing labour, which was then in some degree interrupted by a suspension of the demand for British goods on the continent, would have been likewise obstructed at the same season (a season of peculiar pressure on the common people, from the circumstance of the scarcity) by a more than ordinary difficulty which our manufacturers would have experienced in effecting their payments. The stock of goods in our warehouses, made ready for subsequent exportation, would, in this case, have been smaller; and we might, therefore, on the whole, have had to look forward to a less early rectification of our exchanges. The difficulties of 1793 might have been added to those of the spring of 1801; and if commercial confidence had failed, political credit might in consequence have been shaken at one of the most critical periods of our history.

From the principles recently laid down, some additional inferences may be deduced.

It was the object of several former Chapters to point out the evil of a too contracted issue of paper. The general tendency of the present, as well as of the preceding one, has been to shew the danger of a too extended emission. Two kinds of error on the subject of the affairs of the Bank of England have been prevalent. Some political persons have assumed it to be a principle, that in proportion as the gold of the bank lessens, its paper, or, as is sometimes said, its loans (for the amount of the one has been confounded with that of the other), ought to be reduced. It has been already shewn, that a maxim of this sort, if strictly followed up, would lead to universal failure. A sentiment has prevailed among other persons, which has bordered on a very different extreme. They have complained of nothing, except the too scanty liberality of the bank, and have seen no danger in almost any extension of its discounts, or profusion in the issue of its paper, provided only the bills discounted (that is, the bills received by the bank in return for its notes) were real bills, and were those also of sufficiently safe and responsible houses.

But it will appear from the principles laid down in this and the preceding Chapter, that there may be a disposition among very rich and punctual men to borrow a sum far exceeding that which it may be prudent in the bank to lend. Every additional loan obtained from the bank, if we suppose its gold to remain the same, implies an encreased issue of paper; but the measure of such issue has been shewn to be regulated by a principle which is not even connected with the question of the opulence of the borrowers at the bank, or of the nature of the bills discounted. The borrowers make a promise (and we will suppose that there is no reason to doubt the fulfilment of it) that the loan shall be repaid with punctuality. But in what manner is the payment to be effected? It will be made either in notes furnished by the Bank of England itself, or else in gold supplied by the same company, which notes and gold the bank must take care to render interchangeable for each other; and this is only to be done by keeping down their quantity, and thus maintaining their value.

Objections have been made by some to the monopoly of the bank. And its indisposition to lend to safe houses, on the security of real bills, to an extent which is deemed sufficient, has probably been the circumstance which has induced some mercantile persons to favour the idea of the establishment of a rival establishment. Competition, it is thought, would lead to greater liberality; and, in a variety of respects, would operate beneficially in this case, as it is known to do in many others.

It has been evinced, however, in the present Chapter, that we derive a material advantage from the power enjoyed by the Bank of England of exclusively furnishing the paper circulation of the metropolis. To this very circumstance the bank stands indebted for its faculty of regulating all the paper of the kingdom. On the bank is devolved the task of providing guineas for the whole country: with the bank is lodged the power of so restricting the general paper, as to render bullion purchasable, except in some extraordinary cases of alarm or difficulty. If these excepted cases should arise, and the cash payments of the bank should be suspended, an event of the possible recurrence of which we must not altogether exclude the idea; then the same circumstance of the monopoly of the bank affords to it the means of still sustaining the value both of its own paper and of that of the whole island. It serves also to impose upon the directors of this powerful company a complete responsibility. If a rival institution to the Bank of England were established, both the power and the responsibility would be divided; and, through the additional temptation to exercise that liberality in lending, which it is the object of competition to promote, the London notes, and also the country bills and notes, would be more liable to become excessive. Our paper credit would, therefore, stand in every respect on a less safe foundation.

CHAP. X

Objections to the Doctrine of the two preceding Chapters answered.—Of the Circumstances which render it necessary that the Bank should impose its own Limit on the Quantity of its Paper.—Effect of the Law against Usury.—Proof of the Necessity of restricting the Bank Loans, drawn from the Case of the Transfer of Capital to Foreign Countries.

SINCE it is not improbable that the reasoning of the preceding Chapters may have failed to produce full conviction in the mind of those who have been in the habit of deeming all limitation of the bank paper by the bank itself to be unnecessary; some few pages may be usefully employed in answering popular objections to the doctrine which has been laid down, and in more fully elucidating the subject.

"The encrease of Bank of England paper," we will suppose it to be still said by an objector, "is the effect and not the cause of an "advanced price of commodities. To enlarge the Bank of England "notes merely in proportion as safe and real bills are offered in "return for them, is only to exchange one species of paper for "another, namely, Bank of England notes for bills, which, though "not so current or so safe as bank notes, are sufficiently worthy of "credit. It is, therefore, simply to afford a guarantee to the tran-"sactions of the merchant, and thus to render that accommodation "to commerce which it belongs to the bank to give."

"The depreciation of paper," it may be added, "is apt to arise "not so much from an extension of its quantity, as from a want of "sufficient confidence in it. The great object of the bank should, "therefore, be to maintain the public confidence; to which it "contributes by furnishing, in return for bills confessedly good, a "species of paper still better. The evil of an unfavourable exchange, "and of a consequent high price of gold, arises from an unfavourable

230

"balance of trade, and from that cause only. The true mode of "preventing this evil, or of remedying it, if unfortunately it exists, "is to encrease the national industry. The way to encourage "industry is to give full scope to trade and manufactures by a liberal "emission of paper. The balance of trade will not fail to be rendered "favourable by that abundance of exportable articles which the "labour thus excited must necessarily create. The course of exchange "will, consequently, be supported; all excess of the market price "above the mint price of gold will be prevented; and thus the value "of our paper will be sustained by the very means of its encrease." Suppose a reasoner, on the same side, to add, that when the credit of the assignats of France was overthrown, the fall, especially at the first, was owing rather to the prevalence of distrust than to the excessive quantity of the article, and that the depreciation of assignats rarely bore a regular proportion to the extension of their amount*.

It may, with equal truth, be affirmed by the objector, that if a reference be made to the prices of corn in the London corn-market at various æreas, and also to the account of the quantity of bank notes stated by the bank to have been in circulation at the same or at immediately preceding periods, the price of grain in London will by no means be found to have been high in proportion as the number of Bank of England notes has been great, and low in proportion as it has been small; but that the very contrary has often been remarkably the case.

To these objections it may be answered, that they who represent an unlimited issue of Bank of England paper as having no tendency to produce the evils of a rise in the price of commodities in Great

---

* The following extract from Mr. Arthur Young's Tour through France, seems to establish the abovementioned fact.

"In September 1790, four hundred millions of assignats were in circulation; "but the discount at Bourdeaux never exceeded ten, at Paris six, per cent. "And in May 1791, after many hundred millions more were issued, the dis- "count was from seven to ten per cent. Condorcet, with other theorists, ex- "pected that the prices of corn, and of other necessaries of life, would enormously "advance; but the contrary happened to be the event—the price of corn declined. "The assignats amounted, on the dissolution of the first assembly, to eighteen "hundred millions."—Vol. I. 4to edition, page 520.

Britain, of a fall in our exchange, and of an excess of the market price above the mint price of gold, are bound to prove one of the two following propositions: either, first, that, supposing the directors of the bank to make the most enormous addition to their paper; to raise it, let us suppose, to fifty millions, even this augmentation will not lead to the consequences which have been mentioned; or if they do not affirm this strong position, but admit that there is a certain quantity of notes which will not fail to produce the evils in question, then, secondly, in order to prove that the bank need not place any limit to the issue of its own paper, they are bound to shew that the bank paper has a natural tendency sufficiently to limit itself.

Let us separately investigate each of these two points.

When we assume the fact of the bank paper being raised from its present amount of about fifteen millions to the sum of fifty millions, we are led, in the first place, to enquire in whose hands the additional sum of thirty-five millions would be placed, and what would be the motive for holding it? I admit, or rather it is a point on which I would insist, that the maintenance of the price of the assignats of France by no means rested entirely, nor, for a time, even principally, on their quantity. It depended much on the opinion entertained by Frenchmen respecting the value of the lands declared to be purchasable by means of this particular kind of paper, and respecting the fidelity of the French government to its engagements. Assignats, it is true, bore no interest; but the prospect of an ultimate profit to be reaped by the possessor of them, would operate, for a time, exactly like an accruing interest, in causing many persons to detain them; and, therefore, although they were used as a circulating medium, it is probable that only a part of them was turned to this purpose, and that even that part circulated but slowly. The reader is here desired to recollect a point which was explained in an early part of this work; namely, that the quantity of circulating medium which can be employed without injury to its value, is to be estimated not merely by its proportion to the quantity of trade or of payments, but also by the relative rapidity of its circulation. A species of circulating medium which changes hands once in ten days, will need to be a hundred times as great in quantity as the paper which passes through ten hands in one day. When that sanguine spirit which had at first inspired the holders of assignats subsided, the article would naturally sink in value with considerable rapidity; and in proportion as its price fell, the French government would be under the necessity of extending its issues. It is, therefore, not at all surprising that French assignats should, for a time, have borne a price which was proportionate not so much to their quantity as to their credit. Their quantity, however, after a certain period, operated on their credit, and became a very powerful cause of their depreciation.

Bank of England notes are exactly the converse to assignats in the points which have been mentioned; and their value, on that account, will be found to depend not so properly on their credit as on their quantity. It is true, that when, in consequence of alarm, a run is made upon the bank for guineas, the same confidence which is placed in gold is not reposed in Bank of England paper. Even in this case, however, it is only a small part of the community which is eager for gold: the holders of a very large proportion of the bank paper remain exactly as well contented as before to use it as the medium of their payments. And since the hoarders of gold prefer it not to paper only, but to land, to goods, and to almost every species of property, the paper of the bank cannot be affirmed to fall into discredit in consequence of applications for coin made with a view to hoard it, so properly as gold may be said to come into peculiar demand. In a season of alarm, our guineas are preferred by some persons both to our bank notes and to goods, on the same principle on which, in a state of extreme political convulsion, diamonds, because they may be still more easily transported or concealed, would probably be preferred to gold.

By saying, therefore, that the value of bank notes depends not on their credit, but on their quantity, I mean to affirm that their credit, so far as it affects their value, is always good, and that the common fluctuations of their price, in exchange both for goods and bullion, are not, in the smallest degree, to be referred to variations in the degree of confidence placed by Englishmen in the good faith or the solidity of the Bank of England. The magnitude of its capital is perfectly well known, and not the slightest doubt subsists respecting the sufficiency of its effects to answer much more than all its engagements. If the rise and fall in the public confidence in bank notes were the cause of the gradations in their price, the period at which their value would have been the lowest would have been that which followed the suspension of the cash payments of the bank; an event certainly calculated, more than any other which has been experienced, to affect the reputation of that company. But it is a most remarkable fact, and a fact decisive on the present point, that the exchanges of this country improved, or, in other words, that Bank of England paper rose in value when compared with bullion, in the months subsequent to the suspension of its payments in cash.

Bank of England paper, therefore, is not apt to vary in its value in consequence of the fluctuations of the public confidence in it; but essentially differs in this respect from the late assignats of France. It presents to the holder no hope of future profit from the detention of it. Not only does it bear no interest (in this point, indeed, resembling assignats), but it offers no substitute for interest; it holds out no privileges, certain or contingent, real or pretended, tempting the possessor to detain it. There is, on the contrary, a known and continually increasing loss sustained by keeping it. On this account the quantity held by each person is only that which the amount of payments to be effected by it renders, in his opinion, necessary.

We are at present assuming, for the sake of illustrating the subject, that thirty-five millions of additional bank paper are retained in the hands of the public. Imagine a London banker to acquire his share in them. The supply of bank notes which he chuses to reserve in his drawer is always estimated by the scale of his payments; or, to speak more correctly, by the probable amount of the fluctuations in his stock of notes, which fluctuations are proportionate, or nearly proportionate, to the scale of his payments. So long, therefore, as his payments remain the same (and they will not materially alter while the price of goods suffers no variation, supposing his transactions to retain their former proportion to those of the whole kingdom), he will be perfectly indisposed to hold fifty thousand pounds in bank notes, in the place of each fifteen thousand pounds which he has been accustomed to deem necessary. He will make haste to part with the whole superfluous quantity; he will offer to lend it to any safe merchants, and even at a reduced rate of interest, in case he shall find that borrowers cannot otherwise be invited.

If we imagine the merchants to become possessed of the new paper, the same difficulty of accounting for the detection of it remains; unless we admit that the principles laid down in the two former Chapters are just, and that the larger quantity of circulating medium will cause goods to rise in value, and will thus find for itself employment.

There seems to be only two modes in which we can conceive the additional paper to be disposed of. It may be imagined either, first, to be used in transferring an encreased quantity of articles, which it must, in that case, be assumed that the new paper itself has tended to create; or, secondly, in transferring the same articles at a higher price.

Let us examine the first of these cases.

An encreased quantity of articles can only arise from additional commodities either brought from abroad or produced at home through the exertion of new industry. An extraordinary issue of paper will bring goods from abroad only so far as it enables the country to export either gold, or additional commodities created at home, as the means of paying for the foreign articles. The export of gold has its limit. It is, moreover, desirable, for reasons which have been fully stated, that this limit should be narrow. Whether a very great emission of notes tends to encrease the quantity of goods produced at home, is the point which remains to be considered.

In examining this question, an error into which it is very natural to fall must be developed. When the Bank of England enlarges its paper, it augments, in the same degree, as we must here suppose, its loans to individuals. These favoured persons immediately conceive, and not without reason, that they have obtained an additional though borrowed capital, by which they can push their own particular manufacture or branch of commerce; and they are apt, also, though not with equal justice, to infer, that the new capital thus acquired by themselves is wholly an accession to that of the kingdom; for it does not occur to them that the commerce or manufactures of any other individuals can be at all reduced in consequence of this encrease of their own.

But, first, it is obvious, that the antecedently idle persons to whom we may suppose the new capital to give employ, are limited in number; and that, therefore, if the encreased issue is indefinite, it will set to work labourers, of whom a part will be drawn from other, and, perhaps, no less useful occupations. It may be inferred from this consideration, that there are some bounds to the benefit which is to be derived from an augmentation of paper; and, also, that a liberal, or, at most, a large encrease of it, will have all the advantageous effects of the most extravagant emission.

Let us also consider the mode in which the new paper operates through the medium of these individual borrowers, as unquestionably it does, in giving life to fresh industry. The bank notes convey to them the power of obtaining for their own use, or of destining to such purposes as they please, a certain portion of purchasable commodities. The extraordinary emission of paper causes no immediate difference in the *total* quantity of articles belonging to the kingdom. This is self-evident. But it communicates to the new borrowers at the bank a power of taking to themselves a larger share of the existing goods than they would otherwise have been able to command. If the holders of the new paper thus acquire the power over a larger portion of the existing stock of the kingdom, the possessors of the old paper must have the power over a smaller part. The same paper, therefore, will purchase fewer goods, or, in other words, commodities will rise in their nominal value. The proprietors of the new paper will become greater encouragers of industry than before; the owners of the old paper, being able to command less property, will have less power of employing labour. For industry is excited, strictly speaking, not by paper, but by that stock which the paper affords the means of purchasing. Money of every kind is an order for goods. It is so considered by the labourer when he receives it, and is almost instantly turned into money's worth. It is merely the instrument by which the purchasable stock of the country is distributed with convenience and advantage among the several members of the community.

It may be said, however, and not untruly, that an encreased issue of paper tends to produce a more brisk demand for the existing goods, and a somewhat more prompt consumption of them; that the more prompt consumption supposes a diminution of the ordinary stock, and the application of that part of it, which is consumed, to the purpose of giving life to fresh industry; that the fresh industry thus excited will be the means of gradually creating additional stock, which will serve to replace the stock by which the industry had been supported; and that the new circulating medium will, in this manner, create for itself much new employment.

The supposition which has now been made is admitted to be just. Let the reader, however, take notice, that it assumes the demand both for goods and labour to become more eager than before.—Now the consequence of this encreased eagerness in the demand must, unquestionably, be an enhancement of the price of labour and commodities, which is the very point for which I am contending. Indeed, whatever view we take of the subject, we seem obliged to admit, that, although additional industry will be one effect of an extraordinary emission of paper, a rise in the cost of articles will be another.

Probably no small part of that industry which is excited by new paper is produced through the very means of the enhancement of the cost of commodities. While paper is encreasing, and articles continue rising, mercantile speculations appear more than ordinarily profitable. The trader, for example, who sells his commodity in three months after he purchased it, obtains an extra gain, which is equal to such advance in the general price of things as the new paper has caused during the three months in question:—he confounds this gain with the other profits of his commerce; and is induced, by the apparent success of his undertakings, to pursue them with more than usual spirit. The manufacturer feels the same kind of encouragement to extend his operations; and the enlarged issue of paper supplies both him and the merchant with the means of carrying their plans into effect. Bs soon, however, as the circulating medium ceases to encrease, the extra profit is at an end; and, if we assume the augmented paper to be brought back to its ordinary quantity, we must suppose industry to languish for a time, through the ill success which will appear to attend mercantile transactions.

Mr. Hume has an observation in his Essay on Money, which, in some degree, confirms the remarks which have been made in the text. Having represented an influx of money as exciting industry (and we may presume an encrease of paper to have exactly the same effect), "At first," he says, "no alteration is perceived; by degrees "the price rises first of one commodity, then of another, till the "whole, at last, reaches a just proportion with the new quantity "of specie which is in the kingdom. *In my opinion, it is only in this* "*interval or intermediate situation between the acquisition of money* "*and rise of prices*" (Mr. Hume must mean, no doubt, the completion of the rise, and not the commencement of it) "*that the encreas-* "*ing quantity of gold and silver is favourable to industry**."

* Mr. Hume, in observing that, when money encreases, "the price rises "first of one commodity, then of another, till the whole, at last, reaches a just "proportion with the new quantity of specie which is in the kingdom," appears to me not sufficiently to advert to the tendency of money to go abroad as soon as it shall have raised the gold price of articles above their level in other countries, allowing for the charges of transportation; a subject which will be more fully treated of in the next Chapter. He also describes the operation of an encrease of coin in raising prices as proceeding somewhat more slowly than, perhaps, it would be found to do. An augmentation of Bank of England notes operates, no doubt, in this respect, more quickly than an encrease of money; for the London bankers, who are the great holders of bank paper, are likely to be much less disposed to detain, for example, a double quantity of it, than all the individuals of the kingdom are to detain in their several drawers, or in their pockets, a double quantity of guineas. The banking system, by committing the business

It must be also admitted, that, provided we assume an excessive issue of paper to lift up, as it may for a time, the cost of goods though not the price of labour, some augmentation of stock will be the consequence; for the labourer, according to this supposition, may be forced by his necessity to consume fewer articles, though he may exercise the same industry. But this saving, as well as any additional one which may arise from a similar defalcation of the revenue of the unproductive members of the society, will be attended with a proportionate hardship and injustice. This supposition also implies the acknowledgment of the point for which we are contending, that an encreased issue of paper tends to raise the price of commodities.

It has thus been admitted that paper possesses the faculty of enlarging the quantity of commodities by giving life to some new industry. It has, however, been affirmed, that the encrease of industry will by no means keep pace with the augmentation of paper. The question now to be considered is, whether, if we suppose thirty-five millions of new paper to be suddenly issued, the fresh industry which would, consequently, be excited, would create a quantity of goods, the sale of which would give employment to all the new paper. Let it be admitted, for the sake of illustrating this point, that the thirty-five millions of additional bank notes will have the extraordinary power of calling at once into being thirty-five millions of new goods; still it may be remarked, that even all this additional property would by no means find employment for that equal quantity of paper which is here assumed to have given existence to it.

of payments to few hands, has made much difference in respect to the time within which an encreased quantity of circulating medium may be supposed to raise the price of articles. It has given to many great holders of Bank of England paper a very strong interest on the side of not keeping a superfluous quantity of it.

That an encrease of the circulating medium tends to afford temporary encouragement to industry, seems also to be proved by the effects of the Mississippi scheme in France; for it is affirmed by French writers, that the notes of Mr. Law's bank appeared for a time to have a very powerful influence in extending the demand for labour, and in augmenting the visible and *bonâ fide* property of the kingdom.

We shall be able to explain this circumstance, as well as to throw some new light on the general subject, by supposing an individual, A, to become, in consequence of an extraordinary issue of paper, a new borrower at the bank to the extent of twenty thousand pounds. The twenty thousand pounds, while it is held in the shape of paper, affording him no interest; he will make haste to part with it, by purchasing goods, stocks, land, or some other article, to the extent of the sum in question. Suppose him to make the purchase from B, in three days after he received the notes. B is now in possession of twenty thousand pounds in new bank paper, created by the extraordinary emission; and is, in like manner, in haste to part with it. Imagine him, also, to pay away the same paper in return for goods at the end of three days. Thus the same notes will in six days have effected two purchases amounting together to forty thousand pounds. If we imagine the like transaction to be repeated again and again; the same notes will in twelve days have effected the purchase of goods amounting to eighty thousand pounds; in about a month to two hundred thousand pounds; and in a year to about two millions. Thirty-five millions of new paper will thus effect in a year the sale of goods to the extent of two or three thousand millions. In order, therefore, to account for the employment of the thirty-five millions, we must assume, if we allow no rise in prices to take place, such a new quantity of goods to be called into existence by the magic influence of the new paper, as to become a subject for purchases, amounting, in a year, to no less than these two or three thousand millions. We must assume the creation not of thirty-five millions of property, but of five, ten, or, perhaps, twenty times that sum; or else we must suppose, what is not supposable, that the newly created capital of thirty-five millions changes hands as frequently as the thirty-five millions of bank notes which created it; that is to say, that the new property undergoes a fresh sale on every third day.

The case which has been put is inaccurate, inasmuch as the payments effected by bank notes are on the account not merely of goods and other articles sold, but likewise of numberless sums borrowed and repaid. It is probable, however, that payments of this latter kind will always bear a nearly uniform proportion to those of the other class. The general inference which was intended to be drawn from the case, will, therefore, be just.

In speaking formerly of the reduction of bank paper, much pains were taken to point out the important difference between that limitation of loans which leads to a diminution of paper, and that which produces no such diminution; and it was then observed, that it was by the quantity of Bank of England paper, and not by the amount of loans, or by the amount of loans so far only as they influence the quantity of paper, that a judgment was to be formed of the pressure on the metropolis, and of the reduction of prices. Many of the remarks then made respecting the limitation of bank paper, apply with nearly equal force to the subject of its encrease.

It has now been fully shewn, first, that Bank of England paper is an article of such a nature, that a very superfluous quantity of it will never be for a long time retained in any quarter; and, secondly, that the vast encrease of it, which, for the sake of more convenient discussion, was assumed to take place, cannot possibly create such a new capital as shall furnish the new paper with employment. There remains, therefore, no other mode of accounting for the uses to which the additional supply of it can be turned, than that of supposing it to be occupied in carrying on the sales of the same, or nearly the same, quantity of articles as before, at an advanced price the cost of goods being made to bear the same, or nearly the same, proportion to their former cost, which the total quantity of paper at the one period bears to the total quantity at the other.

We are thus brought, though by a different course, to the point at which we arrived in an early part of a former Chapter. An enlarged issue of paper, it was then observed, produces an encreased facility of borrowing, as well as an opinion of encreased facility; and thus adds to the eagerness of purchasers. It communicates an additional power of purchasing, not only to the original borrower at the bank, but successively, also, as has now been shewn, to all the

Enquiry into Paper Credit 241

other individuals into whose hands the new bank notes pass in the course of their circulation.

Very strong confirmation of the present doctrine may be furnished by a reference to the case of gold. No one doubts, that, in the event of an augmented supply of this article from the mines, the value of it would fall nearly in proportion to the extension of its quantity; especially if it were used for the sole purpose of a circulating medium, and were also the only kind of circulating medium. The metropolis of Great Britain is so circumstanced, that the issue of an extraordinary quantity of bank paper for the purpose of effecting the payments of London, in a considerable degree resembles the creation of an extraordinary supply of gold for the general uses of the world.

It was stated in the beginning of this Chapter, as one objection to the doctrine which I have been endeavouring to establish, that "to enlarge the quantity of Bank of England notes merely in "proportion as sufficient and real bills are offered in return for them, "is only to exchange one species of paper for another, namely, "Bank of England notes for bills, which, though not so current or "so safe as bank notes, are sufficiently worthy of credit. That it "was, therefore, simply to afford a guarantee to the transactions of "the merchant, and thus to render that accommodation to commerce "where it belongs to the bank to give." This objection will be sufficiently answered by repeating an observation which has been already frequently made, namely, that the effect produced by paper credit on the price of articles depends not merely on the quantity of paper in existence, but also on its currency, or, in other words, on the rapidity of its circulation. It was admitted in the objection, that bills are not current like bank notes, and that it is the greater currency of the latter which causes the exchange to be desired.

It was mentioned, as another argument against the doctrine which has been laid down, that corn has not usually borne any sort of proportion to the quantity of Bank of England paper in circulation at the same time. The answer is, that the directors of the bank have never augmented their notes in such a degree as to be likely to produce any material alteration in the general price of goods; that one or more of those circumstances which were dwelt upon in the preceding Chapter, may have counteracted the tendency of the fluctuations of the quantity of paper to produce correspondent variations in the price of commodities; and, above all, that even a small reduction of the supply of grain can hardly fail to lead to a rise in its value when exchanged for paper, so great as to forbid all comparison between the effects of an alteration of the quantity of the one article and of an alteration of the quantity of the other. Paper has been spoken of as raising the cost of commodities, at the most, only in proportion to its encreased quantity. But in the case of a diminished supply of corn, the price rises according to a very different ratio; and for this obvious reason, that we cannot accustom ourselves to the use of a reduced allowance of grain, in the same manner in which we are able, by degrees, to accommodate ourselves to a smaller quantity of circulating medium*.

* The following extract from the work of Sir W. Davenant, who wrote from 1695 to 1712, may give some idea of the vast effect which a small failure of the supply of corn has on the price of this necessary of life.

"It is observed, that but one-tenth defect in the harvest may raise the price "three-tenths; and when we have but half our crop, which now and then "happens, the remainder is spun out by thrift and good management, and "eked out by the use of other grain; but this will not do for above one year, "and would be a small help in the succession of two or three unseasonable "harvests.

"We take it, that a defect in the harvest may raise the price of corn in the "following proportions:

"A defect of		raises the price	above the common rate
"1 tenth			3 tenths,
"2 tenths			8 tenths,
"3 tenths			1 six-tenths,
"4 tenths			2 eight-tenths,
"5 tenths			4 five-tenths.

"So that, when corn rises to treble the common rate, it may be presumed that "we want above one-third of the common produce; and if we should want "five-tenths, or half the common produce, the price would rise to near five "times the common rate."

This scale is not likely to be very accurate. It is, indeed, by no means clear, whether it proceeds on the supposition of a deficiency of the antecedent crop only; or of a deficiency of the total stock, that is to say, of the antecedent crop and of the stock remaining over from a former year taken together; which are two very different questions. And many circumstances may render such calculations, however just, by no means equally applicable to every period. The passage, therefore, is quoted merely for the purpose of giving some general ideas on the subject.

Let the principle which was laid down as regulating the cost of all articles be recollected. The question of prices is a question of power, and of power only; and, in the event of the scarcity of any commodity, the buyers are more or less under the power of the sellers, in proportion as the article in question is of more or less urgent necessity.

That the quantity of circulating paper must be limited, in order to the due maintenance of its value, is a principle on which it is of especial consequence to insist, as it has been overlooked by some writers on paper credit. In the work of Sir James Stewart on Political Œconomy, banks are discussed at considerable length; but little intimation is given of the necessity of confining the total quantity of circulating paper, or of the tendency of an excessive emission to render the exchange unfavourable, and thus to cause gold to be drawn away. On the other hand, the duty of not giving out bank paper, except for sufficient value received (a point on which, at the present time, there is less occasion to enlarge), is strongly urged by this writer, and the security of bills of exchange is implied by him to be inadequate, that of land alone being fully approved. Bank notes emitted without obtaining value in return, are termed by him paper issued for "value consumed;" and are represented as the great source both of loss and danger to a banking company. His mode of expressing himself on this point is such as to make him appear to lend much countenance to the error which it is the object of the present Chapter to expose; namely, that of imagining that a proper limitation of bank notes may be sufficiently secured by attending merely to the nature of the security for which they are given*.

---

* "When paper is issued for no value received, the security of such paper "stands alone upon the original capital of the bank; whereas, when it is issued "for value received, that value is the security on which it immediately stands, "and the bank stock is, properly speaking, only subsidiary.

"I have dwelt the longer on this curcumstance (namely, that of taking "sufficient property in pledge for the notes issued), because many who are "unacquainted with the nature of banks have a difficulty to comprehend how "they should ever be at a loss for money, as they have a mint of their own, "which requires nothing but paper and ink to create millions. But if they con-

Dr. A. Smith, who is a more late writer, has asserted the necessity of a limitation of paper, in the passage which was quoted in an early part of this work; but he has done this in terms which are inaccurate, and he has given an erroneous and inadequate idea of the evil which may result from a very extended emission.

Mr. Locke has lent some countenance to the error which I am endeavouring to expose, by his way of considering the subject of the balance of trade, which is the same mode in which I supposed, in the beginning of this Chapter, an objector to conceive of it. "The evil of an unfavourable exchange," I imagined my opponent to say, "and of a consequent high price of gold, arises from an "unfavourable balance of trade, and from that only. The true way "of preventing this evil, or of remedying it, if it unfortunately "exists, is to encrease the national industry; and the way to encour- "age industry, is to give full scope to trade and manufactures by a "liberal emission of paper. The balance of trade will not fail to be "rendered favourable by that abundance of exportable articles "which the labour thus excited must necessarily be supposed to "create."

Mr. Locke's language respecting an unfavourable balance of trade, and its influence in causing gold to be melted down and exported, is as follows.

"Profit," he says, "can be made by melting down our money, "but only in two cases. First, when the current prices of the same "denomination are unequal and of different weights, some heavier "some lighter; for then the traders in money cull out the heavier, "and melt them down with profit.—The other case wherein our "money comes to be melted down, is a losing trade, or, which is "the same thing in other words, an over great consumption of

"sider the principles of banking, they will find that every note issued for value "consumed, in place of value received and preserved, is neither more nor less "than a partial spending either of their capital or profits on the bank."— Stewart's Political Œconomy, Book IV. Part II. Chap. IV.

Chapter V. is a short chapter, of which the object is to shew that "banks" issuing circulating paper "ought to issue their notes on private not mercantile "credit." By private credit, that of "lands and personal estates" appears to be meant.

245

"foreign commodities. Whenever the over-balance of foreign "trade makes it difficult for our merchants to get bills of exchange, "the exchange presently rises. If the law makes the exportation "of our coin penal, it will be melted down; if it leaves the expor- "tation of our coin free, it will be carried out in specie—one way "or other, go it must. But this melting down carries not away one "grain of our treasure out of England.—*The coming and going of* "*that depends wholly upon the balance of trade**."

The error which I consider as encouraged and supported by this passage of Mr. Locke (and much similar language is to be found in other writers), is this:—the passage implies, that it is the comparative state of our exports and imports which regulates the exchange, and not at all the state of the exchange which regulates the comparative state of our exports and imports. It leads us to suppose, that an unfavourable balance of trade (that is, the excess of the goods imported above those exported) is exclusively the cause, and that the bad state of the exchange is altogether the effect. The passage inclines us not at all to suspect a circumstance which Mr. Hume admits in a note in his Essay on Money, namely, "that an unfavour- "able exchange becomes a new encouragement to export."

The point which I wish here to establish may be still more clearly explained in the following manner. It has been shewn in a former Chapter, and, indeed, it is stated by Mr. Locke, that the selling price of bills determines the rate of exchange. When, therefore, for example, persons abroad wishing to sell bills on England are more numerous than those who are disposed to buy them, the price of bills must drop; and it must continue to fall until it becomes so low as to tempt some individuals to become purchasers of them. They who buy the bills on England, are the buyers of so many orders to receive in England either money or bank notes. The money or bank notes thus received, unless left in some English hand (and they will be so left in some few cases only), must be invested in British articles, and exported. The profit afforded by the fall in the selling price of the bills must, therefore, be sufficient to

* Further Considerations concerning raising the Value of Money.

cause the speculation of the buyers of the bills to answer—the speculation I mean of either bringing over British gold, which would not otherwise have been transferred, or of purchasing and exporting British commodities which would not otherwise have been at that time transported. Thus, therefore, an unfavourable exchange may be considered not only as becoming, according to Mr. Hume's expression, "a new encouragement to export," but as affording all that degree of encouragement to export which is necessary to secure as much actual exportation either of gold or of goods, or both, as shall serve to equalize the exports and imports; unless, indeed, the same cause, namely, the unfavourableness of the exchange, should tempt foreigners to remit money to England, and lodge it for a time in our hands, with a view to the profit to be obtained by this species of speculation.

The principle which I would lay down on the subject now under consideration, is, I think, simple and intelligible, and it applies itself to all periods of time, and to every kind of circulating medium which may happen to be in use. I would be understood to say, that in a country in which *coin alone* circulates, if, through any accident the quantity should become greater in proportion to the goods which it has to transfer than it is in other countries, the coin becomes cheap as compared with goods, or, in other words, that goods become dear as compared with coin, and that a profit on the exportation of coin arises. This profit, indeed, soon ceases through the actual exportation of the article which is excessive.

I would say again, that in a country in which *coin and paper* circulate at the same time, if the two taken together should, in like manner, become, in the same sense of the term, excessive, a similar effect will follow. There will, I mean, be a profit on sending away the coin, and a consequent exportation of it.

I would say, thirdly, that in a country in which *paper alone* circulates, if the quantity be in the same sense excessive, supposing the credit of the banks which issued it to be perfect, the paper will fall in value in proportion to the excess, on an exactly similar principle; or, in other words, that goods will rise; and that a necessity will exist for granting, in the shape of exchange, a bounty on the exportation of them equal to that which would have been afforded in the two former suppositions, assuming the quantity of circulating medium to be excessive in an equal degree in all the three cases.

It thus appears, that "the coming and going of gold" does not (as Mr. Locke expresses it, and as was supposed in the objection at the beginning of this Chapter) "depend wholly on the balance of trade." It depends on the quantity of circulating medium issued; or it depends, as I will allow, on the balance of trade, if that balance is admitted to depend on the quantity of circulating medium issued. Mr. Locke, however, is very far from leading his reader to conceive that the balance of trade depends on the quantity of circulating medium issued; for he describes an unfavourable balance as resulting from a "losing trade," and from an "over great consumption of foreign commodities;" terms which seem to imply an unprosperous state of commerce, and a too expensive disposition in the people, and which naturally lead to the conclusion, that the prosperity of the country will effectually secure us against the danger of the exportation of our coin, whatever may be the quantity of our paper.

It has now, I trust, been made sufficiently to appear, that banks, if they pay in gold, or if, while not paying in gold, they maintain the value of their notes, must observe some limit in respect to their emission of them.

If, indeed, we could suppose a country to have no intercourse with any other, we might imagine an unlimited issue of paper to take place without producing any difference in its value when exchanged for gold. In that case it would be necessary to assume the price of goods to rise indefinitely, but the people to be content to use a less and less proportion of gold to paper, and on that account to continue to consider the relative value of gold and paper as the same. This unlimited rise in the price of goods, and equally indefinite fall in the value of gold, are everywhere precluded by the commercial communications which take place between different parts of the world; gold in exchange for goods, allowing for the expense of transporting them, necessarily bearing that price, or nearly that price, in each country which it bears in all. The variations in the value of bullion, as compared with that of the circulating medium, serve, therefore, to detect and restrain that too great emission of notes to which all countries would otherwise be prone; and those operations of the exchange, which have been described, are the means by which every bank is compelled to make the value of its paper conform itself to the ancient standard.

Let the case of the continental bank notes, already spoken of, be here adverted to. The depreciation of these has been apt to originate, as I conceive, in the state of the exchanges. The unfavourable exchange has produced a difference between the value of bullion and that both of the current paper of those banks and of the current coin; and, when this difference has become permanent and considerable, a discount on the paper has established itself; in other words, coin has ceased to bear the price of paper, and has taken the price of bullion, and from that time the paper alone has passed at the reduced rate. The difference between the value of the circulating medium of this country and that of bullion has always been sufficiently small to prevent the like discount from arising; and so long as we avoid a discount, persons, in general, do not discover that any depreciation of our paper exists. But even the most insignificant of those depressions in the value of our circulating medium, which are indicated by the exchange, are to be referred to the same immediate cause from which the depreciation of the bank paper on the continent has originated. I do not mean that our smaller and their greater depreciations are alike to be referred to an excess of paper. I would affirm, however, that they have equally resulted from the circumstance *of goods, at the time in question, being too high in value* (possibly, in the one case, through an excess of paper, and, in the other, through a fluctuation in the markets) *to bear to be exported in sufficient quantity to satisfy the debt for which payment has been demanded, unless an advantage in the exchange was granted to the exporting merchant.*

249

It may be convenient to the reader here to recapitulate the several points which have been lately dwelt upon.

I have shewn, first, that since Bank of England paper affords no profit to the holder, a very superfluous quantity is not likely to be held in any quarter; and that the additional thirty-five millions, which have been spoken off, must, therefore, be supposed to be employed either in transferring an encreased quantity of goods, which, in that case, it must be assumed to have itself created, or in transferring the same goods at a higher price. I have, then, insisted, that since the fresh industry which is excited cannot be supposed to be commensurate with the new paper, it is necessary to assume (conformably to the principles of a former Chapter), that a great rise in the price of commodities will take place. This rise in the cost of articles in Great Britain must produce, as has been also shewn, a diminution of the demand for them abroad, unless a compensation for their high price is given to the foreigner in the rate of exchange; so that the too great emission of paper will be the cause of a disadvantageous balance of trade, and also of an unfavourable exchange; or, in other words, of a low valuation of the circulating medium of Great Britain when compared with that of other countries.

It has, likewise, been observed, that even the smallest of those depressions in the value of our circulating medium, which are indicated by the exchange, arise out of the same circumstance which has produced the greater depreciations of the continental bank paper; goods, it has been said, being rendered too high (in the one instance, probably, by an excess of paper, in the other by a fluctuation in the markets) to bear to be exported in sufficient quantity to satisfy the debts for which payment has been demanded, unless a bounty, in the shape of the exchange, be granted to the exporting merchant*.

* Some proof of the tendency of a too great emission of paper to render the exchange unfavourable by the means which have been described, and to cause the current coin to be exported, is furnished by the following extracts from arrets of the French government, issued a short time after the establishment of Mr. Law's bank. The reader is desired to take notice, that this bank

We come next to the second topic of enquiry, namely, whether those bounds within which Bank of England paper must be confined, in order to guard against a dangerous depreciation of it, are likely to be observed, in consequence of some natural tendency which it has to limit itself, so that it is unnecessary that the bank should restrain it.

In examining this question, I mean also to enquire whether the adoption merely of such rules as may tend, in a general way, to confine the loans of the bank, may be sufficient; or whether, also, any limitation of the specific sums lent may be necessary.

was instituted on the same professed principles with the Bank of England; was, for a time, independent of the government, though sanctioned by it; possessed a capital of one hundred millions of livres, and lent money on good security. Being, however, permitted to issue notes to the vast amount of about thirty-eight millions sterling, the credit (in some degree a well founded one) which this bank obtained, encouraged the formation of the Mississippi scheme, and led to other doubtful undertakings. The bank paper being rendered exchangeable for the actions (or stock) of the Mississippi company, though at a regulated discount, the value of it, like that of the late assignats of France, was made to depend on the public opinion of the profits of a speculation, and, therefore, on the credit of the circulating article, rather more, perhaps, than on its quantity.

Extract from the King's arret, dated 21st May, 1720.—"The King having "caused to be examined in his council the condition to which the kingdom "was reduced before the establishment of the bank, that he might compare it "with its present condition; it has appeared to the King, that the high rate of "the interest of money had done more damage to the kingdom than all the "expences which the late King had been at during his several wars. By the "establishment of the bank, the King has restored things to good order. The "nobility have found, *in the encrease of the value of their lands,* means to make "themselves easy; manufactures, commerce, and navigation, are re-established; "the lands are cultivated, and the artificer works."

By the arret of the 5th March, his Majesty ordained, "that actions of the "India (or Mississippi) company might be converted into bank notes, and "those notes into actions, according to the proportion which at that time was "reckoned most just with respect to the value of the coin. It remained for his "Majesty to find an expedient *for re-establishing the value of the coin in such* "*proportion as might suit foreign commerce and the vent of the products of the* "*country.* His Majesty has provided for these things by his declaration of "11 March, which *orders the reduction of the value of the coin.*"

This singular arret then proceeds to observe, that since "this *reduction*" of the coin "must necessarily produce a *diminution* of the price of commodities" (a measure calculated to produce its encrease, and which would only fail to have this effect so far as the too great issue of paper had already produced it), "his Majesty," therefore, "has judged the general interest of his subjects

251

First, it is obvious that the principle of lending, simply in proportion to the property of those who desire to borrow, cannot be a safe one. If mere capital were to give a title to bank loans, the borrowers might become beyond measure numerous; even all proprietors of the public funds might prefer a claim for asssistance.

If it should be said that the bank loans ought to be afforded only

"required that the price or *nominal value of actions and of bank notes should be* "lessened *for maintaining them in a just proportion with the coin and other com-* "modities *of the kingdom, for hindering the too high value of coin from sinking* "the *public credit, and for preventing the losses which his subjects might suffer* "in *commerce with foreigners.*"

The arret then directs that actions of 10,000 livres should be reduced to 5,000, and bank notes of 1,000 to 500.

The people, after this arret, which doubled the public injury under the pretence of dispensing equal justice, refused to take the notes, and the arret was revoked. Another arret, reducing the actions alone, was substituted. Still, however (as is observed by Mr. Postlethwaite, from whom this account is taken), "the people having been frighted would not meddle with bank notes except "in payment for their goods which they raised four times above their usual "value or upon a very great discount."

Another ordinance of the King, to the following effect, was then issued.— "His Majesty being informed that many of his subjects, who, in these latter "times, have got considerable fortunes, forgetting what they owe to their "country, have sent the greatest part thereof into foreign countries; and that "some others of his said subjects *keep in the said countries considerable sums in* "specie, with a design to place the same there, which has kept up the course of "exchange to the advantage of foreigners" (the exportation of the gold would tend so far as it went to improve the course of exchange, and was an effect of the unfavourable exchange and not the cause), "and has occasioned the ex- "porting out of the kingdom a considerable quantity of specie. And his Majesty, "considering how much it is important to remedy an abuse so contrary to the "laws of government, though without constraining the liberty of commerce; "his Majesty, with the advice of Monsieur the Duke of Orleans, regent, ordains, "that in general all his subjects shall be *obliged to recall their funds*, and cause "the same to be brought again into the kingdom within two months from the "publication of this present ordinance."

It appears from the first of these arrets, that an encreased emission of paper tends to raise prices as well as to excite industry; from the second that it leads, however, to a very unfavourable exchange, and to the exportation of the coin of a country; and that the reduction of the value of the coin is the remedy which is naturally resorted to. The same point is confirmed by the third arret.

All the three arrets unite in proving the gross ignorance which at this time prevailed on the subject of exchanges and of paper credit, and in shewing, therefore, the unfairness of inferring from the Mississippi project in France the instability of our own paper credit. In the instance of our own South Sea scheme, no new bank was instituted, and the credit of the Bank of England paper was sustained.

to traders, and on the security of real bills, that is to say, of bills drawn on the occasion of an actual sale of goods, let it be remembered that real bills, as was observed in an early part of this work, may be multiplied to an extremely great extent; and, moreover, that it is only necessary sufficiently to extend the customary length of credit, in order to effect the greatest imaginable multiplication of them. If the bank directors were to measure their discounts by the amount of real bills offered, it may be apprehended, that bankers and other discounters, who now take this better kind of paper, might become much more considerable holders of mere notes of hand, or of fictitious bills; and that an opportunity might thus be afforded of pouring a vast additional quantity of real bills into the Bank of England.

It may be imagined, that if the directors were to govern their conduct by a regard partly to the capital of the borrowers, partly to the species of bills offered, but partly, also, to the probability of punctual payment, the addition of this third check to the former might suffice. But it is here to be recollected, that the bank itself, if we suppose a progressive enlargement of notes, must be assumed to furnish perpetually encreasing means of effecting payments, and thus to render punctuality in fulfilling even the most extravagant engagements convenient and easy to the merchants.

It only remains to enquire, lastly, whether any principle of moderation and forbearance on the part of borrowers at the bank may be likely to exempt the directors of that institution from the necessity of imposing their own limit.

It may possibly be thought, that a liberal extension of loans would soon satisfy all demands, and that the true point at which the encrease of the paper of the bank ought to stop, would be discovered by the unwillingness of the merchants to continue borrowing.

In order to ascertain how far the desire of obtaining loans at the bank may be expected at any time to be carried, we must enquire into the subject of the quantum of profit likely to be derived from borrowing there under the existing circumstances. This is to be judged of by considering two points: the amount, first of interest to be paid on the sum borrowed; and, secondly, of the mercantile or other gain to be obtained by the employment of the borrowed capital. The gain which can be acquired by the means of commerce is commonly the highest which can be had; and it also regulates, in a great measure, the rate in all other cases. We may, therefore, consider this question as turning principally on a comparison of the rate of interest taken at the bank with the current rate of mercantile profit.

The bank is prohibited, by the state of the law, from demanding, even in time of war, an interest of more than five per cent., which is the same rate at which it discounts in a period of profound peace. It might, undoubtedly, at all seasons, sufficiently limit its paper by means of the price at which it lends, if the legislature did not interpose an obstacle to the constant adoption of this principle of restriction.

Any supposition that it would be safe to permit the bank paper to limit itself, because this would be to take the more *natural* course, is, therefore, altogether erroneous. It implies that there is no occasion to advert to the rate of interest in consideration of which the bank paper is furnished, or to change that rate according to the varying circumstances of the country.

At some seasons an interest, perhaps, of six per cent. per annum, at others, of five, or even of four per cent., may afford that degree of advantage to borrowers which shall be about sufficient to limit, in the due measure, the demand upon the bank for discounts. Experience, in some measure, proves the justice of this observation, for, in time of peace, the bank has found it easy to confine its paper by demanding five per cent. for interest; whereas, in war, and especially in the progress and towards the conclusion of it, as well as for some time afterwards, the directors have been subject, as I apprehend, to very earnest solicitations for discount, their notes, nevertheless, not being particularly diminished. It is, therefore, unreasonable to presume that there will always be a disposition in the borrowers at the bank to prescribe to themselves exactly those bounds which a regard to the safety of the bank would suggest.

The interest of the two parties is not the same in this respect. The borrowers, in consequence of that artificial state of things which is produced by the law against usury, obtain their loans too cheap. That which they obtain too cheap they demand in too great quantity. To trust to their moderation and forbearance under such circumstances, is to commit the safety of the bank to the discretion of those who, though both as merchants and as British subjects they may approve in the general of the proper limitation of bank paper, have, nevertheless, in this respect, an individual interest, which is at variance with that of the Bank of England.

The temptation to borrow, in time of war, too largely at the bank, arises, as has been observed, from the high rate of mercantile profit. Capital is then scarce, and the gain accruing from the employment of it is proportionably considerable.

The reader, possibly, may think that an extension of bank loans, by furnishing additional capital, may reduce the profit on the use of it, and may thus lessen the temptation to borrow at five per cent. It has been already remarked in this Chapter, that capital by which term *bonâ fide* property was intended, cannot be suddenly and materially encreased by any emission of paper. That the rate of mercantile profit depends on the quantity of this *bonâ fide* capital and not on the amount of the nominal value which an encreased emission of paper may give to it, is a circumstance which it will now be easy to point out.

I admit, that a large extension of bank loans may give a temporary check to the eagerness of the general demand for them. It will cause paper to be for a time over abundant, and the price paid for the use of it, consequently, to fall.

It seems clear, however, on the principles already stated, that when the augmented quantity of paper shall have been for some time stationary, and shall have produced its full effect in raising the price of goods, the temptation to borrow at five per cent. will be exactly the same as before; for the existing paper will then bear only the same proportion to the existing quantity of goods, when sold at the existing prices, which the former paper bore to the former quantity of goods, when sold at the former prices: the power of purchasing will, therefore, be the same; the terms of lending and borrowing must be presumed to be the same; the amount of circulating medium alone will have altered, and it will have simply caused the same goods to pass for a larger quantity of paper. To assume under such circumstances the same rate of mercantile profit to subsist, is only to suppose that the trader will be situated neither more nor less advantageously than before; and that the annual gain which he will obtain by trading with the same quantity of goods, will bear the same proportion as before to their current cost. If this observation be just, there can be no reason to believe that even the most liberal extension of bank loans will have the smallest tendency to produce a permanent diminution of the applications to the bank for discount. It is the progressive augmentation of bank paper, and not the magnitude of its existing amount, which gives the relief. It thus appears, that the moderation and forbearance among borrowers, which were supposed likely to restrain the too great emission of paper, are only to be excited by the means of its perpetual encrease; by the means, that is, to say, of the very evil which it was assumed that they would be sufficient to prevent.

The danger of enlarging the loans of the bank in proportion to the extension of the demand for them, may be nore particularly shewn by adverting to the case of the sudden transfer to foreign countries of capital which had been antecedently lodged in this. Let us suppose the foreign owners, either of British stocks, or of property left in the hands of English correspondents, to draw during the space of three months to a very large amount; and let us imagine that, in consequence of such an event, the exchange turns against Great Britain to the extent of five per cent.; and moreover that at the end of the three months, the drafts ceasing, and the mercantile state of the country improving, the exchange returns to its proper level. In this case any Englishman who can send goods abroad on his own account, and draw for them during the three months in question, will gain an extra profit of five per cent., supposing him to buy them in England for the same English money and to sell them abroad for the same foreign money, for which goods may be bought and sold at the periods preceding, and following the interval of time of which we are speaking. A similar extra profit will be obtainable during the same three months by a variety of other modes of employing capital. It is obvious, for example, that the public funds may be expected to experience a sudden fall through the great sale of foreign property in the stocks, which we have imagined to take place. He, therefore, who shall buy into the funds at the season of depression, and shall sell out at the expiration of the three months, will be likely to derive a benefit from this species of speculation. It is also plain that the quantity of goods in Great Britain will be reduced through the enlarged exportations, as well as through the suspension of imports, to which the state of the exchange will have given occasion. The profit, therefore, on the use of the remaining stock will be generally augmented. The exportation of bullion will afford a gain of the same sum of five per cent. the expence of transporting it being, indeed, deducted. The demand upon the bank for discounts is, therefore, likely to be particularly earnest during the period of which we are speaking; and it is important here to notice, that the ground on which it will be made will not be that which was spoken of in an early part of this work. It will not be the privation of that quantity of circulating medium which is necessary for carrying on the accustomed payments, for these will be very immaterially encreased; the cause of the extraordinary applications to the bank will be the temporary advantage which may be gained, or the loss which may be avoided, by borrowing, during the three months in question, at the rate of five per cent. A pressure, it is true, may be occasioned by the multitude of foreign drafts, and it may resemble that which would arise from a diminution of Bank of England paper. Some of those merchants in whose hands the foreign property had been placed may not be able, with sufficient readiness, to spare from their commerce the sums necessary to answer the bills drawn upon them. Creditors, not being permitted to demand more than five per cent. interest from their debtors, are apt, at particular junctures, to call in their money, for the sake of taking to themselves the extraordinary benefit to be obtained by the use of capital. The disappointments thus brought on persons trading with borrowed wealth are often productive of much evil. The maintenance of the accustomed quantity of Bank of England notes may, therefore, be insufficient to furnish the means of securing the usual regularity of the payments of the metropolis; and a material diminution of paper may be particularly inconvenient. Possibly an augmentation of it may be necessary to the due maintenance of credit. If we suppose, however, a very great encrease of bank notes to take place (and an encrease, probably, equal to the total capital transferred on account of foreigners, will immediately be desired), the result must be a very important fall in the exchange, in addition to the fall of five per cent. already mentioned; and a new and proportionate danger to the Bank of England.

The point which it has been the object here to explain, might have been equally illustrated by imagining either the case of a strong disposition in many British subjects to transfer their own property to foreign countries, in order to lodge it there; or the case of a general eagerness to extend foreign commerce; for we must assume the transfer to foreign parts of an additional British capital to take place on either of these suppositions.

The preceding observations explain the reason of a determination, adopted some time since by the bank directors, to limit the total weekly amount of loans furnished by them to the merchants. The adoption of a regulation for this purpose seems to have been rendered necessary by that impossibility of otherwise sufficiently limiting, at all times, the Bank of England paper, which it has been the design of this Chapter to point out.

The regulation in question I consider as intended to confine within a specific, though in some degree fluctuating, sum, the loans of the bank, for the sake of restricting the paper. The variations in the amount of loans fail of producing exactly correspondent variations in the amount of paper, in proportion as the gold of the bank fluctuates. But the regulation being a weekly one, opportunity is afforded of correcting this attendant imperfection before any material evil can have arisen. The changes which occur in the amount of the loans to government form another ground for taking into weekly consideration the sum which shall, in the succeeding week, be afforded to the merchants.

To limit the total amount of paper issued, and to resort for this purpose, whenever the temptation to borrow is strong, to some effectual principle of restriction; in no case, however, materially to diminish the sum in circulation, but to let it vibrate only within certain limits; to afford a slow and cautious extension of it, as the general trade of the kingdom enlarges itself; to allow of some special, though temporary, encrease in the event of any extraordinary alarm or difficulty, as the best means of preventing a great demand at home for guineas; and to lean to the side of diminution, in the case of gold going abroad, and of the general exchanges continuing long unfavourable; this seems to be the true policy of the directors of an institution circumstanced like that of the Bank of England. To suffer either the solicitations of merchants, or the wishes of government, to determine the measure of the bank issues, is unquestionably to adopt a very false principle of conduct.

CHAPTER XI

Of the Influence of Paper Credit on the Price of Commodities.—Observations on some Passages of Montesquieu and Hume.—Conclusion.

THIS subject has been in so great a degree anticipated by the discussions which have taken place; that it will scarcely be necessary to do more than to remind the reader of the principles which have been laid down, and to point out the manner in which they bear upon the present question.

It was observed in a former Chapter, that a very considerable advance in the price of the commodities bought and sold in one quarter of this kingdom, while there was no such rise in any other, was not supposable; because the holders of the circulating medium current in the spot in which goods were imagined to have been rendered dear, would exchange it for the circulating medium of the part in which they were assumed to be cheap, and would then buy the commodities of the latter place, and transport them to the former, for the sake of the profit on the transaction.

The exchangeableness of our country paper for our London paper was represented as always in this manner preventing the quantity of paper circulating in one place from being very disproportionate to the quantity circulating in another; and as also precluding any great local rise in the price of commodities within our own island.

We may justly extend our views, and conceive of Europe, and even of the world, as forming one great kingdom, over the whole of which goods pass and repass, as suits the interest of the merchant, nearly in the same manner in which they spread themselves through this single country.

In one particular, indeed, the resemblance between the two cases fails. Country bank paper, as compared with Bank of England

260

notes, cannot be, to a material degree, excessive in any part of England; because, by the custom of our country banks, it is convertible, without any discount, into the London paper. But British paper is not exchangeable for the circulating medium of the continent, unless a discount, or difference be allowed. Of this fluctuating discount, or difference, the variations in the course of exchange are the measure.

It is true that the continental circulating medium, like our own, varies in value. Both, however, commonly vibrate only within certain limits; and both may be considered as fluctuating exactly so far as their value differs from that of bullion. To say that bullion varies in its price, is to say that there is an alteration in the general exchangeable value of that article, which constitutes the standard of the world.

We are led, by these observations, to divide our subject into two branches of enquiry: first, into the question how far our paper credit may have raised the price of goods in Great Britain, by causing their current price here (that is to say, their price in British paper, as well as in British coin) to be higher than their bullion price; and, secondly, how far also the bullion price of our commodities here (that is to say, their value in exchange for the article of bullion) may be suspected of having been enhanced by means of the paper credit of Great Britain.

As to the first question; the highest influence which a too extended paper credit can have had in raising the current price of commodities in Great Britain above their bullion price, must be measured by the difference which has subsisted between the market price and mint price of gold; or, which is nearly the same thing, by the fluctuation in the state of our general exchanges. This difference or fluctuation has at no period been more than about ten or twelve per cent. Even this variation, however, has not been fairly referable to a too great issue of paper, but rather to the peculiar circumstances of the country; and, in particular, to our two bad harvests, which sufficiently account for the unfavourable state of our exchanges.

The second question is, how far the bullion price of our commodities may be suspected of having been raised through the influence of the paper credit of Great Britain.

It was formerly stated, that the bullion price of articles may be considered to be their general price: because bullion necessarily bears that value, or nearly that value, in each country, in exchange for goods, which it bears in all, allowance being made for the expence of their transmission, inclusive of export and import duties, ordinary profit of the merchant, freight, insurance, and other customary charges. The expence of the transportation of commodities from the several places of their growth or manufacture, an expence which is great in some cases, and small in others, is the measure of the difference subsisting between the bullion prices of the same articles, at the same time, in different parts of the world. Each addition to this difference implies an extra profit on the transportation either of bullion or of goods; and must be supposed soon to cause the one or the other to be carried over in such quantity as to restore their due relative price. Every rise, therefore, of the bullion price in Great Britain of those commodities which she is accustomed to export, if we suppose the usual exportation to continue, implies an equal, or nearly equal, enhancement of the bullion price of all articles of the same class in every foreign part in which our commodities are sold.

Great Britain so remarkably takes the lead in manufactures and commerce, that she may not unjustly be deemed to have the power, especially in a time of general war, of prescribing to foreign countries the rate at which they shall buy her commodities.

That monopoly of the supply, however, which I am here supposing Great Britain to possess, is, probably, but temporary, and, in every respect, imperfect. In most of her sales abroad she meets with strong competition; for, though other countries may not rival her in the quality of her goods, they can, generally, furnish a substitute, which, if British prices are much lifted up, will gain, by comparative cheapness, the preference. Every great enhancement of the cost of our articles must lessen the foreign demand for them. It must reduce our exported and augment our imported goods. By thus turning tne balance of trade against us, and rendering our exchanges unfavourable, it must cause the rise at home to be a rise not in the bullion price of our articles, the subject which we are now considering, but in the paper or current price, the point which was noticed before. If the advance is in the paper or current price, the bank is compelled to restrict its issues; and the reduction of the quantity of bank notes has a tendency to limit the cost not only of those particular commodities which are the subjects of exportation, but of every commodity in the kingdom.

That the bullion price of some British articles has lately been much encreased, and that the bullion price of all, or of almost all, has in some degree risen, are facts which cannot be doubted. But that this enhancmenet is to be charged to an increase of paper, is not equally to be admitted; for it is plain that other causes have powerfully operated, namely, a state of war, new taxes, and two bad harvests, which, by raising the price of bread, have in some degree lifted up that of labour, and of all commodities. Our prices may have also been partly augmented by the enhancement of the cost of raw materials brought from other countries.

Although it should be granted, as it must, either that the amount of our paper has been enlarged in proportion to the extension of pecuniary transactions; or that an encreased œconomy in the use of it has rendered an equal quantity sufficient for more payments (and it seems of little moment which of these two suppositions is adopted): still, it might be questioned whether the extended issue of paper ought to be deemed the cause of the high prices; or whether the high prices ought not to be deemed the cause, and the encrease of paper the effect.

It was before remarked, that it seems in general more fair to consider the latter to be the case, when the extension of paper is not such as to be the means of reducing its value below that of bullion. To prove the reasonableness of this observation, let us imagine the paper credit of this country to be abolished, and our payments to be conducted by a circulating medium consisting wholly of gold; and let us assume that we still find ourselves able to procure for our

263

commodities sent abroad a higher bullion price than before. In this case the bullion price of articles at home will also experience a rise; for the high bullion prices abroad will have the effect of enlarging our exported and diminishing our imported goods; of rendering our balance of trade favourable, and of bringing gold into the kingdom; which encrease of gold will have precisely the same effect as an augmentation of paper, namely, that of raising British prices. The bullion will continue to flow in until it shall have brought the bullion price of goods in England to a level with the bullion price of the same articles in foreign parts, allowing for charges of transportation. On the ability, therefore, of Great Britain to maintain a high bullion price for her goods abroad, would depend the bullion price of her commodities at home, in the event of her employing gold as her only circulating medium.

If we suppose paper to constitute the circulating medium of Great Britain, and an encreased bullion price for her commodities abroad to be in like manner obtainable, the case will in the main be similar, though in one particular it will differ. The case will be similar, inasmuch as Great Britain will experience, exactly as if she made use only of gold, an encrease in the price of her commodities at home, as well as an enlargement of the quantity of her circulating medium; such an enlargement, I mean, as is necessary for effecting her more extended payments. The case will differ, inasmuch as, instead of importing the additional circulating medium which is wanted, she will create it. The production, therefore, of a rather less quantity of exportable articles will be necessary on the one supposition than on the other; and the state of the exchange itself will be in some degree affected by this variation in the circumstances of the two cases.

It may, perhaps, be thought, that I have considered the bullion price of goods in Great Britain as exclusively depending on the bullion price of the same kind of commodities abroad; and that I ought to have stated the converse to be also in some measure the fact, namely, the bullion price of articles abroad to depend in part on the bullion prices of Great Britain. I have intended thus to represent the case. My position has been this,—that the bullion price of articles in Great Britain conforms itself to the bullion price abroad; but that, in the formation of this bullion price abroad, the British price has some share of influence: and this influence I have considered to be proportioned to the degree of our monopoly of the supply of the foreign markets.

There is an additional mode of considering the influence of paper credit on the bullion price of articles.

The encreased use of paper in each individual country must contribute to lower the price of bullion, by lessening the general demand for it in the world. On every advance in the cost of commodities, it may be suspected that the means of effecting the encreased payments are supplied not by bringing more gold into use but rather by the enlargement of that part of the circulating medium which consists in paper. No inconsiderable portion of British gold coin is employed in effecting the fractional parts of payments; and the total amount of these does not encrease in the same proportion in which the sum total of payments is augmented*. Moreover, the art of œconomizing gold is continually advancing. The very vicissitudes of commerce, probably, tend to improve it. A time of distress, such as was felt in 1793, compels many to resort to new expedients, tending to spare the use both of Bank of England notes

* The bank notes in circulation commonly are notes for five, ten, fifteen, twenty, twenty-five, thirty, forty, fifty, and one hundred pounds and upwards. If we suppose the price of all articles to be doubled, then we may assume every payment of one guinea to be a payment of two guineas, and to employ a double quantity of gold; every payment of two guineas to be a payment of four guineas, and also to employ a double quantity of gold; but every payment of three guineas will be a payment of six, and it may employ a five pound note, the fractional part only being paid in money. This particular payment will, therefore, require less gold. A payment of four guineas will be a payment of eight, and will also require less gold. The payments of more than four guineas, when, in like manner, doubled, will some of them employ a greater and some a less quantity of gold than before. They will employ, taking them together, the same quantity. It is evident from this statement, that an encrease of the quantity of the circulating medium of a country employing paper in its larger payments, and coin only in the smaller, will consist chiefly of paper; a circumstance which may considerably tend to prevent an encreased demand for bullion on the occasion of an augmentation of prices, and which may, therefore, greatly facilitate a rise of the bullion price of articles in the world.

265

and of coin. The measures adopted, at first, through necessity, are afterwards persisted in because they are œconomical. To put the case which we have more recently experienced. An unfavourable balance of trade, arising out of the disadvantageous circumstances of the country, causes our guineas to go abroad. Paper is necessary to supply their place. Experience of the loss incurred by hoarding money, and of the practicability of sustaining both private and public credit during the absence of gold, strengthens the general confidence in a paper currency, and encourages a permanently encreased use of it. If we could suppose as large a substitution of paper in the place of coin to take place in other countries as we have lately experienced in our own; the diminution of the demand for bullion might be such as very materially to affect its general value, and to enhance the money price of articles over the world.

There is, however, a limit to this evil. The annual supply of the precious metals is obtained from mines, of which some afford to the proprietors a higher and others a lower revenue, and some probably no revenue at all. If we suppose the encreased use of paper to lower, in any degree, the value of the precious metals; we must assume those mines which have not yielded any rent, to be no longer worked; and the supply of gold and silver to be, in consequence, somewhat reduced. If we imagine the reduction of the price of the precious metals to be progressive, we must conceive a period to arrive when all mines will be unable to defray the charge of extracting the ore, except those which now yield the very highest rent. At this point the fall will necessarily stop. In other words, gold and silver must continue to bear that price, or nearly that price, at which they are now exchangeable for commodities, a deduction being made of the total present rent derived from the richest mines; a deduction which, if Dr. A. Smith's observations on this subject are just, cannot be very considerable.

Mr. de Montesquieu has represented, in the following manner, the principle which regulates the price of the precious metals. He "compares the mass of gold and silver in the whole world with "the quantity of merchandize therein contained," and "every "commodity with a certain portion of the entire mass of gold and "silver:" and then observes, that, "Since the property of mankind "is not all at once in trade, and as the metals or money also are "not all in trade at the same time; the price is fixed in the compound "ratio of the total of things with the total of signs, and that of the "total of things in trade with the total of signs in trade also." This theory, though not altogether to be rejected, is laid down in a manner which is very loose and fallacious*.

Not to mention the misconception of the subject which may arise from the silence of Mr. de Montesquieu respecting the state of the mines, it may be observed, first, that he alludes, in a manner so imperfect as to be scarcely intelligible, to those effects of the different degrees of rapidity in the circulation both of money and goods, which it has been one object of this work to explain. It is on the degree of the rapidity of the circulation of each, combined with the consideration of quantity, and not on the quantity alone, that the value of the circulating medium of any country depends.

Mr. de Montesquieu also leaves out of his consideration the custom of transacting payments by means of entries in books, and of other expedients. In proportion as contrivances of this sort prevail; and they must abound more and more as commercial knowledge advances in the world; the demand for bullion will be diminished.

He also does not advert to that reserve of gold and silver in the coffers of the banks of various countries which merely forms a provision against contingencies. The amount of this reserve will depend on the opinion which the banks entertain respecting the extent of the sum likely to be suddenly drawn from them, in consequence either of fluctuations in the national balances of trade, or of temporary interruptions of credit among individuals. In proportion, therefore, as the variations in the national balances of trade, as well as in the state of commercial confidence, are greater or smaller, the fund of gold which is kept out of circulation will be

* It is controverted at great length in the work of Sir James Stewart on Political Œconomy.

more or less considerable. On the amount of this fund depends, in no inconsiderable degree, the price of bullion in the world.

Mr. de Montesquieu likewise omits to take into his account that now immense and perpetually encreasing influence in sparing the precious metals which arises from the use of paper credit. The false impression which he gives of this subject, may chiefly be referred to his not having contemplated the effects of the introduction of the banking system.

Mr. Hume has spoken strongly of the influence of paper credit in sparing the use of the precious metals, and in proportionably lowering their value, and raising that of labour and of commodities, He inveighs against bank paper on this account, as well as on some others; but, in so doing, he appears to assume, that paper credit causes a merely local rise in the price of articles; a rise, I mean, which extends itself only over the whole of the single independent country in which the paper is issued. That bank is considered by him as most advantageous to a state, which locks up all the gold received in return for its notes [he admits that it will have no profit on its dealings], and thus causes the total quantity of circulating medium to remain the same. The price of labour, he says, will, in this manner, be kept down. The Bank of Amsterdam is approved by him, on account of its being an establishment of this nature*.

* It has been already observed, that, when the French possessed themselves of Holland, it was discovered that the Bank of Amsterdam had been accustomed privately to lend its deposits of specie to the city of Amsterdam, and, also, to the old Dutch government. The specie thus lent, as soon as goods in exchange for it experienced even a very small rise in Holland, would naturally find its way to other countries. The following are the passages from Mr. Hume, referred to in the text.

"In general we may observe, that the dearness of every thing, from plenty "of money, is a disadvantage which attends an established commerce, and sets "bounds to it in every country, by enabling the poorer states to undersell the "richer in all foreign markets.

"This has made me entertain a doubt concerning the benefit of banks and "paper credit, which are so generally esteemed advantageous to every nation.

"That provisions and labour should become dear by the encrease of trade "and money, is, in many respects, an inconvenience; but an inconvenience "that is unavoidable, and the effect of that public wealth and prosperity which "are the end of all our wishes. It is compensated by the advantages which we "reap from the possession of these precious metals, and the weight which they

268

In thus representing the subject, he appears to forget, that, when the total circulating medium of a country, whether consisting of gold, or of paper, or of both, is rendered excessive; when it has thus lifted up the gold price of articles above the point at which they stand in adjacent countries, the gold is obliged, by the operation

"give the nation in all foreign wars and negotiations. But there appears no "reason for encreasing that inconvenience by a counterfeit money, which "foreigners will not accept of in any payment, and which any great disorder "in the state will reduce to nothing. There are, it is true, many people in every "rich state, who, having large sums of money, would prefer paper, with good "security, as being of more easy transport, and more safe custody. If the public "provide not a bank, private bankers will take advantage of this circumstance, "as the goldsmiths formerly did in London, or as the bankers do, at present, "in Dublin: and, therefore, it is better that a public company should enjoy "the benefit of that paper credit, which always will have place in every opulent "kingdom. But to endeavour *artificially* to encrease such a credit, can never be "the interest of any trading nation, but must lay them under disadvantages, 'by encreasing money beyond its natural proportion to labour and commodities, "and thereby heightening their price to the merchant and manufacturer. And, "in this view, it must be allowed that no bank could be more advantageous than "such a one which locked up all the money it received [this is the case with the "Bank of Amsterdam]; and never augmented the circulating coin, as is usual, "by returning part of its treasure into commerce. A public bank, by this "expedient, might cut off much of the dealings of private bankers and money- "jobbers; and, though the state bore the charge of salaries to the directors and "tellers of this bank (for, according to the preceding supposition, it would "have no profit from its dealings), the national advantage resulting from the "low price of labour, and the destruction of paper credit, would be a sufficient "compensation."—Hume's Essay on Money.

That the encrease of the money of an individual state can have no very great and permanent effect in raising the price of labour, or of commodities, on account of the tendency of so much of the coin as is excessive to transport itself to other countries, as soon as it shall have raised the cost of articles above their general level in the world (the principle contended for in the text), is shewn, on the authority of Mr. Hume himself, in the following passage. Mr. Hume, indeed, names money alone; but his observation is equally applicable to the case of money and paper taken together, of which I have spoken.

"Suppose four-fifths of all the money in Great Britain to be annihilated in "one night, and the nation reduced to the same condition, with regard to "specie, as in the reigns of the Harrys and Edwards; what would be the conse- "quence? Must not the price of all labour and commodities sink in proportion, "and everything be sold as cheap as they were in those ages? What nation "would then dispute with us in any foreign market; or pretend to navigate "or to sell manufactures at the same price which to us would afford sufficient "profit? In how little time, therefore, must this bring back the money which "we had lost, and raise us to the level of all the neighbouring nations; where, "after we have arrived, we immediately lose the advantage of the cheapness of of the exchange, to transport itself to these other parts; and that paper credit, therefore, enhances the prices not of that single spot in which it passes, but of the adjoining places, and of the world. The state which issues paper only in such quantity as to maintain its general exchanges, may be considered as substituting paper in the place of gold, and as gaining additional stock in return for whatever coin it may cause to be exported. It derives, therefore, from its own issue, the whole advantage of this augmentation of capital. It participates with other countries in that inconvenience of a generally encreased price of commodities which its paper has contributed to produce.

That the popular opinion which was lately entertained of the great influence of paper credit in raising the price not only of commodities in general, but of provisions in particular, had no just foundation, is a position which admits of easy proof.

First that opinion has proceeded on the assumption of the fact of a vast encrease of the total circulating medium of the kingdom, within the last two or three years, the period during which the high prices have subsisted. But I have shewn both that the amount of the notes of the Bank of England has lately not been such as to imply a material augmentation of the circulating medium of the metropolis, and, also, that the quantity of circulating medium in the country necessarily conforms itself to that of London, for which it is exchangeable. It has obviously been the use of country bank

"labour and commodities; and the farther flowing in of money is stopped by "our fulness and repletion?

"Again; suppose that all the money of Great Britain were multiplied five-"fold in a night; must not the contrary effect follow? Must not all labour "and commodities rise to such an exorbitant height, that no neighbouring "nations could afford to buy from us; while their commodities, on the other "hand, became, comparatively, so cheap, that, in spite of all laws which could "be formed, they would be run in upon us, and our's flow out, till we fell to a "level with foreigners, and lose that great superiority of riches which has laid "us under such disadvantages?

"*Now it is evident that the same causes which would correct these exorbitant* "*inequalities, were they to happen miraculously, must prevent their happening* "*in the common course of nature; and must for ever, in all neighbouring nations,* "*preserve money nearly proportionate to the art and industry of each nation.*"— Hume's Essay on the Balance of Trade.

270

notes, and especially of the smaller ones, in the place of gold, not in addition to it, which has been the chief occasion of the prevailing suspicion: for the common complaint has been not only that paper has been multiplied, but, also, that guineas have been hardly to be seen: and it has not been considered, that by this double invective some sort of acknowledgment is made that the one article is only that substitute for the other, by which none of the supposed effect on the price of commodities can be produced.

It is sometimes said, that the additional loans which the paper of the country banks has enabled them to furnish, have encouraged mercantile speculation; and that we may ascribe to the spirit thus excited much of the late rise in the price of articles in general, and of corn in particular.

There is an error in the public sentiment on this subject, which it is important to correct.

It has been already shewn, that it is by the amount not of the loans of the Bank of England, but of its paper; or if of its loans, of these merely as indicating the quantity of its paper, that we are to estimate the influence on the cost of commodities. The same remark may be applied to the subject of the loans and paper of country banks. For the sake of more fully illustrating this point, let us examine into the several ways in which a country banker may be supposed to extend his loans, without augmenting the quantity of circulating medium in the kingdom.

He may be enabled to do this, first, through the enlargement of the deposits lodged with him. In this case some of his customers may be considered as leaving with him, or as lending to him, a sum which is lent by him to other customers. This is the same thing as if some individuals were to lend to others, without the intervention of the banker. Loans of this nature will be admitted not to have the supposed influence on prices.

A country banker may also encrease his loans, without augmenting the quantity of the circulating medium of the country, in the following manner. He may extend the issue of his own paper, and then that paper may circulate in the place of gold either hoarded

271

or exported. If the gold is hoarded; if a quantity of coin locked up by one man equals the amount of the new paper issued by another it is plain that there will not be the supposed influence on prices. If the gold is exported, we must consider it in the same light with any other commodity sent abroad. It is true that the paper, according to this supposition, may be said to give existence to an additional exportable article: but so also does every encreased exertion of the national industry, as well as every favourable harvest. An augmentation of prices is no more to be inferred from the creation of a new exportable commodity in the one case than in the others.

The following facts furnish a convincing proof that the late high prices of corn have not been owing to the enlargement of Bank of England paper.

By the account which the bank rendered to Parliament, it appears, that the amount of Bank of England notes was, on the 25th of February, 1795, 13,539,160*l.* In the three months immediately following the 25th of February, 1795, the average price of wheat, in the London corn-market, was about 57*s.* per quarter.

By the same bank account, it appears, that the amount of Bank of England notes was, on the 25th of February 1796, 11,030, 116*l.* In the three months immediately following the 25th of February, 1796 the average price of wheat, in the London corn-market, was about 94*s.* per quarter.

Thus wheat bore a comparatively low price when the amount of bank notes in circulation was greater; and a comparatively high price when their amount was smaller. It bore the moderate price of 57*s.* per quarter, at a time when the amount of Bank of England notes was full as considerable (allowing for about two millions of 1*l.* and 2*l.* notes) as it is known to have been at any period.

Paper credit may be considered as tending, in some respects, to reduce the price of commodities. It was compared, in a former chapter, to a cheap species of machinery, which is substituted in the place of a dear one; and it is obvious, that, in proportion as any instrument of manufactures or commerce is less expensive, the articles which it contributes to produce may be afforded at a lower rate.

Paper credit, also, promotes general cheapness, by sparing much expence and trouble in weighing, counting, and transporting, money; and by thus facilitating more particularly the larger transactions of the merchant. Mr. Hume appears to suppose, that, when a great encrease of it takes place, the augmentation is artificially produced. But it has been shewn, that mercantile persons naturally resort more and more to the use of paper, in proportion as wealth accumulates, confidence improves, and commerce advances. The consumers of commodities may be considered as having an interest in permitting the merchants to follow their own plans of œconomy, in this respect, in the same manner as in all others.

But whatever may be the amount of that influence on the price of commodities which ought to be ascribed to paper credit, one point is clear, namely, that, during the period in which our paper has extended itself, our trade has prospered, the state of our agriculture has advanced, and both the capital and the income of the country have been augmented.

The chief mischiefs which, according to Mr. Hume, are to be apprehended from any considerable addition to our paper currency, may be stated to be the following: first, the great enhancement of the price of British labour and commodities, an evil with which we ought unquestionably to connect that of the diminution of the sale of our manufactures in foreign markets; secondly, the inconvenience to which we may be exposed in time of war through the want of sufficient means of making remittances in bullion to other countries; and, thirdly, the confusion which the failure of paper credit may produce at home in the event of any great disorder in the nation.

That the first consequence (the great enhancement of the price of British labour and commodities) cannot follow from the enlargement of our paper currency in the degree which Mr. Hume supposes, has been proved from the circumstance of our paper causing guineas to go abroad, and tending, therefore, to raise the

Enquiry into Paper Credit

prices of the world rather than those of our own single island. That our prices, however high, have not been such as to lessen the vent abroad of our home-made articles, and have, therefore, not been raised above the prices of other countries, is proved by those documents from our custom-house which state the continually encreasing quantity of manufactures exported by Great Britain*.

That the second evil (that of our being reduced to difficulty in making remittances abroad in time of war through the want of bullion) is one which there is less reason to dread than Mr. Hume has imagined, may likewise be inferred from recent experience. We have been able to maintain the credit of our funds, and to carry on all our financial operations, during the whole of the late expensive and protracted contest, although in the commencement of it our stock of circulating gold was probably less than in many former periods; and although, also, in the last years of the struggle, a period in which we lent considerable sums to Ireland, and had to purchase immense quantities of foreign grain, we were in a great measure deprived of current coin, and the cash payments of the Bank of England remained suspended.

Mr. Hume himself has remarked: "That want of money can "never injure any state *within itself*; for that men and commodities "are the real strength of any community." He might have added, that Want of money can never injure any state *in its transactions with foreign countries,* provided it sufficiently abounds with commodities which are in demand abroad, and which it can afford to sell at a bullion price lower than that for which foreign articles of a similar kind can be afforded. The power of manufacturing at a cheap rate is far more valuable than any stock of bullion. Even the greatest quantity of gold which we can be supposed at any time

* The British manufactures exported in 1785 amounted to—

		£11,082,000	In 1792	to	£18,336,000
In 1786	to	11,830,000	1793	—	13,892,000
1787	—	12,053,000	1794	—	16,725,000
1788	—	12,724,000	1795	—	16,527,000
1789	—	13,779,000	1796	—	19,102,000
1790	—	14,921,000	1797	—	16,903,000
1791	—	16,810,000	1798	—	19,771,000

to possess, bears but a small proportion to our extraordinary expenditure in time of war, and affords a security which is extremely slender in comparison of that which we derive from the commercial capital, the manufacturing skill, and the other resources of the country.

That the third evil (the confusion which the failure of paper credit may produce in the event of any disorder at home) is less a subject for apprehension than Mr. Hume and other British writers have conceived, is a point which a great part of the preceding work will have contributed to establish.

During the late scenes of trouble and consternation on the continent, the possession of a stock of the precious metals probably added little to the security of any nation. When the French armies approached, or when an insurrection was projected, a stock of gold and silver possessed by a government bank might contribute to invite attack; or if the fund should at such a juncture be expended in the public service, it would not long continue to perform the office of a circulating medium. It might even disappear after effecting a single payment.

Our own island has been preserved, through the favour of Providence, from those violent convulsions which have been felt on the continent. We have, however, been exposed to many smaller evils, and, in particular, to the interruption of our mercantile credit. It was probable that the enemy, knowing how much our political strength depended on our commercial prosperity, and our commercial prosperity on the due maintenance of mercantile confidence among us, would direct his endeavours to the very object of exciting alarms over the kingdom, with the view of thus disturbing the course of our trade and manufactures. It therefore became us to protect ourselves by the best means in our power against this species of injury; and the continuance of the law for suspending the cash payments of the Bank of England has been one of the steps which parliament has deemed necessary.

There can be no doubt, that, in the situation in which we have thus found ourselves placed, we have been greatly benefited by the circumstance of our having been previously accustomed to the free use of a paper credit. In a commercial country, subjected to that moderate degree of occasional alarm and danger which we have experienced, gold is by no means that kind of circulating medium which is the most desirable. It is apt to circulate with very different degrees of rapidity, and also to be suddenly withdrawn, in consequence of its being an article intrinsically valuable, and capable of being easily concealed. If, during the war, it had been our only medium of payment, we might sometimes have been almost totally deprived of the means of carrying on our pecuniary transactions; and much confusion in the affairs of our merchants, great interruption of manufacturing labour, and very serious evils to the state, might have been the consequences.

Paper credit has, on this account, been highly important to us. Our former familiarity with it prepared us for the more extended use of it. And our experience of its power of supplying the want of gold in times of difficulty and peril, is a circumstance which, though it ought not to encourage a general disuse of coin, may justly add to the future confidence of the nation.

FINIS

APPENDIX 1

THE EVIDENCE

GIVEN BY

HENRY THORNTON

BEFORE THE

COMMITTEES OF SECRECY OF THE TWO HOUSES
OF PARLIAMENT ON THE BANK OF ENGLAND
MARCH AND APRIL

1797

I

EVIDENCE GIVEN BEFORE THE COMMITTEE OF SECRECY OF THE HOUSE OF COMMONS APPOINTED TO ENQUIRE INTO THE OUTSTANDING DEMANDS OF THE BANK OF ENGLAND*

Veneris, 24° *die Martii* 1797

Henry Thornton, Esquire, a Member of the House, and a Banker of London; called in, and Examined.

Q. Is your House connected with any Country Banks?

A. It is; with several.

Q. Can you specify the places where those Banks are situated?

A. Edinburgh, Glasgow, Liverpool, Bristol, Exeter, Scarborough, Litchfield, Stamford, Tiverton, Totness, Carlisle, Stockton, Winchester, and a few others, which I do not at present recollect.

Q. So far as you know, or have reason to believe, have the Notes of these Country Banks in circulation during six months preceding the 26th of February last, been more or fewer than previous to the commercial difficulties in 1793?

A. I should judge, from occasional conversation which I have had with Country Bankers who have come up to town, that they have been much fewer; but I have not at present correct information from any number of persons on this point. I also incline to think they have been fewer: because, on the occasion of the late alarm, the demand for Guineas from Country Bankers who issue Notes on demand, was much less than on the occasion of the alarm in 1793. I am further confirmed in this opinion, by the circumstance of our having ceased to be connected with some Country Banks which did business with us before the year 1793, on account of our

* [Apart from the original separate edition of 1797 the three *Reports from the Committee of Secrecy on the Outstanding Demands on the Bank of England*, dated March 3, March 7, and April 21, 1797, together with the Evidence and the Report from Committee on the *Restriction of Payments in Cash by the Bank*, dated November 17, 1797, have been reprinted by order of the House of Commons in *Reports from Committees of the House of Commons*, vol. xi, *Miscellaneous Subjects*, *1782, 1799*, 1805, pp. 119–131, and again in 1826. The present reprint is from the edition of 1805, pp. 149–150 and 161–165.]

279

being liable to sudden demands through the circulation of their Notes. Some of these Banks then left off their business.

Q. Have you, or are you likely soon to have, the means of informing the Committee of the amount or proportion of the Notes issued by the respective Banks you have mentioned, previous to the year 1793, since the year 1793, and since the 26th of February last?

A. I yesterday wrote several letters, which I think will bring me information on that subject within three or four days.

Q. Do you apprehend that, for some time previous to the 26th of February last, the quantity of circulating medium had been greater than the convenience of trade required?

A. I am clearly of opinion, that, in the metropolis, it was much less.

Q. Supposing, during any part of the year, preceding the 26th of February, the quantity of circulating medium had been considerably diminished, is it, or is not your opinion, that such considerable diminution would have been highly injurious to public credit?

A. I am clearly of opinion, that, if the circulating medium had been much further reduced, many failures would have been the consequence. I know the distresses of many Merchants, and also of some Bankers, to have been considerable; and have had conversations with some of them on the subject of substituting a new circulating medium, with a view of relieving the existing distress.

Q. Supposing that, during any part of the six months preceding the 26th of February last, Government had wished to repay the whole, or a large proportion of the Bank advances, could Government have done this any otherwise than by a loan from the Public?

A. I conceive it to be self-evident that they could not, except by a loan, or something in the nature of it.

Q. From what source must that loan have been supplied, and in what shape must the advances to repay which the loan was to be made, have been repaid to the Bank?

A. I conceive that the same description of parties who usually furnish loans to Government, would furnish the supposed loan, and in the same manner. The custom now is, for those who are the most opulent, and the most desirous of embarking in a loan, to associate for the purpose of bidding for it; if they succeed in obtaining it, they draw on their Bankers, on the first day of payment, for the amount of that payment; it is usual for the Bankers, a few days antecedent to the first instalment, to request of those friends who have the opportunity of discounting at the Bank, to send Bills there at that period to be discounted, in order to increase the Cash of the Bankers; and I take for granted, that the same means of preparing for the payment of the supposed loan would have been taken, as has been usual in other cases. If the Bank should have been unwilling to furnish discounts on the days antecedent to the first payment on the supposed loan, there would be of course a difficulty in effecting the payment; and the circulating medium which I have already spoken of as too little for the accommodation of the Public, would be rendered, in that case, considerably less. The payments on the loan have usually been made in Bank Notes: in the case of the last loan, however, Exchequer Bills, payable three months after they were issued, have been received in payment of the loan; and these Exchequer Bills, though bearing about $5\frac{1}{4}$ per cent. interest, bore, for a few days antecedent to the 26th of February, a discount of 3 to $3\frac{1}{2}$ per cent., which is equivalent to about 18 per cent. per ann. interest for Money. I understand that Government ceased to issue these Exchequer Bills in consequence of the high discount. Government obtained, by means of these Exchequer Bills, an anticipation of the payments on the loan, for which, however, if they had continued to obtain the same anticipation, they must have paid of course 18 per cent.; and I attribute this high interest to the extreme scarcity of the circulating medium at that time existing.

Q. Supposing a large proportion of the Bank advances to Government had been repaid during any part of the six months preceding the 26th of February last, must not that repayment have diminished the circulating medium, except so far as the Bank had re-issued Notes to the full amount of what should have been paid in?

A. Undoubtedly. I apprehend, moreover, that in order to prevent great commercial distress, it would have been necessary for the Bank to furnish some additional Paper circulation to the Public, antedecent to the first payment on the loan, by which they themselves were to be paid.

Q. If such commercial distress had taken place, is it, in your opinion, probable that the Bank of England Notes, not taken out of circulation by the loan, or any measure in the nature of a loan, would have remained in circulation; or that, on the other hand, by reason of such commercial distress, they must also have been carried to the Bank to be changed for Cash?

A. I apprehend, that, if the distress had become great, and the alarm through the country had risen to any considerable height in consequence, a suspicion of the insecurities of any thing but Guineas, would, in many minds have taken place; and that those persons who were under great alarm, and were possessed of property which they could dispose of, would, in many cases, sell that property, though, at a considerable loss, for Bank Notes, for the sake of exchanging those Bank Notes for Guineas; and that, in that manner, an increased run upon the Bank for Guineas might have

281

taken place, in consequence of a distressing reduction of the circulating Paper of the Bank.

Q. Assuming, that the Paper of the Bank is usually ten millions, if Bank of England Notes to the amount of five millions had, in the course of the last twelve months, been taken out of circulation in the payment of a loan, without any new circulating medium having, previously to such payment, been provided, or without immediate restoration to public circulation of an equal issue of Bank Notes or Specie, is it, or is it not, your opinion, that the commercial distress of the country must in all probability have been very great and general?

A. I cannot conceive that the mercantile world would suffer such a diminution to take place, without substituting a circulating medium of their own; and I happen to know, as I before hinted, that some projects of this sort were on foot, and had been in the minds of several Bankers, whom I understood to have agreed in the general principle, though not actually associated for this purpose. Assuming the circulation of Bank Notes to have been reduced to the extent supposed, and no other circulating medium to have been substituted, I apprehend, especially if the diminution was made suddenly, and was not distinctly known by the Public to have been made, that great, and probably almost universal failures must have been the consequence. In the case supposed, every Banker, on the average, would only have one half of his accustomed Bank Notes in his drawer, which would certainly, in some cases, prove insufficient for the current payments. It is clear also, that in the case supposed, those Bankers who had the most property, whether in Bills or Stock, or other articles convertible into Bank Notes, would eagerly convert them into Notes, at whatever loss, for the sake of securing themselves from the risk of stopping payment. And if some Bankers should thus provide themselves with more than half their usual Paper circulation, other Bankers must be left with less; in which case, nothing is more clear to me, than that the failure of some of those Bankers would have taken place. The failure of even an individual Banker, in such a state of things, would produce the failure of others. It would create a disposition in the customers of other Bankers to take their Bank Notes, for security sake, to their own houses, although possibly some might lodge them in the Bank; in which case, however, it is material to remark, that they would have the right of drawing on the Bank for Guineas just as much as if the Notes were kept at their own houses, and that the balances at the Bank are to be considered therefore very much in the same light with the Paper circulation. I have hitherto spoken only of that part of the Paper circulation of the Bank which is in the hands of Bankers, and which may amount, as I should imagine, to about four or five millions. In case the supposed reduction of Bank Notes should take place, I rather conceive that the Bankers would be obliged to bear more than their share in it, as the private individuals, who have Bank Notes in their possession, would, many of them, be full as earnest, and more able, to retain the same quantity of Notes as heretofore, the sum in the hand of each individual person being small.

Q. In that state of commercial distress, which you represent, in your answer to the former question, to be probably consequent upon the state of facts, therein assumed, if an alarm of invasion had taken place, would it, in your opinion, have been probable, that as great or a greater run upon the Bank of England for Cash would have taken place, as was occasioned by the alarm of invasion, when such an assumed state of facts did not exist, and such a consequent commercial distress did not exist?

A. I think, that the state of facts which has been assumed, is such as might have produced of itself a very great run upon the Bank, in consequence of the commercial failures which would have followed, and of course that it would have exceedingly aggravated any run upon the Bank in consequence of the dread of invasion. These two causes of alarm existing together, would probably have operated with more than double the effects which each would have had separately.

Q. Is it your opinion, that, in the assumed state of facts, the consequent distress could have been avoided by a subsequent restoration, to public circulation, of a quantity of Bank Notes, or Specie, equal to the quantity which had been called in to the Bank in consequence of the proposed loan; or would it not be necessary, in your opinion, in order to avoid that distress, that some new circulating medium should have been provided previously to the Bank Notes having been called in, in the manner supposed?

A. I apprehend, that if the distress, which has been supposed, had taken place, it would take a considerable time, and a large temporary emission of whatever Paper might be received with the greatest confidence, before the natural state of things could be restored.

Sabbati, 1° *die Aprilis* 1797

Henry Thornton, Esquire, a Member of the House; called in, and further Examined

Q. Have you received any information, in answer to the enquiry which you stated you had set on foot, into the comparative amount of the quantity of Country Bank Notes in circulation before and since the commercial difficulties in 1793?

A. I have received a considerable number of letters on that subject; and the following is the substance of the intelligence contained in them:

First, I will state, by itself, the account which I received of the whole circulation of "Notes payable on demand to bearer" at Bristol. The relative quantity circulated at the several periods named, was furnished by the six Bristol Bankers themselves, and I believe it therefore to be very accurate.

Assuming the quantity of "Cash Paper," or Paper for which Cash may be demanded, which was circulated in 1792, and previous to the run on all Country Bankers, to be expressed by the proportion of - - - 10

The amount circulating at Midsummer 1793 and in 1794 (taking the average of these six Banks) will be nearly as - - - - $3\frac{9}{10}$

The amount circulating at Midsummer 1796 to January 1797 will be nearly as - - - - - - - - - - - - - $5\frac{5}{10}$

The amount circulating since the end of February 1797 (being the period of the stoppage of the Cash payments of the Bank of England) will be nearly as - - - - - - - - - - $3\frac{8}{10}$

According to such rough estimate as I am able to form, the amount in *value* of the Bristol Notes, for which Cash may be demanded, circulating in the first of these periods, may have been about - £360,000 sterling.

> In the second period - - - 140,000
> In the third period - - - 220,000
> In the fourth period - - - 130,000

The following may be depended on as a pretty accurate account of the "Notes to bearer on demand," circulated at nearly the same periods, by a considerable Newcastle Bank, before 1793,—about 160 to £180,000

Some time after 1793, the circulation of this House increased, through one of the Newcastle Houses leaving off business, to about - - - - - - - - - - 200,000

Before the stoppage of the Cash payments of the Bank, the circulation was reduced to - - - - - - - - 110,000

Since that time it has been about - - - - - - - 80,000

I am informed by a considerable Bank in the county of Devon, that, according to the best opinion they can form, the quantity of Bankers' "Notes payable on demand to bearer," issued in their county, may have been, in 1792, - - - - - - - - - - £120,000

That in 1793 the difficulties of the times reduced that sum almost to nothing; but that it soon increased to, perhaps, about 60,000

And continued at about that sum till after the stoppage of the Cash payments of the Bank, when it fell to the amount at which it now stands, of about - - - - - - - 20,000

284

I have obtained information on nearly the same points from other Banks in a variety of parts; viz. Ashburton, Carlisle, Exeter, Hinckley, Litchfield, Scarborough, Sleaford, Stamford, Stockton, Tiverton, and Woodbridge. Each of these issue ordinarily "Notes to bearer on demand"; though the quantity issued by several of them is never considerable.

I have endeavoured to compute the relative average quantity of "Notes payable on demand," and issued by all these Banks, at the four several periods I before named; and I conceive that, supposing the amount issued by them all before 1793, to be as - - - - - - 90

The amount for some time after 1793, will
be about as - - - - - - - - 63

The amount before the stoppage of the Cash
payments at the Bank, about - - - 78

And since that time, about - - - - 40

I am informed, that at Manchester no "Notes to bearer on demand," are issued by the Banks; but some small Bank of England Notes begin now to circulate there; and there having been a considerable quantity of Guineas in the Manchester Banks before the stoppage of the Cash payments of the Bank, these Guineas have been paid away whenever they have been demanded since that time. At Carlisle, I am informed that there is usually a premium given by the Bank of that place for Guineas, of $\frac{1}{4}$ to $\frac{1}{2}$ part, which has lately advanced to $1\frac{1}{2}$ per cent. This increase is accounted for by the disposition which there prevails to obtain Guineas, in order to send them over to Ireland. The Bank of Carlisle continues to keep a regular supply of Cash for all the calls upon it.

I am informed, that in Scotland, where the Paper circulation is usually in high credit, and where Guinea Notes are current, it may be calculated, that the additional Guineas lately thrown into circulation, or hoarded by individuals, may amount to about 60,000. This appears to be exclusive of any additional quantity with which the Banks may have supplied themselves, and may have still in their possession. Silver had disappeared from the circulation in Scotland quite as much as Guineas.

Q. Do any observations occur to you, from your late communications from the country, of which you think it will be useful to the Committee to be possessed?

A. It appears to me, that some inferences are obviously to be drawn from the information I have just given; the principal of which I think is, that that part of the Paper circulation of the country, for which, when it is withdrawn, Money becomes naturally the substitute, has been diminished since 1793, and is particularly diminished now; and that, consequently, there is a considerable degree of presumption, that the quantity of Guineas in circulation (not to speak of those which may happen to be hoarded) may have been for some time past, and may now in particular be considerable. I do not conceive, that the very great diminution of Notes, which there is at this time, is likely to have been fully supplied by Guineas; for it is always possible, that for a limited time a very great scarcity of every species of circulating medium, out of London at least, may subsist, and that some suspension of payment, as well as stagnation of trade, may for such interval continue. I should think, however, that the reduction of "Notes to bearer on demand," which I have described as existing for a considerable time, is likely to have been supplied principally by Cash, though partly perhaps by the means of payment made by Bills of Exchange, of which it is not easy to calculate either the diminution or the increase.

Q. Is it understood, that, according to the established principles of banking, a Banker, in order to provide for his own safety, ought to maintain a certain fixed proportion between his Specie and the Notes which may be out against him?

A. I conceive, certainly not; and that his Specie should be proportioned to whatever may be thought, by him, considering all circumstances, to be likely to be the demand for Specie antecedently to the time within which he can provide himself with an additional quantity of it.

Q. According to the best of your judgment and experience, are the principles on which a private Banker acts, in the management of his business, applicable to the Bank of England?

A. I conceive, in many respects, the cases are similar; in others they are different, and even opposite. In forming any comparison between the case of a private Banker and the Bank of England, it will be necessary to take the case of a Country Banker, and not of a London Banker, as the latter does not issue Notes.

Q. What, in your opinion, are the principal differences between the two situations, and the principles which belong to them respectively?

A. I conceive that the cases are different in respect to the issuing of Notes: a Country Banker issues perhaps a small quantity of "Notes to bearer on demand," and a larger quantity of Notes at interest, payable after certain notice; and he likewise has deposited with him very considerable sums, for which he is liable to be suddenly called upon by his customers residing very near to his Bank. In the time of expected distress and danger to the mercantile world, many of the prudent Country Bankers (if circumstanced as I have described) are disposed either to lessen or to suppress the circulation of their "Notes payable to bearer on demand," because these circulate in the hands of strangers at a distance from him, and are con-

286

founded with the Notes of other Bankers; so that if any neighbouring Bank should happen to stop payment, he is particularly liable to a sudden demand for Guineas, in consequence of the country people, through the general alarm, bringing in for payment these Notes; he is also liable to expence and to danger, by its being possible for rival Banks, who have not Guineas enough for their own necessities, to possess themselves of these Notes, and to send them in for payment, with a view of thus supplying their own want of Guineas: the Country Banker therefore may act a prudent part, in relinquishing that source of his profits, which is furnished by the circulation of Notes to bearer, in times of expected difficulty, for the sake of securing himself in other respects. For, if through the pouring in of his Notes, his Cash should be inadequate, the whole body of his creditors would be likely to come for payment of their debts. The Bank of England is not at all circumstanced like the Country Banker in this respect; their Notes are in perfect credit in London, and its neighbourhood, where alone they generally circulate; and I believe it is universally agreed, it is not through any distrust of Bank of England Notes, that the demand upon the Bank for Guineas has taken place. The Bank of England are undoubtedly liable to be called upon for Guineas by Bankers in the country, in the same manner as a great Bank in the country is liable to be called upon for them by a rival Bank: but it is not possible for the Bank of England, unless it is supposed that they suppress their Notes altogether, to exempt themselves from this inconvenience: they are universally considered as the repository for Cash, on which every individual in the country, who is in want of Guineas, has a right to draw, and any person who has property he can sell for what is called ready Money, that is, for Bank Notes, may at any time sell it, and thus possess himself of Guineas drawn from the Bank. Moreover, the Bank of England, by their custom of daily discounting, afford to every individual an opportunity of obtaining Guineas from them; nor is it considered as being at all improper, by the friend of a Country Banker, to discount Bills with a view of thus furnishing Guineas for the relief of a Country Bank: whereas, in the case of two rival Country Banks, the idea of discounting at one Bank for the sake of furnishing Guineas thereby to the other, would not be entertained. I conceive, therefore, that in this respect the Bank of England has no such inducement to suppress or limit its Paper circulation, as a Country Banker has, since it cannot, by such suppression or limitation, secure itself from the inconvenience I have last-mentioned, in the same manner as a Country Banker can. I think, moreover, there is an important difference between the case of a Country Banker and the Bank of England, in this othes respect: if a Country Banker thinks fit to lessen his Paper circulation, or even to reduce or rclinquish his whole trade

287

in a period of expected difficulty, he can do so, without bringing down any great evils on himself: he may possibly contribute to the general distress, by abandoning his profession, or even possibly by diminishing certain parts of his transactions; but he may consider himself as being more than recompensed for his particular share of the general distress which he occasions, by the personal ease and tranquillity, or security, which he obtains. The Bank of England, on the contrary, are engaged in such large transactions, that they cannot relinquish any considerable part of their accustomed business, without giving a general shock to credit, of which they themselves must, as I conceive, be some of the first victims. If they reduce materially their notes in a time of difficulty and distress, there are no other Notes which are ready to supply the deficiency in the circulation; and if it is to be supplied by Guineas, those Guineas must come from the Bank: they are always the possessors of a very large quantity of Bills, which they have discounted, and which are growing due from day to day. It is notorious, that the acceptors of these Bills have not provided themselves with Guineas for the payment of them, but that they depend upon the means of payment on the accustomed liberality of the Bank: in short, the Bank depend, as I conceive, in respect to every part of their receipts, on the maintenance of general credit; whether we consider the taxes, on the receipt of which they rely for the repayment of the loans made to Government, or for the punctual payment of Bills of Exchange, which I have just mentioned, or for any other source of supply which they may be expecting: I conceive, therefore, that the Bank of England can find no safety for themselves, except by seeking it in the safety of the commercial world, in the general support of Government credit, and of the general prosperity of the Nation. It follows, therefore, that if any great suppression of their Notes is injurious to general credit, it must be injurious also to the Bank of England itself; and that the Bank of England, in respect to the issuing of Notes, does not stand on the same footing as an individual Country Banker.

Q. What, according to the best of your judgment and information, is the proportion of Bank of England Notes circulating in the country, to that which circulates in London?

A. I should think that very few circulate more than 20 or 30 miles from London; for there are Country Banks which issue Notes at something more than that distance from London, which supply, as I conceive, the circulation of the surrounding part. The House with which I am connected is in the habit of receiving large remittances from the country, among which they seldom find any thing more than a trifling quantity of Bank Notes.

Q. Assuming, that, in consequence of the Bank having extinguished a very considerable proportion of its Notes in circulation, a new circulating

288

medium should have been created, in order to make up for that deficiency; must not the Bank, supposing it to act on the principle of providing for its own safety, by maintaining a fixed proportion between Cash and Notes, be compelled to make that proportion bear relation, not to its own Notes only which should remain in circulation, but also to the amount of that new circulating medium which should have been so created?

A. In case a new circulating medium in London should take place, I take for granted, that it would pass current every where in payments, exactly like the Bank of England Notes, and that it would be easily exchangeable for them; which Bank of England Notes would then be exchangeable for Guineas. The Bank of England therefore, assuming them to return into circulation a quantity of Bank Notes equal to those which had been brought in through such exchange as I have described, for which I suppose Guineas to have been paid, would again be liable, by the interchange of the new circulating medium for some of these fresh Notes, to have fresh Guineas demanded of them. This observation, however, applies, not merely to any new circulating medium which might be introduced in London, but also to any circulating medium now existing in the country, which is exchange-able for Bank of England Notes, or to any species of Paper, or other article which is convertible into Bank of England Notes. I infer from hence, that the observation I have before made, is indisputable; namely, that the Guineas necessary in order to provide safety for any Bank, should be proportioned, not to the quantity of Notes, but to the probable demand for Guineas, for which, under all the circumstances of the case, the Bank is likely to be called upon antecedently to the time when fresh Guineas can be obtained.

Q. Do you, or do you not conceive, in point of fact, that any considerable reduction of the Paper circulation of the Bank, below its ordinary amount, as often as it has taken place, has commonly produced an increase of discount on Navy and Exchequer Bills and India Bonds, and a fall in the price of Stocks?

A. I am not informed of every diminution in the total amount of Bank Notes, which may at different times have taken place; nor do I conceive that the effect spoken of in this question, is likely so much to follow from a diminution of any given quantity of Notes, as from a reduction of them below that quantity, whatever it may be, at which the circumstances of the time would naturally require that they should stand. It may happen, particularly in times of alarm, that through the depreciation of other Paper, the want of which Bank of England Notes may be wanted to supply, and also through the less œconomical use of Bank Notes, which may result from a disposition in many persons to keep their Bank Notes at home, instead

Enquiry into Paper Credit

of placing them at their Bankers, as well as from their disposition to provide some time before hand for an unexpected payment, that a very increased quantity of Bank Notes may be as necessary as a smaller quantity might have been at another time. I conceive, therefore, that, if in such a period the Bank of England should refuse even to increase their circulation, the effect may be the same, or even greater than their actual reduction of them at another period. I conceive, undoubtedly, that the refusal of the Bank to discount, with a view of reducing their Paper circulation, or of preventing its increase at periods when pressing applications for discounts were made to them, have often been manifestly followed by a great increase in the discounts upon Navy and Exchequer Bills, and upon India Bonds, and even by a fall in the price of Stocks. I apprehend, however, that the effect of such refusal in the Bank, is not so easy to be discerned, in respect to any fluctuation in the Stocks, because many other causes may co-operate in influencing their price.

Q. Have you, in point of fact, remarked, that when the Bank has reduced or limited its discounts within the amount which the convenience of trade required, a rise in the discounts of Government securities, and a fall in the price of Stocks has taken place?

A. I have a general recollection that, early in the last autumn, there was a considerable demand for discounts at the Bank, only a small proportion of which was complied with, and that there was also a great rise on some species of public securities, and I believe also a fall in the price of Stocks. I more particularly know, that at a period ending some weeks previous to the Order of Council, Exchequer Bills payable in three months, and bearing about $5\frac{1}{4}$ per cent. interest, were sold on Government account to the extent of above a million sterling; the interest which was made by the holder being thus about $6\frac{1}{4}$ per cent. I also know, from perfect recollection, that for two days antecedent to the Order of Council, the applications to the Bank for discounts were unusually great, and that a very small proportion of them was complied with, and also that the discounts on Exchequer Bills rose, on the two days preceding the Order of Council, to about 3 and $3\frac{1}{2}$ per cent. per ann. yielding to the holder about 17 to 19 per cent. per ann. interest and that the Stocks fell at the same time; the difference between the price of Stock sold for Money, and the price of the same stock sold for a period distant by a few weeks, was such, as to make the interest paid by the sale and re-purchase of the Stock amount to nearly the same rate. On the Monday succeeding the Order of Council, a very large discount was made by the Bank, with a view of relieving the Bankers from any run upon them, which the alarm arising from the event of the preceding day might occasion; I believe, however, that no such run took place. The price of Exchequer

Bills continued on that day nominally as before, but I believe that few or none of them were sold. On the next day, when some degree of liberality in discounting again took place on the part of the Bank, they fell to 2½ per cent. and the Stocks rose perceptibly. The difference between the ready Money Stock and the price of a future day was such as to afford, if I recollect right, an interest of 8 or 10 per cent. I believe there has been, since that time, some degree of fluctuation in respect to the supply of discounts from the Bank, and a somewhat corresponding fluctuation in the price of the public securities I have already named. It appears to me, that the high rate of discount on Exchequer Bills, which I mentioned to have taken place on Friday and Saturday preceding the Order in Council, was the consequence of the disappointments of the persons applying for discounts on the preceding Thursday, which is the chief discounting day at the Bank; and also, that the fall in the discount of the Exchequer Bills on the Tuesday, was the consequence of the enlarged discount on the Monday; and therefore that the diminution in the value of securities, and the high rate of interest upon them, may be considered rather as being the effect of the conduct of the Bank, than as the cause of the applications being made to them for discounts.

Q. Did the news of the Order in Council, produce any considerable shock on public credit in the metropolis?

A. I conceive the distress, for some time preceding it, and especially for two days before, to have been so great, that the relief given by the unusual discounts on the Monday, more than compensated, in the minds of most of the mercantile world, for any alarm occasioned by the stoppage of the Cash payments of the Bank. It was the want of Bank Notes, and not of Guineas, that had been felt; and no anxiety seemed to be entertained in the city, if Bank Notes were brought into circulation, respecting the manner of contriving to effect the smaller payments.

Q. Must not the reduction of Bank Notes considerably below the amount which the convenience of trade requires, have a tendency to cause manufacturers throughout the whole of Great Britain, to limit their manufactures and turn off their workmen?

A. I should think undoubtedly.

Q. Have any facts fallen within your knowledge, in actual confirmation of that opinion?

A. I recollect to have heard a mercantile person remark, that he had plenty of goods for sale; that he had also a sufficient demand for them abroad, but that a great many of the labouring manufacturers who made those goods had been turned off for some time past, and an increased number just before the Order of Council, on account of his not being able to afford the usual credit, since he could not obtain his usual discounts.

Q. Has not the profit to be made from Cash in the metropolis, for the last year or two, been such, as to afford a strong inducement to all persons having demands on foreign countries, to get in their debts as soon as possible?

A. I conceive the interest on public securities has been so high, and the want of Money so great, as to have been likely to have induced people to urge their correspondents abroad to make them more than ordinary remittances.

Q. Do you recollect the resolution of the Bank of the 31st of December 1795, respecting discounts?

A. Yes.

Q. Was there, at that time, any extraordinary application to the Bank for discounts, arising from any difficulty in procuring private discounts?

A. I believe that private discounts had at that time nearly ceased, if not entirely so; I do not mean by private discounts, the discounts of Bankers, who in general discount for their customers in all periods; I mean, by private discounters, individual merchants, or monied men, who lend out Money upon Bills, for the sake of the interest which they obtain by those Bills.

Q. Were such private discounts, to any considerable amount, previous to December 1795?

A. I believe at some periods, since the war, they were; but I cannot recollect the periods exactly.

Q. Do not private discounts ordinarily diminish in time of war, when considerable profit may be made by floating Government securities?

A. Certainly.

Q. Must not the Bank therefore, in such times, ordinarily supply the defect of private discounts, in order to prevent inconvenience to the Public?

A. Unless it is supposed that a considerable diminution of mercantile transactions takes place in time of war, it appears to me necessary that the Bank should increase their discounts.

Q. Had the resolution of the Bank in December 1795, any effect to create any difficulty or alarm?

A. I do not recollect that any very particular alarm was excited: the Bank, antecedent to that resolution, had, in several ways, narrowed their discount; and I believe it was chiefly considered as an intimation, that they were about to limit them still more by this new regulation.

Q. Is any inconvenience likely to arise from the uncertainty and fluctuation in the conduct of the Bank, respecting their discounts?

A. Undoubtedly it must tend to create an occasion for an increased number of Bank Notes: for those who fear disappointment on the day on which they asked for discounts, will be likely to provide some time before for their expected payments; and Bankers, in proportion as they are in a state of uncertainty, are inclined to furnish themselves with a larger quantity of Bank Notes. I do not conceive that the resolution above-men·tioned implied any fluctuation in the system of the conduct of the Bank, but rather the contrary; it nevertheless occasioned some uncertainty to each individual merchant, as to his means of supply; and I rather think it operated as an intimation to the commercial world at large; I mean, both in the metropolis and in the country, that there was danger of increasing distress.

Q. Supposing Government had, in January last, repaid to the Bank three millions sterling, do you imagine it would have put the Bank in a state of perfect security?

A. I should conceive that it would clearly have made no difference as to the quantity of their Cash. I do not understand whether it is meant, in this question, to assume, that if three millions of Government debt had been paid, the Bank were to suppress in consequence three millions of Notes. If they had taken occasion, at the time of this repayment, to make such a suppression, I conceive, as I have before explained, that they would prejudice essentially all commercial credit, and create a distress as well as an alarm, which would be likely to increase the run upon them for Guineas; but if, on the other hand, they should grant to the commercial world an equal quantity of discounts, that the Bank would then be in much the same circumstances in which they stood antecedent to such repayment.

Jovis, 6° die Aprilis 1797

Henry Thornton, Esquire, a Member of the House; called in, and further Examined

Q. Since your last examination, have you received any further information respecting the quantity of Notes, or of Cash, circulated in the country?

A. I have, from Scotland. I am assured that the Notes now in circulation there, are very much the same as they have been for six months past, and that the amount of the Gold in the possession of the Banks may be computed to be much the same also; consequently, it is presumed, that about £60,000, of Gold which has been lately drawn from the Banks there, and which is about the same sum which the Banks have drawn from London, is not now in circulation there, but is hoarded through fear. The amount of the Paper circulation in Scotland, is computed to be from about £1,200,000 to £1,500,000, and the quantity of Guineas usually circulated, is computed to be not more than £50,000. Seven eights of the Notes is said to be twenty

293

and twenty-one shilling Notes: five shilling Notes have also been lately issued, which are in very great demand, and it is said to be hoped, that the time of their legal circulation may be extended.

Q. In your former examination, you stated some differences between the situation of the Bank of England, and the Country Banker; are there any others, which suggest themselves to your mind; and also, are there any differences between the situations of the Bank of England, and of a Banker in the metropolis or elsewhere, who does not issue "Notes payable on demand"?

A. There is one very obvious and important difference between the case of a Country Banker and that of the Bank of England, to which the existence of the Bank of England itself gives rise. When a Country Banker is in want of Guineas, provided he has no supply of Guineas in the neighbourhood, which in times of alarm will often be the case, he is sure of a resource in the Bank of England: he has only to write to the Banking-house in London with whom he does his business, and to desire that they will send him such quantities of Guineas as he wants by the return of the mail coach: the Country Banker, therefore, has only to provide himself, either with a credit with his London correspondent, or with effects in his hands, or with some kind of property, such as Stocks, Exchequer Bills, or discountable Bills, quickly convertible into Bank Notes, and he may then consider himself as secure of having as many Guineas as his occasions may require. I here assume, that the Bank of England makes payments of Cash as usual. In case the Bank of England should fail in its Cash payments, I would here also remark, that a Country Bank, by suspending its Cash payments, suffers little or no discredit; and, as it appears from the circumstances of the present times, is in no respect very particularly distressed: on the contrary, when the Guineas of the Bank of England are nearly exhausted, it has no repository of Cash, as the Country Banks have, to which it can resort. I apprehend, that there is no quarter to which it can apply, nor any means which it can use, so as to obtain a considerable supply of Guineas, and that its best, and perhaps its only chance of again attracting Guineas to itself, is by strengthening general credit. It may, no doubt, contribute to a favourable balance of trade, and remotely therefore to an accumulation of Guineas in its own coffers, by lending a general aid to commerce; and it may also, more directly and immediately, promote the return of Guineas into its coffers in a time of alarm, by endeavouring to diminish that alarm; which I conceive it may do to a certain degree, and in certain cases, by a considerable increase, rather than by a diminution, of its Bank Notes: I apprehend this is a very important point, in which the Bank of England differ both from a Country Bank, and from every private Bank.

294

2

EVIDENCE GIVEN BEFORE THE LORDS' COMMITTEE OF
SECRECY APPOINTED TO ENQUIRE INTO THE CAUSES
WHICH PRODUCED THE ORDER OF COUNCIL OF THE
26TH OF FEBRUARY 1797*

Die Jovis, 30° Martii, 1797

Lord President in the Chair

Henry Thornton, Esquire, a Banker of London, being attending, he was
called in, and examined

Q. Have you Reason to think there has been a great Increase in the
whole Scale of Publick Income and Expenditure?

A. Undoubtedly.

Q. Has not a similar Increase taken Place in the Scale of Private
Expenditure?

A. If you include several Years past, it certainly has.

Q. Has there not been of late Years a Rise in the Price of Provisions
and of Labour?

A. Certainly.

Q. Has there not been a great Extension in the Manufactures and
Commerce of the Kingdom?

A. Undoubtedly.

Q. Have not the Circumstances, stated in the preceding Questions and
Answers, occasioned a Demand for additional Means of Circulation?

A. Before I reply to that Question, it may be proper to express distinctly
what I shall understand by Means of Circulation. I conceive it to mean,
First, Coin of every Sort; Secondly, Notes to Bearer payable on Demand,
whether issued by the Bank of England or by Country Bankers, which I
consider as exchangeable at all Times for Cash; and Thirdly, Bills of
Exchange. In calling Bills of Exchange a Means of Circulation, I do not

* [The report of this committee, ordered to be printed April 28, 1797,
exists in three forms:

(*a*) in the Journals of the House of Lords, XVI, pp, 186–262.

(*b*) as a separate document, apparently of the same year, 272 pp.

(*c*) reprinted, by order of the House of Commons, February 6, 1810, 151 pp.,
the present reprint is made from (*a*) with corrections.]

295

consider them equally so with the other Two Articles I have mentioned, since they ostensibly serve the Purpose of ascertaining Debts between Buyer and Seller, and of pledging the Acceptor to a punctual Payment, and are often created chiefly with that View, and are used but sparingly and occasionally as a Mean of Circulation. I conceive that the Number of Bills of Exchange which may happen at any Time to exist, bears no necessary Proportion to the Magnitude of the existing Trade, although, I conceive, that the Use of them in Payment does bear a pretty regular Proportion to the Quantity of Commerce. For instance, at Liverpool and Manchester all Payments are made either in Coin or in Bills of Exchange. The Holders of these Bills (since they themselves profit by the Detention of them, the Bills growing more valuable in Proportion as they become nearer due) keep them in their Possession in larger Quantities than they would Notes to Bearer on Demand, the Profit of the Detention of which last goes to the Bank which issues them, and not to the Person who has them in his Possession.

I would now reply to the Question put to me, by answering, that I conceive the increased Trade of the Country has undoubtedly caused a Necessity for an increased Use, either of Bills or Notes to Bearer in Payment; and also that the increased Scale of Expenditure of the Country must have caused, as I conceive, an increased Use chiefly of Notes to Bearer upon Demand, though partly also of Bills of Exhange, and likewise, in some Degree, perhaps of Cash, especially in those Times when Notes to Bearer on Demand come into Discredit. In general, I consider Guineas as furnishing the Means of paying small or broken Sums; and as bearing much the same Relation to Notes which Shillings do to Guineas, and that the Occasion for the Increase of their Quantity does not necessarily keep Pace with the other increased Means of Circulation.

Q. How far have the additional Means of Circulation, stated in the last Answer to have become necessary, been furnished in the Metropolis, either by an increased Proportion of Bank Notes in Circulation, or by any other Means, so as to keep pace with the enlarged Scale of Expenditure, and with the increased Employment of acting Capital?

A. No Notes pass currently in Payment in the Metropolis except those of the Bank of England; nor is it usual there to make use of Bills of Exchange in Payment, as is done often in the Country. Of the Quantity of Bank of England Notes which may have been issued now and at former Periods, I can have no authentic Information; it is commonly understood, however, to have lately decreased; and I should conceive that the high Rate of Interest for Money amounting from Eight to Ten, and even Eighteen per Cent. which has been evident in the Price of Exchequer Bills, India Bonds, and other such Securities, soon convertible into Bank Notes, has arisen in a

296

great Measure from the Scarcity of Bank Notes, the Price paid (if I may so express it) for the Purchase of Bank Notes naturally increasing in Proportion as those Notes are few in Number and in great Demand. In consequence of the assumed Scarcity of Bank Notes, it has been in the Contemplation of several Persons, and particularly of Bankers, to endeavour to provide some additional Means of Circulation for the Metropolis; which it has been thought, that if the Bankers would agree to take, they might become generally current in the Metropolis; but some Doubts have been entertained whether a Project of this Sort would answer, unless the Bankers should guarantee the Notes of each other; in which Case it is a Question, whether it might not be an Infraction or Evasion of the Bank Charter. I consider these Circumstances as Proofs that the Bank Notes in Circulation have not borne a due Proportion to the Wants of the Public.

Q. If, instead of a Decrease of Bank Notes in Circulation, assumed by the last Answer to have taken Place, the Quantity of those Notes had remained as they were, without material Increase or Decrease, would not the Inconveniences resulting from the forced Sale, and consequent Depreciation of other Securities, have then also prevailed, though in a less Degree?

A. I conceive they would; and that the increased Transactions of Commerce in the Metropolis must have required an Increase of the Bank Notes issued. These being the only Means of Circulation in the Metropolis; excepting Guineas which cannot be used in any considerable Dealings.

Q. What Effect would any considerable Augmentation in the Quantity of circulating Bank Notes in the Metropolis have produced?

A. I conceive that the Increase of their Quantity ought to depend not only on the increased Quantity of Trade in the Metropolis, but also on the Occasion for them which might arise from other Causes.

If, for Instance, general Credit should be impaired while Bank Notes sustain their Credit, it follows that there would be a Disposition in many People to hold Possession of Bank Notes, although at some Loss to themselves, who at other Times might be satisfied with the Possession only of Bills of Exchange; for, the Convertibility of Bills of Exchange into Bank Notes being more doubtful, prudent Persons would provide themselves if possible with Bank Notes for their expected Payments, at a Time perhaps much antecedent to the Time of Payment. I conceive, therefore, the Quantity of Notes which it may be proper at any time to issue, to depend much on the State of the Public Mind, that is, on the Dispositions of Persons to detain them. If indeed, a much larger Quantity were issued than would remain in Circulation, I should imagine that the Effect of such excessive Emissions might be to draw Guineas out of the Bank of England.

Q. How far are you of Opinion, that an Increase in the Quantity of circulating Bank Notes, adequately proportioned to the increased Wants and Demands above described, would, or would not, have tended to an increased and inconvenient Call upon the Bank for the Issue of Cash?

A. I think that an increased Quantity of Notes, proportioned to the increased Occasion for them, must tend to prevent a Demand for Guineas rather than to promote it; and if the Quantity of Notes issued should be very considerably less than the Occasion of the Mercantile World requires, I should think a Run upon the Bank for Guineas would be the Consequence; for when Trade is much distressed and Failures are expected, a general Distrust is apt to be excited; and as the Cause of such expected Failures is not distinctly known to be the Diminution of the Bank of England's circulating Notes, there are likely to be at least some Persons in the Country who may wish not only to be possessed of Bank Notes for their Security, but even of Guineas. I further think, that a Scarcity of the circulating Medium of the Metropolis tends to induce some of the Country Bankers, who are the most opulent and respectable, to forbear from issuing their Bank Notes, through the Apprehension of Mercantile Distress: And their Forbearance to issue Country Bank Notes is naturally followed by a considerable Increase in the Use of Guineas, all which are drawn out of the Bank of England.

Q. Is it not for the Interest of the Bank of England, as well as of every private Banker, to issue as many Notes as they possibly can, consistently with due Attention to their Credit and Stability?

A. I conceive that to be self-evident.

Q. Will you proceed to state how far any additional Means of Circulation have been furnished by the Country Banks to keep Pace with the increased Demand described in the preceding Questions and Answers?

A. I have no distinct Information as to the Quantity of Bills of Exchange used in the Country, and which, as I have before stated, in many Cases, answer the Purpose of Notes to Bearer on Demand, and in some Degree also may spare the Use of Guineas. I conceive, however, that the Use of Notes and Bills of Exchange depending in a great Measure on the Custom of each particular Place, which does not often vary, the Circulation of Notes and Guineas when combined must, generally speaking, supply the Means of Circulation in those Parts where Notes and not Bills of Exchange have been ordinarily current, as a Means of Circulation. I am well assured, that in many Parts the Notes of Country Bankers have, since the Year 1793, diminished rather than increased, and that they are in particular much decreased at this Time. I infer, therefore, that the Means of Circulation have been supplied, to a considerable Extent, by Guineas.

Q. Will you assign the Reason why you state the Year 1793 as the Time at which the Diminution of Country Bank Notes began to take Place?

A. That was the Period of very considerable Failures in this Country, and especially of the Country Bankers. Having been desired to enquire into the State of Paper Circulation in the Country, I some Days ago wrote to about Fifteen or Sixteen Country Bankers in different Places, with whom I was either acquainted or connected, and I desired them to state to me the comparative Amount of their Notes payable to Bearer on Demand, naming particularly to them the Period preceding the Failures in 1793, and also the Period subsequent to it as well as the present Time.

Q. Will you state the Result?

[The answer to this question repeats *verbatim* the first answer given to the House of Commons Committee on April 1st, from the paragraph beginning "First, I will state . . ." to the end of that answer (pp. 284–5 above), only adding at the end the following paragraph:]

The Paper Circulation of Scotland continues much the same as it was before the Failure of the Cash Payments of the Bank of England.

Q. When the Country Banks are in general in a high state of Credit, has it not been the Practice of the Country Bankers to discourage the Circulation of Bank of England Notes in the Country, in order to increase their own Circulation?

A. I rather think it has; I am well convinced that very few Bank of England Notes have in ordinary Times circulated far from London, because if they had so, the Banking House with which I am connected, receiving, as they do, large remittances of Paper of various Sorts from the Country, would have received sometimes Bank Notes among them, and would also probably have been desired sometimes to send Bank of England Notes into the Country, neither of which has been the Case in any considerable Degree except indeed that since the Stoppage of the Cash Payments of the Bank, we have sent, I think, between 40 and £50,000 in Bank Notes, some Part of which have been 5*l*. Notes, the rest chiefly 20*s*. or 2*l*. Notes.

Q. Did not the First Alarm, on the late Occasion, with respect to the State of general Credit, take its Rise from some of the Country Banks?

A. A considerable Alarm was created about Three Weeks before the Stoppage of the Cash Payements of the Bank, through the Suspension of the Payments of the Newcastle Banks. But a considerable Distress in the Mercantile World prevailed antecedently to that Time.

Q. When this Alarm first prevailed in the Country, did the Country Bankers apply to their Correspondents in London for a Remittance of Cash or Bank Notes?

A. It did not happen to the House with which I am connected, to have any very considerable Demands for Cash made to them in consequence of the Stoppage of the Newcastle Banks, and still less for Bank Notes; the Application for Guineas to us, was from only One or Two Banks in the Neighbourhood of the Newcastle Banks, and also from Scotland, which Demands we had partly anticipated; the Demand for Guineas subsequent to the Stoppage of the Newcastle Banks was but small and gradual, so far as respected the House with which I am connected, the Effect of those Stoppages seemed not to be felt in some Parts on the Western side of England, till some Days after the Issue of the Order in Council.

Q. Did the late Alarm of Invasion occasion a great Demand of Guineas from the Country Banks?

A. I have always understood that it did so at Newcastle, and I presume it to have been probable that it did so, more or less, at other Places.

Q. Are you of Opinion, that the Check given to the Credit of some of the Country Banks in 1793, the subsequent Diminution of Country Bank Notes payable on Demand, the Effect of the late Alarm of Invasion, and the other Circumstances mentioned by you, have, altogether, occasioned the carrying of a considerable Quantity of Guineas from the Metropolis into the Country, beyond the Proportion which had been before employed in the Country?

A. I am not well informed as to the Transmission of Guineas at any particular Time from London into the Country, but I am well persuaded, that, in Point of Fact, a very considerable Quantity of Guineas are in various Parts of the Country at present. I have received Information in the Course of Business, from four or five Bankers in the Country, of their having either a Sufficiency or a Surplus of Guineas, and I have heard no Complaint lately of the Want of them. As the Notes of the Country Bankers to Bearer on Demand, now in Circulation, appear by the foregoing Statement to be at this Time particularly small, and as I have learnt from many Places that Guineas are abundant, I think it fair to infer, that the Quantity of Guineas now in the Country is, on the whole, likely to be considerable.

Q. Do you think, that the Distress in the Mercantile World, which you say preceded the Alarm from Newcastle in February last, did occasion an increased Demand for Cash on the Bank?

A. I conceive that it may have done so in the Manner which I before partly stated. The respectable Country Bankers knowing the Distress in London, and, anticipating future Mischief, restraining (as I well know in some Places) their Paper Circulation. The general Apprehensions of the Public being also aggravated by the Distress of the Commercial World, might also tend to produce in some Persons a Disposition to hoard Guineas;

300

and it is obvious, that if only a few Persons of timid Minds choose to invest a large Portion of their Property in Guineas, instead of using them merely as that Means of Circulation for which they are intended to serve, that the Effect will be considerable.

Q. Did not the great Increase of Commerce in this Country for the last three Years, require a proportional Increase of Capital in the Commercial World, and was not that Want of Capital one of the Causes of the Distress amongst Commercial Men?

A. I conceive that it may have been so.

Q. Does not any given Quantity of Commerce in Time of War, require a greater Capital to carry it on, arising from the increased Expense of Freight, Insurance, and Mercantile Charges, than the same Quantity of Commerce in Time of Peace?

A. Undoubtedly it does.

Q. If any considerable Proportion of the Bank Advances to Government had been rapaid in the Course of the last two Years (suppose to the Extent of 4 or 5 Millions), are you of Opinion, that a Reduction in the Quantity of Bank Notes to that Extent could have been made without occasioning great Public Distress? and give your Reasons?

A. I am clearly of Opinion that a Reduction of Bank Notes to the Extent of £5,000,000 less than their hitherto existing Amount, which I understand may have been about 9 or 10 Millions, would either produce the Substitution of other Paper nearly to the same or perhaps to a still greater Amount, or, assuming no such Substitution to take place, that it would produce very general, if not universal Failures in the Metropolis. In the Case supposed, one Half of the Bank Notes now in Circulation are to answer the Purpose that is now answered by the Whole; I apprehend that the Bankers of London may on a rough Estimate be supposed to have 4 or 5 Millions of Bank Notes, and possibly rather more, in their Possession, and that is the Sum which they deem it prudent if not necessary to keep for their current Payments; in whatever Degree they can reduce that Sum, they save in ordinary Times 8, 10, and occasionally 18 per Cent. per Annum, on the Sum reduced, so that it is obvious that they do not keep more than is necessary. If the supposed Diminution of Bank Notes were to take place, I may consider the General Body of Bankers to be provided only with about One-Half of their accustomed Quantity of Bank Notes; some of these, however, would in that Case be able to possess themselves of more than Half, and others of less; the certain Failure therefore of those whose Resources are the least, would be the Consequence, and the Failure of one Banker in such a State of Things would be quickly followed by that of others.

301

I have as yet said nothing of that Part of the Bank Notes in Circulation which would be in private Hands. I conceive, however, that Bankers would suffer at least as great a Diminution of the Sum possessed by them as private Persons, for as the Occasion for Bank Notes, and also the Alarm would in such a Case be as great or nearly so in the Minds of many private Individuals as in the Minds of Bankers, and as private Individuals would be more able each of them to possess themselves of a small Quantity of Bank Notes, by selling at whatever Loss any Property that was marketable, I think the private Persons would retain more than their accustomed Half of the Notes in Circulation. The Circumstance of Government paying off their Debt to the Bank, which has been supposed in the Question put to me, would evidently, as I apprehend, make no Difference in any Part of the Case which I have described. The Debt which Government would pay to the Bank would be paid by a Loan from the publick, and would be raised immediately from the Banking or mercantile World. I apprehend that the very Negociation of a Loan in Times of great Difficulty and Distress, since it occasions the Payment of large Instalments on particular Days, would be the Cause of peculiar Apprehensions antecedently to those Days, and of very eager Endeavours in some Bankers to provide Bank Notes for the Payment of whatever might be their expected Share of the Instalments, which Share they would not know distinctly before Hand, since they are not informed of the Proportion of the Loan which each Customer may have. Some Bankers might be therefore led through their Fears, or through unavoidable Mistakes in their Calculations, to provide more Bank Notes for their expected Payments than might prove necessary, while others might provide less, and might be in peculiar Danger of failing in their Payments in consequence. I consider that there is always an Occasion for some Increase in the Emission of Bank Notes at the Period antecedent to each Instalment, on a Government Loan, on Account of this Uncertainty which the Bankers feel in respect to the Drafts which will be drawn upon them. I consider also that if a Loan were made by Government, with a View to pay the Bank, and if the Bank, in consequence, were to lend the same Sum to the Merchants, it would merely be like a Transfer of their Debt from one Person to another, and that the Bank would not be relieved by it. On the other Hand, if we suppose the Bank not to lend out the same Sum to Merchants, but to take that Opportunity of reducing their Paper Circulation, then the probable Mischief of such Reduction would, as I think, be what I have already stated.

Withdrew.

Die Veneris, 31° Martii 1797

Lord President in the Chair

Henry Thornton, Esquire, being attending, he was called in, and examined.

Q. You having stated, that in Time of general Mercantile Difficulty and Apprehension of Failures, it is the Custom of the respectable and prudent Country Bankers to lessen or suppress the Quantity of their Notes payable on Demand, what is the Reason that, on the same Principle, the Bank of England ought not to lessen their circulating Notes at the same Time?

A. I take the Case of a Country Banker and of the Bank of England to be in several Respects extremely different, and that the Explanation of the Differences I allude to in their Circumstances, will best furnish an Answer to that Question.

First, I would observe, That a Country Banker who issues Notes to Bearer on Demand has, in many Cases, also several other Branches of Business which he follows, and which are very important to him. He has perhaps large Deposits in his Hands from his own immediate Customers, amounting in some Cases possibly to many Times the Sum in Notes which he has in Circulation; and he is liable to be called upon at any Time for immediate Payment of the whole Amount of these Deposits. His Customers, however, having Confidence in him, and being personally known to him, are not very likely to take Alarm, unless some special Cause of Alarm should be given them; his Notes on the contrary circulate through the Hands of Strangers, and, consisting in small Sums, they are often in the Hands of the lowest Class of People. These Notes, moreover, are often confounded in the Minds of the Holders of them, with the Notes of other Bankers of less Credit; insomuch, that in the Event of the Failure of any neighbouring Bank, it is probable that the most respectable Banker in the Country would suffer some Run upon him from the Holders of his Notes. In order, therefore, to prevent his Credit from being wounded in that Part where it is most vulnerable, a prudent Country Banker, in Times of apprehended Danger, is apt to lessen or suppress his Notes to Bearer on Demand, for the Sake of better securing his Credit in other Respects. This is one Circumstance in which a Country Banker differs from the Bank of England. The Bank of England Notes possess undoubted Credit in the Metropolis and its Neighbourhood, where alone they chiefly circulate, and are not confounded with the Paper of other Banks. It is obviously not through any Distrust of the Bank of England Notes that any considerable Quantity of Guineas has been demanded for them, and that there is no Occasion, therefore, in Times of Danger to suppress them, for the Reason operating in the Minds of the Country Bankers which I have just stated. I would remark that, in the next Place, the Country Banker withdraws his Notes in a Time of Danger, partly because they expose him to a sudden Demand for Guineas in the following Manner: Rival Banks, when in want of Guineas, have only to possess themselves of his Notes, in order to obtain a Supply of Cash for themselves, which, when his Notes are every where in Circulation, are easy to be obtained, and he is thus exposed both to the Expence and the Risk of supplying Guineas to other Banks who have not sufficiently supplied themselves. If he withdraws his Notes, the rival Banks cannot so easily obtain Guineas from him by the Means of Guineas paid for the Deposits of his Customers; for his Customers will not assist them in any such Attempt. In this respect, the Case of the Bank of England is widely different. I here assume indeed, that the Bank of England will in no Case totally suppress their Paper Circulation; and, if they do not, it is obvious that any one who has Property which he can sell for what is called ready Money, (that is Bank of England Notes,) may possess himself of Guineas; and thus the Bank of England, as long as they issue Notes at all, are liable to be drained of their Cash just as much as any Country Bank that is the most exposed by his Paper Circulation. Moreover, the Bank of England are liable to have Cash demanded of them for the Amount of whatever may be their Deposits, and for all the Sums which they discount also, assuming that they continue to discount at the Rate, for Instance, of £100,000 a Day, they are liable to a daily Demand for Guineas to that Amount; and this Demand may be made upon them by Persons immediately connected with Country Banks who want those Guineas, without the Bank being able to prevent it; for, from the Extent of their Transactions, and from the Effect of the general Rules which they lay down, from the little private Attachment which can be supposed to be between them and their Customers, and, above all, from their being considered as the chief Repository of Cash on which every Individual in the Country supposes himself to have a Right to draw, they are, through the Necessity of their Situation, obliged to furnish Guineas to all the Persons who may be in Want of them. As no Reduction of their Notes can remove from them this Hardship, they have in this Particular no such Inducement to lessen their Paper Circulation, as the Country Banker has.

In the next and last Place I would remark, that when a Country Banker lessens or suppresses his Notes payable to Bearer on Demand, either some other Kinds of Paper or Guineas naturally supply their Place, and no general Distress results from such Conduct of one individual Banker: He may contribute possibly, by too great a Reduction of his Business, to produce general Commercial Difficulty, but the Advantage in the Way of Ease and Security, and, perhaps, of Profit also, which he individually derives from the Suppression of his own particular Notes, may be greater than his Share of the Disadvantage which results from his own particular Conduct. In this respect, the Case of the Bank of England is totally different. When the Bank of England materially lessens or suppresses its Notes, there are no other Notes, as I said before, which can supply their Place. Their Place, indeed, may be supplied partly by Guineas; but these Guineas must be furnished by the Bank of England itself; the Distress which the Suppression of Bank of England Notes, to any considerable Degree, causes in the Metropolis, produces Distress through the whole Kingdom: It is the Means, as I before explained, of producing the Suppression of much of the Paper of the Country, and a consequent Demand for Guineas from the Bank; in short, the Suppression of the Bank of England's Paper, to any considerable Extent, must, unless some other Paper is substituted, in my Opinion, pull down the Price of Exchequer Bills, of India Bonds, and other Government Securities, which will be sold by those who possess them, in order to secure a sufficient Quantity of Bank Notes to carry on their Payments, and which a Variety of Bankers will be selling at the same Time, each endeavouring, though in vain, to possess himself of the notes held by the others. It must produce, therefore, Discredit to the Government, a consequent Distrust in the Minds of the Public, who will not understand the Cause of this Depreciation of the Stocks; it must produce, at the same Time, Commercial Failures, and an Appearance of Bankruptcy, even in Times when the Individuals in the Nation, and the Nation itself, might be rich and prosperous; and in the general Alarm and Difficulty which must ensue, the Demand for Guineas must of course rise, and perhaps to a considerable Height: In this Manner I think that the Bank of England, by its powerful influence on the Affairs of the Country, must, by the Suppression of its Notes, both prejudice the Country, and materially involve itself.

I conceive that the Principle of lessening the Paper Circulation of the Bank, in Proportion as Difficulties threatened it, and as Guineas were drawn out, may possibly at its first Origin have been a prudent Principle, for the same Reason that it is now a prudent Principle in the Country Bankers; but that since the Bank of England have obtained the Monopoly of supplying the Metropolis with its whole Means of Circulation, and have, by their superior Credit, excluded entirely all other Paper, and have also bound themselves, as far as long Custom can bind them, to a Number of General Rules, such as that of discounting daily for the Public; and since they have also become so considerable, that their individual Conduct operates upon the Credit of the whole Nation; it is no longer prudent in them to attempt

Enquiry into Paper Credit

to pursue their own individual Interest, by any Means which are contrary to the general Interests.

Q. Do Country Bankers, notwithstanding the peculiar Difficulties which you have stated they are exposed to, usually proportion the Number of their Notes to the Demand which they know is likely to be made for them in Payment of Rent and other large Remittances?

A. In ordinary Times, I conceive they do.

Q. In One of your Answers, you suppose £10,000,000 of Bank Notes to be in Circulation; will you explain how far that Amount is equal in its Operation as a Means of Circulation when compared to the same Quantity Five or Ten Years ago? and also how far you think it is equal to the increased Demands of the Kingdom described in the preceding Questions and Answers?

A. I should think that the increased Expenditure of the Country, and the very large Transactions on Government Account, which a State of War occasions, may (exclusively of the Distrust of other Paper, resulting from the War) occasion an increased Want of Bank of England Notes. I apprehend that in the Transactions of Government many Bank Notes are used, which, strictly speaking, are not in Circulation; and I have before stated, that during the Time of a Loan, a larger Quantity of Notes than usual appears to me to be wanted by the Public. I think, however, that the chief Cause of the Want of an increased Number of Bank Notes arises from the Distrust of other Paper, and in particular I conceive, that, at the present Time, a considerable Increase of Bank Notes is wanted for the Supply of the Country, and also as a Substitute for Guineas in many Places, for I do not find that Country Bankers are much disposed to become the Issuers of 20*s.* Notes on Account of the heavy Penalties to which the late Act for permitting their Issue is supposed to subject them, and, moreover, they refrain from issuing £5 Notes, because there is now no general Repository from which they can obtain Guineas in case the Notes should come in upon them. For all these various Reasons, I conceive there is an urgent Occasion for an Increase in the Issue of Bank of England Notes beyond the Amount to which they stood Five or Ten Years ago.

I cannot, however, calculate what that Increase ought to be, but I conceive it ought to be considerable.

Q. Supposing the Bank of England, for the Purpose of diminishing the Quantity of Bank Notes in Circulation, or from any other Motive, to reduce their Discounts considerably below the Demand for Discounts, what would be the Effect as well in the Metropolis, as with respect to the Country Banks, and the Commercial and Manufacturing Towns?

A. I should think there would be no great Difficulty in answering that

Question, if the unnaturally low Interest of Money resulting from the Usury Laws which confine the Rate of discounting at the Bank to 5*l*. per Cent. did not perplex the Question. I am afraid that in the present Times, and supposing also the Stocks to continue at nearly the present Price, there might be a much greater Disposition to borrow of the Bank at 5*l*. per Cent. than it might become the Bank to comply with. I apprehend, however, that, generally speaking, the too great Limitation of the Bank Discounts, by producing too great a Limitation of the Bank Notes in Circulation, would draw after it the evils which I have already pretty fully described. I think the Country has a common Interest with the Metropolis in this respect; I conceive it is not the Limitation of Discounts or Loans, but that it is the Limitation of Bank Notes or of the Means of Circulation that produces the Mischiefs I have spoken of, and that, whether the Bank lend more to Government, and less to Individuals, or less to Government and more to Individuals, the Quantity of the Bank Paper which comes into Circulation, and therefore the Effect upon the Public also, will be much the same. Indeed, I consider the Government in the light of one great discounting Customer, to whom the Bank lends Money just as it does to Individuals, but with this Difference, that it lends to Government Sums which are to be repaid at the Distance of Twelve Months, and perhaps a longer Period, while the Sums which it lends to Merchants are, according to the present ordinary Rules of the Bank, repaid in Two Months. I here take for granted, that the Notes which the Bank pays to Government do not remain locked up in the Hands of Government to any considerable Extent, and if they do not, it is perfectly clear to me that they very soon find their Way into the Hands of the Bankers, who are of course the Bankers to those who receive the Payments made by Government. For Instance, I will suppose a particular Banking House to be Bankers to an Army Agent who owes to that Banking House £10,000, it clearly matters not whether that Agent relieves the Banking House of the Load of that Debt, by paying in £10,000, which the Agent himself procures from the Bank of England by discounting, or whether the Agent obtains Payment of £10,000 of Arrears due from Government which the Government by a Loan of the same Nature, though in another Form, obtains from the Bank of England. The Relief granted to the Bankers in general, and to the Commercial World and to the Publick at large, is much the same, in my Opinion, whether the Bank of England's Paper (which I say is necessary as the Means of Circulation) comes to the Bankers and the Publick through the Medium of Government from the Bank of England, or whether it comes from the same Bank of England through the Medium of Individual Discounters. I think however that the Merchants, from a superficial View of this Subject,

307

may very naturally be led to suppose that a large Extension of discounts to them must of course operate materially to their own Relief. I am clear, however, that if it is duly considered, that in order to effect this Increase of Discount, a Quantity of Bank Notes, equal in its Amount, must first be paid into the Bank by the same Bankers who are in the Habit of accommodating these Merchants with Discounts, and who must reduce their Accommodations to the Merchant in Proportion, that this Misconception must cease. I do not here mean to imply any Opinion on the Subject of the Propriety on other Grounds of paying off Part of the Government Debt to the Bank, and of distributing the Amount of it by the Means of Discount to the Merchants; but I mean distinctly to say, that I conceive such a Measure would not produce any particular and direct Relief to the Merchants. I think, however, it might perhaps indirectly produce Benefit to them by improving general Confidence. I have thought it necessary thus fully to explain for what Reasons I conceive, that even an Increase of Discounts, if it is no greater than the Sum paid to the Bank by Government, will, in Fact, be no Increase of Accommodation to the Publick. I apprehend, on the other Hand, that some Diminution of Discounts would not hurt the Merchants, if a Loan were afforded to Government by the Bank to a still greater Extent; for Bank Notes to the Amount of that Loan would come into the Hands of the Bankers, and be lent by the Bankers to the Merchants, instead of being lent to the Merchants by the Bank of England.

Q. Is the Committee to understand, that you conceive the Opinion you have given to the preceding Answer to be consonant to the general Sentiments entertained by the Mercantile Body?

A. I conceive that many Persons of the Mercantile Body having heard that the Bank are likely, in the Event of a Loan made with a View of paying off the Bank, to increase their Discounts, have satisfied themselves to a certain Degree with that Information, not adverting to the Suppression of Bank Notes to as great, or possibly a still greater Amount, which the Bank of England might take Occasion to make at the Time of the Loan. Many of the Mercantile Body seem to me not at all to have considered the Whole of the Subject: Those Individuals of them, with whom I have conversed at large upon this Topic, have been very much of my Opinion.

Q. Is it not generally understood, that the Bank encreased their Discounts to a considerable Amount, subsequent to the Order of Council?

A. They accommodated both the Bankers and others with an unusually large Discount early on the Monday Morning, subsequent to the Order of Council. A Representation was made to them by some of the City Bankers, that they were doubtful whether to open on the Monday Morning, and to make their Payments as usual, unless some extraordinary Discounts were afforded with a View of providing against the Demand on them for Bank Notes, which the Consternation, arising from the Event of the Sunday, was thought, by some of the Bankers, not unlikely to produce. I believe that the Bank also continued their Liberality, though not on the same Scale, for some of the succeeding Days in that Week, but I conceive not through the Whole of it, and I rather think, that antecedently to the Day of the Order of Council, they had particularly contracted their Discounts.

I believe, that during the last Week or Ten Days, they have also enlarged their Discounts.

Q. Is it not generally understood, that if the Bank had not increased their Discounts at the Period mentioned in the preceding Question, considerable Failures would have ensued in the mercantile World?

A. I believe that such an Apprehension did prevail, though I rather think it prevailed more for some Days preceding the Order of Council, than it did for some Days after it.

Q. If the Bankers in London had, in consequence of an assumed Scarcity of Bank Notes, provided some additional Means of Circulation for the Metropolis, what Effect, in your Opinion, would such a Measure have had on the publick Credit?

A. I think the good or bad Effect which it would have had would have depended considerably on the good or bad success of the Plan. An Attempt to substitute in the Place of Bank Notes a new circulating Medium, if unsuccessful, would be likely to produce additional distrust. If, on the other Hand, it should be successful, and should be carried to any considerable Extent, whatever Evil had arisen from the too small Quantity of Bank of England Notes, would, of course, be cured; and if Payments were made with Facility in the Metropolis, and its Fears relieved, I should think that the Circumstance of the Creation of new Paper, through the acknowledged Deficiency in the Quantity of the Paper of the Bank of England, might not produce any considerable Prejudice to general Credit. I assume that the Plan I have alluded to would have been effected without much previous Agitation in the public Mind, and without the Suspence occasioned during the passing of an Act of Parliament.

Q. If, from an acknowledged Diminution in the Quantity of the Paper of the Bank of England, arising from the Pressure of the Times, such a Plan, as has been described in the preceding Question should be attempted, and should prove unsuccessful, would the Failure of such a Plan affect, in your Opinion, the future Interests of the Bank?

A. I am not aware that such Failure would particularly affect them.

Q. Would it not have the Effect of increasing their Credit?

A. I consider the Credit of the Bank of England already so high in the

Minds of all those who have Transactions with them, or who are Possessors of their Notes, that it is hardly capable of Increase. I conceive that they have more Credit than they make use of, and that their Credit is material only in Proportion as in some Way or other it is expected to be used.

Q. Did the Pressure of the Times, in your Opinion, render it necessary to diminish the Number of Bank Notes in Circulation?

A. My own Opinion is, that for the Reasons which I have already given, the Pressure of the Times was likely rather to require an extension of their Number.

Q. Have not Merchants as well as Bankers occasionally engaged in the discounting Business, and has not that Business considerably diminished since the Bank have limited their Discounts?

A. There are a few Merchants who at some Periods have been great Discounters, but I believe they have for some Time almost entirely ceased to discount.

Q. Has not the low Price of the Funds and other Government Securities, by affording an higher Interest than Five per Cent., operated as an Hindrance to Mercantile Discounts?

A. It undoubtedly has operated in that Manner very effectually.

Q. Did there appear any Mercantile Distress previous to the Determination of the Bank to limit their Discounts by their Resolution in December 1795?

A. I apprehend there was, and that the large Demand for Discounts made to the Bank arising from that Distress, gave Occasion to the Resolution of the Bank.

Q. Explain what you think gave rise to that Resolution of the 31st of December 1795?

A. I conceive that formerly the Bank of England were accustomed to afford Discounts to as many Persons as brought in Bills which they considered as sufficiently secure, and that their Notes of course at that Time proportioned themselves to the Demands for them; but that the Directors, wishing not to continue the same Proportion between their Paper and the Demands for it which had antecedently existed, established the Rule that has been referred to, with a View of enabling themselves to limit their Discounts, and thus to limit their Paper without Prejudice to the Credit of any individual Discounter. Antecedently to that Time they had established some other Rules tending to facilitate the Limitation of their Paper.

Withdrew.

APPENDIX II

MANUSCRIPT NOTES

BY

HENRY THORNTON

To Lord King's Thoughts on the Effects
of the Bank Restriction

(April 1804)

The copy of Lord King's *Thoughts on the Effects of the Bank Restriction.* The Second Edition enlarged, including some remarks on the coinage. London, 1804 (viii + 178 pp.), from which the following manuscript notes are reproduced, is in the Goldsmiths' Library of the University of London. It bears on the top of the title page the inscription "James A. Maconochie 1805" and beneath the title the statement, "The Manuscript Notes in this copy are by Henry Thornton Esq. M.P." This is supplemented by the further statement in the same hand on the back of the title page, that "This Copy with his own MS Notes was sent to Mr. Scott Moncrieff by Mr. Thornton and given by him to me. J. A. M." As it appears from Henry Thornton's Diary that he was acquainted with a Mr. Scott Moncrieff, and as the marginal notes in the volume are at least in part in a hand which resembles that of Henry Thornton, there seems to be no reason to doubt the correctness of the ascription.

The notes are partly written on the margin of the book and partly on separate sheets pasted in. The latter may be in a different hand, but have probably been transcribed from rough notes on loose slips. A number of very short marginal notes, mostly consisting of single words expressing approval of, or doubt about, a particular passage have not been reproduced.

It should be noted that the page references given refer to the second edition of Lord King's *Thoughts,* the pagination of which is different from the first edition of 1803.

F. A. v. H.

MANUSCRIPT NOTES BY HENRY THORNTON TO THOUGHTS ON THE EFFECTS OF THE BANK RESTRICTIONS BY LORD KING

THE SECOND EDITION ENLARGED, INCLUDING SOME REMARKS ON THE COINAGE LONDON 1804

p. 5, line 14   There can be no doubt that a well regulated Bank having the exclusive supply of paper over a certain district in which the use of paper is necessary may by a due limitation of that paper ensure its "supplying" with sufficient exactness "the place of that Coin which it represents."

p. 6, line 9   It does not follow from the circumstance of "*many* European Governments" and the American States having suffered their Paper through various causes to be depreciated that the Bank of England must also *necessarily* become depreciated which seems to be the point assumed.

p. 7, line 6   It is not shown by this occasional Discount. The Discount results from a different Cause namely from the Interest on the Exchequer Bill being an insufficient Equivalent for the delay of Payment. An Exchequer Bill is not *circulating* Paper and the fluctuations in its Value depend chiefly on the variations in the current rate of Interest.

p. 8, line 24   They probably were not aggravated by an extension of its *Issues* to Government. This term indeed is inaccurate. Does it mean "by its *Loans* to Government" or its *Issues of Paper* in consequence of those loans. If it means Issues of Paper then the question is whether the paper was *on the whole* excessive. And it is the *general* Excess of Paper arising from Issues to Government, Issues to Merchants etc. that ought to be represented as the cause of the Evil. I doubt whether the Issue of paper for some time antecedently to the Suspension had been on the

313

whole too great—I have no doubt that when reduced to 8½ Millions it was too small.

p. 9, line 8   This reduction tended as I conceive to prevent the restoration of Confidence. I admit, however, that it tended slowly and gradually to improve the Exchange. The Reduction tended to produce an immediate immense demand for Guineas and to promote perhaps after some Months interval of time an influx of Gold into the Country.

p. 10, line 16   The run on the Bank did not arise properly speaking from a want of Credit in the Bank and was not therefore to be prevented by any association. It arose from a discredit cast on *Country* Bank Notes and a demand for gold in consequence of Country Bank Notes being called in which demand the Bank of England is through the peculiar circumstances in which it stands under a necessity of supplying even to any extent. It arose also from a preference given to Gold over even Bank of England Paper at the moment of an alarm of Invasion a preference however not arising from a distrust of the Bank which any Association could cure, but from an idea that in case the Enemy should land or possess the Country Gold would be the most portable kinds of Goods and also the most universally current Medium.

p. 11, line 9   A new Coinage would have been to little purpose if Bank Paper had been suffered to be excessive for it would then have been exported as soon as issued and if Bank Paper was not rendered excessive the limitations of paper would secure the Influx of Gold and the purchase of it at a saving price. Still however the limitation of paper could not be counted on as sufficient to produce an Influx of Gold sufficiently prompt and large to supply the demands of the whole public when agitated by the dread of Invasion. The actual demand on the Bank for Gold was as I suspect no less than half a Million a week (perhaps still more) for some weeks preceding the Suspension and it was proceeding in an encreasing Ratio. A similar demand might be expected to recur again and again in a War such as that in which we were engaged and the very expectation of its recurrence, if the Bank of England had again been opened would have produced an Irregularity in the Issues of the Paper both of the Country Banks and of the Bank of England and a State of Apprehension among the Merchants which might have been extremely distressing to Commerce.

p. 12, line 14   Probably not because it was not fully understood that the measure would be so free from bad consequences as it proved.

p. 13, line 10   The Profits of the Bank can hardly fail to be enlarged when Notes under £5 are issued in addition to their other Notes.

line 23   It was the limitation of Bank Paper and the known Solvency of the Bank, rather than any particular effect of an Association which sustained the Credit of Bank Notes.

p. 16, line 10   It is not accurate to infer from the general magnitude of our Commerce that 16 Millions of Notes are not too much. If with 16 Millions the Exchanges are favourable 16 Millions are not too much. If with 10 Millions the Exchanges were greatly and permanently unfavourable we might pronounce 10 Millions to be too much.

p. 17, line 18–   perfectly just
20   State of Exchanges

p. 20, line 1–4   Apply the observation in this Passage which I think just to what is said in page 9—If more paper is wanted in time of Alarm it could not be "necessary" in 1797 to reduce the Paper of the Bank to 8½ Millions.

p. 23, line 8   This credit is now limited much in the same manner and degree in which it would be limited if the Bank paid in Gold.

p. 27, line 1   In times however of great alarm (such for instance as that of an actual landing of the Enemy) an augmentation of Paper may be necessary.

line 19   Say rather by the State of Exchanges.

p. 28, line 11   A paper circulation which is not convertible into Specie will as much maintain its Value as a paper circulation which is convertible provided its quantity is equally limited and the credit of the issuing Bank equally perfect in both cases.

p. 28, line 17   It is also probable that they will not be exactly right when their paper is convertible into Specie. The State of the Exchange will equally be the criterion by which they must judge in both cases.

315

p. 29, line 10   It is the total of their Loans (consisting of Issues in part to Government and in part to Merchants) which constitutes the Excess and there is much more temptation to issue too much to the Merchants than to the Government. The Interest of the Bank Directors in the *Profits* of the Bank is a very trifling consideration. The chief danger of an over-issue arises from the circumstances of the Directors perhaps not sufficiently perceiving that a limitation of Paper will improve the Exchanges and that it is necessary if the Exchanges continue long unfavourable to make this reduction even against the general sense of the merchants.

p. 30, line 18   This is a remarkable erroneous position of Dr. A. Smith. It seems to imply that there must be some clipping of the Coin or some adulteration of it whenever the Coin is for any considerable time of less value than the quantity of Gold professedly contained in it. And Dr. Smith in a passage connected with that which is here quoted, shows this to be his meaning. This inferiority in the Value of Gold in Coin to Gold in Bullion may however arise and commonly does arise from the circumstance of the whole circulating medium being too great in quantity and being therefore depreciated, for Gold in Coin (if the depreciation is not great) will in such case pass even for a long time at the depreciated Paper price. If indeed the general Depreciation is great the Coin will go abroad and after a time the Banks must stop—The general Inference however both of Dr. A. Smith and of Lord King (namely that the Market price of Gold and Silver are the test of a depreciated currency) is just.

p. 31, line 18   A Currency in specie may be degraded in a small degree. This degree, supposing the exportation to be free, will not exceed the Charges of Exportation.

p. 32, line 22   Mr. Boyd in his letter to Mr. Pitt insisted that the *Nonconvertibility* of Paper into Gold was the cause of a depreciation of it which he assumed to be so great as to account "more than any other cause" for the high price of Bread. He did not measure the degree of the Rise which an Excess of paper occasioned by the variation in the Exchange as he ought to have done and he did not seem to consider that this Nonconvertibility of Paper into Gold

316

does not necessarily produce a depreciation of paper, but produces only when it serves to encourage the Issues of Paper to issue it to excess. A non-convertible Paper *which is limited* and is in full credit may maintain its price just as if it were convertible.

p. 33, footnote, line 11 — That the Bank of England ought to limit its "paper in the case of Gold going abroad and of the general Exchanges continuing long unfavourable" is one of the practical principles laid down by Mr. T. (See Page 295 of Mr. H. T.'s work [p. 259 of the present volume]).

p. 33, line 16 — This fact proves the truth of the important principle which I have before asserted namely that a nonconvertible paper if limited may maintain its price exactly in the same manner as a convertible paper. This point however seems to be denied in many parts of this Pamphlet.

p. 35, line 4 — Gold (not Silver) is the Test by which Depreciation of English Paper should be tried, for Gold Coin is the chief English Coin and the only actually Current Coin of which the standard is maintained. Much of the reasoning in the pamphlet proceeds on the supposition that the price of Silver is the Test.

p. 37, line 11 — Lord King does not take into his consideration the addition made to the Bank Paper by the Issue of £1 and £2 Notes circulating in the place of Gold which was either carried abroad or hoarded and which therefore would not have any influence. He continues also to estimate the Depreciation by the price of Silver Bullion and not of Gold Bullion. The latter as I believe never was more than 10 or 11 Per cent above the Mint price. I agree however with Lord King that it is probable there may have been about this time a somewhat too great issue of Bank of England Notes.

p. 38, line 1 — I think this Correspondence (vide Tables at the end of this book) has not so remarkably existed. In July 1802 for example when Bank Notes were at the highest namely 17.254.100 an English Pound Sterling was worth 34 Hamburgh Shillg. whereas in February 1800 when Bank Notes were 15.120.000 the English Pound was worth only 30/6.

The effect of a too great issue of Paper followed at so great a distance of time from its cause and is so obscured

317

by interfering circumstances that a very discernible correspondence is not to be expected. Some general Correspondence, however, appears from the annexed tables. It is to be regretted that Lord King in stating the quantity of Bank of England Notes has not distinguished the quantity of £1 and £2 notes. Before the Restriction there were no Notes of this Class. Some time after it they amounted to 2 Millions and by the last account rendered to 4 Millions—It is farther to be considered that Bank of England Notes are now kept as a fund standing in the place of Gold by Banks in the Country. On the other hand I suspect that in London there is a continually increasing economy in the use of Bank Paper.

p, 39, footnote line 18–22   Does not this passage a little contradict what is said above of the discernible Correspondence between the State of the Exchanges and the quantity of Bank of England Notes in circulation.

p. 41, line 6–9   Is this precisely the fact?

p. 42, line 6   I understand that the relative prices of Silver and Gold Bullion have varied of late years.

line 22   This I take to have been nearly its highest price.

p. 46, line 16   Is this the case? Is there I mean any difference?

p. 51, line 5   There is I think some truth in the Remark though it is perhaps put too strongly.

54, line p. 21 (after "balance of trade")   with the Continent.

p. 55, line 15 to end of page   Ought not Silver (which is here considered as imported in order to be exported) to be classed among Commodities and not represented as indicating, when thus imported with a view to Exportation, a favourable balance of Trade. Lord King seems to me to adopt in part that erroneous language respecting Balance of Trade which he himself condemns. Silver as I apprehend is often purchased abroad on account of the India Company at whatever may be the existing price in order to be exported to India. Is it in such case to all intents and purposes an Article of Commerce and its transmission to England in order to be put on board India Ships is then no more indication of a favourable Balance of Trade than the similar transmission of any other article. This observation

318

may perhaps supply an answer to the discussion with which this Work closes.

p. 58, line 21   It will be reduced to Equality except so far as either the Debt subsisting between Great Britain and foreign Countries may vary, or the quantity of precious metals in Great Britain may fluctuate. It is probable that neither of these will alter materially and it is clear that neither of them will perpetually and indefinitely encrease.

p. 61, line 23   This is a very unfair mode of describing the Encrease of Bank of England Paper. The 16 Millions include as I rather think no less than 4 Millions of £1 and £2 Notes which circulating in the place of Gold withdrawn form no addition to the circulating Medium.

p. 62, line 13   This subject certainly demands explanation. There can be no doubt however that a large part of the Irish Bank Paper is a mere substitute of paper for gold which has disappeared.

p. 67, line 23   I should conceive them to have had no effect.

p. 69, line 25   An enlargement of the profits of the Bank is not proof of misconduct. The Issue of £1 and £2 Notes must necessarily be profitable and of the propriety of this Issue there can be no doubt.

p. 70, line 9   It ought to be considered on behalf of the Bank of Ireland that that Bank not having the monopoly of the Supply of paper Currency in Dublin (other Bank Paper circulating in the same place) has not the same power which the Bank of England has of limiting the circulation of the Country and that the limitation of the Bank of Ireland paper in the present circumstances of Ireland might possibly have little other effect than that of leaving to the other private Banks (which are completely rival Establishments) those profits which the Bank of Ireland should relinquish.

p. 73, line 13   An obligation to give Bills on London at a fixed Exchange, or a voluntary Agreement in all the Dublin Banks to give them, would answer the same purpose and would perhaps be a less objectionable Remedy.

p. 77, line 12   Though the plan proposed might not much extend the *circulation* of English Bank Notes in Ireland it would create a necessity of keeping a certain quantity of English Bank Notes in the hands of the Irish Banks.

p. 79, line 15 It deserves consideration whether this limitation of the Paper of the Bank of Ireland *alone* would have the effect proposed. Might not the void occasioned by the extinction of Bank of Ireland Paper be filled by proportionately encreased Issues of the private Banks of Dublin which seem to be complete competitors of the National Bank. This is a difficult question. The much surer remedy would be to compel or in some way to induce *all* the Dublin Banks to give in Exchange for their paper bills on London at a fixed date. Query indeed whether all the Dublin Banks should give Bills on London (as the Edinburgh Banks do) or whether the private Dublin Banks should merely continue to give Bank of Ireland Notes, and the Bank of Ireland alone Bills on London.

p. 86, line 7 Landholders and Stockholders resident in Ireland are unproductive Laborers—in other words are consumers at home of the Produce of the labor of others. If these unproductive Laborers reside in England and spend their income here, a proportionably greater quantity of the produce of Irish Labor is exported, and the Exportation of this Produce is to be set against the drafts which they draw on Ireland.

p. 99, footnote, line 1 There were some [i.e. failures]. Alarm among holders of Country Bank Notes existed in both cases and a free issue of the *best* paper is certainly at all times the best means of allaying an alarm. In 1797 when an alarm existed not only were the Bank of England Notes not encreased, they were diminished in a very extraordinary degree namely at the rate of about $\frac{1}{2}$ Million a week for several weeks together.

p. 100, line 5 It is limited through the circumstances of the Notes being exchangeable for Bills on London or Bank of England Paper. The value of Country Paper in Great Britain necessarily therefore conforms itself to whatever is the value of Bank of England Paper and if the Value of Bank of England Paper is maintained (as it may be by the limitation of its quantity and the exclusive circulation in London which it enjoys) the value of Country Paper must be maintained also. If A (the London Paper) is equal to B (the current coin) and if C (the Country Paper) is equal to A., then C must also be equal to B.

p. 108, line 6   The quantity did not perhaps increase in both cases in exactly the same proportion, but they must have been *excessive* in the same degree. I suspect that a large sum in Bank of England Notes is now kept by the Country Banks (perhaps 1 Million) which used not to be kept by them before the Bank Restriction as a fund for paying those who demand to have Country Bank Paper exchanged for Bank of England Paper. Bank of England Paper stands in the place of a fund of Gold.

p. 126, line 2   It does not appear to me to be expedient now to determine the period when the Bank Restriction Bill shall cease, except indeed that it ought to be made to cease in a moderate time after the termination of the War. While the War lasts (a War in which we shall be subject to many serious alarms of Invasion) the Bank of England ought as I conceive to be protected from the danger of having Gold demanded in indefinite quantities for the purpose of hoarding, a danger which Lord King has almost entirely omitted to treat of in his pamphlet. The Bank however ought not to be protected against that demand for Gold which results from the long continuance of an unfavourable Exchange.

Lord King himself admits in many parts of his book that the Bank of England is able by the restriction of its Paper to remedy the unfavourableness of the Exchange. If then the restriction of its paper will not fail to rectify the Exchange, it can only be necessary that Parliament should resort to such measures as shall be sufficient to secure this Restriction. Measures short of that of compelling the Bank soon to open, let the alarm of Invasion be what it may, would unquestionably produce the Restriction desired. Indeed it may be doubted whether the Bank has not at this time (April 1804) almost sufficiently confined its paper to turn the Exchanges in our favor. I conceive that if the Committee of the House of Commons on Irish Currency now sitting were to state in their Report to the House in distinct language that they are persuaded that a reduction of Bank Paper must have a tendency to improve the Exchange even this hint coming from such a quarter and applying itself as it necessarily [would] to the Bank of England as well as that of

Enquiry into Paper Credit   321   X

Ireland would have all the desired effect. The Directors of the Bank of England if they have erred at all, have erred but a little and their Error has resulted from the circumstance of their not sufficiently perceiving the great and important principle which Lord King has so well laid down, namely that an Excess of Paper is the great radical cause of a long continued unfavourable Exchange.

p. 134, line 14   Does not this passage show the unfairness of estimating the depreciation of Bank of England Paper by a comparison between the Market price and Mint price of *Silver*.

APPENDIX III

TWO SPEECHES

OF

HENRY THORNTON, ESQ.

ON THE

BULLION REPORT

MAY, 1811

PREFACE

THE first of the two following Speeches was delivered soon after the opening of the debate in the House of Commons on the Report of the Bullion Committee; the question then under consideration being the first of the Resolutions moved by Mr. Horner, the Chairman of that Committee. The general object of his Resolutions may be stated, briefly to have been, First, to declare what was the standard of the country; secondly, to affirm the depreciation of Bank paper; thirdly, to suggest the limitation of it, as the means of improving its value and preparing for a return to cash payments; and, lastly, also to recommend that the Bank should open in two years. It was chiefly to the third point, namely, the practical measure of limiting the Bank paper, that the first Speech was directed.

The second Speech was delivered after a debate of five days had taken place. The Resolutions of Mr. Horner had then been negatived, and the counter Resolutions, moved by Mr. Vansittart, were under consideration.

The imperfect manner in which the very extended debates on the Report of the Bullion Committee have been given to the public, and the importance of spreading sound opinions on the fundamental principles of the system of our paper credit, are the considerations which have led to the present publication.

It contains the substance of the facts and arguments adduced, as far as they could be recollected, though the order may have been in some degree changed; and a few passages, which appear to have been misunderstood, are rendered more clear.

The substance of these Speeches is submitted more especially to those numerous Constituents, to whose favour the individual who delivered them stands indebted for the opportunity which he has had of expressing his sentiments on this subject before the House;—a subject which has long engaged his careful attention, and on which he has been most anxious to form a sound and dispassionate, as well as disinterested, judgment.

TWO SPEECHES OF MR. HENRY THORNTON

MAY 7, 1811.

MR. H. THORNTON said, that however ably, as well as fully, the Learned Gentleman (Mr. Horner), who opened this discussion, had treated the subject, he conceived that there were some important points which required amplification; and he should prefer entering on these, to the examination of those numerous and smaller questions respecting the accuracy of the Report of the Bullion Committee, on which the Right Hon. Gentleman who preceded him (Mr. Rose) had principally dwelt. A time would come, when the respective merits of the several propositions intended to be submitted by different members would be brought into minute discussion, and an answer to the Right Hon. Gentleman might then, perhaps, be more conveniently given. He trusted the House would agree with him in the propriety of his confining himself, for the present, to great and broad principles; he should apply himself to the spirit of some of the first resolutions now proposed, and to the main point at this moment in issue. That main point was, not whether the Bank should open at any particular time, or any change be made as to the law in this respect, which would be a second consideration; but whether with a view to facilitate such opening if it should be prescribed, or with a view to secure the due maintenance of our standard during the long continuance of the restriction of cash payments, if the continuance should be deemed advisable it was or was not expedient that the Bank should regulate the issues of its paper with a reference to the price of Bullion, and the state of the Exchanges. The Bank and the Bullion Committee were at variance on this leading and essential point. The Committee affirmed, that the quantity of paper had an influence on the price of Bullion, and the state of the Exchanges; all the Directors of the Bank who had been examined, affirmed that it had not. The Right Hon. Gentleman over the way (Mr. Rose) likewise insisted . that it had not. "None whatever," were his words. This was a great practical question. If the Bank had in their own hand the power of improving the Exchange, and lowering the price of Bullion, and did not use it, if they had the means of restoring, or contributing to restore, the standard of the country, and did not at all believe that they possessed it, then it became the House, who had exempted them from the necessity of making payments in cash, supposing it to agree with the Bullion Committee, to take care that

327

the Bank should resort to the proper remedy of the present evil, by interposing some suggestion of their own on the subject.

He would now proceed to prove, that quantity of paper had an influence on the price of Bullion and the Exchanges. There were two steps in this argument. First, he had to shew that quantity of paper influenced its value, or, in other words, the relative value of commodities exchanged for it. Could it be doubted, on the first mention of the proposition, that the quantity of all articles affected their value? This was unquestionably true of the precious metals, for the augmented supply obtained from the mines of the new world, was acknowledged to have produced that general lowering of the value of money, which had been experienced in Europe for many years. And why was paper, the substitute for gold, to be exempted from this universal law? He had never yet found any man, who, when the simple question was put to him, whether an augmentation of paper had a tendency to reduce its value, or raise that of commodities, had been so singular as to refuse his assent to the proposition. One of the Bank Directors of Dublin, when examined before the Committee on the State of the Irish Exchange, though firmly persuaded that an extension of paper currency had no influence whatever on Exchanges, had been very ready to agree that it must have an effect on the price of commodities, and one of the Directors of the Bank of England had then, if he rightly recollected, made a similar admission.

This point had been conceded only the other day in the House; for in debating the question of granting Exchequer Bills to the distressed manufacturers, it was generally affirmed and understood that the supply of these bills, which would operate in some measure as circulating medium, and would facilitate their obtaining it, would enable them to maintain their prices at a point higher than that to which they otherwise would have fallen. He himself well remembered having in 1796 observed the influence upon prices, which the restriction of the Bank discounts at that period had produced. He recollected to have then heard a West-India merchant, who had failed to obtain from the Bank the whole of his usual and expected accommodation, declare his intention of proceeding in consequence to sell some of his sugar at a somewhat reduced rate; half an hour after which, he heard a sugar-baker express his indisposition to buy sugar in consequence of the same scarcity of money, which he also had experienced. Was it not obvious, that when these two men met in the sugar-market, some fall in the price of that commodity would be the result? When money was generally scarce, an influence of this kind would diffuse itself over all commodities: it was thus, in short, that general prices were regulated; and it was absolutely necessary to set out in such an investigation as the present, with the establishment of some great and fixed principles in the mind; for a thousand points would then become manifest and simple, which otherwise would be contradictory and perplexed. He did not mean to say, that equal quantities of paper would affect the value of equal quantities of goods in an exactly equal degree, under all the varying circumstances which might arise. Far from it. He insisted, however, that augmentation of paper always *tended* to the diminution of its value, and diminution to its increase. The principle was always operative: its tendency was uniform, though not always productive of an equal effect.

A great fall of prices had at one time been experienced in Dublin, in consequence of the suppression of a large part of the currency of the place, as one of the Irish Bank Directors had incidentally observed.

Mr. H. Thornton admitted that great pressure, and even calamity, might arise from any sudden and very violent diminution of the circulating medium: he had himself complained, of what he thought too great and rapid a reduction of the paper of the Bank of England, in the year 1797, when called upon to give evidence before the Secret Committee of the Lords and Commons on that point. He was as earnest as any man to prevent severity of pressure in any quarter, and having already shewn this disposition in the Bullion Committee, he was anxious to express it also in the House. But he was not investigating principles: he was aiming to shew the tendencies of things; and such tendencies were often most clearly evinced by the palpable effects manifested in some strong and striking case.

Assuming, then, the tendency of every increase of paper to lower its own value, or, in other words, to augment that of commodities exchanged for it; a point, as he had just observed, admitted on all hands, and so plain as scarcely to demand proof; he had, in order to establish the second and concluding part of his argument, merely to prove something which was as undeniable as any mathematical proposition, as plain as any common question in arithmetic, and of which he felt just as confident as of his own existence.

This was, that supposing an increase of paper to take place, and to augment the general price of commodities in exchange for that paper, it must influence also the state of the Exchanges, and raise the price of Bullion. For what, in the first place, do we mean by the rate of our Exchanges? We mean the rate at which the circulating medium of this kingdom passes in exchange for the circulating medium of other countries. Supposing, then, the circulating medium (the gold or silver coin for example) of other countries to remain as before, that is, to bear the same price as before in exchange for commodities, while the value of our currency, in exchange for commodities, has been altered, it follows that our currency must exchange for a new quantity of such foreign coin. It also follows equally, that it must exchange for a new quantity of Bullion; for foreign coin is itself made of Bullion, deviates from it in only a limited degree, and is almost identified with it. Bullion, indeed, is a commodity: it comes from America in the same manner as other commodities—is subject to those laws which govern their rise and fall—and consequently, when it is affirmed that an increase of circulating medium, raises the price of commodities, Bullion must be considered as included among their number. It could not be supposed that one article would be affected by an increase of the general currency, and not another;—the produce of manufacturing industry, for example, and not the produce also of the surface of the earth, and of the mines. All things, it is manifest, must ultimately partake in that increase of price which an augmentation of currency tends to produce, as well as in that depression of price which a reduction of it occasions.

Mr. H. Thornton next proceeded to observe on the doctrine which was maintained that the present high price of Bullion and state of the Exchanges resulted from the unfavourable circumstances of our commerce, and the present extraordinary state of the world. The evil was referred to what is called the unfavourable balance of trade or of payments, and was thought to have nothing to do with quantity of paper inasmuch as this balance of trade and payments was deemed a separate and independent cause. He was willing freely to admit the influence of the present circumstances of our trade and expenditure, on Exchanges and the price of Bullion; but he could not allow that these had a separate and independent operation.

He should best explain himself, on this difficult but important subject, of the influence of balance of trade, as it is called, or balance of payments, by putting three several cases; in each of which cases, he would suppose that we had to struggle with political and commercial difficulties exactly resembling the present.

First, he would assume that we had no laws forbidding the melting and exportation of our coin, or limiting the rate of interest, or protecting the Bank against cash payments, it being the simple policy of the country to let every thing take its own course. By thus adverting to what might be called a state of nature, we should be able to discover what was the natural limitation of the evil to which we were now subject; and what the kind of corrective which administered itself. He was not examining whether it was wise to commit ourselves to this state of nature; he was now only investigating principles, that we might thus obtain some light to guide us amidst those difficulties of our own artificial system, in which our understandings seemed to be lost.

His second case would be, the actual case of this country before the cash payments of the Bank were suspended; and his third, our case at present.

First, then, he would suppose, that we were paying in cash, and that we had no usury laws, and no law forbidding the melting or exportation of coin; the King merely affixing his stamp to those pieces of gold which were the current circulating medium, in order to certify their quantity and fineness. For the sake of simplifying the subject, he would also assume the same circulating medium to be employed in surrounding countries. If, while we were thus circumstanced, the same evils of which we now complain were to arise, what would be the consequence? Doubtless much of our gold coin would be taken from us; and, perhaps, a larger quantity of this than of other articles. The whole, however, would not leave us; a high rate of interest would arise, and this extra profit on the use of gold, which would increase as its quantity diminished, would contribute to detain it here—some foreigners, probably, transferring property which would take the shape of the precious metals, or continuing to afford to us the use of it for the sake of this high interest. Such portion of our coin would be transferred, as would cause the remaining quantity to bear the same value in exchange for our remaining commodities, which the same coin in foreign countries bore to commodities abroad. In other words, gold and commodities would be exported in that relative proportion in which the exportation answered; and since every diminution of the quantity of our gold would produce an augmentation of it abroad, the relative value of gold to goods, in this and in foreign countries, would soon find one general level; and thus would remain the standard of value among us all. This, indeed, was simply to suppose the same case to occur in respect to Europe, which usually exists in respect to the different provinces of the same kingdom. He repeated, that he was merely putting a case for the sake of illustration; and the great point which he meant to press was this, that according to what he had denominated the state of nature, there would *be a reduction of the circulating medium of this country under the present circumstances of our trade*—a reduction which would tend to bring down our prices to the level of the prices which similar commodities, allowing for all expenses of transportation, were found to bear in exchange for gold in the general market of the world.

He would now put the second case. He would suppose our laws to forbid both the melting and exportation of coin, and to limit the rate of interest to five per cent.; and the Bank to be paying in cash. In other words, he would assume that we were circumstanced as we were before 1797, and that exactly the same political and commercial difficulties which we now experience were to arise.

The effect of these difficulties upon the quantity of our currency, would resemble the effect assumed to be experienced in the former case, though it might not be exactly equal in degree. There would arise a similar demand for cash, with a view to exportation; and though the law would interpose some obstacle to its transmission, yet some of our gold would probably go abroad, and it would serve, as in the former case, both as a remittance which would contribute to pay our debts, and as the means of augmenting the circulating medium of foreign countries, as well as of diminishing our own. The Bank, in this event experiencing a drain, would, in some degree, contract its issues. It would not only not increase them, as it has in some degree done during the last two or three years of the very unfavourable state of our exchanges; it would diminish them; it would feel itself, in consequence of our new circumstances, under the painful necessity of straitening its accommodation either to merchants or government, or both; and some difficulty in effecting the limitation would arise out of the necessity under which the Bank would consider itself to be placed of still continuing to lend at only five per cent. It was only by limiting its paper that it could maintain its own cash payments. The reduction would undoubtedly be an evil, but it would be an evil to be balanced against another evil otherwise to be incurred, that of stopping payment, and ceasing to abide by the standard of value which the King and the law had prescribed.

He was aware that this view of the case was not the most gratifying, and might not be welcome to some gentlemen around him; but it was the truth, and it was only by the right knowledge of the nature of our situation, that we could expect to come to any just conclusion. Thus, in this second case, exactly as in the first, there would be a reduction of the total quantity of circulating medium, which would be carried so far as to equalize, or nearly equalize, the relative value of our currency and commodities with the relative value of currency and commodities in our countries. Doubtless a pressure might arise which possibly might be considerable: (*A cry of Hear! Hear!*) He wished to know whether his principles were admitted. Was it acknowledged, that if we were now paying in cash, as before 1797, the Bank would thus limit its issues, and by such limitation would lower the price of Bullion, and rectify the Exchange? He should be glad to have a distinct affirmative or negative to this question. What degree of pressure might result, was not the main point now under consideration. He did not care at this moment what gentlemen said as to that point. He was in search of a principle. Did they or did they not admit his fundamental position, namely, that when a very unfavourable exchange, resulting from what is called an unfavourable balance of payments, arises, the limitation of the currency of the country serves to limit the evil? He had shewn, first, that this was the corrective which applied itself in what he had called the state of nature; and, also, secondly, that this corrective applied itself under that partly artificial system, under which we lived before our cash payments were suspended.

He now advanced to his third, which was the present case. The Bank, since they became protected against the necessity of making cash payments, not unnaturally thought that they might use more liberality than they would have ventured to exercise under the same circumstances of our trade, if they had been subject to a drain for cash. They, perhaps, were not much to be blamed on this account. Indeed, they appear not to have believed that a reduction of their paper would mend the Exchange, for they had not examined very deeply or philosophically into the subject. They had continued, although the exchanges turned much against us, gradually a little to augment their notes, as they had done for a long time before, they appearing to themselves not to increase, but merely to maintain the existing prices; and they hoped that the evil of the unfavourable exchange would correct itself. Possibly some new latitude might fairly be allowed under the new political circumstances in which we were placed. It was, however, important not to mistake leading principles, and not to fancy that an exchange running against us with all countries for two or three years, and reaching the height of 25 and 30 per cent., accompanied with a corresponding high price of gold, ought at no time and in no degree to be checked by that limitation of the currency to which nature, as it were, as well as our own practice before 1797, taught us in such cases to resort. He was aware that before 1797, if our coin was sent abroad, it went illegally. (*A cry of Hear! Hear!*) The illegality of the transaction, however censurable it might render the individuals engaged in it, was no reason for dismissing the consideration of this part of the subject. It was by this illegal melting and exportation of our coin that the drain on the Bank used heretofore to be produced; and it was by the operation of that drain on the mind and practice of Bank Directors, that the evil of a high price of gold, and an unfavourable exchange, was checked.

It was affirmed in the resolutions to be proposed by his Right Hon. friend (Mr. Vansittart), that there was a want of correspondence between the amount of bank paper in circulation at a vareity of periods, and the state of the exchanges, the exchanges being often more favourable when the notes were higher, and less favourable when they were lower in amount. This might be the case in certain instances which might be selected; for a variety of undefinable circumstances would lead to little fluctuations, both in the exchange and the amount of notes. It, however, was remarkable, that three cases had occurred, and only three within the memory of persons

333

now living, in which the experiment of a restriction of discounts had been made; and in each of these the effect had been comformable to the principles which he was affirming. He meant to say, that at three several times—namely, first in 1782 and 1783; secondly, in the end of 1795 and the beginning of 1796; and, thirdly, in February 1797; and only at these three times the Bank had experienced a material drain of their cash;—that in each of these cases they had been led by the drain, as they themselves professed, to restrain their supply of discounts;—and that not long after each of these three periods, the exchange and the price of bullion manifestly improved. Perhaps a question might arise, whether the improvement of the exchange through the year 1797, might not be referred to the restriction of paper in 1795 and 1796, rather than to that in the single month of February 1797: on which supposition the cases might be said to be two, instead of three; the effect of the limitations in the two latter periods being considered as combined.

That in the first period, namely, in 1782 and 1783, the experiment both was made and answered, was proved by the testimony of the late Mr. Bosanquet before the Secret Committee of 1797, who referred the improvement to this cause. The improvement of the exchange in 1796 and 1797 would be seen in the papers now before the House, and would also be found to be stated in the evidence of Mr. Pitt before the Secret Committee; by whose testimony it also would appear how earnestly the Bank had previously insisted on his repaying them some large advances, on the alleged ground of the existing drain; of which advances only a part was afterwards afforded in the way of accommodation to the merchants. A resolution of a new and very strict kind had been passed by the Directors, on 31st December 1795, with a view of limiting the total amount of mercantile discount, and served remarkably to show how much their liberality had been restrained, before the suspension of cash payments, by a drain of gold.

The limitation of paper in February 1797 was sudden and very great, and arose from a drain occasioned, not by an unfavourable exchange, but a totally distinct cause—an alarm produced through fear of an invasion. He had always thought, and still was of opinion, that the sudden limitation of paper at that period tended not to mitigate the alarm, but rather to increase it; but it unquestionably served to manifest the general habit of the Bank of reducing their issues when they found their gold taken from them. Since 1797, the Bank, having been subject to no drain, in consequence of their being under no obligation to pay in cash, the experiment of limitation of discounts had not been tried, and it had not been likely to be tried between 1783 and 1795, for that was an interval of peace, when exchanges are less subject to fluctuation, and when, moreover, the current rate of interest in the market being lower than in war, and as low perhaps as the rate charged by the Bank, there would be less disposition than in war to borrow of the Bank to an extent which should lead to an excessive issue of notes. It was in evidence before the Secret Committee of 1797, that the Bank had, at one period of the peace, deliberated, whether they should not lend at a less rate of interest than five per cent., so small was then the demand for discount.

This subject, of the rate of interest, was one to which he wished to call the attention of the House; it seemed to him to be a very great and turning point. If the principle adopted by the Bank was that which they professed, of lending to the extent, or nearly to the extent, of the demand made upon them by persons offering good mercantile paper, the danger of excess was aggravated in proportion to the lowness of the rate of interest at which discounts were afforded; and one cause, as he conceived, of the somewhat too great issues of the Bank, during the present war, had been the circumstance of their lending at five per cent., when rather more than five per cent. might in reality be considered as the more current rate paid by the merchants. Private bankers had generally found, during the war, that the growing demand of their customers on them, for discounts at five per cent. on very good bills, was apt to exceed the supply which any means of theirs could enable them to afford. If they gratified every wish, there would be no bounds to the gradual increase of applications. They therefore gave the preference to some applicants, and the persons who obtained the accommodation conceived themselves to be receiving a favour. The usury laws forbid the banker to charge more than five per cent.; but he who borrowed from a private banker, naturally, and of his own accord, bestowed the benefit of his running cash, which was often an important consideration; while, in the case of his discounting at the Bank, he kept a running cash which was extremely insignificant, and therefore borrowed at the rate of exactly five per cent. in that quarter. Again, if he borrowed in what is called the money market, he gave to a broker a small per centage on every bill; and thus paid not less than five and a half or six per cent. per annum, in the way of interest.

It was material to observe, that there had, since the beginning of the war, been a continual fall in the value of money: he meant, of money commonly so called, whether consisting of cash or paper. This had been estimated by some at 60 or 70 per cent., and certainly was not less than 40 and 50 per cent.; which was, on the average, 2 or 3 per cent. per annum: it followed from hence, that if, for example, a man borrowed of the Bank 1000*l.* in 1800, and paid it back in 1810, having detained it by means of successive loans through that period, he paid back that which had become worth less by 20 or 30 per cent. than it was worth when he first received it. He would have paid an interest of 50*l.* per annum for the use of this money; but if from this interest were deducted the 20*l.* or 30*l.* per annum, which he had gained by the fall in the value of the money, he would find that he had borrowed at 2 or 3 per cent., and not at 5 per cent. as he appeared to do. By investing his money either in land or in successive commercial undertakings, in the year 1800, and then finally selling his land or his commodities in the year 1810, he would find the produce amount to 200*l.* or 300*l.* above the 1000*l.* which he had borrowed; which 2 or 300*l.* being deducted from the 500*l.* interest which he had paid, would make the neat sum paid by him to be only 200*l.* or 300*l.* It was true, that men did not generally perceive, that, during a fall in the price of money, they borrowed at this advantageous rate of interest; they felt, however, the advantage of being borrowers. The temptation to borrow operated on their minds, as he believed, in the following manner:—they balanced their books once a year, and, on estimating the value of those commodities in which they had invested their borrowed money, they found that value to be continually increasing, so that there was an apparent profit over and above the natural and ordinary profit on mercantile transactions. This apparent profit was nominal, as to persons who traded on their own capital, but not nominal as to those who traded with borrowed money; the borrower, therefore, derived every year from his trade, not only the common mercantile profit, which would itself somewhat exceed the 5 per cent., interest paid by him for the use of his money, but likewise that extra profit which he had spoken of. This extra profit was exactly so much additional advantage, derived from the circumstance of his being a trader upon a borrowed capital, and was so much additional temptation to borrow. Accordingly, in countries in which the currency was in a rapid course of depreciation, supposing that there were no usury laws, the current rate of interest was often, as he believed, proportionably augmented. Thus, for example, at Petersburgh, at this time, the current interest was 20 or 25 per cent., which he conceived to be partly compensation for an expected increase of depreciation of the currency.

The observations which he had made had been suggested to him by his attention to a variety of facts; and he would now trouble the House with the statement of some specific cases, which would contribute to establish the truth of the doctrine which he had asserted—namely, that an increase of the quantity of paper tended to diminish its value; and a reduction of its quantity, to improve it;—that when the quantity became too great, a drain of cash arose; that this drain was checked by a limitation of paper;—

and that the excess, and cons quent drain, were most likely to accrue when any circumstances rendered the rate of interest taken, less than the current and actual rate at the time in the common market.

The case of the Bank of Paris was remarkably in point, and it was full of instruction to the parliament and people of this country. That Bank stopped payment in 1805, the year when the war had again broken out. It was a Bank as independent as any such institution in France could be, of the French government. It had a good capital, and circulated notes around the metropolis of France; which it emitted only in the way of discounts, and, as far as he understood, only on the security of bills at short dates, and of a good character: it thus exceedingly resembled the Bank of England, though inferior in the extent of its transactions. The French government having occasion in 1805 for some advances on the security of what they call their anticipations, a species of security on which it was not consistent with the rules of the Bank of Paris to lend, borrowed the sum in question of some French merchants and capitalists, who then contrived to fabricate among themselves, and proceeded to discount at the Bank, as many securities as were sufficient to supply their occasions; so that the Bank was the true lender. The object of thus borrowing at the Bank, was to save something in the way of interest; for if these anticipations had been sold in the market, the price would have been very disadvantageous. The consequence of this transaction was, an augmentation of the paper of the Bank of Paris; a drain of their cash followed; the diligences were found to be carrying off silver into the departments, which the Bank, with a view to its own safety, had continually to bring back, with much expense and trouble. The circulating medium of the metropolis had now plainly become excessive. Greater facilities were afforded for borrowing in that quarter than in other places, and the country wished to partake in those opportunities of extending purchases which the metropolis enjoyed. But the paper of the Bank would not circulate in the departments: it was therefore necessary first to exchange it for coin; and the coin being then carried away from Paris, the plenty of of circulating medium would equalize itself through the French territory. In England we had country bank paper, which was interchanged for Bank of England paper, and proportioned itself to it; but no part of the English paper would circulate out of the country. What therefore the departments of France were to Paris, that Europe was to Great Britain. If large opportunities of borrowing were afforded in London, and over England, by a free emission of paper, there would arise a disposition to exchange that paper for gold, because the gold might then be sent abroad, and it would tend to diffuse over the continent that plenty of circulating medium which we had introduced into our own territory.—It might, perhaps, be thought

Enquiry into Paper Credit   337   Y

that the cases were dissimilar, inasmuch as we had an unfavourable course or exchange, and a high price of gold, into which the evil which we suffered appeared to resolve itself. But it would be found that there arose also a premium on silver at Paris, and an unfavourable exchange between Paris and the departments of France; and this was proportionate to the expense and trouble of bringing back the silver from the departments. There was, therefore, a similarity in the two cases. The Bank of Paris at length stopped payment; the Government was consulted; the Bank was directed to reduce its paper; and in the course of three months, having pursued this principle, it opened without difficulty. The discount on its paper, or, in other words, the premium on coin, had varied from 1 to 10 or 12 per cent.; but after the reduction of paper it ceased. The exchanges of France with foreign countries had also turned about 10 per cent. against that country.

A special commission, of which M. Dupont de Nemours was the secretary, was subsequently appointed to inquire into the causes and effects of this stoppage of the Bank of Paris; and it was from the French Report published by this gentleman that he collected the facts which he had stated. The report proceeded to suggest the means of preventing the recurrence of a similar evil, and it advised three things; first, that the Government should never solicit any loans from the Bank, on the ground that such an application amounted to a demand, and might lead to issues inconsistent with the true nature of a banking establishment. It was unnecessary to observe, how unlike our circumstances, in this respect, were to those of France. Our Bank Directors had sufficiently shewn, in 1796, their complete independence of the Government; for they then peremptorily refused to afford to Mr. Pitt even the continuance of the existing advances. The second suggestion of the commission was, that the Bank of France should lend only on securities coming due within two months; and this, as well indeed as the other, was for the purpose of enforcing the third and principal admonition,—namely, that the Bank should always "draw in its discount as soon as it perceived the existence of a more than ordinary disposition to exchange bank paper for money."* "For what," added the Report, "mean these applications for money? They imply that there are more bank notes on the spot than the circumstances of the time demand. And how are you to provide against this evil? By diminishing their quantity, through a reduction which shall exceed the new emissions."† It is then added, that

* "Reserrer l'éscompte, aussitôt que l'on s'apperçoit qu'il se presente à la Caisse plus de billets à réaliser en argent que de coutume."

† "Qu'est-à-dire que ces demandes d'argent? Qu'il y a sur la place plus de billets que les affairs du moment n'en exigent. Et comment y pourvoir? En diminuant leur quantité par un retrait plus fort que l'émission nouvelle."

if the Directors of the Bank will but be attentive to the first signs of superabundance, if they will moderate the evil in the first instance, they will almost always retain the mastery; and thus the horseman (it is said) will not be thrown out of his saddle.

Many of the principles urged by the Bullion Committee, would be found to be remarkably confirmed by this Report. It appeared by it, that the French over-issue arose from an attempt to turn certain securities into cash, at a rate of interest lower than that which was the natural one at the moment. The Report dwelt much on the error committed in this respect. The anticipations, it said, ought to have been sold, though at a losing and discreditable price, at whatever might have been the rate in the market.

Again, the Report stated that the limitation of the French bank paper did not produce an instantaneous, or exactly corresponding effect; but yet that after three months it issued in the expected consequences. All this was in exact conformity with the doctrines of the Bullion Committee. They had never said that every small fluctuation of Bank of England paper would be attended by either an immediate, or an exactly proportionate, influence on the exchanges, or on the price of gold. They had only affirmed that the unquestionable tendency of limitation was to improve exchanges; and had recommended that the Bank should feel its way. The discount of 10 per cent. on the French paper was not completely removed till the amount was reduced from 90 to 54 millions of livres; a scale of reduction unquestionably greater by far than would be found necessary here, under all the circumstances of our metropolis.

The Report affirmed another principle of the Bullion Committee, namely, that it was not merely the numerical quantity of bank paper which evinced either its deficiency or excess; the true test being the disposition of the public to demand payment for bank notes in cash. At one time the Report observed that one hundred millions of bank paper had circulated at Paris, and that there was not a note too much, because there occurred no extraordinary demands for cash; but that at the period of the failure, 90 millions evidently were excessive; that at the time of publishing the Report, 44 millions was the whole amount. Circumstances were described as occurring from time to time, which called for a diminution of currency, or an increase.

The Bank of Sweden supplied another example which it might be useful to consider. It was not, properly speaking, a government bank, being a bank only of the States: and it issued its notes in the way of loan, at a moderate interest, and their amount, as he had been informed, there was reason to think had been much extended. This bank had ceased, for some time, to pay in cash, and its paper had fallen to about 70 per cent. discount. Sweden,

339

in one respect, was circumstanced somewhat like ourselves: it had experienced great obstacles to the exportation of many articles, with which it abounded; and, probably, the desire of keeping up the nominal price of those commodities, contributed to dispose both the government, the states, and the people to the existing system. The public in Sweden, according to what he had heard, were not fully persuaded of the depreciation of their paper; for many of their commodities, their iron in particular, had not risen in any proportion to the fall of their currency. Indeed, nations in general were usually insensible at first to the declension of the value of their circulating medium. They were accustomed to experience fluctuations of exchange, and they naturally referred, at first, even a serious depreciation of their paper, to the same commercial causes which they were in the habit of contemplating. He well remembered to have been himself, twenty or thirty years ago, employed in a Russian counting-house, where he had often heard conversations on the Russian Exchange. It used at that time generally, and on the whole, to decline; but as it occasionally rose, and evidently fluctuated a little, with each political or commercial event, the general tendency to depression, as far as he remembered, was never ascribed to an increase of the quantity of Russian paper; but it was now plain, that quantity had had a leading and permanent influence upon it. The ruble, originally, was worth 48 pence sterling; at the time when he was in the Russian counting-house, it passed for 35 or 40 pence: it was now worth only 12 or 14 pence. Was it possible, that merely what is called balance of trade, or political events, could in thirty years have reduced the ruble from 48d. to 12d.? It was not perfectly well known, that the late Empress, as well as the succeeding emperors of Russia, had, from time to time, greatly augmented the quantity of paper money; and hence, in truth, arose the depression. Many of those who narrowly watched the exchange, were the most misled on the subject. Thus, if a man watched the falling tide, he might be deceived by seeing a few occasional waves rise higher than the preceding ones, and might infer that the tide was rising when it was falling.

It was reasonable to suppose, that men should generally mistake in this respect. We naturally imagine that the spot on which we ourselves stand is fixed, and that the things around us move. The man who is in a boat seems to see the shore departing from him, and it was the doctrine of the first philosophers that the sun moved round the earth, and not the earth round the sun. In consequence of a similar prejudice, we assume that the currency which is in all our hands, and with which we ourselves are, as it were, identified, is fixed, and that the price of bullion moves; whereas in truth, it is the currency of each nation that moves, and it is bullion, the larger article serving for the commerce of the world, which is the more fixed.

It was remarkable, that when the American banks, about the year 1720, issued their excessive paper, the merchants of America ascribed the consequent fall of the exchange to something in the state of trade; a circumstance which is noticed, in the recent history of General Washington, by Mr. Marshall.

All the banks which he had mentioned, except that of Russia—namely, the Bank of France, the Bank of Sweden, and the Banks of America, were establishments more or less independent of the government: they all emitted their paper in the way of loan, furnished at a moderate or low interest; and they had all issued it to excess. The adversaries of the Bullion Committee had grounded a great part of their argument on the following distinction between the Bank of England and all those Banks of which the paper had been depreciated:—The Bank of England, they said, issues nothing, except in return for something valuable: they receive a bill, representing real property, for every note which they emit; and therefore they cannot issue to excess. Now the French Bank, the American Banks of which he had spoken, and he believed also the Swedish Bank, issued paper only in the way of loan; they received something valuable in return for every note which they put out—in this respect resembling the Bank of England. It was true, that the Austrian and the Russian Banks issued paper simply in discharge of the expenditure of the government: they were, strictly speaking, government banks; and the excess in their case was more likely to be great. But it was of the utmost consequence to understand, that, even when a supposed equivalent is received in return for the paper issued, excess might arise; and the excess, as he had already said, was likely to be great in proportion as the rate of interest was low.

The Bank even of Mr. Law, in France, issued its paper only in the way of loan. This bank had been adverted to by the Learned Gentleman who opened the debate; and the Right Honourable Gentleman who spoke next to him had complained of the comparison between the establishment of that projector and the Bank of England. Undoubtedly the name of Mr. Law, and that of the present Directors of the Bank, ought not to be mentioned on the same day, if the general nature of the two establishments, or the comparative character of the persons presiding over them, were the only subject for consideration. It was, however, not improper to point out what was the main error of Mr. Law. It very clearly exposed itself in a small Essay on Money and Credit, published by him in Scotland, containing a plain, submitted to the Scotch Parliament, which was apparently not unlike to that which he had more successfully recommended in France. Mr. Law considered security as every thing, and quantity as nothing. He proposed that paper money should be supplied (he did not specify in his book at

341

what rate of interest) to as many borrowers as should think fit to apply, and should offer the security of land, estimated at two thirds of its value. This paper, though not convertible into the precious metals, could not, as Mr. Law assumed, be depreciated. It would represent, as he said, real property, and would be worth even more than the precious metals, because land was not subject to the same fall in value as gold and silver. He forgot that there might be no bounds to the demand for paper; that the increasing quantity would contribute to the rise of commodities: and the rise of commodities require, and seem to justify, a still further increase. Prices in France rose to four times their antecedent amount; great seeming prosperity was experienced for a time; but in the end, the fall of exchanges, and the exportation of money, served to detect the error of the system; and successive alterations of the standard of the coin were among the means of recovery to which the government resorted. The Bank of Mr. Law preceded the French Mississippi scheme, and was formed, in some measure, after the example of the Bank of England; but its notes, after a short time, were made a legal tender, and they were lent at the low rate of 3 per cent. interest. In the progress of the scheme, the Bank became confounded with the Mississippi Company, for whose actions the bank notes were interchangeable; so that it was not easy to trace causes and effects through the whole progress of those extraordinary speculations.

The present state of the currencies in Surinam and Demerara afforded another proof of the tendency of an increase of paper to influence exchanges. In one of these places, the circulating medium consisted of paper; in the other, of coin; and before these colonies came into our possession, the coin of Demerara had even been of less value than the paper of Surinam, that paper having been carefully limited. Through the facility of the government of Surinam, the paper, as he had heard, had been exceedingly augmented, and it was now of only about one-third its former value, and one-third the present value of the coin of the neighbouring settlement. In Austria there had been a manifest excess of paper, and a corresponding fall in its value, indicated by the exchange. The case was somewhat the same at Lisbon. Indeed, in all parts of Europe, Hamburgh, Amsterdam, and Paris excepted, the principle of a standard seemed to have been lost; a suspension of cash payments had every where taken place; and paper had been issued to excess, and had also been depreciated. It belonged, therefore, to Great Britain to take care that she did not follow the course of so many nations on the Continent; and it would be most presumptuous in her to assume that her Bank, on account of some undefined difference in its constitution, could act on their principles, and yet not share in their fate.

The Directors of the Bank of England, as he had already shewn, before the suspension of their cash payments, had been used to lessen their paper when they experienced a drain of their cash. The quantity of currency, indeed, when gold was in circulation, in the event of a very unfavourable exchange, lessened itself, for a part of it was transported to other countries. No such natural corrective now existed; and it therefore was important that the general and permanent state of the exchange should be regarded as the index of an excess of paper, and that the Bank Directors should not continue to act on the principle that a limitation of paper had no influence whatever on the exchange. This was the point on which they were at issue with the Bullion Committee. That Committee, as he conceived, would have rendered an essential service, even though guilty of all the errors with which the Right Honourable Gentleman had charged them—errors, however, which he was by no means ready to admit—if they had merely called the attention of Parliament to this important subject. The Parliament had now to decide on this point of difference between the Committee and the Bank. He would not affirm it to be totally impossible that the exchange should improve, or even recover itself, without any change of system; but his fears predominated. The circumstance that most encouraged hope, was the fact of our exchanges having been restored, after a great depression, in 1800 and 1801, and apparently without any effort to improve them made by the Bank. There were, however, three points of difference between that case and the present. First, the exchanges did not fall, in the years of scarcity of 1800 and 1801, more than about 8 or 10 per cent. below par— they had now fallen 25 or 30, and even more than 30 per cent., and had continued much depressed for nearly three years. Secondly, we had in 1800 and 1801 a great quantity of gold in circulation, the clandestine transmission of which undoubtedly contributed to improve the exchange, by constituting a remittance; perhaps also to diminish the sum total of the currency remaining in this kingdom; and it should be remembered, that it is the amount of currency in general, and not of paper in particular, which regulates the value. Thirdly, we had, after the fall of exchange in 1801 and 1802, the benefit of an interval of peace. If the Right Honourable Chancellor of the Exchequer would assure the House of the approach of peace, he would contribute much to dissipate the present fear.

The Right Honourable Gentleman over the way (Mr. Rose) had spoken of the balance of payments as having lately been peculiarly unfavourable to this country. A short time before the appointment of the Bullion Committee, the same Right Honourable Gentleman had stated in his place, from documents to which he only had then access, how uncommonly favourable the balance of trade appeared to be up to that time. He was right in his statement; for, upon an inspection of the

343

annual Custom-house accounts of the year 1809, afterwards presented to the House, it appeared that the balance of that year was no less than about sixteen millions in our favour, if reckoned according to the official value—a balance greater by several millions than it had been in any preceding year. The balance, computed according to the real value, proved to be nearly as considerable, and equally exceeded the balance in real value of any preceding year. He admitted that the Committee had fallen into inaccuracy in stating some parts of this topic; but it was a subject on which he defied any man to arrive at any thing like precision, and he had chiefly to lament that they had attempted too much specification. They had been betrayed into this course by too great a wish to follow their adversaries into a detail of discussion of this sort, which he was happy to find that the resolutions of his Right Honourable Friend did not much countenance. He was convinced that it was impossible to form any estimate of the amount of precious metals which went out of the country, or of what was called the balance of trade, by instituting calculations of the value of exports and imports, and by then combining with these the amounts of drafts drawn on Government account, and all the other items which remained to be added to the two sides of the statement. The errors committed by those who had gone the furthest in such attempts were a warning on this subject. The Right Honourable Gentleman had remarked, that the sum paid for foreign freights had been erroneously stated by the Committee, as being to be deducted from the favourable balance; and he was right to a certain extent, in this observation. It, however, only followed from hence, that the Committee had represented the balance somewhat less favourably than they should have stated it. The year which had passed subsequently to their Report, was certainly much more adverse than that to which they adverted, the large importations of corn in 1810 having materially augmented our imports. Neither this circumstance, nor the burning decrees of the enemy, on which much stress had been laid, were known at the time when the Committee made their Report.

He must advert, before he concluded, to the important subject of the standard of our currency. There was great danger of our finally departing from it, if we suffered the present depreciation of our paper to continue. The first resolution of his Right Honourable Friend appeared to him to be liable to the construction of laying in some claim to depart from it, if such a measure should hereafter be deemed expedient; for it asserted the King's right to alter the standard: and the very mention of such a right, at a period when the temptation to exercise it was occurring, might naturally excite apprehension among the public. Indeed the argument in favour of a deterioration of our coin (or of a change of its denomination, which was the same

344

thing), would, while the present state of things continued, grow stronger every day. To change the standard when the paper has been long depreciated, is only to establish and perpetuate a currency of that value, to which we already are accustomed, and may also be made the means of precluding farther depression. The very argument of justice, after a certain time, passes over to the side of deterioration. If we have been used to a depreciated paper for only two or three years, justice is on the side of returning to the antecedent standard; but if eight, ten, or even fifteen or twenty years, have passed since the paper fell, then it may be deemed unfair to restore the ancient value of the circulating medium; for bargains will have been made, and loans supplied, under an expectation of the continuance of the existing depreciation. If, therefore, we were in earnest in our professions of attachment to the standard, we ought not to place ourselves in a situation of irresistible temptation. By the present decision of the House, the question of adherence to the standard might be determined. It had been said, that, by our present contest in Portugal, we were in truth defending England, since we were preventing a conflict which might otherwise take place on English ground. We might, by the parliamentary contest of this day, prevent a struggle for the maintenance of the standard of our coin. We were now, perhaps, fighting that battle, and at a time the most favourable for it. If the limitation of paper had been urged when the exchanges were only six or eight per cent. against us, it might have been said, that the evil was not sufficiently considerable to deserve attention. If we waited till they were fifty or sixty per cent. against us, it might have been insisted, that the time for administering such a remedy was past, and that the mischief was become too formidable for us to deal with. Was it not at least prudent to take the side of limitation? He had no idea, that all that embarrassment would result from a moderate reduction of Bank paper, which some gentlemen might suppose. Let the whole subject be fairly understood, for much depended on the general prevalence of sound opinions on this question;—let the contending parties yield a little to each other;—let it be known that the Bank proposes to do nothing sudden or violent; that they are determined to guard carefully against extensive failures; and to afford to the mercantile world reasonable facility for fulfilling the pecuniary engagements into which they might have already entered; —let it be seen through the country, that there was no party spirit, or heat, in our discussions:—he should, in that case, have little fear of disastrous consequences. If, on the other hand, the question was to be carried with a high hand, and there was to be a triumph of the Bank over the Bullion Committee; if the Bank were to be encouraged in the extension of their issues for the sake of the temporary ease which these might afford to the

345

merchants and to the government; and we were resolved to shut our eyes to the remoter consequences; the light might possibly, at length, break in upon us, as Mr. Burke, on another occasion, had observed, not through the ordinary apertures, but through flaws and breaches; and we might then lament, too late, that we had not made timely efforts to restore the value of our currency. Gentlemen, he feared, had not sufficiently considered the present state of the law on this subject. A question was suspended, the decision of which was expected every day, and might lead to the establishment of two prices. We were, moreover, at the mercy of events. Many persons seemed to think that there was no particular evil to be apprehended from perseverance in the present system; and were unwilling to resort to a limitation of paper, because it was safer not to change our course: but they ought to reflect, that, though a small depreciation of paper produces little or no evil, and even may, for a time, operate beneficially; and though a great depreciation may not bring on at once any striking mischief; yet the long continuance and the growth of it, might lead to the most serious dangers. To the consequences of excess of quantity distrust might add itself: new laws might become necessary to enforce the receipt of the depreciated currency; and in order that they might be effectual, their severity must increase as the depreciation extended itself. This had been the course in other countries. At the same time, there probably would not be wanting ill-affected persons, who would endeavour to aggravate the evil, and would be glad to connect with the temporary discredit arising from the excess of our circulating paper, the discredit of the whole mass of our stocks, which had nothing to do with it. Surely it became the Parliament to anticipate the possible occurrence of such a state of things, and not to wait the uncertain course of events, as if we had no power whatever to provide for our own safety, or contribute to the improvement of our condition.

On these grounds he now supported the first set of the Resolutions of the Learned Gentleman, which affirmed the doctrine of a standard, and which recommended, as the means of expediting and insuring our return to it, a cautious restriction of the paper of the Bank of England.

On the 14th of May, Mr. H. Thornton observed, that having, when he before addressed himself to the House, spoken antecedently to all those gentlemen to whom he was opposed, excepting only one Right Hon. Gentleman (Mr. Rose), who had chiefly dwelt on the details of the Report; and having now the advantage of distinctly knowing the grounds on which their argument rested; he was anxious to be permitted once more to offer himself to their notice.

The speech of his Right Honourable Friend (Mr. Vansittart), in support of the Resolutions now proposed by him to be substituted in the place of those of the Chairman of the Bullion Committee, had particularly urged him to rise. In the conclusion of that speech, his Right Honourable Friend had enumerated the various circumstances to which he looked as the means of producing an improvement of the exchange:—first, a continental peace; secondly, a better understanding, and, consequently, an open trade with America; thirdly, some extension of our commercial intercourse with Europe;—all of them, especially the first, events which he did not much encourage us to expect:—but it was remarkable that he totally omitted any mention of a limitation of paper, in this enumeration of the means of meliorating our exchanges. His Right Hon. Friend, in one part of his speech, as well as the Right Hon. Chancellor of the Exchequer, had admitted that a limitation of paper had a tendency to produce this effect; but it was plain, from the concluding part of it, that the principle was practically disregarded. Indeed, his resolutions were in the same spirit: they were silent on this point: they did not venture to deny the doctrine, that quantity of paper had an influence on its value; but they seemed to throw a doubt upon it; for they specified a variety of facts, with the evident view of discrediting the principle; and thus were calculated to lead men, less enlightened than the Mover, to suppose that the tenets of the Bullion Committee, in this respect, were completely visionary and erroneous.

He rejoiced that his Right Hon. Friend was the person who led the opposition to the Report of the Bullion Committee, because he was confident, that, with such an adversary, the discussion would be amicable, and free from party spirit, and because the House was sure of hearing so much ability employed on that side of the subject. He could not, however, help remarking, that his Right Hon. Friend himself had been a party in an administration which had twice extended the term of the continuance of the restriction act on a principle which, if Parliament would now give its attention to the subject, he could not help thinking that they would perceive to have been very objectionable.

Twice, under the administration of Lord Sidmouth, of whom he wished to speak most respectfully—namely, once in peace, and once after the recommencement of the war—the act for restricting the cash payment of the Bank was renewed, upon the professed ground of the unfavourableness of the exchanges. This was not the principle on which the first act had passed, and he much questioned whether the Parliament would have ever consented to institute such a measure merely on that plea. It was by means of an unfavourable exchange, and a high price of bullion, that an excess of bank paper was detected and restrained, as he trusted that he had already sufficiently shewn. The ground on which the restriction bill had passed was much more justifiable, namely, that of an alarm arising out of the idea of an immediate invasion, which caused a violent run upon the Bank, and threatened suddenly and unavoidably to exhaust its coffers. The State, for political reasons, on that occasion interfered. To extend the suspension because the exchange was unfavourable, was to adopt a new and dangerous course. He recollected to have himself, on one occasion, remarked on the insufficiency of this motive for the renewal; but the subject did not always particularly attract the attention of the House; it now, therefore, became them, and especially since they were resolved to continue the suspension, to look well to the general principles on which both they and the Bank proceeded, and not to consider themselves as debating merely on a temporary measure.

One great security to the Bank of England, heretofore, had been its independence of the Government: its paper had been properly restrained, because the Government had felt no interest and taken no part in the extended issue of it; and he submitted, whether, if the subserviency of large issues from the Bank to the purposes of the war, and the convenience of the State, were, during the suspension of cash payments, to be a principle recognised by Parliament, the State and the Bank might not become identified in point of interest, somewhat in the same manner as those government banks on the Continent, whose paper had become first excessive and then depreciated.

It might not be improper to take a slight survey of the whole period which had passed since the first Bank Restriction Bill in 1797. Probably, in consequence, as he had before shewn, of a limitation of paper which was antecedent to that area, and perhaps in consequence also of the caution which the Bank would naturally exercise for some time after it, the exchanges in 1797 and 1798 were peculiarly favourable, and a great tide of gold flowed into the country. In the years 1800 and 1801, when the scarcity of corn occurred—a commercial event more likely, perhaps, than any other to prejudice the exchange—the tide turned quite as much against us: the exchanges then fell below the point which they had ever reached while the Bank was open. The Bank did not at that time limit its issues, which it certainly would have done if it had been liable to make its payments in cash. The exchange, however, recovered itself in 1802, but it did not improve so much as to bring back gold into the country. After a few more years, the exchange turned much against us; and it had now, for the space of nearly three years, continued more unfavourable than it was ever known to be before the suspension. Thus the only influx of gold, of which we had had the benefit, since the suspension act of 1797, was, apparently, in consequence of a limitation of paper antecedent to that period. There would naturally be a tendency to excess during the suspension of cash payments; but the first consequences of such excess, as well as the peculiar pressure of 1801 and 1802, would undoubtedly be mitigated by the exportation of a large portion of that immense fund of gold, with which the providence of the time preceding the suspension had enriched us; and the recovery of the exchange in 1802 was thus facilitated. When the second great pressure, of 1808 and 1809, arose, it found us stripped of a great part of our coin; and this probably was the reason why it proved so serious. It soon carried off our little remaining gold; and we were therefore now arrived at a period when we were no longer protected against the most fearful fall of our exchanges. As long as the foreigner knew that the bill on England which he bought, could be turned into cash, which cash was of a given value, and subject, though contrary to law, to be transported, there was a limit to the depression of the price of the bill; and this limit would exist even during the suspension of the cash payments of the Bank, provided there was a moderate quantity of gold coin actually circulating; for, in that case, if the exchange fell below a certain point, some men would clandestinely collect our guineas, and thus furnish a remittance: but now a man must walk a mile before he can collect a guinea, he must incur great expense in gathering, as well as in purchasing, the very trifling quantity of coin which remained among us. The limit, therefore, to the fall of the bill, was no longer what it had been: we were ceasing to have any limit, and were therefore now arriving at a new state of danger; so that it was difficult to say, in case untoward circumstances should arise, what might be the extent to which the exchange possibly might run down. Such had been the effect of the long continuance of the Bank Restriction Bill, and of the system under which we had acted during the fourteen years of its existence. The House had now decided against the repeal of it, and seemed to intend that the bill should remain in force until the period

349

already assigned to it, of six months after the ratification of a treaty of peace. He was not eager as to the question whether the Bank should now be required to open at any early period. He would willingly have agreed to suspend the determination of that point, if he could but have seen a disposition to act, in the mean time, in such a manner as to facilitate the opening. But the misfortune was, that the Directors of the Bank seemed to consider the suspension as exempting them from the necessity of pursuing the principles on which they would have acted if no suspending bill had passed, and on which also they could not fail now to act, if they were liable to pay in cash. To one of them the question was put, "Supposing the Bank to pay in cash, and a great drain to arise (and there could be no doubt that a great drain would now arise if the Bank were liable to pay in cash) should you advise some diminution of bank paper?" The answer was, "I must recommend it from necessity, though in my opinion it would not improve the exchange. I think it one of the advantages of the Restriction Bill, that we are not driven to that necessity." The Parliament, if they voted the resolutions of his Right Hon. Friend, would fortify the Bank in these opinions. They had, indeed, already indicated their approbation of them, by negativing all the first resolutions of the Learned Gentleman; and in consequence of that vote, which he had considered to be a vote against any limitation of paper, he had reluctantly joined in the subsequent vote for opening the Bank in two years;—a vote which he should have been glad to have had an opportunity of qualifying, by specifying certain accompanying measures, by which he thought that the apparent severity of it might have been mitigated, and the opening much facilitated. He had, when in the Bullion Committee, expressed a wish to soften the terms used in that part of the Report which suggested that the restriction should cease in two years. He was clearly against a period so indefinite as that of six months after the ratification of a treaty of peace, considering all the experience we had had. He was for returning to the principle on which we had set out, that of allowing to the Bank only a short term; possibly renewing it, if necessary, but not as a matter of course, and on the mere ground that the exchanges were unfavourable. He was aware that the gentlemen opposed to him had gained a great advantage by turning the attention of the public to the opening of the Bank; as if that were the only thing recommended by the Bullion Committee. This was not the sole object of their Report. There had been many shades of opinion upon that part of it, among men agreed in all their fundamental principles. The Bullion Committee had been far more united on the other point on which he had dwelt—the propriety of limiting the bank issues with a view to the improvement of the exchange. The Parliament was now taking part with the Bank against their own

350

Committee, in respect to this important principle; and the Right Hon. Chancellor of the Exchequer, in exerting himself on the same side, appeared to him to be taking on himself a fearful responsibility.

It had appeared in the course of the present debates, that the chief circumstance which had led the Directors of the Bank to embrace the opinion that the quantity of their paper had no influence on the exchange, was the doctrine which they entertained respecting what is called the Balance of Trade. The state of the exchange was, according to them, the unavoidable consequence of an unfavourable balance: he therefore requested leave to enter somewhat fully into this topic.

An inaccurate use of words had served to confuse many parts of the general subject under discussion; and the term balance of trade, in particular, had contributed to this perplexity. He would endeavour to expose the error involved in this expression; and in order to do this, it might be convenient to remark how it first obtained currency.

Our ancestors, eager for the acquisition of the precious metals, exploring, as is well known, new continents, chiefly with a view to this article; and accustomed to consider trade as profitable or otherwise, in proportion as it brought in or took out gold and silver, were naturally led to denominate that part of our exports or imports which consisted of these metals *a balance*. In truth, however, this was not a balance. Bullion was an article of commerce, rising or falling in value according to the supply and the demand, exactly like any other, transporting itself in greater or less quantities according to the comparative state of the market for that and for other articles, and forming only an item on one side of the general account. Corn, or any other commodity, might just as properly be said to pay the balance as gold or silver; but it would evidently be inaccurate to affirm that corn discharged it, because it would imply that the amount of all the articles except corn was fixed; and that these having first adjusted themselves with relation only to each other, a given quantity of corn was then added to pay the difference. It was, for the same reason, inaccurate to affirm, that gold or silver paid the difference. He was aware that many of our older writers of great name had used expressions of this sort, and that a phraseology borrowed from such respectable authority ought not to be too much censured. They had written, however, at a time when paper currency scarcely had an existence; they had not contemplated the consequences of the introduction of so much paper credit: they had therefore not guarded or measured their expressions, as they probably would have done, if they had foreseen the use which was now made of them.

The Governor of the Bank (Mr. Manning) had in his speech quoted a passage in Mr. Locke, containing the term on which he had just animadverted, and had grounded himself on what he inferred from this expression to be the principles of that author. The words of Mr. Locke were these;—"The coming and going of our treasure depends wholly upon the balance of trade;"—a mode of speaking which certainly countenanced the doctrine of the Honourable Gentleman and other Bank Directors, namely, that there is no possibility of preventing the departure of our gold by any measures which the Bank can take, inasmuch as it is balance of trade, and balance of trade alone, which regulates both its coming and its going, over which balance the Bank has no controul. It would be found, however, that Mr. Locke could not be so completely claimed as an authority, on the side of the Governor of the Bank, as might at first view be supposed; for Mr. Locke in the part of his work immediately preceding that from which the quotation was taken, speaks of "two cases" in which profit may be made by melting down our money: "First, when the current prices of the same denomination are unequal and of different weights, some heavier, some lighter; the other that of a losing trade, or an overgreat consumption of foreign commodities;" and then goes on to say, that "the coming and going of our treasure depends wholly on the balance of trade."

Mr. Locke, therefore, refers to either of two causes the disappearance of coin. Agreeing in this respect with Sir Isaac Newton and others, whom his Honourable Friend (Mr. Huskisson) had quoted, he affirms that two kinds of circulating medium, if of different value, cannot long continue to pass interchangeably, because the heavier and more valuable pieces will be melted down, with or without law, and the light ones only will remain. Did gentlemen allow the truth of what Sir Isaac Newton and other high authorities, not excepting Mr. Locke, had laid down as a fundamental maxim in this science? If they did, they ought to admit not only that silver currency would disappear, if of more value than gold; and gold currency, if of more value than silver; and heavy pieces, if light ones were allowed equally to pass; but also that gold currency would vanish if a paper currency of inferior value was circulating at the same time. Silver coin was not now a legal tender for more than a limited amount; gold coin and paper were therefore the only two currencies in use for the payment of large sums; Gold was now to paper what it had formerly been to silver, and what the heavier pieces of gold had been to the lighter pieces of the same metal. Thus, the present disappearance of our gold coin, might be ascribed to the first of the two causes mentioned by Mr. Locke, namely, the difference in value between the two kinds of currency in the country; and not to the second cause, the unfavourable balance of trade.

Still, however, the language of Mr. Locke was certainly inaccurate, when he said, that the "coming and going of our treasure depends wholly on the balance of our trade," and served to countenance that dangerous doctrine which now prevailed. According to this doctrine, the fact of the disappearance of our guineas attended with the highest imaginable price of gold, was no indication of an excess of paper or of a depreciation of it, but was simply an evidence of an unfavourable balance of trade; and the only remedy was generally to promote national industry and œconomy. It might, indeed, be imagined by some, that according to this view of the subject, even additional issues of paper would operate as a remedy; for it might be said that an increased emission of it tended to encourage manufactures, an augmented quantity of manufactures supplied the means of enlarging our exports, and more extended exports improved the balance of trade; and thus an increased issue of paper might be assumed to be the means of rectifying the exchange, instead of prejudicing it. This was exactly the course of argument into which the Noble Lord over the way (Lord Castlereagh) appeared in one part of his speech to be running. It was an error to which he himself had once inclined, but he had stood corrected after a fuller consideration of the subject. There must obviously be a fallacy in this way of reasoning. It proved too much. It implied, that indefinitely to increase our paper, was the way indefinitely to improve its value in exchange for the circulating medium of other countries, as well as in exchange for bullion and for all commodities. The utmost admission which he was disposed to make was, that in proceeding to limit our paper with a view to the improvement of the exchange, we ought to avoid that severity of pressure by which manufacturing industry might be seriously interrupted.

According to the same erroneous doctrine, the export of our gold coin in each of those instances of which Sir Isaac Newton and others spoke, was referable to balance of trade, and not to the cause to which they ascribed it. When in the reign of King William, our gold coin went abroad, in consequence, if we were to credit Sir Isaac Newton, of its having become more valuable than our silver, through a change in the relative value of the two articles, it went to pay a balance of trade; for it was balance of trade, and balance of trade alone, according to the tenets in question, which caused the precious metals to transfer themselves to other countries. When in a subsequent year a similar difference between the two kinds of currency occurred, it was in order again to pay a balance of trade that the better coin quitted the kingdom. He would put another case. Suppose a fisherman on our southern coast, to collect a thousand guineas, and exchange them in the channel with some French fisherman for as much French brandy as should be deemed an equivalent, the gold, according to the doctrine in fashion, would have gone to pay the balance of trade. It would have been employed to discharge a previously existing national debt. It was always, according to these tennets, the brandy which forced out the gold, and not at all the gold which forced in the brandy. By the Frenchman's putting the brandy into his boat, the Englishman was compelled to put the gold into his. The brandy always went before; the gold always followed after. It was one of the peculiar properties of gold that it always served to pay a balance.

The truth was, that our paper currency having become less valuable by nearly twenty per cent. than the gold contained in our coin, the coin could no longer circulate interchangeably for it, but went abroad, because there was a profit of nearly twenty per cent. on the transmission. This profit operated as effectually in withdrawing it from circulation, and causing that part of it which was not bought at a high price for manufacturing uses, to be exported, as if an actual bounty of twenty per cent. were given on the export of it; and as much prevented the importation of gold for the purpose of serving as currency—the only purpose for which large quantities of gold were usually imported—as if a tax of twenty per cent. were levied on the import of it. We deplored the loss of our gold coin; but by not limiting our bank notes, we were thus, in substance, laying a tax on its importation, and giving a bounty on its exportation: and then, referring its absence to balance of trade, we imagined that we had no power of recalling it.

He admitted that something was to be conceded on the ground of an unfavourable state of trade and a bad harvest, as well as on account of large drafts in discharge of the foreign expenditure of Government. Our manufactures, and other exportable commodities, might happen not to be in such demand abroad as to supply, on such occasions, the whole of the remittance advantageously. The precious metals were in more universal request than any other article; and the transmission of a certain quantity of these might prevent so low a selling price of our commodities, in the foreign market, as might otherwise be necessary. But our gold was now gone, and that disadvantage of which he was speaking, was therefore one against which we were beginning to be quite unprotected. Our coin had for the most part left us in 1801. The state of our trade and foreign expenditure seemed not likely to improve materially. The exchange could not be corrected, as heretofore, by the transmission of specie. The cautious limitation of our paper was, therefore, a principle to which every consideration of prudence should lead us to resort.

Several of the first Resolutions of his Right Hon. Friend (Mr. Vansittart) were intended to shew that there was no correspondence between the variations in the exchange for some time past, and the existing quantity of notes. He had in his former Speech remarked, in reply, that at three several periods—in 1783, 1795 and 1796, and 1797—the Bank had experienced a drain of gold, had consequently restrained their issues, and had experienced a subsequent improvement of the exchange. His Right Hon. Friend erroneously assumed that the Bullion Committee deemed the effect of a limitation of paper to be instantaneous; an error which was exposed by the amendments intended to be offered by the Chairman of the Bullion Committee. The influence both of a reduction and increase of paper, though sure, might be slow, and probably would be various, both as to the degree and time of its operation: it would affect, first, one kind of commodity, then another; probably operating more early on those articles of which the sale was for ready money, reaching slowly the land, and still more slowly the labour, of the country. When an over-issue of paper had produced a general alteration in the price of labour, and, through the price of labour, on that of commodities, the improvement of the exchanges became more difficult and hopeless; and this consideration ought to induce us not to delay the reduction of our bank notes till the wages of labour had become materially affected. In the case of an alteration in the value of the coin of a country, the operation on prices, though in like manner sure, was also in like manner slow and irregular. Mr. Hume, in speaking of the successive deteriorations of the French coin, in the reign of Louis XIV., had remarked, that they did not at once produce a proportionate rise of prices. He says, "Though the high price of commodities be a necessary consequence of the increase of gold and silver," (as it surely must also be of the increase of paper currency), "yet it follows not immediately on that increase, but some time is required before the money circulates through the whole state. At first, no alteration is perceived: by degrees the price rises, first of one commodity, then of another; till the whole at last reaches a just proportion with the new quantity of specie in the kingdom. In my opinion," he adds, "it is only in interval between the acquisition of money and rise of prices, that the increasing quantity of gold and silver is favourable to industry."—Those gentlemen who are eager to maintain an extended paper circulation, with a view to serving commerce, would do well to bear in mind this very sound observation of Mr. Hume. They should remember, that it is only by the perpetual increase of paper that their object can be fully effected. They should also reflect, that, in proportion to this increase, the exchange will be prejudiced, and the standard of the country forsaken. Mr. Hume goes on to specify some facts in proof of his general position. "And that the specie," says he, "may increase to a considerable pitch before it have this latter effect" (of raising prices), "appears, amongst other instances, from

355

the frequent operations of the French King on the money; where it was always found, that the augmenting of the numerary value did not produce a proportional rise of prices, at least for some time. In the last year of Louis XIV., money was raised three sevenths, but prices augmented only one."

The impression intended to be conveyed by his Right Hon. Friend (Mr. Vansittart) was this; that, inasmuch as there was no exact correspondence between the quantity of paper and the state of the exchanges, at the periods which were specified by him, the evidence of facts was against the doctrine of the Bullion Committee, that a diminution of paper tended to meliorate the exchange. His Right Hon. Friend, if reasoning at the time of Louis XIV., might have shown the evidence of facts to have been against the corresponding doctrine of Mr. Hume, that a debasement of the quality, and consequent enlargement of the quantity, of the coin of a kingdom, tended to raise prices. He would have only had to select some day almost immediately following the debasement, in order to shew that no perceivable consequence had followed. It then took a year to produce an effect amounting to 1-7th, when the whole ultimate effect ought plainly to be, and doubtless was, 3-7ths. The case of the Bank of France, in 1805, might, in like manner, have been turned by his Right Hon. Friend to the purpose of proving his own point. The restriction of its paper was not effectual at once; it was not operative in any kind of regular proportion to its degree. These two cases served, nevertheless, on the whole, to establish the doctrine of the Bullion Committee. They shewed both the general effect and the irregularity of it. Nothing, indeed, was more easy, than for one who, in a case like this, had the choice of the days on which he was to make his comparisons, to state facts which would seem to prove almost any thing, In one instance, his Right Honourable Friend, arguing from the amount of bank notes on a single day, had stated them three millions higher than a note supplied by a Bank Director (Mr. Raikes) had allowed them to be; of which error he had become so convinced, as to have altered his resolution. It was only by averages of the amount, and not by the amount on single days, and it was by looking to periods subsequent to the limitation of paper, that any sound inference could be made.

There was another species of unfairness in the Resolutions. They stated the fluctuations in the exchange and the price of bullion, for a long time preceding the suspension of cash payments; and then spoke of the variations since that period, as if these were somewhat similar *in their degree*. But was the House aware of the different extent of the fluctuations in the two periods? He would specify the fluctuations in the price of bullion. This was a surer test of depreciation than the exchanges. Many circumstances perplexed our inquiry into the true par of exchange; it was necessary to know, first, the exact standard in foreign countries;—secondly, the degree of wear of the current foreign coin; for it was with the coin actually circulating, and not with that which was fresh from the foreign mint, that the comparison with our own was to be made;—we ought likewise to be informed whether there was any, and what, foreign seignorage; and also, indeed, what obstacles to the exportation of the foreign currency. But, besides these sources of inaccuracy, many of which were continually varying, there was another most fruitful cause of error, namely, the circumstance of the standard of this country having now for some time been gold, while that of Hamburgh in particular, as well indeed as of Amsterdam, was silver. There had been a very varying disproportion between the prices of gold and silver in the world; and this variation, as he believed, would serve to account for much of that occasionally great depression of our apparent exchange with Hamburgh, in times preceding 1797, on which the opponents of the Bullion Committee had relied. The people of this country were not bound to examine into all the intricacies of the exchange, in order to know whether their standard was adhered to. The state of the exchanges merely afforded a confirmation of a depreciation of our currency : a generally high price of bullion of itself distinctly established it. What, then, was the price of bullion before 1797, and what was it now? It had never, before 1797, except in the South Sea year, and at the time when our coin was deteriorated, risen higher than 4*l*. 1s. 6d. per oz. and had scarcely ever reached that point; that is to say, it had never fluctuated more than from 3*l*. 17s. 10d. to 4*l*. 1s. 6d.—it was now 4*l*. 14s. It had not exceeded its proper mint price by more than 3s. 8d. or 2 to 3 per cent. in the one period—it exceeded it by 16s. 2d. or fitfeen to twenty per cent. in the other. Was it fair, then, to infer, or to imply, that because we had occasionally departed from the standard before 1797, to the extent, at the utmost, of two of three per cent.; we need not now regard a departure from it of fifteen or twenty per cent.? The Bullion Committee had never intended to say, that no deviation from the standard of our coin, however small, ought to be tolerated. They were not in this respect the theorists which they were sometimes represented to be. They, indeed, affirmed bullion to be the standard, and the more the subject was examined, the more did it appear that we had either this standard or none; but they allowed of a moderate departure from it. Nothing human was perfect. The very mint, though it professed to convert a pound of gold into forty-four and a half equal parts, or guineas, did not effect their object with mathematical precision, and to their deviation was given the technical name of a Remedy. Even the most minute departure of this kind below the

357

standard might be called a depreciation. Through the wear of guineas there arose a further depreciation, which the Parliament had taken care to limit, by making them cease to be a legal tender when their weight fell below about one per cent. The strictness of this limit shewed the principle in the mind of Parliament; it proved that depreciation to a certain extent was contemplated, and that depreciation beyond that point was thought an evil to be carefully provided against. The operation of our laws, which prevented the melting and exportation of coin, had led to a further increase of the difference between the market price and mint price of gold, or, in other words, to a further depreciation. The effect produced by all these causes had never, before the suspension of cash payments in 1797, been such as to cause the actual currency of the country to differ from bullion more than to that extent of two or three per cent. which he had stated, except on the two occasions which he had spoken of. The people, therefore, up to that time, were secure of having the value of their currency thus far sustained. The liability of the Bank to pay in cash, guaranteed to them a paper incapable of departing below bullion further than in the degree which he had mentioned. At the present time this paper was fifteen or twenty per cent. below bullion, and they had no security against a further, and even indefinite, depression. It was said, that gold itself had risen; but even if it had, gold being the standard, we were bound to hold to it: we had held to it in its general fall, and we ought to abide by it in its general rise also. The argument that gold had risen would justify an adulteration of the gold coin, just as much as it would justify the present depreciation. On the whole, he thought, that to confound the little differences between the market price and mint price of bullion before 1797, with the great difference at present, was most unfair. The difference, it was true, might be said to be only in degree, but degree was every thing in this case; and it was remarkable, that the Resolution of his Right Hon. Friend studiously forbore to specify the amount of the difference between the market price and mint price of bullion at the two periods.

There remained only one other topic on which he had to remark.—The Resolutions of his Right Hon. Friend assumed that the notes of the Bank of England were not excessive, because the difference between their numerical amount now and in 1797, was not greater than the comparative trade and expenditure at the two periods would fairly justify.

The notes of 5*l*. and upwards, for the average of three years before 1797, were about ten millions seven hundred thousand pounds; and, for the average of the last three years, were about fourteen millions two hundred thousand pounds. He would fairly say, that if he had been asked to pronounce them excessive on the simple ground of their relative quantity at the two periods, he might have hesitated to do it. He should have inquired what was the state of the exchanges and the price of bullion, and should have formed his judgment chiefly by the answer to this question. He was, however, very far from admitting, on the other hand, that the due limitation of them could be presumed from what was called the small extent of their increase. There was much misconception on this subject, which those who, like himself, were acquainted with the money transactions of the metropolis, were best able to remove. A very increased degree of economy was practised in the use of notes. Gentlemen uninformed on this topic naturally assumed, that when our trade and revenue and public expenditure were extended, the amount of notes requisite for these enlarged payments must be nearly proportionate. But this was very far from being the case. In the infancy of paper credit, the circulation of such an establishment as the Bank of England might regularly and uniformly increase: a time, nevertheless, would come when it would begin to diminish; but exactly at what period, and in what degree, this change would take place, was not easily ascertained. When the Bank was instituted, and for some time afterwards, the fund which private bankers, who were then goldsmiths, kept in store as a provision against emergency, consisted chiefly of gold; but by slow degrees it became Bank of England notes. The papers before the House would accordingly shew how very trifling was the circulation of the Bank at an early period of their establishment, and how greatly it after a time advanced. But it was not regularly progressive in proportion as confidence increased. The banker suffered a loss of interest proportionate to the amount of Bank paper in his possession; for which, therefore, he would be disposed to substitute a paper from which no such disadvantage accrued. Exchequer bills furnished one provision of this sort. They yielded interest to the banker, and yet were convertible by a very short and sure process into bank notes. Bank paper, therefore, was by no means the perfection of the system; it was not his "last and best supply." The last and best supply had been furnished from the Bank of the Right Hon. the Chancellor of the Exchequer, who well knew to what an extent his issues of this kind had been recently carried. Bills of exchange also, and other articles of a similar nature, served exceedingly to spare the use of notes; and a variety of devices was resorted to for the same purpose. As in many manufacturing concerns there had been a perpetual exercise of ingenuity, and a consequent abridgment of labour; so in the banking system there had been an exertion of the talents of individuals in producing the necessary quantity of notes. Evidence had been given before the Bullion Committee of the increasing number of money-brokers, who passed from one banking-house to another, and supplied the daily and hourly wants of one quarter, by carrying away the superfluity of another. If we could suppose the sixty or seventy bankers of the metropolis to be reduced to six or seven, it was obvious that a very diminished quantity of notes would suffice for the same business. The improvements in the banking system tended to unite, as it were, into one house, for the purpose of which he was speaking, even those bankers who held no direct communication with each other.

The quantity of notes kept by private families was also, as he believed, continually diminishing, through the increased habit of employing bankers, and of circulating drafts upon them, in and round the metropolis. The circulation of Bank of England notes in the country (he still spoke of those of 5*l*. and upwards), had probably also diminished, in consequence of the immense increase of country banks. The sum total of the stock of Bank of England notes kept in store by these banks might be augmented; but that stock consisted, in a great degree, of those 1*l*. and 2*l*. notes, which he had left out of his calculation.

Mr. H. Thornton concluded with observing, that he was conscious of having left almost untouched many important parts of this extensive subject. The material point, however, of the nature of the standard, over which so much obscurity was thrown by the present Resolutions, had been so very ably and satisfactorily treated by the Right Hon. Gentleman over the way (Mr. Canning), as well, indeed, as by the Honourable Gentleman near him (Mr. Huskisson), that he had felt little inclination to dwell upon it: but he could not sit down without adverting once more to the first of the Resolutions now proposed, in which the right of the Crown to vary the standard, both with and without the concurrence of Parliament, seemed to be asserted. It might be true, that to the King, generally speaking, was committed the regulation of the coin of a country; but the language which he should be disposed to use, would be that, not of his Right Hon. Friend, but rather of Sir Thomas Rowe, at the council table of Charles I. ;—a language, indeed, in the first words of it a little resembling the Resolution on which he was animadverting, but far different in its conclusion. "The regulating of coin," said Sir T. Rowe, "hath been left to the care of princes, who have ever been presumed to be the fathers of the commonwealth. *Upon their honours they are debtors and warrantees of justice to the subject in that behalf.*"

Dr. A. Smith had observed, that "in every country the avarice and injustice of princes and sovereign states, abusing the confidence of their subjects, has by degrees diminished the real quantity of metal in their coin." This was an evil to which, in times of difficulty, like the present, all nations were prone. The Romans (observed the same author), in the later and worse times of their country, reduced their coin to one twenty-fourth.

England had reduced her pound only to one third. Scotland enjoyed the honour, and had also had the advantage—for such the principles of the Right Honourable Baronet over the way (Sir John Sinclair) would probably lead him to consider it—of having reduced its coin to one thirty-sixth; France to one sixty-sixth. He had always deemed it highly creditable to England, that the deterioration of her standard had been comparatively so small; but we seemed to be now willing to expose ourselves to the danger of giving way to this temptation, while Hamburgh and Amsterdam, and our great adversary in France, were superior to it. Their several standards were sustained. That we might not yield in this respect to the pressure of our present circumstances, was the chief object for the sake of which he had spoken. A country seldom was sensible of the first steps taken in this downward course; and it therefore belonged to those who possessed an extensive knowledge of such subjects, and adverted to the history of other nations, to point out the approaching danger.

He feared that the members of the Administration, partly, perhaps, through their having taken in the first instance a too transient view of the question, in consequence of their multiplied employments, and of their having then committed themselves too hastily upon it; partly also through a wish to enjoy the present benefit of an extended issue of paper in their financial and political concerns, were not the safest guides on the present occasion. He had endeavoured, for his own part, to fulfil his duty, both as an individual of the Bullion Committee and as a member of Parliament; and though he had not dwelt in his speech on the difficulties by which we were encompassed, he had not formed his judgment without taking them fully into his consideration.

INDEX RERUM

Assignats, 231–234.

BALANCE OF TRADE, 141–145, 150, 153.
Its effect on gold reserves, 111–112.
Its increase, 166.
Effect thereupon of increase of currency, 198.
On difficulties of calculating it, 344.
The Directors of the Bank and the Balance of Trade, 351.

BANK OF ENGLAND
Its nature, 105.
Its relations with Government, 106, 128–129, 254, 348.
Its actions in the crisis of 1797..127, 131–140.
Its note circulation, 214.
Objections to its monopoly, 228–229.
Contrasted with private banks, 286–288, 294, 303–305.

BANK NOTES, 90 et seq.
Their velocity of circulation, 96 et seq, 232–233.
Effects of their abolition, 100.
Of the effects of a diminution, 113–128, 280–283, 301, 305.
Of changes in their quantity, 124, 195–200.
Democratic objections thereto, 171 *n*.
Relation to quantity of country paper, 215–217.
Effects of an excessive issue, 218, 226.
Economy thereof, 222, 263, 359.
Of person advocating no limit to their issue, 227, 231.
Causes of an increase in issue, 230–233, 240, 241.
On the value of Bank of England notes, 233–235.
Effects of an increased issue on home production, 235–240.
Methods of restraining the note issue, 251–254.
On substitutes for bank notes, 282, 289, 297, 309.
Of the relative proportions of Bank of England notes and country
  bank notes in circulation, 288, 299.
Effects of a reduction in circulation on the price of Government
  securities, 289–305.
Their reduction a cause of unemployment, 291.
Of the use of guineas when notes are scarce, 298.
That their quantity be increased when payments of Government
  loans become due, 302, 306.
That an increased issue thereof raises prices, 329, 342–344.

363

Bank of Paris, 337–338.
Bank of Sweden, 339.
Barter, 81.
BILLS OF EXCHANGE
　Their function, 82.
　Monetary use thereof, 92, 296.
　Advantages to merchants, 93.
　In international trade, 145.
　As security for bank loans, 252.
BULLION
　See also "Gold."
　Of a high price, 103, 145–150, 201, 221, 261, 330.
　Bank of England's holding thereof in 1797..136.
　Effects of balance of trade on its price, 225, 330.
　Price lowered through increased use of notes, 265, 329, 339.
　Whether note issues should be regulated by the price of Bullion, 327.
　As a commodity, 330.
　The Bullion Committee, 343, 345, 350, 355–361.

CAPITAL
　Its definition, 79.
　Increase through use of paper credit, 176–177, 301.
　Scarcity in war-time, 255.
　Its export, 256.
Cash Ratio, 286, 289.
Coin, 243, 272, 349.
COUNTRY BANKS
　Their number, 168.
　Their origin, 169.
　Their notes, 169.
　Their multiplication, 172–173.
　Advantages and disadvantages thereof, 174.
　Danger of depreciation of their notes, 189–192.
　The influence of their notes on prices, 193, 270.
　How they increase their loans, 271.
　Quantity of their notes in circulation from 1793–1797..284.
　Reasons for decreasing their note-issues, 287, 304.
CREDIT
　Commercial, 75.
　Term thereof, 76.
　Relation to national wealth, 78.
　Limitation thereof, 122.
Crisis of 1793..97–99, 113, 181 *n*, 265, 279, 299, 334.
Crisis of 1797..134, 135, 279, 299, 334, 348.

DEFLATION
Its effects, 113–128, 291, 280–283.
Advocated in 1811..345.
Demand and Supply, 193–197.
Demand, increased through expansion of note issue, 237.
Discounts, 306–309.

EXCHANGE
Unfavourable state thereof, 141, 143, 156–159.
That the rate determines balance of trade and not vice versa, 246–248.
Effect thereupon of increased quantity of money, 329, 332, 354.
That state of exchanges should be criterion of excess of paper, 343.

Forced saving, 239.
FOREIGN TRADE
In bullion, 117.
Effect of scarcity of bank-notes, 117.

GOLD
See also "Bullion."
Of the velocity of circulation of gold guineas, 99–101.
Of substitutes for gold currency, 101.
As the standard of value, 111, 357.
Of gold reserves at the Bank, 111.
As an internationally traded commodity, 145, 160, 262, 331, 351.
Difference between mint and market price of gold, 148–150, 193,
    200–203, 218, 220, 261, 353–355, 358.
Of attempts to increase the fund of gold in times of crisis, 161, 167.
Fall in value with increased output, 242, 328.
Not the best medium of currency, 275–276.

Hoarding, 97, 266, 300.

Inflation, 107–108, 195–200.
INTEREST RATE, 335.
Its effect on demand for money, 254–258.
Its relation to the quantity of money, 281, 296–297, 336, 338.
Its relation to the value of money, 336.
Of its natural rate, 339.

LOANS
Their relation to note circulation and gold currency, 125, 133, 137.
Of security for loans, 251–252.
Mechanism of Government borrowing, 280–281.

365

LONDON BANKS
Their number and system, 113.

MONEY
See "Bank notes."
The demand for money, 194.

PARLIAMENT
Interference in 1797 thought improper, 138–140.
Precious Metals, their monetary use, 81.
PRICES
High prices result of too great quantity of bank-notes, 220–224, 230, 263.
Profits, increased at times of rising prices, 237–238.

Scotland, state of its proper credit, 285, 299.
SECURITY
Relative importance of security and quantity in determining value of bank-notes, 341.
Land as security for note-issue, 342.
Suspension of cash payments, 112, 132–140, 196–197, 215 *n, et passim*.

Unemployed resources, 236.
Usury laws, 307.

Value, 193–194.

INDEX NOMINUM

Anderson, A., 37.
Angell, J. W., 15.

Baring, Sir Francis, 38, 45, 107.
Bentham, J., 31, 50, 59.
Black, W. G., 15.
Bogatsky, C. H. von, 13.
Bowdler, J., 20.
Bowdler, T., 20.
Boyd, Walter, 44, 45, 92, 214–216, 316.
Brougham, H., 32, 34.
Burney, Fanny, 18.

Cannan, E., 62.
Cantillon, R., 37.
Canton, W., 23.
Clarkson, T., 20.
Condorcet, 231.
Coupland, R., 21.
Cowper, W., 13, 14.

Davenant, Sir W., 243.
Dicey, A. V., 21.
Dupont de Nemours, 338.

Eliot, Edward, 21.

Fitzjames, J., 21.
Forster, E. M., 21, 32, 60, 61.
Fox, C. J., 19, 31.

Galiani, 37.
Gisborne, T., 19, 20.
Grant, Charles, 20–22, 29, 32, 33.
Grant, Robert, 22.

Halévy, E., 11.
Harris, Joseph, 37.
Hastings, Warren, 20.

Hawtrey, R. G., 62.
Hesketh, Lady, 23.
Horner, Francis, 47, 51, 53–55, 325, 327.
Hume, David, 37, 49, 68, 238, 247, 268–270, 273–275, 355, 356.
Huskisson, W., 54, 55, 353.

Inglis, R. H., 11, 26, 31, 33.

Johnson, C. B., 23.
Jones, M. G., 23.
Joplin, T., 34, 36.

King, Lord Peter, 52, 313, 316–318, 322.
Klingberg, F. J., 21.
Knutsford, Lady, 23.

Law, John, 239, 250, 341–342.
Lloyd, Henry, 37.
Locke, John, 37, 68, 245–248, 351, 353.

Macaulay, T. B., 21, 33.
Macaulay, Zachary, 20, 22, 23, 31, 33, 48.
MacCulloch, J. R., 14, 15, 41, 59.
Malthus, T. R., 32.
Mill, J. S., 48, 58.
Miller, G., 57.
Montesquieu, 37, 68, 266–268.
More, Hannah, 20, 23, 33.
Morgan, A. de, 23.

Newton, Sir Isaac, 352–353.
Newton, J., 13, 14.
Nightingale, Florence, 21.
North, Lord, 18.

367

Oldfield, T. H. B., 55.

Palmer, J. H., 35.
Parnell, H., 54.
Pennington, J., 33.
Pitt, William, 17–19, 29, 31, 39, 41, 44, 92, 316.
Postlethwayt, 37, 252.
Pym, Dorothy, 21.

Ricardo, D., 32, 36, 41, 48, 57, 58, 62.
Rowe, Sir Thomas, 360.

Seeley, M., 31.
Sharp, Granville, 20.
Smart, W., 55, 62.
Smith, Adam, 38, 62, 68, 90, 91, 94–96, 100, 103–104, 113, 127, 148, 150, 152, 176, 177, 200, 202–208, 245, 266, 316, 360.
Smith, W., 20, 21.
Stephen, Leslie, 21, 28, 29.
Steuart, James, 37, 68, 244, 245, 267.
Stock, E., 23.
Sykes, Marianne, *see* Thornton, Marianne.

Taussig, F. W., 48.
Teignmouth, Lord, 20.
Telford, J., 13, 21.
Thompson, F. W. B., 22.
Thornton, Godfrey, 12, 16.
Thornton, Henry, *passim*.
Thornton, John, 12.
Thornton, J., 12–14, 19.
Thornton, Marianne, 12, 28, 30.
Thornton, P. M., 12.
Thornton, R., 12, 15.
Thornton, S., 14, 15, 36.
Thrale, H., 18.
Tooke, T., 40, 62.
Trevelyan, G. O., 21.
Turgot, 37.

Venn, H., 13, 20, 21.
Venn, J., 13, 20, 21.
Viner, Jacob, 36, 58, 62.

Wedgwood, J., 29.
Wicksell, Knut, 50.
Wilberforce, S., 21.
Wilberforce, W., 11, 17, 19, 21, 22, 29, 33, 42, 61.
Woolf, Virginia, 21.

Young, Arthur, 231.